London Stage

in the
NINETEENTH
CENTURY

Robert
Tanitch

London Stage

in the
NINETEENTH
CENTURY

*Robert
Tanitch*

for Brian Dallamore

Also by Robert Tanitch

A Pictorial Companion to Shakespeare's Plays; *Ralph Richardson, A Tribute*;
Olivier; *Leonard Rossiter*; *Ashcroft*; *Gielgud*; *Dirk Bogarde*; *Guinness*;
Sean Connery; *John Mills*; *Brando*; *Clint Eastwood*; *The Unknown James Dean*;
Oscar Wilde on Stage and Screen; *Blockbusters!*; *London Stage in the 20th Century*

London Stage in the Nineteenth Century

Text copyright © Robert Tanitch, 2010

The illustrations are drawn from the collections of Westminster City Archives
and are reproduced here with their permission

First published in 2010 by
Carnegie Publishing *in association with* Westminster City Archives

Carnegie Publishing Ltd
Chatsworth Road,
Lancaster LA1 4SL
www.carnegiepublishing.com

British Library Cataloguing-in-Publication data
A catalogue record for this book is available from the British Library

ISBN 978-1-85936-208-2   *hardback*

Designed and typeset in Bembo and Lysandria by Carnegie Publishing
Printed and bound in the UK in association with Jellyfish Solutions Ltd

FRONTISPIECE

*The Proscenium of the English Opera House in the Strand (formerly the Lyceum)
as it appeared on the evening of 21 March 1817 when Adam Walker exhibited his
eidouranion, a form of entertainment that used back-projection to give astronomical
effects. Walker, who had invented the eidouranion in the 1780s, is seen here on
stage, lecturing to a musical accompaniment played on a glass organ. The majority
of the chattering audience does not seem to be looking at the stage.*

Contents

Foreword

London Stage in the Nineteenth Century is a unique survey of one of the most exciting periods in British theatre history. This was a time of growth, innovation and diversification for the capital's theatre scene, during which London asserted itself as the leading player on the world's cultural stage. With lively period detail, witty quotations and evocative images from the archives of the City of Westminster, each page of this book brings to life the thrilling story of London's nineteenth-century theatreland.

The heart of the Victorian entertainment industry lay in districts that now form part of the City of Westminster. New theatres sprang up in the West End at a staggering rate, ever more breath-taking in conception and palatial in appearance. Architects competed to design the optimum in theatre-going experiences, and fitting settings for celebrity actor-managers to tread the boards. Audiences flocked to theatres not only to see their favourite plays and performers, but also to marvel at the technical innovations that transformed stage drama into spectacle.

The illustrations for Robert Tanitch's fascinating account of the nineteenth-century London stage have been sourced exclusively from the Westminster Libraries and Archives Theatre Collection, one of the most significant collections of performing arts material in the United Kingdom. Beautifully crafted souvenir programmes, rare playbills, and exquisite artworks from the collection are showcased here to evoke the golden age of London theatre.

Westminster City Archives welcomes enquiries on the history of performance in London. The Archives Centre at 10 St Ann's Street, provides a purpose-built research space for visitors to explore the cultural heritage of the West End and other London theatres through first-hand contact with original material.

We hope that this book will inspire you to delve deeper into London's rich theatre history and discover more treasures of the capital's Theatreland.

Judith Bottomley, Local Studies Librarian
Westminster City Archives
May 2010

Henry Irving as Mathias in the most famous of all Victorian melodramas, Leopold Lewis's The Bells, at Lyceum Theatre. The play premiered on 25 November 1871. To this day the agonised cry of 'The Bells! The Bells!' remains part of theatre-goers' collective consciousness, a remarkable testimony to the mesmerism of Irving's acting. This caricature was by Ape (Carlo Pelligrini) and appeared in Vanity Fair on 19 December 1874.

Introduction

London Stage in the Nineteenth Century is an illustrated record, year by year, decade by decade, day by day, of great actors, famous performances, major premieres, celebrated revivals, and spectacular productions.

Theatre has never been as popular again as it was in the nineteenth century, and yet, from the number of revivals seen on the stage today, theatre-goers might well be forgiven for thinking that there was nothing worth reviving between Sheridan and Goldsmith and Oscar Wilde. Today the most regularly produced nineteenth-century works are Wilde's *The Importance of Being Earnest*, the Savoy Operas of Gilbert and Sullivan, and Brandon Thomas's *Charley's Aunt*.

Interestingly, the criticisms that are made today against Wilde's society plays — too much melodrama and too many epigrams — were the very things that were said about the original performances. Wilde's society plays, *Lady Windermere's Fan* and *An Ideal Husband*, nevertheless, remain constantly in the repertoire and do well at the box office. Audiences like melodrama, and they like wit.

What characterised the London stage during this period? For one thing, the major London theatres at the beginning of the nineteenth century were big (too big), and the only way to bring in the public to fill them was by providing genuinely popular entertainment. The emphasis, therefore, tended to be on the sensational, both in action and scenery. Pantomimes, extravaganzas, burlesques, burlettas, equestrian dramas and aquatic dramas were what the public wanted to see. Burlettas were musical farces in three acts, each of which had five songs, and they were extremely popular with theatre managers because, unlike straight plays, they did not have to have a licence to perform them. Pantomimes were completely transformed by Joseph Grimaldi's clowning, by J. R. Planché's scenic wonders and by H. J. Byron's outrageous puns. 'Joey' is still remembered with affection by clowns to this day. Planché was one of the great costumiers, and what he produced on stage was very beautiful. Byron's prolific output included the hugely successful comedy, *Our Boys* (1875), which ran for four years, one of London's longest runs.

Actors in the nineteenth century often gave 'big' performances. The theatres were not designed for subtlety. Poets such as Lord Byron, Robert Browning and Alfred Lord Tennyson, who attempted to revive tragedy, met with no lasting success. Byron didn't want his plays staged; in fact, he even tried to take legal action to stop performances.

Melodrama has always been the most popular form of theatre. It is no surprise that the novels of Charles Dickens were staged instantly. Many were published in weekly instalments and they were often adapted for the stage even before Dickens had finished writing them. Nowadays directors and actors, not trusting the genre, generally fail to take melodrama seriously and parody it crudely. Modern audiences, too, usually feel – mistakenly so – that the proper behaviour is to cheer the hero, boo the villain, weep tears for the heroine and greet dialogue and actions with ironic laughter. The word melodrama immediately conjures up thoughts of absurd over-acting and classic utterances, such as 'Dead! Dead! And never called me mother!'

In one sense melodrama typifies the period. Dion Boucicault (1820–90), the Irish-born playwright and actor-manager, was one of its leading practitioners. Famous for his sensation scenes, he provided shipwrecks, earthquakes, erupting volcanoes, floods and burning houses. Heroines were saved from drowning and from fates worse than death. Heroes were saved from being run over by trains and from falling down crevices. 'Sensation is what the public wants,' said Boucicault, 'and you can't give them too much of it.'

Sometimes, of course, things were a bit too sensational. One of the hazards of nineteenth-century theatre-going was that theatres were liable to burn down, not once, not twice, but even three times. Rowdy and vulgar behaviour in theatres was the norm, and riots often took place, especially when billed actors failed to appear, or seat-prices were raised.

The London stage was undoubtedly popular, but unevenly so. Victorian music halls were a good place to pick up prostitutes, and for much of the century the respectable middle classes went only to operas.

Only a tiny fraction of the nineteenth-century repertoire is performed today. It could well be argued that there ought to be a theatre in the West End whose artistic policy would be to revive neglected playwrights and neglected plays and not, of course, just from the nineteenth century and not just British writers.

There would be no shortage of material. Boucicault alone wrote 200 plays. *The Poor of New York* (re-titled according to the city and town in which it was playing), *The Colleen Bawn* and *The Shaughraun* have been produced from time to time, but his other successes have been completely ignored. *The Corsican Brothers* (1852), *Jessie Brown* (1858), *The Octoroon* (1859), *Formosa* (1869) and *Arrah-na-Pogue* (1864) deserve at least to be considered for revival.

The arrival of Tom Robertson (1829–71) in the 1860s was as major a turning-point in the nineteenth century as was the arrival of John Osborne in the 1950s in the twentieth century. Robertson established the drawing-room drama, which dealt with contemporary issues in a realistic manner. He also directed his own plays and always insisted that the actors acted in a naturalistic manner and rejected bombast, tradition and cliché. W. S. Gilbert, who wrote and directed his and Sullivan's Savoy Operas, said that when he was a young man he attended Robertson's rehearsals and had learned how to direct from watching him in action. Robertson made his name with plays such as *Society* (1865), *Ours* (1866), *Caste* (1867), *Play* (1868) and *School* (1869). The story of his life in the theatre has been sentimentalised by Arthur Wing Pinero in *Trelawany of the 'Wells'* (1898), a play that has always been much loved by the acting profession. A reappraisal of Robertson's œuvre is long overdue.

Tom Taylor (1817–80), editor of *Punch*, was also the author of such successes as *Still Waters Run Deep* (1855), *The Contested Election* (1851) and *The Overland Route* (1860), and yet only *The Ticket-of-Leave Man* (1863) is ever revived today.

Plagiarism was rife. A great number of plays were adapted from the French without the permission of their authors. Theatre managers would pay for people who could do shorthand to go to the theatres and take down the text verbatim during the performance; and since there were no copyright laws, there was nothing playwrights could do about it. Interestingly, a major surprise of the period is how rarely playbills advertised the name of the playwright – unless the play was by Shakespeare.

Shakespeare was regularly performed throughout the nineteenth century, but it was not the Shakespeare that we perform today. The texts were cut brutally, re-written with happy endings and, of course, bowdlerised. Spectacular scenes, which Shakespeare had reported but failed to stage, were interpolated. The texts were constantly sacrificed for visual histrionics. The public flocked to see George Frederick Cook's *Richard III*, and if they were lucky he might appear on stage; and if they were even luckier he might not be too drunk to perform. Edmund Kean's Shylock was one of those legendary occasions when an actor makes his name overnight. In his memorable London debut, he rejected tradition, which went right back to the sixteenth century and Richard Burbage, and found a completely new way to play the role. Coleridge's observation that watching Kean act was like reading Shakespeare by lightning has been much quoted; less well known or reported is the fact that Kean not infrequently kept audiences waiting while he fornicated in his dressing-room.

Sarah Siddons' Lady Macbeth sleep-walking has been vividly recorded for posterity in words and art, most famously by, respectively, William Hazlitt and Johann Heinrich Fussli. At her official farewell performance the play stopped on her exit, and those who wanted to know what happened to Macbeth had to come back another day. But Siddons, the greatest English tragedienne, was not the sort of actress who could give up the stage, and she kept on coming back, to the despair of many of her former admirers.

Dorothy Jordan was an adorable and exuberant Rosalind. Nineteen-year-old Fanny Kemble made her reluctant debut as Juliet to improve the box-office at Covent Garden Theatre and to help her actor-manager father, John Philip Kemble, who was in financial difficulties. Helen Faucit's Cordelia was much admired; Isabella Glyn's formidable Cleopatra was the talk of the town; and Charlotte Cushman's Romeo was said to be better than any man's.

Ellen Terry's performance as Imogen must, surely, have been one of the reasons why Alfred Lord Tennyson asked (in his last will and testament) for a copy of Cymbeline to be buried with him. Samuel Phelps' Coriolanus was considered the finest of his generation, and Ada Rehan's Katherina was for many theatre-goers and critics quite simply the best shrew ever. Henry Irving's Shylock was so sympathetic that many people didn't think he was Shylock at all. Johnston Forbes-Robertson, a great Hamlet, never enjoyed acting and claimed there was never a performance when he didn't long for the final curtain to come down.

William Charles Macready was probably the greatest male tragedian of the nineteenth century, and in his position of actor-manager actively raised the standards of the acting profession by insisting on rehearsals for the full company. His two great roles were Macbeth and Lear.

Other actor-managers such as Madame Vestris and her husband Charles Mathews at the Olympic, and Mary Wilton, and her husband Squire Bancroft at the Tottenham Theatre, did much to raise standards. So did Samuel Phelps at Sadler's Wells, and Charles Kean at Princess's and Henry Irving at Lyceum. Vestris was responsible for the box set in 1832, and the realism seen in her theatres anticipated the work of Tom Robertson in the 1850s. Her high production values at Covent Garden and Lyceum were so costly that she and Mathews were bankrupted three times. Mathews ended up in prison.

Wilton turned a theatre that was described as a 'dust-hole' into a small and respectable theatre, which was perfect for the intimacy of Robertson's tiny 'cup-and-saucer' plays. Phelps produced all of Shakespeare's plays at Sadler's Wells Theatre, bar four, and transformed the theatre and its audiences out of all recognition.

Kean became a Fellow of the Society of Antiquaries as a direct result of his productions, which were always notable for their meticulous research and historical accuracy. He was much criticised for illustrating Shakespeare; but it was the spectacle which brought in a public who would almost certainly have stayed away without it. His spectacular productions required large numbers. Kean employed 500 people, which meant that, financially, he was often struggling.

There were visitors from abroad: Edwin Forrest and Edwin Booth from America, Sarah Bernhardt from France, and Eleanor Duse from Italy. Forrest blamed Macready for his bad reviews, and their rivalry was such that when Macready appeared in *Macbeth* in New York on the same night as Forrest was appearing in *Macbeth* there were riots. Booth famously alternated Othello and Iago with Irving. They were both better as Iago. Bernhardt and Duse were great rivals. While Duse was naturalistic, Bernhardt was flamboyant on stage and off. The Prince of Wales dallied with her (often making her late for rehearsals). Wilde wrote *Salome* for her. The Lord Chamberlain banned the play while it was in rehearsal. Biblical figures were not allowed on stage.

Ira Aldridge, who had left America because of racial prejudice at the age of 17, initially had to overcome the same hostility on the London stage; he succeeded triumphantly, not only in black roles, such as Othello and Aaron in *Titus Andronicus*, but also in white roles, and in Europe and Russia, too, winning many awards and honours.

Theatre managers strove for the new, the dramatic, the extravagant. Animals, lions, tigers and elephants trod the boards of London's theatres. Plays were even written for dogs to show their skills. One versatile dog, indeed, played the cat in *Dick Whittington*.

Equestrian drama was particularly popular, and Andrew Ducrow's horsemanship made him a big star. *Richard III* was re-written so that the horse became the leading role. There were rumours that an admirer sent a bouquet of hay to every single performance.

No theatre lover would have wanted to miss Charles Mathews' brilliant one-man shows, when he transformed himself, and at extraordinary speed, into an amazing range of characters, both male and female. T. P. Cooke was the salt of the sea, and cornered the sailor market for life when he played Long John in Douglas William Jerrold's *Black Eyed Susan*.

John Martin Harvey, exquisitely pathetic, was the definitive Sydney Carton, just as Coquelin, all panache, was the definitive Cyrano de Bergerac. Herbert Beerbohm Tree was a master of make-up, and he loved playing Svengali, although he was under no illusions as to the play's qualities.

If there had to be just one performance that would serve to define the Victorian stage, it would, surely, have to be Henry Irving's performance as Mathias in *The Bells*, which is so embodied in theatrical consciousness that no great actor has appeared in it since. The agonised cries of 'The bells! The bells! The bells!' continue to ring out in the nation's collective memory.

Irving was, in fact, the first actor to be knighted, an act that honoured not only him but the whole profession. Queen Victoria, incidentally, loved the theatre and was a regular theatre-goer until Prince Albert died in 1861 and she went into permanent mourning.

Hopefully, in the not too distant future, someone might think not only about reviving *The Bells* and the plays of Tom Robertson, Dion Boucicault and Tom Taylor, but also such plays as W. S. Gilbert's charming *Engaged* (which Oscar Wilde obviously drew on when he came to write *The Importance of Being Earnest*) or Henry Arthur Jones' *The Liars*, one of the most successful comedies of the 1890s.

Arthur Wing Pinero's *The Profligate* would certainly make a change from his usual farces. It might be foolhardy to revive Edward Bulwer Lytton's *Richelieu*; but it could well be fun to revive Charles Reade's *The Lyons Mail*.

The chronology which follows, with its nostalgic drawings, photographs, playbills and caricatures, recalls and celebrates famous productions, famous personalities and famous theatre buildings.

London Stage in the Nineteenth Century is both a reference book and a book for theatre lovers to dip into for the sheer pleasure of looking at the pictures and the sheer fun of reading the often rude and acerbic reviews of the critical fraternity. But at the same time it is to be hoped very much that the running commentary and the quotes from the critics, and the actors, and the playwrights themselves, will also encourage theatre practitioners to take a more serious look at the neglected works of the nineteenth century and to restage the best of them.

Acknowledgements

Robert Tanitch would like to put on record his sincere appreciation to his publisher, Alistair Hodge. He would also like to thank the staffs of the Theatre Museum and Westminster Reference Library for their invaluable help and, as always, for making his frequent visits so pleasurable. He would also like to thank Westminster City Archives, and Rory Lalwan in particular, for the endless trouble he went to in giving him access to Westminster's wonderful collection of drawings, photographs and playbills and who was responsible for scanning all of the images that appear in this book.

RIGHT

Sarah Siddons as Queen Katharine in Shakespeare's Henry VIII. Siddons was probably the greatest tragedienne in English theatre. Her other great Shakespearian roles included Lady Macbeth, Constance in King John, Isabella in Measure for Measure and Volumnia in Coriolanus. William Hazlitt described her as 'not less than a goddess, or than a prophetess inspired by the gods'.

The
1800s

The playbill for John Gay's The Beggar's Opera at Theatre Royal, Covent Garden, in 1800. The Spoil'd Child was a farce by Isaac Bickerstaffe.

Gay's hugely successful ballad opera had been premiered in London at Lincoln's Inn Fields in 1728, making so much money for John Rich, the theatre owner, that he felt able to invest in the construction of the Theatre Royal, Covent Garden, which opened four years later.

The Beggar's Opera was a mainstay of the London stage well into the twentieth century.

THEATRE ROYAL, COVENT GARDEN,
This prefent WEDNESDAY, Sept. 24, 1800,
Will be prefented

The BEGGAR's OPERA.

Captain Macheath by Mr. INCLEDON,
Peachum by Mr. DAVENPORT,
Lockit by Mr. THOMPSON,
Mat o'the Mint, Mr. Denman, Ben Budge, Mr. Klanert,
Wat Dreary, Mr Street, Nimming Ned, Mr Atkins,
Harry Paddington Mr Claremont, Robin of Bagfhot Mr Wilde,
Jailor Mr Blurton, Drawer Mr Abbot, Filch Mr SIMMONS,
Lucy by Mrs. MARTYR,
Mrs. Peachum by Mrs. DAVENPORT,
Jenny Diver, Mrs Caftelle, Mrs Coaxer, Mrs Follett,
Dolly Trull, Mrs Blurton, Mrs Vixen, Mrs Norton,
Betty Doxey, Mrs Sydney, Mrs Slammekin, Mifs Leferve,
Sukey Tawdry, Mrs Watts, Molly Brazen, Mrs Lloyd,
And Polly by Mifs DIXON,
(From the Opera Houfe, Pupil of Mrs. CROUCH, being her firft Appearance on this Stage)
In Act III. a HORNPIPE in Fetters by Mr. PLATT.
To which will be added (by Permiffion of the Proprietors of Drury Lane Theatre) the FARCE of

The SPOIL'D CHILD.

Little Pickle by Mrs. MILLS,
Mr Pickle Mr EMERY, John Mr Abbot, Thomas Mr Street
And Tag by Mr. KNIGHT,
Maria by Mifs SIMS,
Sufan, Mifs LESERVE, Margery, Mrs. WHITMORE,
and Mifs Pickle by Mrs. DAVENPORT.

No Money to be Returned.   Printed by F. MACLEISH, 2. Bow-ftreet.

In confequence of the univerfal Applaufe with which Mr. BRUNTON
was honored on his firft Appearance in the Character of
Frederick in LOVER's VOWS; and the loud and general Teftimonies
of Approbation beftowed on Mrs. BASTAR in the POOR SOLDIER,
both thofe Pieces will be repeated on Friday.
On Monday, Mr. BRUNTON will perform the Part of HAMLET—after
which will be revived the Opera, in one Act, of DAPHNE & AMIN-
TOR—Amintor by Mr. INCLEDON, and Daphne by a YOUNG LADY,
who never appeared on any Stage.
On Wednefday, Mr. BLANCHARD, from the Theatre Royal, Norwich,
will make his firft appearance on this Stage, in the Characters of ACRES
in the Comedy of the RIVALS, and CRACK, in the Comic Opera
of the TURNPIKE GATE.   A New Comedy called LIFE; and
a New Mufical After-piece called the TWO FARMERS, is in rehearfal

1800

JANUARY 3. William Thomas Lewis as Goldfinch in Thomas Holcroft's **The Road to Ruin** at Covent Garden Theatre. John Emery as Silky. Romantic sentiment and cynical opportunism: the hero is willing to marry a rich old woman in order to save his bankrupt father. Premiered in 1792, it remained enormously popular throughout the nineteenth century.

FEBRUARY 8. John Fawcett, Alexander Pope and Mary Davenport in Thomas Morton's **Speed the Plough** at Covent Garden Theatre. Seduction, adultery, duels and bloodshed: a knight believes erroneously that he has killed his brother. This sentimental comedy is only remembered, if remembered at all, for Mrs Grundy, a character, who is much talked about, yet never appears. Mrs Grundy became synonymous with middle-class prudery and propriety, and 'What will Mrs Grundy say?' became a popular catchphrase.

> The sentiments are instructive and patriotic, and those indelicate allusions and paltry double-entendres which have unfortunately been allowed to degrade the theatre by insulting common sense, and undermining common decency have been carefully avoided … It is unquestionably superior for rustic honesty and independence of mind, to any other of the same class in modern drama. *The Times*

MARCH 28. Premiere of Haydn's Oratorio, **The Creation**, at Covent Garden Theatre. This joyous celebration of the universe was an antidote to the misery of the Napoleonic wars.

MARCH 29. John Philip Kemble and Sarah Siddons in Joanna Baillie's **De Montfort** at Drury Lane Theatre. Blank verse tragedy. De Montfort's hatred is totally irrational. When he suspects his sister, for whom he has incestuous feelings, is going to marry his former friend he murders him. Kemble

gave a powerful performance. Siddons enjoyed her role enormously. The scenery – especially the convincing set for the cathedral aisle in the final scene – was highly praised. The play, however, a typical example of the romantic Sturm and Drang movement, was heavy-going, and the public didn't like it and hissed. There were only eleven performances. It was revived at Drury Lane, 21 years later, by Edmund Kean. It was a total failure.

APRIL 3. John Philip Kemble as Valentine in William Congreve's **Love for Love** at Drury Lane Theatre. Dorothy Jordan as Miss Prue. Jane Pope as Mrs Frail. John Palmer as Tattle.

> [*Love for Love*], notwithstanding the ample curtailment, is still too gross for public representation. In other respects we readily concede to it its just portion of praise for wit, humour, sprightliness of dialogue, and happy delineation of character. *Dramatic Censor*

APRIL 6. John Fawcett, John Emery and Edward Knight in George Colman the Younger's **Heir of Law** at Haymarket Theatre.

> Mr Colman calls *Heir of Law* a comedy but Mr Fawcett certainly exerts himself to make it farce; and so it will always be while an actor's chief study is to make his characters merely laughable. LEIGH HUNT

APRIL 14. Joseph Grimaldi and Baptiste Dubois in Thomas Dibdin's **Peter Wilkins or Harlequin in the Flying World** at Sadler's Wells Theatre. Grimaldi, in his first big success, rejected the traditional rosy-faced clown and wore a white face with scarlet half-mooned cheeks.

MAY 15. James Hadfield, an ex-soldier, attempted to assassinate King George III in Drury Lane Theatre during a performance of Colley Cibber's

World premieres
Friedrich Schiller's *Maria Stuart*
in Weimar

Deaths
William Cowper, poet
(b. 1731)

Births
Frederick Lémaître, French
actor
Thomas Babbington Macaulay,
British essayist, historian
William Fox Talbot, British
photographer

History
Napoleonic Wars continue
Act of Union passed, bringing
Ireland into United
Kingdom
Napoleon Bonaparte invades
Italy

She Would and She Would Not. The king, showing admirable sangfroid, refused to leave. After Hadfield had been arrested the audience sang 'God Save the King' twice. Hadfield was mad, and confined in Bedlam for the rest of his life.

MAY 21. William Barrymore, George Wathen and Dorothy Jordan in Oliver Goldsmith's ***She Stoops to Conquer*** at Drury Lane Theatre.

JUNE 13. Mr Quick as Mendoza in Richard Brinsley Sheridan's ***The Duenna*** and Mrs Jordan in ***The Sultan*** at Covent Garden Theatre. Jordan sang 'Blue Bell of Scotland', a patriotic song she had written about fighting the French.

JULY 5. Charles Kemble in John Fawcett's ***Obi or Three Finger'd Jack, The Terror of Jamaica*** at Haymarket Theatre. Music by Samuel Arnold. A pantomimic melodrama, with a political agenda, related the rebellious activities of an escaped Jamaican slave.

OCTOBER 6. James Brunton and Jane Pope in Shakespeare's ***Romeo and Juliet*** at Covent Garden Theatre. William Thomas Lewis playing Mercutio stole the plaudits.

OCTOBER 20. John Philip Kemble in Shakespeare's ***Hamlet*** at Drury Lane Theatre. Joseph Grimaldi played the Second Gravedigger. Two days earlier his wife had died in childbirth.

> Such, indeed, are the unrivalled beauties of Mr Kemble's personification of the character that frivolous and debauched as is the public taste, the play never fails to attract a crowded audience; and never were we persuaded was morality more impressively, more successfully inculcated from the pulpit, than it is by this Gentleman from the stage. *Dramatic Censor*

OCTOBER 30. George Frederick Cooke made his London debut in Shakespeare's **Richard III** at Covent Garden Theatre. He had already made his name in Dublin and the English provinces. He was 46 years old. *The Sun* thought his performance was too jocose and familiar for tragedy. *The Morning Post* complained that, 'his voice is uncommonly harsh, and at times unmusical. It even seems in some notes to be cracked.' But such was Cooke's success that Kemble never acted Richard again.

> His [Cooke] superiority over all others, in the confident dissimulation, the crafty hypocrisy, and the bitter sarcasm of the character, is acknowledged by every writer who has criticised his acting. WILLIAM DUNLAP, *Memoirs of George Fred. Cooke Esq.*

> The singularity of his utterance was that he spoke with two voices, one of which was harsh and acrimonious, the other mild and caressing. The great secret of his effect in speaking was a rapid transition from one of these sounds to the other. JAMES BOADEN, *Memoirs of the Life of John Philip Kemble*

> Cooke is perfect caricature. He gives you the monster, but not the man Richard. ... He gives you no other idea than of a vulgar villain, rejoicing in his being able to overreach, and not possessing that joy in silent consciousness, but betraying it, like a poor villain, in sneers and distortions of the face, like a droll at a country fair. CHARLES LAMB, *Morning Post*

OCTOBER 30. William Barrymore in Mrs Francis Plowden's **Virginia** at Drury Lane Theatre. The drama, set in America during Elizabethan times, was so bad and the resulting uproar so great that hardly a word of the text was heard after the second act. Finally, Kemble, manager of the theatre, came forward to say the play would not be performed ever again. The announcement was received with universal applause.

NOVEMBER 10. George Frederick Cooke as Shylock and Mrs Murray as Portia in Shakespeare's **The Merchant of Venice** at Covent Garden Theatre.

NOVEMBER 20. John Philip Kemble in Shakespeare's **King John** at Drury Lane Theatre. Sarah Siddons as Constance. Charles Kemble as Faulconbridge. The play was popular because of its anti-French sentiments.

NOVEMBER 28. John Philip Kemble as Othello and George Frederick Cooke as Iago in Shakespeare's **Othello** at Covent Garden Theatre. 'Mr Cooke,' said Leigh Hunt in *News*, 'is the Machiavell of the modern stage.'

DECEMBER 5. George Frederick Cooke and Harriet Litchfield in Shakespeare's **Macbeth** at Covent Garden Theatre. 'He spoke,' said *Theatre*, 'in a tone rather too familiar for the dignity of tragedy.'

DECEMBER 6. Sarah Siddons as Lady Randolph in Rev. John Home's **Douglas** at Drury Lane Theatre. This romantic tragedy had been rejected by Garrick in 1749, who declared it was totally unfit for the stage. It was, however, a huge success in Edinburgh, provoking a memorable reaction from the audience: 'Whaur's yer Wully Shakespere noo?' Its success in London was due entirely to Siddons.

DECEMBER 13. John Philip Kemble and Sarah Siddons in **Antonio or The Soldier's Return** at Drury Lane Theatre. The performance was pompous and extravagant, without either energy or accuracy of meaning. 'The only sensation they produced,' reported *The Times*, 'was a regret that such talents should be lavished on such a production.'

DECEMBER 17. George Frederick Cooke as Kitely and John Fawcett as Captain Bobadil in Ben Jonson's **Every Man in His Humour** at Covent Garden Theatre.

1801

JANUARY 9. Charles Kemble in George Farquhar's **The Inconstant** at Drury Lane Theatre. Charles was John Philip Kemble's son.

> The audience was surprised with his [Kemble] manner and style of acting and the newspapers reverberated his praise the next morning in strains of the most delightful panegyric. There are some stomachs that will swell on anything – no matter how rank and fulsome the fumes of adulation. *Dramatic Censor*

JANUARY 27. George Frederick Cooke and Harriet Litchfield in Benjamin Thompson's **The Stranger** at Covent Garden Theatre. Based on August von Kotzebue's *Misanthropy and Repentance*. Wife runs off with her lover, leaving her children behind. When she returns, she finds they have forgotten her.

> He [Cooke] fails because his habits, his manners, his disposition and his whole train of thought and action are not so totally absorbed in self as to render him as adequate and perfect a representative of a misanthrope. *Dramatic Censor*

FEBRUARY 11. William Thomas Lewis, Joseph Munden and Isabella Mattocks in George Colman the Younger's **The Poor Gentleman** at Covent Garden Theatre. A decent but penniless lieutenant wins the girl he loves despite the machinations of a wealthy and mendacious knight. Colman was criticised for writing for 'the depraved palate of the town'.

FEBRUARY 12. Sarah Siddons as Imogen and John Philip Kemble as Posthumus in Shakespeare's **Cymbeline** at Drury Lane Theatre. Charles Kemble as Guidarius. Elegant rusticity.

FEBRUARY 24. Thomas Holcroft's **Deaf and Dumb or The Orphan Protected** at Drury Lane Theatre. The 8-year-old orphan, deaf and dumb, heir to a fortune and palace, is dumped on the streets of Paris by his wicked guardian, who wants the money and the estate all for himself.

MARCH 12. Dorothy Jordan as Peggy in David Garrick's **The Country Girl** at Drury Lane Theatre. Garrick's sanitised version of William Wycherley's *The Country Wife*. Peggy, first acted by Jordan in 1785, was one of her favourite roles.

> Though she [Jordan] was neither beautiful, nor handsome, nor even pretty, nor accomplished, nor 'a lady', nor anything conventional or comme il faut whatsoever, yet was so pleasant, so cordial, so natural, so full of spirits, so healthily constituted in mind and body, had such a shapely leg withal, so charming a voice, and such a happy and happy-making expression of countenance, that she appeared something superior to all those requirements of acceptability, and to hold a patent from nature herself for our delight and good opinion. LEIGH HUNT

MARCH 28. George Frederick Cooke as Sir Giles Overreach in Philip Massinger's **A New Way to Pay Old Debts** at Covent Garden Theatre.

> In his convulsive agony, he was only noisy; his face refused to supply what breath failed to utter. JAMES BOADEN, *Memoirs of the Life of John Philip Kemble*

APRIL 11. George Frederick Cooke in Colley Cibber's version of Shakespeare's **Richard III** at Covent Garden Theatre. 'Perfect caricature,' said Charles Lamb. 'He gives you the monster Richard but not the man Richard.' When the audience complained they could not hear him, Cooke's reaction was to walk off stage in the middle of the fourth act.

MAY 4. Charles Kemble and Dorothy Jordan in Matthew 'Monk' Lewis's **Adelmorn, The Outlaw**, at Drury Lane Theatre. The critics dismissed the play, which was based on a true murder story, as insufferable, stupid, absurd, uninteresting and blasphemous. The high spot was when the Ghost's costume accidentally caught fire and had to be extinguished.

> I sincerely hope my readers may discover more merit in it than I have hitherto been able to find myself. MATTHEW LEWIS, Preface to the published play

SEPTEMBER 27. George Frederick Cooke in Shakespeare's **Hamlet** at Covent Garden Theatre. Disastrous.

OCTOBER 8. Henry Siddons (son of Sarah Siddons and nephew to John Philip Kemble) made his debut in **Integrity**, an adaptation of a German comedy, at Drury Lane Theatre. Moral insipidity and poor speaking didn't help. No author was listed, but

1801

World premieres	Births	History
Friedrich Schiller's *Die Jungfrau von Orleans* in Leipzig	Cardinal Newman, British theologian	London Stock Exchange is founded
Frederick Schiller's *Maria Stuart*	Johann Nestroy, Austrian dramatist	Battle of Copenhagen
		First national census: London has a population of 860,035

everybody presumed that the play had been written by Henry Siddons.

> It is a very honourable recommendation of the piece that a single sentiment does not occur which is not calculated to promote the interests of virtue. *The Times*

DECEMBER 4. John Philip Kemble as Zanga in Dr Young's **Revenge** at Drury Lane Theatre. The performance had a noisy reception. Kemble remained cool, and addressed the audience directly and sarcastically: 'We cannot express how much we feel obliged to you for the honour of your attendance; but at this rate the object of your visit must be completely frustrated. We must therefore, entreat you to *condescend* to favour us with a *little more* of your ATTENTION.'

DECEMBER 26. Riot at Covent Garden Theatre during Shakespeare's **Richard III**. Despite the arrest of the main troublemakers, the audience's continued bad behaviour made the performance impossible. Missiles – including wine glasses, quart bottles, apples and oranges – were repeatedly thrown, and it wasn't until six guardsmen with fixed bayonets arrived in the gallery that the drunken mob was dispersed.

> I could always wish the Military to act on such occasions; because when the storm rages, any other action is very *bad acting* indeed. Nothing but the fear of their lives will alarm our rabble sufficiently to quiet them. JAMES BOADEN, *Memoirs of the Life of John Philip Kemble*

John Philip Kemble (1757–1823) was actor and theatre manger of Covent Garden Theatre. His most famous roles were Hamlet, Brutus and Coriolanus. 'Mr Kemble,' said William Hazlitt, 'sacrifices too much to decorum. He is chiefly afraid of being contaminated by too close an identity with the character he represents.'

1802

JANUARY 2. Miss Murray as Rosalind in Shakespeare's *As You Like It* at Covent Garden Theatre. George Frederick Cooke as Jaques. 'Instead of the pensive philosophic Jaques,' said *The Morning Post*, 'we seemed to behold the ploughman from the ale house.'

JANUARY 8. George Frederick Cooke in Shakespeare's *King Lear* at Covent Garden Theatre.

JANUARY 15. George Frederick Cooke and Harriet Litchfield in Monk Lewis's *Alfonso, King of*

Castile at Covent Garden Theatre. Treason, lust, murder, parricide, suicide and bombastic extravagance: Cooke revelled in all the guilt and horror.

MARCH 24. John Philip Kemble as Leontes and Sarah Siddons as Hermione in Shakespeare's ***The Winter's Tale*** at Drury Lane Theatre. Mrs Powell as Paulina. Siddons, according to one critic, was 'one of the noblest statues that even Grecian task ever invented ... Upon the magical words pronounced by Paulina, "Music; awake her: strike", the sudden action of the head absolutely startled as though such a miracle had really vivified the marble; and the descent from the pedestal was equally graceful and affecting.'

APRIL 10. George Frederick Cooke as Sir Partinax Macsycophant in Charles Macklin's ***The Man of the World*** at Covent Garden Theatre.

APRIL 30. Dorothy Jordan in Arthur Murphy's ***Three Weeks after Marriage*** at Covent Garden Theatre.

' *It was not as an actress but herself that she charmed every one. Mrs Jordan was the same in all her characters, and inimitable in all of them, because there was no one like her. Her face, her tears, her manners were irresistible. Her smile had the effect of sunshine, and her laugh did one good to hear it. Her voice was eloquence itself: it seemed as if her heart was always in her mouth. She was all gaiety, openness and good nature. She rioted in her fine animal spirits, and gave more pleasure than any other actress, because she had the greatest spirit of enjoyment in herself.* '

WILLIAM HAZLITT

The report in a Morning Paper of Mrs Jordan having entered into an engagement with the proprietors of Drury Lane Theatre for a salary of forty-five guineas a week is without the smallest foundation. Much as we admire her talent were such salaries given it would excite no surprise to hear Managers were ruined.   *The Times*

1802

Births	Deaths	Notes
John Baldwin Buckstone, British actor, dramatist, manager	George Romney, English artist (b. 1734)	Madame Tussaud gives her first exhibition of waxworks at Lyceum Theatre
Benjamin Disraeli, British Prime Minister	*Literature*	
Alexandre Dumas, père, French dramatist, novelist	Wordsworth and Coleridge's *Lyrical Ballads*	*History*
Victor Hugo, French poet, dramatist, novelist	Wordsworth's poem 'Westminster Bridge'	Treaty of Amiens ends war with France, temporarily London's West India Docks open

MAY 1. Dorothy Jordan as Miss Lucy in Henry Fielding's **The Virgin Unmasked** at Drury Lane Theatre. Musical farce. Lucy accepts numerous proposals of marriage from the gentry, but finally marries a footman. (Jordan was mistress to the Duke of Clarence, later King William IV, and she bore him ten children.)

MAY 11. George Frederick Cooke attempted to play Orsino in Shakespeare's **Twelfth Night** at Covent Garden Theatre. Cooke was so inebriated that he was hissed off the stage.

> When the tragedian was intoxicated he was overbearing, noisy and insufferably egotistical, asking questions and answering them himself. Thus; Who am I? Sir George Frederick Cooke, sir. What am I, sir? The Tragedian, not Black Jack, sir. *Records of a Stage Veteran*

MAY 17. Dorothy Jordan in Richard Steele's **The Tender Husband** at Drury Lane Theatre. William Charles Macready said she had 'a spirit of fun that would have out-laughed Puck himself'.

SEPTEMBER 27. George Frederick Cooke in Shakespeare's **Hamlet** at Covent Garden Theatre.

> Such a text as Mr Cooke then spoke in the part of Hamlet, I never yet read; and doubt whether it could be found in print. JAMES BOADEN, *Memoirs of the Life of John Philip Kemble*

OCTOBER 7. Stephen Kemble as Falstaff in Shakespeare's **Henry IV Part 1** at Drury Lane Theatre. Kemble was so obese he didn't need any padding. J. R. Planché said, 'his reading of the part was irreproachable, but he lacked the natural humour, and was too ill at ease to portray the mere animal spirits of the jovial knight.'

NOVEMBER 13. Charles Farley and H. Johnstone in Thomas Holcroft's **A Tale of Mystery** at Covent Garden Theatre. This was the first play to be advertised as a melodrama. It was based on Pixerecourt's *Coelina ou L'enfant de Mystère*, and offered a combination of dialogue and dumb show. The hero was dumb, but Farley managed to make his dumbness

A portrait of Dorothy Jordan (1761–1816) in The Country Girl. The portrait is by George Romney, and engraved by F. Bartolozzi. Jordan was born Dorothy Bland. She assumed the name Mrs Jordan; there was no Mr Jordan. She was the mistress of the future George IV.

highly articulate. An anti-Semitic song caused offence.

NOVEMBER 20. Dorothy Jordan as Mrs Sullen and Charles Kemble as Aimwell and Mr Dwyer in George Farquhar's ***The Beaux' Stratagem*** at Drury Lane Theatre.

DECEMBER 18. Dorothy Jordan as Rosalind in Shakespeare's ***As You Like It*** at Drury Lane Theatre. One of Jordan's most popular roles. Playwright Elizabeth Inchbald described her as 'the Rosalind of both art and nature'.

1803

JANUARY 29. William Downton in Thomas Holcroft's ***Hear Both Sides*** at Drury Lane Theatre. The comedy was a satire against lawyers and got bad reviews. Holcroft accused the Press of being false, ludicrous and insipid. *The Times* recommended he should write no more plays.

MARCH 5. George Frederick Cooke as Peregrine in George Colman the Younger's ***John Bull or An Englishman's Fireside*** at Covent Garden Theatre. Sentimental comedy. Peregrine runs away from home, goes abroad, makes his fortune, returns to England to find the man, who had once lent him ten guineas when he was destitute, is bankrupt. Colman had great difficulty finishing the play, and it was only by locking him in his room and not giving him any money that he completed it. *Theatre Journal* was impressed with the final result: 'For wit, humour, repartee, equivoque and genuine pathos it is one of the best efforts of the English comic drama.'

The play is a monument of genius, left rather unfinished, a bold illustration of national character, and a noble lesson of high morality. As such it was and continues to be, received by the public of England and America. Its great object is to excite a just detestation of the character of a seducer and to inculcate mercy and forgiveness to the seducer. WILLIAM DUNLAP, *Memoirs of George Fred. Cooke*

JUNE 10. Jane Pope had an apoplectic fit on stage while playing Desdemona in Shakespeare's ***Othello*** at Covent Garden. She died on 18 June.

SEPTEMBER 24. Charles Kemble in Shakespeare's ***Hamlet*** at Covent Garden Theatre.

Later actors have played the part with more energy, walked more in the sun – dashed more at effects, piqued themselves more on the girth of a foil, but Kemble's sensible, lonely Hamlet has not been surpassed. WILLIAM HAZLITT

SEPTEMBER 27. Sarah Siddons as Isabella in Shakespeare's ***Measure for Measure*** at Covent Garden Theatre. Siddons was old and overweight. In Act V, when she had to kneel down and plead for Angelo's life, two attendants were needed to

World premieres	Births	History
August von Kotzebue's *The German Provincial* in St Petersburg	William Douglas Jerrold, British dramatist Edward Bulwer-Lytton, British novelist, dramatist, politician Charles Mathews, British actor	Napoleon assembles huge fleet at Boulogne and an army of 15,000 at Dunkirk in preparation for the invasion of Britain

1803

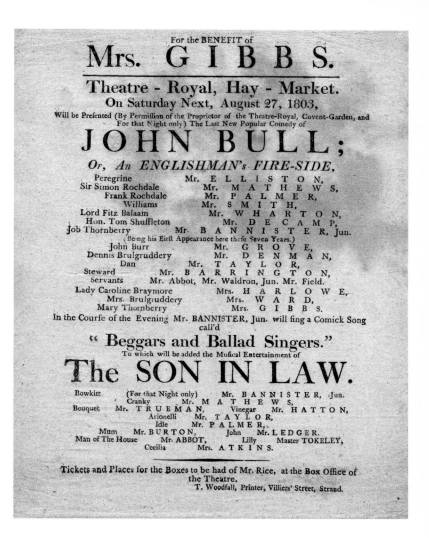

A playbill for George Colman the Younger's John Bull and John O'Keefe's The Son in Law at Theatre Royal, Haymarket, in 1803.

help her rise. So that this was not too obvious to the audience, the other two actresses on their knees were also helped up.

OCTOBER 17. George Frederick Cooke, Sarah Siddons and John Philip Kemble in Richard Brinsley Sheridan's *Pizarro* at Covent Garden. Cooke was too drunk to speak his lines, let alone act them. Kemble apologised to the audience.

NOVEMBER 5. William Thomas Lewis as Jeremy Diddler in James Kenney's *Raising the Wind* at Covent Garden Theatre. Kenney was 23 years old. The farce was a success due to the popularity of Diddler, who (coining a new word) diddles everybody, never pays back a loan, outwits a family,

and gets the better of his rival in love with a series of deceptions.

NOVEMBER 17. Sarah Siddons in Thomas Otway's *Venice Preserv'd* at Drury Lane Theatre.

I never played more to my own satisfaction than last night in Belvidera: if I may say so, it was hardly acting, it seemed to me, and I believe to the audience, almost reality. SARAH SIDDONS

DECEMBER 5. John Bannister Jr, William Downton and Harriot Mellon in Frederick Reynolds' *The Caravan or The Driver and His Dog* at Drury Lane Theatre. The dog, to tumultuous applause, leaped into a stream of real water and saved a child. The dog was the main attraction, bringing in huge audiences and saving the theatre from financial ruin.

DECEMBER 19. Joseph Munden, William Blanchard and Julia Glover in Thomas Dibdin's *The English Fleet in 1342* at Covent Garden

Theatre. Historical comic opera: a patriotic piece to support the English war effort. Music by John Braham.

DECEMBER 26. First performance of Charles Dibdin's *Little Red Riding Hood* at Sadler's Wells Theatre.

1804

JANUARY 3. First performance of *Cinderella or The Little Glass Slipper* at Drury Lane Theatre. Billed as 'A New Grand Allegorical Pantomime'. Music by Michael Kelly. The book was said to have been written by 'a young Oxonian'. Theresa De Camp played Cinderella. 'It is,' said one critic, 'perhaps the happiest tale that could possibly be selected to instruct and amuse the rising generation. How lovely is virtue! How base and degrading is vice!' Joseph Grimaldi played Pedro, servant to the Ugly Sisters.

' *He [Betty] furnishes another proof of the superiority of British genius over the genius of any other country.* '

The Times

APRIL 2. John Conway, Mr Smith and Mr Ingle in Charles Dibdin's *The Siege of Gibraltar* at Sadler's Wells Theatre. The scenery was painted by R. C. Andrews. There was real water. The ships were built and rigged (on an inch scale) by shipwrights and riggers for His Majesty's Dockyard at Woolwich. In his memoirs Dibdin boasted that he didn't think anybody who had witnessed it would not have asserted that 'it was one of the most novel, imposing and nationally worthy exhibitions' they had ever seen.

APRIL 3. Charles Farley and Baptiste Dubois in Thomas Dibdin's *Valentine and Orson* at Covent

Garden Theatre. Billed as 'Grand serio-comick romantick melodrama in two acts'. Overture and music by Mr Jouve. Valentine was a foundling. Orson was a wild man. The production included a Grand Pageant representing a meeting between the Emperor of Constantinople and the King of France.

APRIL 16. William Downton as Dr Cantwell in Isaac Bickerstaff's *The Hypocrite* at Drury Lane Theatre. English version of Molière's *Tartuffe*. Downton was said to be inimitable in the role.

MAY 27. Robert William Elliston, John Palmer, Charles Mathews, Theresa De Camp and Mrs Gibbs in Thomas Dibdin's *Guilty or Nor Guilty* at Haymarket Theatre. An adaptation of a French farce.

A high minded young man, who has been expelled the university, obliged to leave the army under the imputation of cowardice, who has leagued with gamblers, who is charged with the crime of seduction, and of having attempted his father's life, and his step-mother's honour, and yet acquiesces under all calumny consequent upon such vices, without an effort of exculpation, is a character, perhaps, within the range of dramatic possibility, but certainly England is not the soil which is liable to produce him. *The Times*

JUNE 20. Thomas Dibdin's *The Enchanted Island* at Haymarket Theatre. A picturesque, spectacular and magical prequel to Shakespeare's *The Tempest*. 37 performances.

NOVEMBER 24. Robert William Elliston and Dorothy Jordan in James Kenney's **Matrimony** at Drury Lane Theatre. Leigh Hunt said it was the best amorous quarrel he had ever witnessed.

DECEMBER 1. Master Betty as Achmet in Dr John Brown's **Barbarossa** at Drury Lane Theatre. Huge box office success. The 12-year-old William Henry Betty was hailed as Garrick reborn and The Infant Roscius. A detachment of Guards and constables was sent to control the crowds who had come to watch the arrival of the distinguished audience which included the Prince of Wales, Prime Minister Pitt, MP Fox and Lady Caroline Lamb. A legend grew that Pitt had adjourned the House of Commons so that MPs could attend a performance. The audience was predominantly male. Betty's salary was 150 guineas for the first three nights. Thereafter it was raised to 100 guineas a night. He played 28 nights and earned £17,210 11s. Betty was painted by John Opie, James Northcote and Henry Heath. His success was absurd. He had no expression and his voice was sing-song, but the public, female and male alike, fell in love with him. His career lasted just over a year.

> He [Betty] was at times too rapid to be distinct; and at others too noisy for anything but rant … The wonder was how any body, who had just completed his 12th year, could catch passion, meaning, cadence, action, expression and the discipline of the stage in ten very different and arduous characters. JAMES BOADEN, *Memoirs of the Life of John Philip Kemble*

DECEMBER 4. Master Betty as Young Norval in Rev. John Home's **Douglas** at Drury Lane Theatre.

Robert Elliston (1774–1831) was actor-manager of the Surrey, Olympic and Drury Lane theatres.

Based on the ballad of Gil Morrice, Home's play was a lot of artificial rhetoric. John Philip Kemble and Mrs Siddons refused to act with a child, but George Frederick Cooke, being short of cash, had no option but to do so. He was heavily criticised for stooping to bully a boy.

> The popularity of that baby-faced boy, who possessed not even the elements of a good actor, was a hallucination in the public's mind, and a disgrace to our theatre history. THOMAS CAMPBELL, biographer of Sarah Siddons

World premieres
Ludwig van Beethoven's Eroica Symphony (originally named Bonaparte)

Births
Samuel Phelps, British actor

Deaths
John Tobin, British dramatist (b. 1770)

Literature
William Blake's *Jerusalem*

History
Richard Trevithick tests world's first locomotive

1804

HAMLET.

THE YOUNG ROSCIUS,

MASTER BETTY as HAMLET.

Ham. *Whither wilt thou lead me? Speak. I'll go no fur*

The Young Roscius: Master Betty, 13-year-old child prodigy, as Hamlet at Drury Lane Theatre in 1805. Betty (William Henry West, 1791–1874) was the most popular child actor of the nineteenth century.

1805

JANUARY 8. Rebecca Duncan and Robert William Elliston in Dr Hoadly's **The Suspicious Husband** at Drury Lane Theatre.

We are sorry to be obliged to renew our objections to his [Elliston's] deportment and attitudes; they are too studied and mechanical. They have more the stiffness and precision of a Maître de Ballet than the unaffected ease of a well-bred gentleman.
The Times

JANUARY 15. George Frederick Cooke, Charles Kemble, Joseph Munden, William Thomas Lewis, John Emery and Harriet Litchfield in Thomas Morton's **The School of Reform or How to Rule a Husband** at Covent Garden Theatre. Emery was so funny that he was encored in the middle of the play.

JANUARY 31. Robert William Elliston, Charles Mathews, Rebecca Duncan, Harriet Mellon in John Tobin's **Honey Moon** at Drury Lane Theatre. A very popular re-working of Shakespeare's *The Taming of the Shrew*.

Miss Duncan is covered with splendid elegancies for the envy or admiration of the ladies. The high Argus Pheasant feathers in her hat wave without any motion of the head and play from side to side with a breath of air. *Theatre*

FEBRUARY 9. Master Betty in Shakespeare's **Romeo and Juliet** at Covent Garden Theatre.

We are persuaded, long before he [Master Betty] shall have reached maturity, his native genius and boundless capabilities will have placed him far, very far, above every co-rival in the art. *The Times*

FEBRUARY 19. Master Betty in Elizabeth Inchbald's **Lover's Voice** at Drury Lane Theatre.

Such is the rage of the multitude that a new play even from Shakespeare could hardly contend against him … I hate all prodigies – partly I fancy because I have no faith in them … This is a clever little boy, and had I never seen boys act, I might have thought him exquisite. MRS INCHBALD

MARCH 18. Master Betty in Shakespeare's **Hamlet** at Drury Lane Theatre.

Is it not almost a crime to make a child of thirteen years of age act every night, in a large theatre, the most arduous parts of the tragedies represented? *Morning Post*

APRIL 20. Master Betty as Osman and Henry Siddons as Zara in Voltaire's **Zara** at Covent Garden Theatre. Osman is the Sultan of Turkey and Zara is a Christian slave.

There is too much dry, monotonous declamation in the part; this is not the forte of this extraordinary youth [Master Betty]. In forcible and natural delineation of the passions, he is even, at this early age, excelled by few of the

---

World premieres	Deaths	History
Ludwig van Beethoven's *Fidelio* in Vienna	Thomas Murphy, Irish playwright (b. 1727)	London Dock opens for commercial traffic: the first vessel, *London Packet*, brings wine from Oporto
Births	**Notes**	First Trooping of the Colour
Maria Ann Kelley, British actress	Surrey Theatre is destroyed by fire	Battle of Trafalgar; death of Horatio Nelson
Alexis de Tocqueville, French historian	'Tailors Riot' at Haymarket Theatre	Battle of Austerlitz

1805

The playbill for Thomas Morton's *Speed the Plough*
and George Colman the Younger's *Children in the
Wood* at Theatre Royal, Haymarket, in 1805.

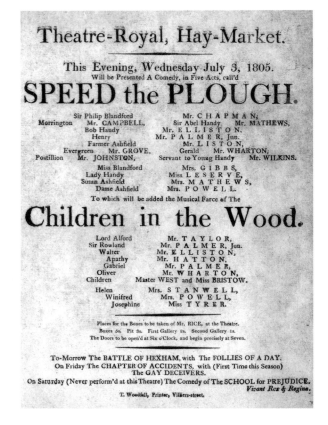

most accomplished proficients in the profession;
but accomplished as he is, he cannot give effect
to the pompous monologues which so often
occur in the play. *The Times*

MAY 8. Master Betty in Shakespeare's ***Richard III***
at Drury Lane Theatre. Betty's performance was
much derided.

SEPTEMBER 30. John Philip Kemble, Harriet
Litchfield and Charles Kemble in Dr Young's
The Revenge at Drury Lane Theatre. Based on
Shakespeare's *Othello*. Kemble's figure didn't look
too good in his tight-fitting costume, but his
performance during Act V produced repeated
'Bravos!' and prolonged applause.

There is always something sublime in the sudden
contemplation of great objects, and perhaps there
is not a sublimer action on the stage than the
stride of Mr Kemble as Zanga, over the body
of his victim, and his majestic exultation of
revenge. LEIGH HUNT, *Dramatic Essays*

NOVEMBER 7. Charles Dibdin's ***Nelson's Glory***
at Covent Garden Theatre. Billed as a 'Royal
Musical Impromptu.' Dibdin wrote it in one day
to celebrate Horatio Nelson's naval victory in the
Battle of Trafalgar.

NOVEMBER 8. John Philip Kemble as Falstaff
in Shakespeare's ***Henry IV Part 1*** at Drury Lane
Theatre. Henry Siddons as Hal. Robert William
Elliston as Hotspur.

We lament to observe that the Hotspur of Mr
Elliston expressed everything but the fire and
animation of a rough soldier … Mr Siddons
was highly interesting but when ringing in the
midnight revels of the Boar's Head on Eastcheap
the gay madcap, nimble-footed Hal dwindled
down to the dull posing of a Methodist Preacher
at a Conventicle. *News*

NOVEMBER 10. Drury Lane Theatre commem-
orated ***The Victory at the Battle of Trafalgar
and the Death of Lord Viscount Nelson*** with a
'new melodramatic piece and appropriate scenery'.
The overture music was by M. P. King and John
Braham.

NOVEMBER 23. Miss Mudie in David Garrick's
The Country Girl at Covent Garden Theatre.
Eight-year-old Ann Mudie attempted to jump
on the band wagon of 12-year-old Master Betty's
success and was hissed off the stage.

DECEMBER 3. Miss Bristow in the first
performance of Sir Lumley Skeffington's ***The
Sleeping Beauty*** at Drury Lane Theatre. 'Very
little skill or ingenuity,' said *The Times*, 'has been
shown in adapting it for the stage. The early scenes
are dull and monotonous.'

1806

JANUARY 4. Master Betty in Shakespeare's *Macbeth* at Drury Lane Theatre.

His [Master Betty] efforts to extend his voice beyond its natural powers caused a hoarseness of delivery, or mouthing, which most often rendered him unintelligible to those who are not immediately acquainted with the text. His performance did not pass without instances of violent opposition but they were silenced by much more violent plaudits.   *Observer*

JANUARY 10. Master Betty and Miss Smith in James Thomson's *Tancred and Sigismund* at Covent Garden Theatre. Heroic tragedy: love, honour and duty in Sicily in the twelfth century.

JANUARY 27. John Philip Kemble and Sarah Siddons in Richard Brinsley Sheridan's *Pizarro* at Covent Garden Theatre. The second most popular play of the nineteenth century.

FEBRUARY 25. John Philip Kemble and Sarah Siddons in Shakespeare's *Macbeth* at Covent Garden Theatre.

We can conceive of nothing grander. It was something above nature. It seemed almost as if a being of superior order had dropped from a higher sphere to awe the world with the majesty of her appearance. Power was seated on her brow. Passion emanated from her breast as from a shrine; she was tragedy personified. In coming in on in the sleep walking scene, her eyes were open but their sense was shut. She was like a person bewildered and unconscious of what she did. Her lips moved involuntarily – all her gestures were involuntary and mechanical. She glided on and off the stage like an apparition. To have seen her in that character was an event in any one's life not to be forgotten.
WILLIAM HAZLITT

SEPTEMBER 18. Olympic Pavilion opened with *Feats of Horsemanship* followed by a pantomime called *The Indian Chief or British Heroism*.

OCTOBER 9. Joseph Grimaldi and Charles Farley in Thomas Dibdin's *Orson and Valentine* at Covent Garden Theatre.

As soon as the act-drop fell, he [Grimaldi] would stagger off the stage into a small room behind the prompter's box, and there sinking into an arm-chair, give full vent to the emotions which he found impossible to suppress. He would sob and cry aloud and suffer so much from agonizing and violent spasms that those about him, accustomed as they at length became to the distressing scene, were often in doubt up to the very moment of his being called whether he would be able to go upon the stage for the second act. He never failed, however.   *Memoirs of Grimaldi* edited by BOZ (Charles Dickens)

NOVEMBER 18. John Philip Kemble in Shakespeare's *Coriolanus* at Covent Garden Theatre. An apple was thrown on the stage while Sarah Siddons, in her role of Constance, was on her knees pleading with Coriolanus not to destroy Rome. Kemble picked up the apple and, addressing the audience, offered 100 guineas to any man who

Births	*Literature*	*History*
Edwin Forrest, American actor	Webster's Dictionary	Napoleon begins 'Continental System' to blockade British ports
Deaths	*Notes*	Cape Colony becomes British colony
William Pitt, British Prime Minister (b. 1759)	Surrey Theatre is re-built Olympic Theatre is built Sans Pareil Theatre opens	

1806

> *Grimaldi appears, every face wears a smile,*
> *As his comical tricks he exhibits the while.*
> *His looks are so queer, and his singing is droll*
> *There are none can look grave for he pleases the*
> *whole.*
>
> Amusements of London

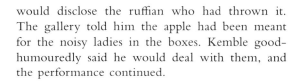

would disclose the ruffian who had thrown it. The gallery told him the apple had been meant for the noisy ladies in the boxes. Kemble good-humouredly said he would deal with them, and the performance continued.

NOVEMBER 20. Robert William Elliston in Thomas Holcroft's **The Vindictive Man** at Drury Lane Theatre.

> Mr Holcroft's friends were not idle for as soon as any one hissed – shewed any public marks of dissatisfaction there was a preconcerted cry of 'turn him out!' and so violent were these monitors that they appeared like a parcel of constables. *News*

DECEMBER 8. John Philip Kemble as Prospero in John Dryden's version of Shakespeare's **The Tempest** at Drury Lane Theatre. Miss Meadows as Ariel. John Emery as Caliban. Louisa Brunton as Miranda. Charles Kemble as Ferdinand. Joseph Munden as Stephano. John Fawcett as Trinculo.

> [Dryden] has filled the dialogue, if not with direct ribaldry, with obscene double meanings and innuendos which he has contrived to render as disgusting as possible by putting them into the mouths of two innocent virgins. *News*

In some of the solemn passages he [Kemble] was extremely impressive; but his forte is not declamation and Prospero offered little room for anything else. *Monthly Mirror*

DECEMBER 29. Joseph Grimaldi as the aged Squire Bullface Bugle and also as the Clown in Thomas Dibdin's **Harlequin, Mother Goose or The Golden Egg** at Covent Garden Theatre. The pantomime established him as the foremost low comedian of his day. Samuel Simmons played Mother Goose. John Bologna played Harlequin. The music was by William Ware. According to Charles Dickens, Grimaldi didn't think much of the production – there was no gorgeous scenery, no beautiful costumes – and he always considered his own performance one of the worst he had ever given. The pantomime, nevertheless, ran for 92 performances and earned more than £20,000 for the theatre. Dibdin complained that Thomas Harris, Covent Garden's theatre manager, had never given him 'a cheering clap on the back'.

> All former pantomimes were eclipsed by this masterpiece of fun, as all former clowns were by Joe [Grimaldi]. It is impossible to describe what he did. A thousand masks would not portray the grotesque proportions of his countenance. J.S.MUNDEN, *Memoirs*

1807

FEBRUARY 17. Alexander Pope and Julia Glover in George Colman's ***The Jealous Husband*** at Covent Garden Theatre.

FEBRUARY 19. Robert William Elliston, John Bannister and Rebecca Duncan in John Tobin's ***The Curfew*** at Drury Lane Theatre. The drama was set during the time of William the Conqueror.

MARCH 7. John Phillip Kemble in Shakespeare's ***Hamlet*** at Covent Garden Theatre. Miss Bolton as Ophelia.

> Kemble turned his head so slowly that people might have imagined he had a stiff neck while the words came so slowly that people thought he might have been reckoning how many words he had got by heart. LEIGH HUNT, *News*

> Neither in voice nor action can we regard Mr Kemble as a model upon which the candidates for dramatic excellence should form themselves. He has two or three remote (very remote) and expressive tones; and two very remote styles of action and deportment, which he alternately plays off in their full force (and generally, it must be admitted, in their right places, though not always right degrees); but he seems to have neglected all the intermediate modifications. *Theatre*

MARCH 10. Charles Kemble in John Maddison Morton's ***Town and Country*** at Covent Garden Theatre. Dissipated young man of fashion elopes with a girl of fortune. John Fawcett as a cockney

stockbroker. Blanchard as a cotton manufacturer. Louisa Brunton as the girl.

MARCH 30. Robert William Elliston in William Dimond's ***The Young Hussar or Love and Mercy*** at Drury Lane Theatre.

APRIL 9. Rebecca Duncan in Andrew Cherry's ***A Day in London*** at Drury Lane Theatre.

APRIL 27. Junius Brutus Booth in William Thomas Moncrieff's ***The Lear of Private Life!, or Father and Daughter*** at Royal Coburg Theatre. A daughter sings a song for her father, who has been mad these last five years, and he recovers his sanity.

John Fawcett (1769–1837) was an actor and dramatist. His most famous role was Dr Panglos in George Colman the Younger's The Heir-in-Law.

Births
Ira Aldridge, African-
American actor

Literature
Thomas Bowdler's *Family
Shakespeare*
Charles and Mary Lamb's
Tales from Shakespeare

History
Abolition of slave trade
Gas street lighting is
introduced to Pall Mall in
London
Congress of Vienna

JUNE 22. Charles Mayne Young in Shakespeare's **Hamlet** at Haymarket. Harriet Litchfield as Gertrude.

The articulation was not nice, and he laboured under a lisp whenever the letter 's' occurred. But there was great ardour, vast animation, powerful action, untiring energy, and good sense. JAMES BOADEN, *Memoirs of the Life of John Philip Kemble*

SEPTEMBER 16. Charles Incledon as Macheath in John Gay's **The Beggar's Opera**. Mary-Catherine Bolton as Polly. Mrs Charles Kemble as Lucy. Joseph Munden as Peachum. Mary Davenport as Mrs Peachum. John Emery as Lockit.

SEPTEMBER 24. Robert William Elliston and Mrs Powell in Matthew Gregory Lewis's **Adelgitha or The Fruits of a Single Error** at Drury Lane Theatre.

SEPTEMBER 28. Miss Norton as Imogen in Shakespeare's **Cymbeline**. John Philip Kemble as Posthumus. Alexander Pope as Iachimo.

OCTOBER 5. Sarah Siddons as Queen Katharine and John Philip Kemble as Cardinal Wolsey in Shakespeare's **Henry VIII** at Covent Garden Theatre.

Mrs Siddons has an air of never being an actress; she seems unconscious that there is a motley crowd called a pit waiting to applaud her, or that there are a dozen fiddlers waiting for her exit. This is always the mark of a great actor … She unites with her noble conceptions of nature every advantage of art, every knowledge of stage propriety and effect. This knowledge, however, she displays not with the pompous minuteness of Mr Kemble, but with that natural carelessness which shows it to be the result of genius rather than grave study. … These are the effects Mr Kemble should study, and not the clap-provoking frivolities of ending every speech with an energetic clash of the fist, or of running off the stage after a vehement declamation, as if the actor was in haste to get his pint of wine. LEIGH HUNT

OCTOBER 15. Panic at Sadler's Wells Theatre. The audience thought the building was on fire. Nineteen people died in the crush to the exits.

NOVEMBER 11. Joseph Munden as Autolycus in Shakespeare's **The Winter's Tale** at Covent Garden Theatre. One of Munden's most famous roles.

When you think he [Joseph Munden] has exhausted his battery of looks, in uncomfortable warfare with your gravity, suddenly he sprouts out an entire new set of features, like Hydra. He is not one, but legion. Not so much a comedian, as a company. If his name could be multiplied like his countenance, it might fill a playbill. He, and he alone, literally makes faces. CHARLES LAMB, *On the acting of Munden*

NOVEMBER 19. Henry Siddons in James Kenny's **Ella Rosenberg** at Drury Lane Theatre. Melodrama.

DECEMBER 1. James Kenney's **The Blind Boy** at Covent Garden Theatre. Melodrama. The boy was played by Theresa De Camp.

DECEMBER 26. William Godwin's **Furibond or Harlequin Negro** at Drury Lane Theatre.

1808

JANUARY 12. George Frederick Cooke, Miss Smith and Charles Kemble in Charles Kemble's *The Wanderer or The Rights of Hospitality* at Covent Garden Theatre. Adaptation of a play by August von Kotzebue.

FEBRUARY 11. John Braham and Miss Lyon in John Reeve and John Braham's *Kais or Love in the Desert* and Mrs Maddocks and Miss de Camp in Henry Fielding's *The Virgin Unmasked* at Drury Lane Theatre.

FEBRUARY 12. William Thomas Lewis, Alexander Pope, Charles Kemble, John Fawcett, Miss Smith, Miss Norton, Mary Davenport in Frederick Knowles' *Begone Dull Care or How Will It End?* at Covent Garden Theatre.

FEBRUARY 25. John Fawcett, John Liston, Mrs Liston and Theresa De Camp in Mr Condell's *Who Wins or The Widow's Choice* at Covent Garden Theatre. Musical Farce.

MARCH 31. Mr Simmons and John Liston in *Bonifacio and Bridgetina or The Knight of the Hermitage or The Windmill Turrett or The Spectre of the North East Gallery* at Covent Garden Theatre. The production deserved a better audience than it got. Not everybody realised that it was meant to be a burlesque of a burlesque.

An author may furnish fun for the sensible part of the audience; he cannot furnish brains for the foolish that they may comprehend it. The spectators in the theatre, especially the fashionable part, have their several ends to answer by coming hither. Young women come to shew themselves – old ones to shew their daughters – men come, one to see those they love, and others to be loved by those who see them. In short, in the side boxes and the private boxes, the stage is the last consideration. *Theatre*

MAY 3. Harriet St Leger in George Colman the Elder's version of Francis Beaumont and John Fletcher's *Bonduca Queen of the Ancient Britons* at Covent Garden Theatre. The production included a Grand Procession to the Temple of the Druids and a Triumphal March to the Roman Camp.

MAY 27. John Emery sang T. P. Cooke's *Lunnun is the Devil!!!!* at Covent Garden Theatre.

MAY 30. Michael Kelly made his last appearance as Frederick in Prince Hoare and Stephen Storace's *No Song, No Supper* at Drury Lane Theatre. Musical farce. Kelly was 45 and had been principal soloist at Drury Lane since 1787.

JUNE 29. Francis Beaumont and John Fletcher's *Rule a Wife and Have a Wife* at Drury Lane Theatre. *The Times* thought that since much of the play was 'totally unfit for the perusal of the female eye', the text was in need of still further expurgation.

JULY 28. George Colman the Younger's *The Africans or War, Love and Duty* at Haymarket Theatre. Topical, heavy-going drama about slavery. (A Bill to abolish the slave trade in the British Empire had been passed in 1807.)

World premieres
Heinrich von Kleist's *The Broken Jug* in Weimar

Literature
Goethe's *Faust I*

Notes
Covent Garden Theatre (built in 1732) is destroyed by fire on 20 August

History
Peninsular War between Britain and France begins: the Duke of Wellington assumes his first major military command

1808

AUGUST 31. Mr Grove, John Liston, Charles Farley, Charles Mathews, Mary Davenport and Maria Ann Kelley in Isaac Pocock's **Yes, or No?** at Haymarket Theatre. Musical farce.

> Conscious of inability and inexperience, my sole attempt in this little piece, was to contrive a few ludicrous incidents – and a few comic situations, to display the peculiar powers of the performers.   ISAAC POCOCK

SEPTEMBER 19. The Covent Garden Theatre is destroyed by fire. Twenty-two died, including firemen, when the roof fell in. Scenery, properties, stage jewellery, armour, costumes, wines and original manuscripts of scores for operas, including those by Handel and Arne, were all destroyed. So, too, was Handel's organ which Handel had bequeathed to actor-manager John Rich and was worth 1,000 guineas. Seven adjacent houses and a public house, The Smugglers, were burned to the ground. Sarah Siddons lost her entire wardrobe, including a piece of lace which had belonged to Marie Antoinette and which she valued at £1,000. Joseph Munden also lost his wardrobe. The fire illuminated London and drew huge crowds to the theatre. The tops of houses in all directions were covered with people observing the destruction. The pillar of fire was not less than 450 feet in breadth.

> Everything I had in the world of stage ornament is gone and literally not one vestige of all that has cost me so much time and money to collect.
> SARAH SIDDONS

DECEMBER 30. Stone laid by Prince of Wales for a new building to replace the old Covent Garden Theatre.

The Olympic Pavilion on Drury Lane opened on 1 December 1806, and was licensed for dancing, music and equestrian entertainments. The theatre manager was Philip Astley, who is generally considered to be the founder of the modern circus.

THEATRE ROYAL, HAY-MARKET,

This present FRIDAY, Jan. 20, 1809, will be acted the Tragedy of

The GAMESTER.

Beverley (2d time) by Mr. YOUNG,
Stukely by Mr. COOKE,
Lewson by Mr. C. KEMBLE,
Bates by Mr WADDY, Dawson by Mr. CLAREMONT,
Jarvis by Mr. MURRAY, Waiter by Mr FIELD,
Mrs. Beverley by Mrs. SIDDONS,
Charlotte by Ms. St LEGER,
Lucy by Mrs WHITMORE.

After which (19th time this season) with additional Splendour, the celebrated Pantomime of

Harlequin & Mother Goose;

Or, the GOLDEN EGG.

The Overture and Musick composed by Mr Ware.
The Scenery painted by Mess. Phillips, Whitmore, Hollogan, Lupino, Grieve, Hodgins, and their Assistants.
The Pantomime produced under the Direction of Mr FARLEY—The Dances by Mr BOLOGNA, Jun.
Mother Goose, Mr. SIMMONS,
Colin, afterwards Harlequin, Mr. BOLOGNA, Jun.
'Squire Bugle, afterwards Clown, Mr. GRIMALDI,
Avaro, afterwards Pantaloon, Mr. T. BLANCHARD, Counsellor Crumpy, Mr. W. MURRAY
The Little Sailor-Boy (with a Hornpipe) Miss WORGMAN,
Colinette, afterwards Columbine, Miss ADAMS,
The whole to conclude with THREE ENTIRE NEW SCENES—The First representing the

RUINS

Of the late Theatre Royal, Covent Garden,
The Second,—An exact representation of the Laying of the

FOUNDATION STONE,

As it appeared on Saturday, the 31st of December last;
Which change to a

NEW THEATRE.

Boxes 6s. Second Price 3s—Pit 3s 6d. Second Price 2s.—Gallery 2s. Second Price 1s.—Up. Gal. 1s.
Ma . . . . VIVANT REX ET REGINA

Tomorrow, 29th time, the Opera of The EXILE.
WITH KATHARINE and PETRUCHIO
Petruchio by Mr. LEWIS, Katharine, Mrs. C. KEMBLE.
On Monday, Shakspeare's Tragedy of
KING RICHARD the THIRD.
King Richard by Mr. COOKE.
To which will be added, HARLEQUIN and MOTHER GOOSE.
On Tuesday, Shakspeare's Historical Play of KING HENRY the FOURTH—PART I.
Prince of Wales. Mr. C. KEMBLE, Hotspur, Mr. YOUNG, Sir John Falstaff, Mr COOKE.
After which (for the last time this season) the Pantomime of
HARLEQUIN and MOTHER GOOSE.
On Wednesday, Shakspeare's Tragedy of MACBETH.
Macbeth by Mr. KEMBLE,
(Being his first appearance since his late severe Indisposition)
Lady Macbeth by Mrs. SIDDONS.
To which will be added the Burletta of TOM THUMB the GREAT.
On Thursday, (30th time) the new Grand Melo-Dramatick Opera of The EXILE.
After which will be revived, the Grand Historick Pantomime Drama of
DE LA PEROUSE; or, The DESOLATE ISLAND.
With entire new Scenery, Dresses, & Decorations.

1809

FEBRUARY 24. Drury Lane Theatre is destroyed by fire. Richard Brinsley Sheridan, the lessee, sat in the Piazza Coffee House drinking wine with Michael Kelly. When somebody expressed surprise at his sitting there he famously replied: 'May not a man be allowed to drink a glass of wine by his own fireside?'

' *I acknowledge Shakespeare to be the world's greatest dramatic poet but regret that no parent could place the uncorrected book in the hands of his daughter and therefore I have prepared the Family Shakespeare … many words and expressions occur which are of so indecent a nature as to render it highly desirable that they should be erased.* '

THOMAS BOWDLER

[The expurgation was in fact performed by his sister, Henrietta Maria, but the edition came out under his name, since no respectable lady could possibly admit she knew such words and expressions.]

AUGUST 14. Joseph Grimaldi in Charles Dibdin's **The Wild Man or Water Pageant** at Aquatic Theatre – Sadler's Wells. The last scene had real water. 'The aquadrama,' said Dibdin 'showed the powerful influence of music over even the savage mind.' Grimaldi danced with a fury, and his mirth was as extreme as his grief.

AUGUST 30. Richard William Elliston in **The History, Murders, Life and Death of Macbeth** at Royal Circus. Burletta. Adaptation by John Cross. 'With the exception of the dialogue,' said *The Morning Chronicle*, 'the performance was almost exactly the play of Shakespeare.'

SEPTEMBER 18. The new Theatre Royal Covent Garden opened with John Philip Kemble and Sarah Siddons in Shakespeare's **Macbeth**. Kemble raised the price of seats to cover the £150,000 cost of the new building. The boxes, which used to cost 6s., now cost 7s. The pit, which used to cost 3s. 6d., now cost 4s. The third tier, normally reserved for the public, was converted into private boxes at a rent of £300 a year. People who sat in the gallery could only see the actors' legs. Hissing, hooting, groans and catcalls broke out the moment Kemble spoke. The rest of the cast were greeted with applause to indicate that the anger was not aimed at them. The play proceeded in pantomime. Not a word was heard. Siddons went through it all with wonderful composure. 'Perhaps,' said *The Public Advertiser*, 'a finer dumb show was never heard.'

When the performance came to an end the audience refused to leave. Kemble called in the magistrates. The audience, furious, did not disperse until gone two o'clock in the morning. They returned on the next night with banners and placards which read:

OLD PRICES. OPPOSITION, PERSEVERE, YOU WILL SUCCEED.

JOHN BULL'S OPPOSITION TO JOHN KEMBLE'S IMPOSITION.

OLD PRICES OR EMPTY BENCHES.

FAIR ACCOUNTS AND FAIR PRICES.

NO ITALIAN DEPRAVITY OR FRENCH DUPLICITY BUT NATIVE TALENT. NO PRIVATE BOXES. LET THERE BE NO INTRIGUE, NOR PRIVATE PERFORMANCE IN THE ANTI-ROOMS BEHIND THE PRIVATE BOXES.

A contemporary cartoon shows magistrates reading the Riot Act during the Old Price (OP) Riots at Theatre Royal, Covent Garden, in 1809.

A coffin with cross bones was delivered with the inscription:

HERE LIES THE BODY OF NEW PRICE,
AN UGLY CHILD AND BASE BORN.

The shouts of 'O P' (that is, Old Price) were accompanied by a beat or a blow on the floor with a stick, a foot or a bludgeon.

On one night Kemble brought in Joseph Grimaldi, and that quelled the house; however, the ploy only worked once. When Grimaldi came on stage the following night, the uproar was greater than it had ever been.

On another night Kemble asked Charles Incledon to pacify the rioters. Incledon, a big burly singer whose forte was nautical and patriotic ballads, refused: 'I attempt to stop the riot. I might as well bolt the door with a boiled carrot.'

The audience's fury increased when Kemble hired two pugilists – Dan Mendoza and Dutch Sam – to deal with trouble-makers.

Kemble distributed leaflets which read as follows:

CAUTION. Lord Mansfield, on the trial of the Rioters in the café of Mr Macklin, stated, a British audience has a right to express approbation or disapprobation of plays and actors in the usual way, but if it could be proved that any person or persons went night after night to the theatre for the purpose of preventing an actor exercising his performance or to injure the managers or proprietors, such person or persons would not only be subject to an action at law but might be indicted for the offence. And in the case of the prisoners of the King's Bench, Lord Mansfield stated, if the parties concurred in doing an act, although they were not previously acquainted with each other, IT IS A CONSPIRACY.

The so-called OP Riots lasted 75 nights. *The Times* and *The Morning Post* supported Kemble. *The Morning Chronicle* sided with the rioters.

1809

Births	Deaths	History
Charles Darwin, British naturalist	Thomas Holcroft, British dramatist (b. 1745)	Battle of Corunna
Nikolai Gogol, Russian dramatist	Thomas Paine, British radical (b. 1737)	Battle of Talavera
Fanny Kemble, British actress, daughter of Charles Kemble		Dartmoor Prison opens, at first to hold French prisoners of war
Felix Mendelssohn, German composer	*Notes*	George Canning and Lord Castlereagh argue over military deployments, culminating in a duel on 21 September on Putney Heath in which Canning is shot in the leg.
Edgar Allan Poe, American novelist	Drury Lane Theatre (built in 1794) is destroyed by fire	
Alfred Lord Tennyson, British poet	Lyceum Theatre opens	
	Covent Garden Theatre re-opens	

The
1810s

Mr KEAN.

in the Character of Macbeth?

Stars, hide your fires.

Let no light see my black and deep desires.

Theatre Royal, Covent Garden, which had been rebuilt after the fire of 1808, re-opened in 1809 with John Philip Kemble in Shakespeare's Macbeth. Seat prices were raised to cover the cost of the re-building, and this led to more than three months of riots.

The new interior of Theatre Royal, Covent Garden, was capable of seating 2,800.

1810

JANUARY 5. John Philip Kemble in Shakespeare's *King Lear* at Covent Garden Theatre. Miss Bristow in her stage debut as Cordelia. Charles Kemble as Edgar. This was one of the last performances of *Lear* to be staged and many critics rated it as among his best. Actors and managers, on account of King George III's madness, didn't feel it was appropriate to stage the play.

A prettier Cordelia was never seen than Miss Bristowe [sic] and to do her justice, a worse was never heard. *Monthly Mirror*

FEBRUARY 20. John Baldwin Buckstone, Charles Mathews and William De Camp in Isaac Pocock's *Hit or Miss* at Lyceum Theatre. 'We never saw so bad a piece so well received,' said *The Monthly Mirror*. The play ran for 33 performances.

To Mr Mathews I am obliged for the assistance he afforded me in heightening the character of Cypher as well as for his extraordinary exertions in the representation of a part which he invariably excited the most unqualified bursts of laughter and applause. ISAAC POCOCK

MAY 5. George Frederick Cooke as Henry, John Philip Kemble as Cardinal Wolsey and Sarah Siddons as Katharine in Shakespeare's *Henry VIII* at Covent Garden Theatre.

It is not easy to conceive a more defective performance. Instead of the noble, frank, boisterous look and manner of Henry, he [Cooke] had the look of Richard III or the bearded head of Shylock, and the artful manner of Iago. Nothing could or can be worse. *Monthly Mirror*

JUNE 25. John Philip Kemble in Shakespeare's *King John* at Covent Garden Theatre. Sarah Siddons as Constance. Charles Kemble as Faulconbridge. The performance was followed by *Mother Goose*.

Mr Kemble's King John, with its theatrical tone of dignity and its mixture of confidence and whining, is one of his happier performances … but there is too much pantomimic rolling of the eyes. Charles Kemble, always elegant, with a chivalrous air, and possessing a strong taste for contemptuous irony, is as complete a Faulconbridge as one can desire … The Constance of Mrs Siddons is an excellent study for young actresses to whom it will shew the great though difficult distinction between rant and tragic vehemence. LEIGH HUNT, *Examiner*

AUGUST 7. William Barnes Rhodes's *Bombastes Furioso* at Haymarket Theatre. Highly popular burlesque. Rhodes was the Chief Teller at the Bank of England.

SEPTEMBER. *The Monthly Mirror* published an Ode to John Philip Kemble exhorting him to give up the tier of private boxes at Covent Garden Theatre:

O Kemble, again you are tost on the seas.
For Mercy sake, what are you doing?
Return to harbour, assuage the O.P.s
The tempest may end in your ruin.

Births

Phineas T. Barnum, American circus showman
Mme Celeste, French dancer
Fryderyk Chopin, Polish composer

Alfred de Musset, French dramatist
Robert Schumann, German composer

Literature

Walter Scott's *The Lady of the Lake*
George Crabbe's *The Borough*

1810

September 24. T. P. Cooke as Roderick Dhu, Robert William Elliston as Fitzjames and Sarah Booth as the Lady in Thomas Dibdin's ***The Lady of the Lake*** at Surrey Theatre. A melodramatic ballet based on Walter Scott's poem, which had been published in May and had sold 25,000 copies. The music for 'Hail to the Chief' was set by James Sanderson.

October 4. Astley's Royal Amphitheatre advertisement read as follows: Olympic Games by Double Troop. Clown Mr Usher who will throw 59 flip flaps. The Blood Red Knight. Equestrian Agility by the Double Troop, and Peasant's Frolic and Flying Wardrobe by Mrs Muken. A military hornpipe by Mr Collet. Also Sweet Fanny that Lives in the Valley by Mr Jones. To which will be added The Pindar of Wakefield or Gog and Magog. In the course of the pantomime, a Clog Hornpipe by Mr Usher. Half price at half-past eight.

December 26. Joseph Grimaldi in Charles Farley's ***Harlequin Asmodeus and Cupid on Crutches*** at Covent Garden Theatre. 46 performances. Grimaldi created a pugilistic figure out of cabbage, turnips, carrots, parsnips, radishes and fruit and then beat him off the stage.

Charles Kemble (1775–1854) was the younger brother of John Philip Kemble, and married to Marie Therese De Camp. Charles William Macready thought that Kemble was 'a first-rate actor of second-rate parts'.

1811

FEBRUARY 4. John Philip Kemble in Joseph Addison's **Cato** at Covent Garden Theatre.

All the hopes of Rome seemed to be concentrated in his tower-like figure. He [Kemble] seemed to convey the idea of vast dignity; he filled the stage. *News*

FEBRUARY 20. Sixteen white horses were introduced for the first time at Covent Garden Theatre in a revival of Michael Kelly's **Bluebeard or Female Curiosity**. The appearance of a dog on stage caused a sensation. Leigh Hunt lambasted the management for using the horses. The stench, he said, was so abominable; it was like sitting in a stable. Pictorial high spot was a journey across a mountain with the people and the animals getting larger on every entrance.

MARCH 26. Charles Kemble as Captain Absolute and Joseph Munden as Sir Anthony Absolute in Richard Brinsley Sheridan's **The Rivals** at Covent Garden. Charles Mayne Young as Faulkland. Joseph Grimaldi as Bob Acres.

APRIL 1. John Philip Kemble in Shakespeare's **Richard III** at Covent Garden Theatre. His performance was aristocratic, austere and statuesque.

In Richard III, which he played with great vigour, he could not look villainous enough.

He seemed more like a country gentleman; and say what evil he would of himself, the audience would not believe him. SIR WALTER SCOTT

APRIL 4. Sarah Siddons as Margaret of Anjou and Alexander Pope as Warwick in Paul Hiffernan's **The Earl of Warwick** at Opera House. Robert William Elliston as Edward. John Braham sang 'Said a smile to a tear'.

The character is still one of those to which she [Siddons] can still render justice. She looked ill and I thought her articulation indistinct and her voice more than usually drawling and funereal during the first act; but as she advanced in the piece, her genius triumphed over the natural impediments … Her advancing old age is really a cause of pain to me. She is the only actor I ever saw with a conviction that there never was nor ever will be her equal. Elliston played Edward: a wretched Tragedian – his attempts at dignity are ludicrous. He is a fine bustling comedian but he bustles in tragedy also. HENRY CRABB ROBINSON, *Diary*

APRIL 11. Joseph Grimaldi in **Dulce Domum or England the Land of Freedom!** at Aquatic Theatre – Sadler's Wells Theatre. Advertised as 'Staged to prove the Superiority of our Native Country over all others by a Comparison existing of Existing Circumstances (in general too palpably true to be contradicted.)'

Births	*Deaths*	*Notes*
Charles Kean, British actor, theatre manager, son of Edmund Kean	George Frederick Cooke, actor (b. 1756)	Percy Bysshe Shelley is sent down from Oxford
John Maddison Morton, British dramatist	Heinrich von Kleist, German dramatist (b. 1777)	*History*
Ambroise Thomas, French composer	*Literature*	George III is declared insane
	Jane Austen's *Sense and Sensibility*	Prince of Wales becomes Regent
		Luddite riots in Yorkshire and Nottinghamshire

MAY 18. John Braham in M P King and John Braham's *Americans* at Lyceum Theatre. The playbill promised a chorus of sailors, Indians and Africans. Braham, whose voice was said to have rung like a trumpet, also appeared in *The Death of Nelson*. The patriotic libretto was by J. S. Arnold. Lady Hamilton, Nelson's former mistress, who was sitting in one of the private boxes, became hysterical during the performance, and had to be escorted out.

JUNE 3. *Alfred the Great or England Invaded* at Surrey Theatre. Grand Patriotic Melodrama.

DECEMBER 3. John Philip Kemble as Pierre, Charles Kemble as Jaffier and Sarah Siddons as Belvidera in Thomas Otway's *Venice Preserv'd* at Covent Garden Theatre.

Kemble treads the stage with peculiar grace and dignity; his figure is tall and imposing … His countenance is noble; in a word, he has a most majestic presence … Kemble's great disadvantage is his voice; it wants deep, rich bass tones and has not sufficient effect.
WASHINGTON IRVING

DECEMBER 15. John Philip Kemble in *Coriolanus* at Covent Garden Theatre. Lord Byron said Kemble 'was glamorous and exerted himself wonderfully'.

DECEMBER 25. Joseph Grimaldi in *Harlequin and Padmanaba or, The Goldfish* at Surrey Theatre. Joseph Grimaldi, playing a Persian cook, was upstaged by Chuny, the largest elephant yet seen in London.

1812

FEBRUARY 29. John Philip Kemble as Brutus, Charles Kemble as Marc Antony and Charles Mayne Young as Cassius in Shakespeare's *Julius Caesar* at Covent Garden Theatre. John Fawcett as Casca, Mrs Powell as Portia. The spectacular production employed up to 106 actors.

This artificial actor [John Philip Kemble] does so dole out his words, and so drop his syllables one by one upon the ear, as if he were measuring out laudanum for us that a reasonable auditor … has no alternative between laughing and being disgusted. LEIGH HUNT, *Examiner*

MARCH 17. Henry Phillips, William Downton and Rebecca Duncan in James Kenney's *Turn Out* at Lyceum Theatre. *The Times* was not impressed: 'In this misshapen work, everything that Mr Kenney probably ever heard or saw, or dreamed of, as a means of exciting an unwilling laugh has been forced into service.'

MAY 2. London premiere of Mozart's *The Marriage of Figaro* at Pantheon Theatre. Sung in Italian.

JUNE 5. Charles Kemble in John Milton's *The Masque of Comus*. Sarah Siddons as Lady. Kemble lacked sensuality and was said to look like Lady's lackey.

Sarah Siddons in her most famous role in her most famous scene: Lady Macbeth sleep-walking in Shakespeare's Macbeth.

JUNE 12. Joseph Grimaldi played Bob Acres for one performance in Richard Brinsley Sheridan's **The Rivals** at Covent Garden Theatre.

JUNE 15. Charles Mathews in Walley Chamberlaine Oulton's **The Sleepwalker or Which is the Lady?** at Haymarket Theatre. Mathews ('A man of genius,' said Leigh Hunt in *The Examiner*) played an actor, who acts the roles he dreams of acting when he is asleep.

JUNE 29. Sarah Siddons made her farewell appearance as Lady Macbeth at Covent Garden in Shakespeare's **Macbeth**. The performance ended on her sleep-walking scene, her final scene. 'Nothing ever was, or can be like her,' said Lord Byron.

> Her gestures – the depth and richness of her tones – the melancholy and thoughtful beauty of her smile, were all tragic – and in tragedy she found no equal.   *The Times*

> While the stage lasts there will never be another Mrs Siddons who will walk in the sleepless ecstasy of the soul and haunt the mind's eye ever after with the dread of suffering and guilt …
> Who will make tragedy once more stand with its feet upon the earth, and with its head raised above the skies weeping tears and blood? That loss is not to be repaired.
> WILLIAM HAZLITT, *London Magazine*

JULY 6. Charles Mathews as Goldfinch in Thomas Holcroft's **The Road to Ruin** at Haymarket Theatre. One of Mathews's most famous roles.

JULY 6. Robert William Elliston and Mrs Edwin in John Tobin's **Honey Moon** at Surrey Theatre. Buffoonery. 'Let us,' said *The Theatre Inquisitor*, 'have no more of these illegitimate species of drama.'

NEW OPERA and PANTOMIME.

THEATRE ROYAL, LYCEUM,

This present THURSDAY, August 6, 1812,

Will be performed, for the 14th time, a NEW COMIC OPERA in Three Acts, called

RICH AND POOR,

The OVERTURE and MUSIC composed and selected by Mr. HORN.

The Principal Characters by—Mr. FAWCETT,

Mr. PYNE, Mr. HORN, Mr. OXBERRY, Mr. KNIGHT,

Mr. PENSON, Mr. PENLEY, Mr. FISHER, Mr. WEWITZER,

Mrs. ORGER, Miss GRIGLIETTI, Miss KELLY,

Mrs. HARLOWE, Mrs. BLAND, Miss JONES,

☞ The Opera of RICH and POOR is published, and may be had in the Theatre,
or of Sherwood, Neeley and Jones, Paternoster Row.

The MUSIC is also published and may be had of J. POWER, 34 Strand.

After which will be performed, for the 7th time, a new Splendid Harlequinade which has been in
preparation previous to the Summer Season, called

Jack and Jill;

OR, THE CLOWN'S DISASTERS.

Invented and produced under the direction of Mr. KIRBY.

With entirely new Scenery, Machinery, Dresses and Decorations.

The Overture and Music entirely new, composed by Mr. George W. REEVE.

CHARACTERS Jack, (afterwards Harlequin) Mr. HOLLINGSWORTH,
Watty Wildgoose, (Suitor to Jill, afterwards Lover) Mr. WEST,
Watty's Guardian, (afterwards Pantaloon) Mr. MALE,
Watty's Lacquey, (afterwards Clown) Mr. KIRBY,
Old Dame-Gill, the reputed Grandmother to Jill, (afterwards the Goddess Fortune)
Miss E. BOLTON, And Jill, (afterwards Columbine) Miss VALANCEY.
Owner of Waste Ground, Mr. BUXTON, China Man, Mr FRANKLIN,
Cheese Monger Mr. APPLEBY, Mr. Sweet, (the Grocer) Mr. COST,
Pastrycook, Master SEYMOUR, Organ Man, Mr. REECE,
Showman, (of a Non-descript) Mr. JAMIESON,
The Non-descript, Master E. PARSLOE,
Sailor, Mr. LEE. Soldier, Mr MADDOCKS,
Beau, Mr. MILLER, Alderman, Mr. JONES,
Millers, Messrs. Buxton, Mathews, Hope, Cost, Appleby,
Thrashers, Messrs. West, Chappel, Jamieson.
Crab, Master C. PARSLOE, Batch, the Baker, Mr. FRANKLIN,
Grasshopper Master I. PARSLOE, Fishmonger, Mr. APPLEBY,
Tradespeople, Mesds. Jones, Minton, I. Boyce, Carlyle, &c. &c.
Watchmen, Messrs. West, Reece, Perkins, &c. &c. &c.

In the course of the Pantomime, the following New and Splendid Scenes will be exhibited.

1. Outside of Dame Gill's Cottage, and distant Village by Sun-set.
2. Interior of the Cottage. changes to
3. The abode of the Goddess, Fortune, with her Cornucopia, which changes again to
4. The interior of the Cottage.
5. A piece of Waste Land, with a grand Mechanical change to
6. Harlequin's Villa,
7. A fanciful Garden which the Clown is elevated on a spout of real Water.

8. Outside of Harlequin's Villa, turned topsy-turvy."
9. Grocer's Shop.
10. A Corn-field, with a Stack of Wheat, which changes to
11. A Wind-Mill. afterwards to
12. Pastry-Cook and Baker's Shop.
13. A Fishmonger's Shop.
14. Road-side, and Pot-house by a Brick-field,—a Storm, with Clown's ascent into the air.
15. Best Room in the Pot-house, Clown's descent.

And to conclude with (16) a splendid Scene, representing

The ABODE of FORTUNE in the REALMS of RICHES.

The SCENERY and MACHINERY designed by Mr. MORRIS,
and executed by him, Mr. UNDERWOOD, and numerous Assistants.

The DRESSES by Mr. BANKS, Mrs. ROBINSON, &c.

The DANCES by Mr. HOLLINGSWORTH.

☞ Books of the Pantomime may be had in the Theatre.

OCTOBER 10. Drury Lane Theatre re-opened. Since the fire the company had been performing at the Lyceum Theatre. 3,060 people came to see Robertson Elliston in Shakespeare's **Hamlet** and a musical farce, **The Devil to Pay**.

NOVEMBER 20. John Liston as Lubin Log in James Kenney's **Love, Law and Physic** at Covent Garden Theatre. Farce. Liston was one of the great comedians and Lubin Log, the conceited cockney who thought himself 'tolerably pretty', was one of his most famous roles. Liston went on to become the highest paid comedian in London, earning between £60 and £100 a week.

> Mr Liston has more comic humour, more power of face, and a more genial, happy vein of folly, than any other actor we remember. His face is not caricature. WILLIAM HAZLITT, *Examiner*

DECEMBER 26. Joseph Grimaldi as Dragoon in **Harlequin and the Red Dwarf** at Covent Garden Theatre. Richard Norman as Pantaloon. The star was the llama from Peru, but the llama refused to act. The high spot was Grimaldi riding to Epping Forest on a huge carthorse.

Births	*Deaths*	*Notes*
Charles Dickens, British novelist, dramatist	Isaac Bickerstaffe, Irish dramatist (b. 1735)	Drury Lane Theatre re-opens
Robert Browning, British poet, dramatist	George Frederick Cooke, British actor (b. 1756)	Last shipment of Elgin Marbles arrives in London
Edward Lear, British artist and nonsense writer		Waltz craze
Christopher Mayhew, British journalist	*Literature*	*History*
	Grimm Brothers' *Fairy Tales*	War between Britain and USA
		Napoleon invades Russia

1812

1813

JANUARY 23. Mr Rae and Julia Glover in Samuel Taylor Coleridge's **The Remorse** at Drury Lane Theatre. Improbable Gothic drama set in medieval Spain. Two brothers, one good, one wicked. Goodness triumphs.

> Mr Coleridge combines in a pre-eminent degree the various peculiarities and absurdities of the school of poetry ... his images are generally unnatural and incongruous; his diction uncouth, pedantic and obscure; he mistakes abruptness for force, and supposes himself to be original when he is only absurd. *Theatre Inquisitor*

> Coleridge's great fault is that he indulges before the public in those metaphysical and philosophical speculations which are becoming only in solitude and with select minds.
> HENRY CRABB ROBINSON, *Diary*

FEBRUARY 10. Dorothy Jordan in Susannah Centliver's **The Wonder: A Woman Keep a Secret** at Covent Garden Theatre. There was a vicious attack on Jordan's morality in *The Times* accusing her of 'bringing shame to the art she practices and double shame on those who must have it in their power to send her back to penitence and obscurity.' Most newspapers and the public sided with Jordan.

> How Mrs Jordan acted in the great Theatre of the World is not a question for the public. *Morning Post*

> To the amusement of the public Mrs Jordan appears as the servant of the public – and in that light only should she be judged. *News*

MARCH 18. John Philip Kemble as Valentine in William Congreve's **Love for Love** at Covent Garden Theatre. Dorothy Jordan was absurdly old to be playing the romping wanton Miss Prue.

> No man could deliver brilliant dialogue – the dialogue of Congreve or of Wycherley – because none understood it – half so well as John Kemble. His Valentine, in *Love for Love*, was to my recollection, faultless. CHARLES LAMB, *Elia*

Harriet Mellon (1777–1837), actress, married the banker Thomas Coutts and retired.

JUNE 12. Master Betty, now a young man, appeared in Shakespeare's **Richard III** at Covent Garden Theatre. He was not a success.

OCTOBER 21. Charles Farley as Grindoff in Isaac Pocock's **The Miller and His Men** at Covent Garden Theatre. Spectacular melodrama. Music by Henry Bishop. The dialogue was subservient to the scenery. The hero joins a band of Bohemian bandits in order to blow up their stronghold so that he can rescue the girl he loves. The explosion made for a spectacular finale.

NOVEMBER 15. Charles Mayne Young and Harriet Faucit in **Antony and Cleopatra** at Covent Garden Theatre. The text was derived from Shakespeare and Dryden. The critics thought it a 'miserable patchwork'. The authenticity of the settings and costumes, based on Hope's *Costumes of the Ancients*, published a few months earlier, made far more impression than the performances did. There was no orgy aboard Pompey's boat and Cleopatra's death scene was much curtailed. There was, however, a sea-fight and an eight part choir with over forty singers for the joint funerals. Faucit's Cleopatra was described by *The Examiner* as pretty and genteel.

> Spectacle is the order of the day; the intellect yields precedence to the eye, and to painting, and the contrivance of machinery; truth and taste and sentiment, are the melancholy sacrifice. *Examiner*

> A succession of incidents and scenes in which there is more bustle than business, and more pomp than nature. *Bell's Weekly Messenger*

World premieres	Births	History
Gioachino Rossini's *L'Italiana in Algeri* in Venice	Georg Büchner, German dramatist	John Nash presents his plans and designs for the development of Regent Street, London
Literature	Giuseppe Verdi, Italian composer	Leigh Hunt begins a two-year sentence for insulting the Prince Regent
Jane Austen's *Pride and Prejudice*	Richard Wagner, German composer	Cape of Good Hope becomes British colony
Robert Owen's *A New View of Society*	David Livingstone, Scottish missionary and explorer	East India Co. loses monopoly
Robert Southey is appointed Poet Laureate		

1813

1814

JANUARY 15. John Philip Kemble in Shakespeare's **Coriolanus** at Covent Garden Theatre. Sarah Siddons as Constance. Joseph Munden as Menenius. 'A noble and unequalled performance,' said *The Theatre Inquisitor*. 'The lady and her brother are nature and art personified,' said *News*. Some critics found Kemble pedantic and asthmatic, and his eccentric pronunciation was made the subject of endless satires. (He pronounced hideous as hijust, bird as beard, earth as airth, Rome as room, virgin as vargin, sovereign as suvran, aches as aitches and gave Coriolanus five syllables.) Julian Charles Young, son of Charles Mayne Young, recorded in his memoir of his father that 240 persons had marched across the stage in stately procession. Siddons 'towered above all around, and rolled and almost reeled across the stage; her very soul as it were dilating and rioting in its exultation; until her action lost all grace and yet became so true to nature, so picturesque and so descriptive, that pit and gallery sprang to their feet, electrified by the transcendent execution of an original conception.'

Edmund Kean made his name overnight with his sensational London debut, in which he played a totally original Shylock in Shakespeare's The Merchant of Venice. This painting was by W. H. Watt.

'EDMUND KEAN: *If he was irregular and unartistic-like in his performance, so is Niagara compared with water waves of Versailles.*'

FANNY KEMBLE

JANUARY 26. Edmund Kean made his triumphant debut as Shylock in Shakespeare's **The Merchant of Venice** at Drury Lane Theatre. 'If I succeed I shall go mad,' he had said. To the amazement of the rest of the cast he abandoned the traditional red wig and wore a black wig and beard. When Kean got home, flushed with success, he said to his wife: Mary, you shall ride in a carriage yet and Charley [his son] shall go to Eton.' *The Times* was unequivocal:

'We have seldom seen a much better Shylock.' The general consensus was that, 'For voice, eye, action, expression, no actor has come out for many years at all equal to him.'

His Jew is more than half a Christian. Certainly our sympathies are much oftener with him than with his enemies. He is honest in his vices; they are hypocrites in their virtues … His style of acting is, if we may use the expression, more significant, more pregnant with meaning, more varied and alive in every part, than any we have almost ever witnessed. The character never stands still; there is no vacant pause in the action; the eye is never silent.

WILLIAM HAZLITT, *Morning Chronicle*

THEATRE ROYAL, DRURY-LANE.

This present MONDAY, October 3, 1814,

An Occasional Address,

Will be spoken by Mrs. EDWIN.

After which, their Majesties' Servants will perform (1st time this season) SHAKSPEARE's Tragedy of

King Richard the Third.

King Henry, Mr. POPE,
Prince of Wales, Miss CARR,   Duke of York, Miss C. CARR,
Duke of Gloster, Mr. KEAN,
(Being His First Appearance this Season)
Buckingham, Mr. HOLLAND,
Richmond, Mr. RAE,
Norfolk, Mr. WALDEGRAVE,   Lord Stanley, Mr. POWELL,
Catesby, Mr. ELRINGTON,   Ratcliffe, Mr. CROOKE,
Oxford, Mr. I. WEST,   Lieutenant of the Tower, Mr. R. PHILLIPS,
Tressel, Mr. I. WALLACK,   Lord Mayor, Mr. CARR,
Tyrrel, Mr. COOKE,   Blunt, Mr. EBSWORTH,
Forest, Mr. LEE,   Dighton, Mr. EVANS,
Queen, Mrs. GLOVER,
Lady Anne, Miss BOYCE, Duchess of York, Mrs. BRERETON.

The following Scenes will be exhibited in the Course of the Tragedy.
In Act II. an Ancient Street in Westminster, composed chiefly from Remains of the Fifteenth Century.
State Chamber of King Edward III.—Vaulted Chamber of King Henry VI.
Crosby Council Chamber—Baronial Hall.—Tudor Hall. *By Mr. CAPON.*
Exterior of the Tower.—King Richard's Camp.
And the Camp of the Earl of Richmond. *By Mr. GREENWOOD.*

To which will be added, the Musical Farce of

LOCK AND KEY.

Brummagem, Mr. MUNDEN,
Captain Vain, Mr. DE CAMP,
Cheerly, Mr. PYNE,
Ralph, Mr. KNIGHT,
Laura, Miss POOLE,
Fanny, Miss KELLY,
Selina, Mrs. CHATTERLEY, Dolly, Miss HORRIBOW.

Doors to be opened at half-past Five o'Clock, the Performance to begin at half-past Six precisely.

☞ Boxes and Places to be taken of Mr. SPRING, Box Office,
Little Russell Street, from TEN till FOUR,
and of whom may be had a Private Box, (Nightly).
Boxes 7s.—*Second Price 3s 6d.*—Pit 3s. 6d. *Second Price 2s.*
Lower Gallery, 2s.—*Second Price 1s.*—Upper Gallery 1s. *Second Price 6d.*

⁂ **No Orders will be admitted.**

VIVANT REX ET REGINA.   NO MONEY TO BE RETURNED.   [C. Lowndes, Printer, Marquis Court, London.

To-morrow, the Comedy of MAN AND WIFE, with the Musical Entertainment of
THE CHILDREN IN THE WOOD.
On Thursday, Mr. KEAN will make his Second Appearance, and perform, for the first time this
Season, the Character of OTHELLO.
After which, the Farce of HONEST THIEVES.
On Saturday, the Comedy of EVERY ONE HAS HIS FAULT, with (2d time this season) the
Melo-Drama of THE WOODMAN'S HUT.

A NEW COMEDY,

In Five Acts, is in rehearsal, and will be speedily produced.
The Grand Melo-dramatick Oriental Romance of ILLUSION; or, *The Trances of Nourjahad*,
is in preparation; and will be revived, with renewed Splendour, in a few days.

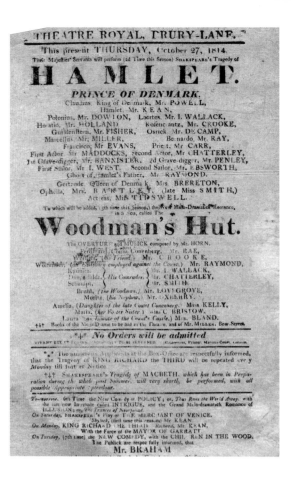

The playbill for Shakespeare's Hamlet and Samuel James Arnold's The Woodman's Hut at Theatre Royal, Drury Lane, in 1814.

'EDMUND KEAN's attitude in leaning against the pillar was one of the most graceful and striking positions ever witnessed. It would serve a Titian, Raphael, or Salavator Rosa to model. The transition from the fiercest passion to the most familiar was a quality which Kean possessed over every other actor that ever appeared. Many attempted this style and all have most egregiously failed.'

WILLIAM HAZLITT

I cannot imagine better acting. It appeared to me as if there were no fault in him anywhere and in his scene with Tubal there was exquisite acting. JANE AUSTEN

FEBRUARY 12. Edmund Kean in Shakespeare's *Richard III* at Drury Lane Theatre. Kean looked like a Tartar Amazon and was delighted with his performance: 'I could not feel the stage under me,' he said.

In his diary Lord Byron wrote: 'Life, nature, truth, without exaggeration or diminution. Richard is a man, and Kean is Richard.' Byron gave Kean a present of a gold snuff box. The lid had a boar hand-worked in mosaic.

The whole performance was the most perfect of anything that had been witnessed since the days of Garrick … The concluding scene, in which he is killed by Richmond, was the most brilliant. He fought like one drunk with wounds and the attitude in which he stands with his hands stretched out, after his sword, is taken from him, had a preternatural and terrific grandeur, as his will could not be disarmed, and the very phantoms had a withering power. The audience sat in silence, awed by the sublimity of the scene.

WILLIAM HAZLITT, *Morning Chronicle*

His death scene was the grandest conception and executed in the most impressive manner; it was a piece of noble poetry, expressed by action, instead of language. He fights desperately; he is disarmed, and exhausted of all bodily strength; he disdains to fall, and his strong volition keeps him standing: he fixes that head, full of

intellectual and heroic power, directly on his enemy; he bears his chest with an expansion, which seems swelling with more than human spirit; he holds his uplifted arm in calm but dreadful defiance of his conqueror.
THOMAS BARNES, *Examiner.*

Elliston as Richmond in a new suit of shining armour strutted about the stage, grasping a terrific pole axe and a bright shield, very much to his own delight, Kean's annoyance and the amusement of the audience. *Theatre Inquisitor*

FEBRUARY 21. Dorothy Jordan as Rosalind in Shakespeare's **As You Like It** at Covent Garden Theatre. William Conway as Orlando. Charles Mayne Young as Jaques.

The triumph of mind over matter in this wonderful performance was complete. Her voice, and manner, and look, were all perfect conformity with the character: the depredation of time, and disadvantages of person, are forgotten in our admiration of that naïveté, vivacity, and irresistible expression of nature, which characterizes every tone, look and motion. There is no actress whose loss will be more generally felt or less easily supplied.
Theatre Inquisitor

MARCH 12. Edmund Kean in Shakespeare's **Hamlet** at Drury Lane Theatre. 'The finest example of the art of acting that has ever been seen on the modern stage,' said *The Champion.* The theatre was so packed that not only were women fainting but men also.

MAY 5. Edmund Kean in Shakespeare's **Othello** at Drury Lane Theatre. 'The finest piece of acting in the world,' said William Hazlitt. 'The masterpiece of the living stage,' said Leigh Hunt. 'Depend upon it, this is a man of genius,' said Lord Byron. Kean alternated Othello and Iago with Alexander Pope.

No, sir, I did not see Kean. I saw Othello, and further I shall not act the part again.
JOHN PHILIP KEMBLE

Pope by dint of mere lungs got his full share of applause in Othello – Indeed it is too clear that violent gesticulation and loud bawling is a pretty sure road to success.
HENRY CRABB ROBINSON, *Diary*

Kean was unquestionably a man of genius, in Shylock, Richard III, Othello, in Sir Giles Overreach and in Zanga he was great. In other roles he never approached within any measurable distance of the learned, philosophical and majestic Kemble. In comedy he was detestable. *Quarterly Review*

MAY 7. Thomas Sowerby Hamblin as Othello and Edmund Kean as Iago in Shakespeare's **Othello** at Drury Lane Theatre.

He [Hamblin] was greeted with one deserved and universal hiss, and we hope that this decisive testimony of public opinion will teach him to estimate more correctly his own attainments and abilities. *Theatre Inquisitor*

JUNE 18. John Philip Kemble in Shakespeare's **Othello** at Drury Lane Theatre

My head is satisfied and even astonished, yet my heart is seldom affected. I am not led to forget that it is Kemble, the actor, not Othello, the Moor. WASHINGTON IRVING

I think him [Kemble] a very great one; and those who say to the contrary are envious men, and not worthy as actor, to wipe his shoes. GEORGE FREDERICK COOKE

AUGUST 31. *Frederick the Great* was followed by **Harlequin Hoax** at Lyceum Theatre. John Liston as Harlequin. Fanny Kelly as Columbine.

SEPTEMBER 30. Charles Farley in William Barrymore's **The Forest of Bondy or The Dog of Montagaris** at Covent Garden Theatre. Murder story. Andrew Ducrow had a big success as the dumb boy. The dog was the star turn, ringing a doorbell, carrying a lantern, digging up a grave, and pursuing a murderer.

Edmund Kean in one of his great roles: Shakespeare's Richard III. The engraving was by J. Heath from a picture by De Wilde.

Of Mr Conway's Romeo, we cannot speak with patience. He bestrides the stage like a colossus, throws his arms into the air like the sails of a windmill, and his motion is as unwieldy as that of a young elephant.

WILLIAM HAZLITT, *Champion*

OCTOBER 13. Eliza O'Neill as Belvidera, William Conway as Jaffier and Charles Mayne Young as Pierre in Thomas Otway's **Venice Preserv'd** at Covent Garden Theatre. 'Mr Conway's fine figure,' said *The Times*, 'is rather too athletic for the weak and tender-minded Jaffier.' O'Neill was compared unfavourably to Sarah Siddons.

NOVEMBER 5. Edmund Kean and Mrs Bartley in Shakespeare's **Macbeth** at Drury Lane Theatre. Hazlitt was not impressed. Kean was said to have 'fought more like a modern fencing-master than a Scottish chieftain of the eleventh century'. The production was notable for the large number of witches.

OCTOBER 6. William Conway and Eliza O'Neill in Shakespeare's **Romeo and Juliet** at Covent Garden Theatre. O'Neill's debut.

It was not altogether the matchless beauty of form and face, but the spirit of perfect innocence and purity that seemed to glisten in her eyes. And breathes from her chiseled lips.

WILLIAM CHARLES MACREADY, *Diary*

DECEMBER 26. Joseph Grimaldi in **Harlequin Whittington or Lord Mayor of London** at Covent Garden Theatre. When Grimaldi announced the news of the end of the war with America he wasn't taken seriously and was hissed.

1814

Births
Mikhail Lermontov, Russian poet, novelist
Charles Reade, British dramatist, novelist
Mrs Henry Wood, British novelist

Deaths
Philip Astley, British equestrian, theatre manager (b. 1742)

Marquis De Sade, French writer, sadist (b. 1740)
Charles Dibdin, British director, actor, song-writer (b. 1745)

Literature
Jane Austen's *Mansfield Park*
Walter Scott's first novel, *Waverley*, is published anonymously

Notes
First cricket match at the present Lord's Ground

History
Abdication of Napoleon; he is exiled to Elba
Treaty of Ghent
British sack and burn Washington DC
George Stephenson builds the first steam locomotive

1815

JANUARY 2. Edmund Kean and Sarah Bartley in Shakespeare's ***Romeo and Juliet*** at Drury Lane Theatre. Kean was miscast and disliked the role intensely. 'Never,' said Henry Barton Baker in *Our Old Actors*, 'was anything more leaden or unlovable than their balcony scene.'

FEBRUARY 4. Charles Mayne Young and Eliza O'Neill in Benjamin Thompson's ***The Stranger*** at Covent Garden Theatre. 'The audience,' said *The Theatre Inquisitor*, 'paid her the noblest tribute of praise, "they drowned the stage in tears".'

MARCH 9. Edmund Kean in Shakespeare's ***Richard II*** at Drury Lane Theatre. Robert William Elliston as Bolingbroke. Alexander Pope as John of Gaunt.

> He [Kean] is always at full stretch – never relaxed. He expresses all the violence, the extravagancies, the fierceness of the passions, but not their helplessness, and sinkings into despair. WILLIAM HAZLITT, *Examiner*

> The flashes are so brilliant and so frequent, that the mind is actually lost in the splendour which surrounds him. *Chronicle*

> Pope as usual raved and whined alternately by turns ludicrous and by turns annoying. He is in fact a sort of monster upon the stage, a pantomime elephant who is entirely out of his proper sphere and comes on solely for the amusement of the galleries. *Theatrical Inquirer*

Charles Mayne Young (1777–1856) became the leading English tragedian after the retirement of John Phillip Kemble.

Geo. Jones. del.

INTERIOR _OF THE_ LITTLE THEATRE, _HAYMARKET._

I. Stow. sculp.

FRONT _OF THE_ ABOVE.

London. Published 1st Dec.r 1815, by Robert Wilkinson. No 58. Cornhill.

Geo. Jones del.

Wise sculp.

ARENA *OF* ASTLEY's AMPHITHEATRE, *SURREY ROAD.*

London. Published 1st Dec.r 1815

FRONT *OF* THE ABOVE.

by Robert Wilkinson. N.o 58. Cornhill.

World premieres	Births	History
Gioachino Rossini's *Elisabetta, Regina d'Inghilterra* in Naples	Eugène Labiche, French playwright Anthony Trollope, British novelist	Battle of Waterloo Treaty of Vienna Corn Law passed, preventing import of cheap wheat

' *We look upon Grimaldi, in his way, as excellent as Kean ... he is as energetic, and perhaps, even excels the tragedian in tricks and activity.* '

Champion

MARCH 11. Joseph Munden as Dozey, the old sailor, in Thomas Dibdin's **Past Ten O'Clock and A Rainy Night** at Drury Lane Theatre. Lovers thwart their parents. Broad farce. Munden created one of his most famous roles.

APRIL 28. William Conway in John Milton's **The Masque of Comus** at Covent Garden Theatre. Mrs Faucit as Lady. Music by George Frederick Handel, Henry Bishop and Dr Arne. 'Barbarous amputation of the text,' said *The Theatre Inquisitor*. 'Conway had no idea at all on the subject; he repeats the lines as a schoolboy repeats his morning task, that is, as if it had no meaning.'

APRIL 29. Charles Mayne Young and Eliza O'Neill in Arthur Murphy's **Grecian Daughter** at Covent Garden Theatre. Leigh Hunt in *The Examiner* was not impressed: 'A tissue of commonplace ideas and commonplace expressions; the incidents which he has borrowed from tragedy are affecting; but he has very little else of tragedy except it's [sic] language which abounds in pompous lines and hackneyed invocations to the gods.'

OVERLEAF, LEFT

The interior and exterior of Little Theatre, Haymarket, in 1815. The artist was George Jones.

OVERLEAF, RIGHT

Astley's Theatre, Westminster Bridge Road, Lambeth: its interior and exterior in 1815. One of the theatre's most popular performers was the equestrian, Andrew Ducrow.

MAY 17. Charles Mathews, John Liston and Isabella Mattocks in James Kenney's **The Fortune of War** at Covent Garden Theatre. Farce. The theatre managers, Augustus Harris, John Fawcett, Charles Farley and Frederick Reynolds were lambasted by *Theatre Inquisitor*:

> They have disgraced the stage by monstrous exhibitions at one time: they have brought forward a troop of horse, and at another an elephant; at one time dogs to bait a fictitious bull, and at another to follow a real stag. Nor in the last of their offences, let it be forgotten they have forced on the public the trash of Pocock, of Reynolds and of Harris.   *Theatre Inquisitor*

JULY 3. Joseph Grimaldi in Charles Dibdin's **Harlequin Brilliant** at Sadler's Wells Theatre. 'The exuberance of animal spirits was really miraculous,' said Leigh Hunt in *The Examiner*.

DECEMBER 26. **Harlequin and Fortunio or Shing-Moo and Thum Tom** at Covent Garden Theatre. Joseph Grimaldi played a voracious Tartar called Munchikoff. His 13-year-old son made his debut. The production included the Plain of Waterloo after the battle, and had an exact replica of Bonaparte's carriage.

1816

JANUARY 12. Edmund Kean as Sir Giles Overreach in Philip Massinger's *A New Way to Pay Old Debts* at Drury Lane Theatre. Sir Giles foamed, rage and cursed. 'The last scene was absolutely terrific,' said John William Cole in his *Life of Kean*. 'It threw ladies in the boxes into hysterics and gave Lord Byron himself a convulsive fit.'

FEBRUARY 16. Fanny Kelly was in the middle of the first act of William Shield's comic opera, *Rosina*, at Drury Lane when George Barnett, a jealous and deranged admirer, who didn't approve of her appearing in breeches' roles, shot at her from the pit. He missed and was arrested.

APRIL 23. Shakespeare's birthday was celebrated with a pageant of characters acted by the leading actors of the day.

APRIL 26. John Philip Kemble as Sir Giles Overreach in Philip Massinger's *A New Way to Pay Old Debts* at Covent Garden Theatre. Sir Walter Scott thought Kemble, who was booed, was 'too handsome, too plausible and too smooth. He came not a hundred miles of Cooke.'

MAY 9. Edmund Kean as Bertram in Charles Robert Maturin's *Bertram or The Castle of Aldobrand* at Drury Lane Theatre. Popular Gothic tragedy. Bertram was the leader of a band of pirates. *The Times* thought Kean was extremely successful, but now and again a little exaggerated. Maturin was an Irish clergyman and had sent his play to Lord Byron who was on the plays committee at Drury Lane.

JUNE 8. John Philip Kemble and Sarah Siddons in Shakespeare's *Macbeth* at Covent Garden Theatre.

SEPTEMBER 16. William Charles Macready's London debut as Orestes in Ambrose Philips's *The Distrest Mother*, a translation of Racine's *Andromaque*, at Covent Garden Theatre. Julia Glover as Andromaque. One critic said that Macready 'is one of the plainest and most awkwardly made men that ever trod the stage. His voice is even coarser than his person.'

> We have not the slightest hesitation in saying, that William Macready is by far the best tragic actor that has come out in our remembrance, with the exception of Kean.
> WILLIAM HAZLITT, *Examiner*

> The last act, the most impassioned was the happiest test of William Macready's talents. Subtlety, terror, age, despair and triumph were successively displayed by him with truth and energy. *Observer*

OCTOBER 13. William Charles Macready in Shakespeare's *Othello* at Drury Lane Theatre. He was accused by some critics of lacking in grandeur and being deficient in majesty of character and passion.

OVERLEAF, LEFT

The Opera House: its interior and entrance in Haymarket in 1816. Mozart and Rossini had their London premieres here.

OVERLEAF, RIGHT

Olympic Theatre: its interior and exterior in 1816. The artist was Errol Sharson.

G. Jones del.

H. Cook sculp.

PROSCENIUM *OF THE* OPERA HOUSE.

ENTRANCE *IN THE* HAYMARKET.

London Published 1st Oct.r 1816

by Robert Wilkinson 125 Fenchurch Str.

Schnebbelie del.   H.Cook sculp.

INTERIOR OF THE OLYMPIC THEATRE NEAR DRURY LANE.

EXTERIOR OF THE ABOVE THEATRE.

London Published 1st Oct.1816. by Robert Wilkinson, 125 Fenchurch Street.

194

G. Jones del.

S. Springsguth Jun.r sculp.

INTERIOR *OF THE* SANS PAREIL THEATRE,

THEATRE

THE SANS PAREIL

ENTRANCE *IN THE* STRAND.

London *Published* 1.st Oct.r 1816 *by* Robert Wilkinson 125 *Fenchurch Str.*

Schnebbelie, del.t   Cook, sculp.t

INTERIOR OF THE REGENCY THEATRE, TOTTENHAM STREET, TOTTENHAM COURT ROAD.
BUILT ON THE SITE OF THE KINGS CONCERT ROOMS.

EXTERIOR OF THE ABOVE THEATRE.

London, Published 1 October 1817, by Robert Wilkinson, 125, Fenchurch Street.

Sarah Siddons as Lady Macbeth.
Portrait by G. H. Harlowe, engraved by C. Rolls.

'Mrs Siddons has retired once from the stage. Why should she return to it again? She cannot retire twice from it with dignity. Any loss of reputation to her is a loss to the world. Has she not had enough glory? To have seen Mrs Siddons was an event in every one's life and does she think we have forgotten her. Or would she remind us of herself showing us what she was not? In the sleeping scene she produces a different impression from what we expected. It was more laboured, and less natural. In coming on formerly, her eyes were open, but the sense was shut. She was like a person bewildered, and unconscious of what she did. She moved her lips involuntarily; all her gestures were involuntary and mechanical. At present she acts the part more with a view to effect.'

WILLIAM HAZLITT, *Examiner*

OVERLEAF, LEFT

The Sans Pareil Theatre: its interior and its entrance in the Strand in 1816. The theatre, founded by John Scott and his daughter Jane, was licensed for musical entertainment, pantomime and burletta only.

OVERLEAF, RIGHT

The interior and exterior of Regency Theatre in Tottenham Street, Tottenham Court Road in 1817.

1816

World premieres
Gioachino Rossini's *Il Barbere di Siviglia* in Rome

Births
Charlotte Bronte, British novelist
Charlotte Cushman, American actress

Deaths
Dorothy Jordan, British actress (b. 1762)
Richard Brinsley Sheridan, British dramatist (b. 1751)

Literature
Jane Austen's *Emma*

Notes
Lord Elgin sells the Elgin marbles to the British Museum

History
Sir David Brewster invents the kaleidoscope

NOVEMBER 4. Edmund Kean in Shakespeare's **Timon of Athens** at Drury Lane Theatre. James Wallack as Alcibiades.

We suspect that Timon will not rank as one of his first performances; it wants sufficient variety and flexibility of passion for him... We must protest however against the dance of young Amazons, clashing their swords and shields. Shakespeare, we allow, has specified Amazons for the occasion; but if Amazons there must be, they should at least have lutes.
LEIGH HUNT, *Examiner*

NOVEMBER 12. William Charles Macready as Gambia in Thomas Maddison Morton's **The Slave** at Covent Garden Theatre. Music by Henry Bishop.

William Macready's black slave was no bad specimen of his peculiar talent, which seems to lie in the broad and boisterous ostentation of tempestuous passion, for which he has only one language; nervous, certainly, but rather monotonous; though we must do him justice to say that he uttered many passages of the play with extreme tenderness, pathos and delicacy. *Observer*

1817

JANUARY 20. Edmund Kean and Miss Somerville in Aphra Behn's **Oronooko** at Covent Garden Theatre.

This is a very offensive play – A whole stage filled with blacks is a disgusting scene, though one may be interesting – Kean was finely coloured – he was quite varnished so that the deception was complete – he acted very finely though he appeared to great disadvantage by the side of Miss Somerville who played Imoinda. She is a beautiful creature though wretched actress. HENRY CRABB ROBINSON, *Diary*

FEBRUARY 12. Junius Brutus Booth in Shakespeare's **Richard III** at Covent Garden Theatre. Booth gave a very good imitation of Edmund Kean in the role.

FEBRUARY 20. Edmund Kean enticed Julius Brutus Booth away from Covent Garden Theatre to come and play Iago to his Othello. Booth, completely upstaged, realised he had made a bad career move, broke his contract, and returned to Covent Garden to play Richard III. The audience gave him a rotten time, hurling expletives, so much so that it was impossible for him to act the role.

Kean is all effort, all violence, all extreme passion: he is possessed with a fury, a demon that leaves him no repose, no time for thought, or room for imagination.
WILLIAM HAZLITT, *Examiner*

FEBRUARY 27. Maria Theresa Bland and John Pritt Harley in Wally Chamberlayne Oulton's **Frighten'd to Death!** at Drury Lane Theatre. Musical farce. Music selected and composed by Thomas Simpson Cooke. A dissipated youth is knocked out. When he regains consciousness everybody treats him as if he were a ghost.

MARCH 8. Junius Brutus Booth as Sir Giles Overreach in Philip Massinger's **A New Way to Pay Old Debts** at Covent Garden Theatre. Booth gave his imitation of Kean in the role.

APRIL 7. Charles Farley in Robinson Crusoe and **The Bold Buccaneer** at Covent Garden Theatre. Joseph Grimaldi as Man Friday.

He [Grimaldi] literally does nothing because he has nothing to do. Farley, who plays Robinson Crusoe, acted the pantomimic part with great skill but when he opened his mouth to

MR. KEAN AS OTHELLO.

LEFT

Mme Vestris (1797–1856), actress-singer, became a star overnight when she played the leading role in Giovanni in London in 1817. Later she would become theatre manager of Olympic Theatre and of Covent Garden Theatre. She was married to Charles Mathews.

ABOVE

Edmund Kean in Shakespeare's Othello. Samuel Taylor Coleridge said, 'To see Kean act was like reading Shakespeare by flashes of lightning'.

moralize, which he did very often, he became ridiculous. *Theatre Inquisitor*

APRIL 12. Giuseppe Ambrogetti in London premiere of Mozart's **Don Giovanni** at Her Majesty's Theatre. 'Absolute perfection, the recitatives were masterly, full of variety,' said *The Observer*; 'will amply reward those who have the opportunity of enjoying so pure a treat.'

MAY 2. William Charles Macready, Charles Kemble, Charles Mayne Young and Eliza O'Neill in Charles Lalor Sheil's **The Apostate** at Covent Garden Theatre. Spain during the Inquisition. Moorish lover becomes a Christian. Hazlitt didn't approve of the violence and horror.

> He [Macready] personates a villain of the very first order; even Richard III, Iago or any of the most treacherous characters in our plays are angels of light compared with this most pernicious, flagitious and cruel hypocrite. *Observer*

' *We cannot without some repugnance see her [Eliza O'Neill] tear her hair and strain her eyeballs and rattle her throat, and utter shrieks like mandrakes, and dig for her husband's grave with her nails. The pain is greater than the pleasure: the physical horror overpowers the poetical interest.* '

THE TIMES

JUNE 17. Sarah Siddons as Lady Macbeth in Shakespeare's **Macbeth** at Covent Garden Theatre. Both Kemble and Hazlitt thought her return to the stage was a mistake.

> We certainly thought her performance the other night inferior to what it used to be. She speaks too slow, and her manner has not that decided, sweeping majesty which used to characterize her as the Muse of Tragedy … An actress who appears only once-a-year cannot play so well as if she was in the habit of acting once a week. We therefore wish Mrs Siddons would either return to the stage or retire from it altogether. By her uncertain wavering between public and private life she may diminish her reputation while she can add nothing to it.
> WILLIAM HAZLITT, *Examiner*

JUNE 19. Francois Joseph Talma in concert at King's Theatre. The great French actor, a favourite of Napoleon, gave extracts from his best roles, which included plays by Racine, Voltaire and Corneille. The principal actors of Covent Garden had given him a celebratory lunch two weeks earlier at the Caledonian Hotel.

> To my judgement he was the most finished artist of the times, not below Kean in his most energetic displays, and far above him on the refinement of his taste and extent of his research, equalling Kemble in his dignity, unfettered by his stiffness and formality.
> CHARLES WILLIAM MACREADY

> Of M. Talma's acting we can hardly speak highly enough. Neither his face nor his person

1817

World premieres
Gioacchino Rossini's *La Cenerentola* in Rome

Births
Helen Faucit, British actress
George Henry Lewes, British critic, dramatist
Tom Taylor, British dramatist

Deaths
Jane Austen, British novelist (b. 1775)

Literature
William Hazlitt's *Characters of Shakespeare's Plays*
Walter Scott's *Rob Roy*

Notes
Gas lighting introduced at Covent Garden, Drury Lane and Lyceum Theatres

History
'Blanketeer' Protests: fear of insurrection leads to suspension of Habeas Corpus

is much in his favour; the one is flat and round, the other thick and short; nor has his voice much to boast of, except a manly strength and depth ... His acting displays the utmost force of passion regulated by the clearest judgment. It is the triumph of art. *The Times*

JUNE 23. John Philip Kemble took his farewell in Shakespeare's **Coriolanus** at Covent Garden Theatre. A laurel wreath with a white satin scroll deploring his retirement was thrown from one of the boxes. It landed in the orchestra area of the stalls and Talma picked it up and handed it to Kemble.

He plays the part as well as ever he did, with as much freshness and vigour. There was no abatement of spirit, energy, none of grace and dignity. His look, his actions, his expression of the character, were the same as they ever were; they could not be finer.
WILLIAM HAZLITT, *Examiner*

DECEMBER 26. Madame Vestris in Thomas Moncrieff's **Giovanni in London** at Olympic Theatre. A burlesque of Mozart's opera was specially written for Vestris, who always looked good in breeches roles:

What a breast! What an eye! What a foot, leg
   and thigh
What wonderful things she has shown us!
Round hips, swelling sides, and masculine
   strides
Proclaim her an English Adonis.

RIGHT

Edmund Kean as Lucius Junius Brutus in John Howard Payne's Brutus at The Little Theatre, Haymarket, in 1818.

LEFT

Edmund Kean as Barabas in Christopher Marlowe's The Jew of Malta at Theatre Royal, Drury Lane, in 1818.

1818

William Farren in the role with which he was particularly identified, and which he played all his career: Sir Peter Teazle in Richard Brinsley Sheridan's The School for Scandal, first seen at The Little Theatre in 1818.

M.ʳ W. FARREN,
as Sir Peter Teazle.

FEBRUARY 6. Edmund Kean and Mrs Marydn in William Dimond's adaptation of Lord Byron's **The Bride of Abydos** at Drury Lane Theatre. 'Lord Byron's genius,' said *The Times*, 'is not of a dramatic nature'.

MARCH 6. First performance of Mozart's **The Marriage of Figaro** in English at Covent Garden Theatre. Henry Bishop wrote additional music and rearranged Mozart's score. John Liston as Figaro. Miss Stephens as Susanna. William Jones as Almaviva. Mrs Dickons as Countess.

> Liston played Figaro and, though the part is a little too serious for him, gave it in a very effective manner. Jones personated Count Almaviva with his usual spirit; the occasional substitution of a deputy for him, on account of his not being able to sing, is embarrassing and it requires all the fascination of the finest music in the world to redeem the absurdity. *The Times*

MARCH 10. Signor Garcia as Almaviva, Signor Naldi as Figaro and Madame Fodori as Rosina in London premiere of Gioacchino's Rossini's **The Barber of Seville** at King's Theatre.

> As an actor [Gracia] he is extremely clever; he plays with spirit and animation; but his action is rather too exuberant and is somewhat ungraceful. As a singer we think very highly of him. *Observer*

MARCH 12. Charles William Macready in **Rob Roy Macgregor or Auld Lang Syne** at Covent Garden Theatre. Isaac Pocock's operatic adaptation of Walter Scott's novel. There were songs by Robbie Burns and William Wordsworth plus some Scottish airs.

APRIL 2. Charles Mathews in **Mail Coach Adventures** at English Opera House. Mathews,

THEATRE ROYAL, COVENT-GARDEN

. This Theatre during the Recefs has been NEWLY DECORATED and EMBELLISHED throughout, and no Pains or Expenfe have been fpared to afford that elegant Accommodation *before* the Curtain, and by the Engagement of a Company, fraught with the higheft Profeffional Talent, to enfure that fuperior Dramatick Entertainment on the Stage, which the Inhabitants of this Great City have a right to expect in their National Theatre.

The Publick are refpectfully informed that

THIS THEATRE
WILL BE OPENED

This prefent MONDAY, September 7, 1818,

When will be performed Shakfpeare's Tragedy of

MACBETH.

The Overture and Symphonies between the acts by Mr Ware—the Vocal Mufick by Matthew Lock.

Duncan, King of Scotland, by Mr. CHAPMAN,
Malcolm by Mr. ABBOTT, Donalbain by Mr. MENAGE,
Macbeth by Mr. YOUNG,
Macduff, Mr C. KEMBLE Banquo. Mr EGERTON, Fleance Mafter C. Parfloe
Lenox by Mr. JEFFERIES, Roffe by Mr. COMER,
Siward, Mr CRUMPTON, Seyton Mr CLAREMONT, Phyfician Mr TREBY
Officers, Meff. King & Atkins, Chamberlains, Meff. Heath & Collet
Gentlemen, Meff. Goodwin, Grant, Louis, Platt, Sutton, White

Lady Macbeth by Mrs. YATES,
(From the Theatre Royal, Dublin—being her firft appearance in London,)
Gentlewoman by Mifs LOGAN,
Ladies, Mefdames Bologna, Chipp, Corri, Norman, Penn, Robinfon
Hecat' by Mr TAYLOR, Witches, Meff. Blanchard, Farley, Simmons
Apparitions, Mr. Norris, Mafters Parfloe and E. Parfloe.
The principal Vocal Witches,
Meff. Durufet, Everard, George, Guichard, Lee, Montague, Norris, Pyne, I. S. & C. Tett, Tinney
Treby, Watts, Watfon, Williams, &c.
Mefdames Matthews, Lifton, Bifhop, Sterling Coates, Emery, Green, Grimaldi, Herbert, Hibbert, Iliff,
Lelerve, Parrin, Port, Norman, Sexton, Smith, Tokely, Watts, Whitmore, Wood, &c. &c.

To which will be added the Melo-Drama of The

Miller & His Men.

The Mufick compofed by Mr. BISHOP.
Grindoff, (the Miller) by Mr. FARLEY,
Count Frederick Friberg, Mr. CONNOR, Karl (his fervant) Mr. LISTON
Lothair, Mr. ABBOTT,
Kelmar (an old Cottager) Mr. CHAPMAN,
Riber and Golotz (two Banditti) Meff. JEFFERIES & KING, Zingra by Mr Norris
Lindoff Mr. Tinney, Coburg Mr. Treby
Claudine by Mifs FOOTE, Laurett, Mifs GREEN.
Ravina by Mrs. FAUCIT.

☞ *NOT AN ORDER can be admitted.*
A Private Box may be had for the Seafon, or nightly, of Mr. Brandon at the Box-office
Boxes 7s. Second Price 3s 6d.—Pit 3s 6d. Second Price 2s.
Lower Gallery 2s. Second Price 1s —Upper Gallery 1s. Second Price 6d.
The DOORS to be opened at SIX o'Clock—the Play to begin at SEVEN
Places for the Boxes to be taken of Mr. BRANDON at the Box-office, Hart-ftreet, from Ten till Four.
E. MACLEISH, Printer, 2. Bow-ftreet, Covent-Garden Vivant Rex et Regina

On *Wednefday*, the Opera of GUY MANNERING; or the Gipfey's Prophecy. In which
Mr. PYNE
will make his firft appearance at this Theatre in the Character of HENRY BERTRAM.
With the new Ballet of LA CHASSE—and the popular Farce of HUSBANDS and WIVES.
On *Thurfday*, the Comedy of The SCHOOL for SCANDAL. In which
Mr. W. FARREN,
Of the Theatre Royal, Dublin, (who is engaged at this Theatre) will make his firft appearance
in the Character of SIR PETER TEAZLE.

The playbill for Shakespeare's Macbeth and F. Talfourd and H. J. Byron's The Miller & His Men at Theatre Royal, Covent Garden, in 1818.

famed for his ventriloquism, impersonated different characters travelling on the coach. 60,000 theatregoers came to see his virtuoso solo performances. His monologues, a mixture of comic singing and droll stories, became an annual feature.

> For joyousness of manner, amusing eccentricity and what may be denominated the sublime of farce, we know of nothing more amusing than these sketches. *Drama*

APRIL 24. Edmund Kean as Barabas in Christopher Marlowe's **The Jew of Malta** at Drury Lane Theatre. The poisoning of the whole convent was omitted. Leigh Hunt in *The Examiner* said Kean's performance was 'in his very best taste of self-hugging revenge and triumphal Machiavelism'.

> Nothing can more strongly show the power and popularity of Kean than his having been able to illumine and render tolerable so dark a portrait as Barabas. He introduced a song in the 4th act, but though encored, we cannot help think it a perversion of talent. *Athenæum*

JUNE 1. Edmund Kean in Shakespeare's **King John** at Drury Lane Theatre. James Wallack as Faulconbridge. Miss Macaulay as Constance. It was not wise of Kean to play John so soon after Kemble's big success in the role.

JUNE 8. Edmund Kean in Nathaniel Lee's **Alexander the Great** at Drury Lane Theatre. The pageantry and scenery were superb. Kean withdrew the play when the management wouldn't pay for the costumes and decorations.

AUGUST 12. Vauxhall Gardens opened with a Fête for the Prince Regent's birthday. High spots included a concert, fireworks and Madame and Mlle Saqui dancing an allemande on two ropes. The gardens were illuminated with thousands of additional lamps. The price of admission was 3s. 6d.

SEPTEMBER 14. William Farren and Elizabeth Brunton as Sir Peter and Lady Teazle in Richard Brinsley Sheridan's **The School for Scandal** at Covent Garden Theatre. Farren's London debut.

> His tone is clear and capable of great variety of modulation; his enunciation distinct, his countenance expressive, and wonderfully flexible. He is comic without an effort and his humour is chaste. *Observer*

OCTOBER 4. Edmund Kean in Shakespeare's **Othello** at Drury Lane Theatre. William Cleary as Iago. Mrs West as Desdemona. 'William Kean's Othello,' said Leigh Hunt in *The Examiner*, 'is the masterpiece of the living stage.'

> From the third act onwards all was wrought out with a mastery over the resources of expression such as has been seldom approached. In the successive unfolding of these great scenes here presented with incomparable effect, the lion-like fury, the deep and haggard pathos, the forlorn sense of desolation, alternating with gusts of stormy cries for vengeance.
> G.H.LEWES, *On Actor and the Art of Acting*

OCTOBER 8. **The Lady of the Lake** at Surrey Theatre. Romantic drama. This adaptation of Walter Scott's novel was followed by a representation of **The Battle of Trafalgar** with ships of war going though a regular engagement.

1818

Births	Literature	Notes
Emily Bronte, British novelist	Jane Austen's *Northanger Abbey* and *Persuasion*	The Royal Coburg Theatre opens
Ivan Turgenev, Russian dramatist	William Hazlitt's *A View of the English Stage*	Ludwig van Beethoven becomes completely deaf but continues to compose
Deaths	Mary Shelley's *Frankenstein*	
Matthew Gregory 'Monk' Lewis, British novelist (b. 1775)	Thomas Bowdler's expurgated *Family Shakespeare* is published	*History* First blood transfusion

The Royal Coburg Theatre was founded by James King, David Dunn and John Thomas Serres in 1818. They had secured the patronage of Princess Charlotte and Prince Leopold of Saxe-Coburg.

OCTOBER 14. William Farren as Lord Ogleby in David Garrick and George Colman's **The Clandestine Marriage** and as Sir Fretful in Richard Brinsley Sheridan's **The Critic** at Covent Garden Theatre.

What a mixture of shrewdness and infatuated self-complacency, of causticity and courtesy, of puerile affectation and manly judgment, of selfishness and chivalry! I say that Farren realized and harmonized all those aspects, is in effect to say he was one of the great comedians. He possessed to perfection the nuances of expression, apprehended with the finest delicacy the effect of semitones.

JOHN WESTLAND MARSTON, *Our Recent Actors*

OCTOBER 18. William Farren as Sir Anthony Absolute in Richard Brinsley Sheridan's **The Rivals** at Covent Garden Theatre. Louisa Brunton as Lydia. John Liston as Acres. Charles Mayne Young as Faulkland.

OCTOBER 31. Edmund Kean in Howard Payne's **Brutus or The Fall of Tarquin** at Drury Lane Theatre. Henry Kemble as Tarquin was so bad that he was booed. *The Theatre Inquisitor* lambasted Payne for failing to acknowledge his blatant plagiarism of plays by Richard Cumberland and Nathaniel Lee:

The money he has pocketed by this barefaced and scandalous piracy and imposture let him exult over; but as to fame and reputation, he has plunged them down an abyss from which they can never rise. *Theatre Inquisitor*

DECEMBER 5. William Charles Macready in Shakespeare's **Coriolanus**. Helen Faucit as Volumnia. 'Mrs Faucit belongs to melodrama,' said Leigh Hunt in *The Examiner*. 'A Roman matron does not think it essential to her dignity to step about with her head thrown back, as if she had contempt for her own chin.'

1819

JANUARY 26. London premiere of Gioacchino Rossini's **L'Italiana in Algeri** at His Majesty's Theatre. Sung in Italian.

FEBRUARY 10. Eliza O'Neill and William Charles Macready in Charles Lalor Sheil's **Evadne or The Statue** at Covent Garden Theatre.

MARCH 8. Charles Mathews' **Trip to Paris** at English Opera House. A virtuoso solo performance of vividly drawn character sketches.

He was Charles Mathews in everything he did. Now he would change his clothes, anon his character, but his personality was always the same – quick, delightful effervescing, impulsive. In his own line, a somewhat limited one it is true, he was incomparable. In the very distinct line of business of being oneself upon the stage, Charles Mathews has evidently never been surpassed and possibly will never be.
HAROLD SIMPSON and MRS CHARLES BRAUN, *A Century of Famous Actors*

Charles Matthews (1776–1835) was famous for his one-man shows.

Elizabeth O'Neill (1791–1872) was hailed as the new Siddons. Her career lasted but five years. Shelley wrote The Cenci especially for her, but she never played it.

APRIL 3. Frederick Yates as Falstaff, Charles Kemble as Hal and William Charles Macready as Hotspur in Shakespeare's **Henry IV Part 1** at Covent Garden Theatre. Mrs Davenport as Mistress Quickly. This was the first time Macready played Hotspur in London, one of his great roles. *The Times* praised his 'very effective manly representation of the character'.

APRIL 19. Joseph Grimaldi in **The Talking Bird** at Covent Garden. Grimaldi sang one of his most popular songs, 'Hod Codlins', a lyric about an old woman who sells apples. The audience sang the chorus: 'Ri tol iddy, iddy, iddy. Ri tol iddy, iddy, Ri tol lay.'

AUGUST 15. Fanny Kelly in G. Ware's **Belles without Beaux or The Ladies Among Themselves** at English Opera House.

AUGUST 29. John Emery in John Maddison Morton's **A Roland for an Oliver** at Covent Garden Theatre. Blow for blow, a farce. Music by Henry Bishop.

William Charles Macready as Hotspur in
Shakespeare's Henry IV Part 1 at Covent
Garden Theatre in 1819.

OCTOBER 25. William Charles Macready in Colley Cibber's version of Shakespeare's **Richard III** at Covent Garden Theatre. 'I never saw the gayer part of Richard to such advantage,' said *The Examiner*.

Macready is of a warm temperament; his ardour frequently becomes too great for his discretion, and in the heat of action he sometimes goes further than he himself intended; though few actors are possessed of greater power, he husbands his resources with so little reserve, that a long part like that of Richard is sure to exhaust him before the conclusion. *The Times*

It was perfectly original, yet there was no apparent struggle after originality, no laborious effort to mark the difference in passages of small importance. *Morning Chronicle*

NOVEMBER 19. William Charles Macready in Shakespeare's **Coriolanus** at Covent Garden Theatre. There was high praise for the mob and the siege of Rome.

William Macready aware no doubt that his figure, face and manner combined would not inspire awe in vulgar souls, or strike a plebeian dumb by a single motion, gave excessive business to his words and violence to his action. *News*

William Charles Macready in one of his great roles: Shakespeare's Richard III.

DECEMBER 11. John Liston and William Farren as the Dromio twins in Frederick Reynolds' musical version of Shakespeare's **The Comedy of Errors** at Covent Garden Theatre. Reynolds drew on songs from Shakespeare's other plays and also selections of music from Dr Arne and Mozart.

> The admirers of Shakespeare having long regretted that most of his lyrical compositions, have never been sung in a theatre, The Comedy of Errors (one of the shortest and most lively of his comedies) has been selected as the best vehicle for their introduction – A few additional scenes and passages are absolutely necessary for this purpose; and however deficient these may be found, it is hoped they will be readily pardoned, as having served to bring to the stage, more of the 'native wood notes wild' of our Immortal Bard. FREDERICK REYNOLDS, *Playbill*

DECEMBER 17. Miss Macaulay in Frederick Schiller's **Mary Stuart, Queen of England** at Covent Garden Theatre. First performance in London. Avona Bunn as Queen Elizabeth. William Charles Macready as Leicester. The audience was divided as to whether the performance should be repeated.

DECEMBER 27. Eliza Povey as Idle Jack, John Peter 'Jack' Bologna as Harlequin and Chevalier Southby as Clown in **Jack and the Beanstalk or Harlequin and the Ogre** at Drury Lane Theatre. Povey was one of the first women to play Principal Boy in pantomime.

Births
George Eliot, British novelist
Jacques Offenbach, French
  composer
John Ruskin, British art critic
Queen Victoria

Deaths
August von Kotzebue, German
  dramatist (b. 1761)

Literature
Lord Byron's *Don Juan* is
  published, 1819–24
John Keats' *Ode to a Nightingale*
John Keats' *Eve of St Agnes*
William Hazlitt's *Lectures on
  the English Comic Writers*

Notes
Sans Pareil Theatre is renamed Adelphi Theatre

History
'Peterloo' massacre in
  Manchester
Cotton Mills and Factories
  Act outlaws employment of
  children under age of nine

1819

The
1820s

1820

JANUARY 3. William Barrymore's **Wallace, the Hero of Scotland**, at Astley's Amphitheatre. Historical melodrama. The advert read: 'Horsemanship by William W. Davis. The infant prodigy, Miss Clarke, only five years old, will go through her wonderful and pleasing evolutions on a Tight Rope.'

JANUARY 20. Death of King George III. The theatres closed until February 17, which meant a serious loss of revenue to proprietors and actors.

JANUARY 25. Edmund Kean in Shakespeare's **Coriolanus** at Drury Lane Theatre. Julia Glover as Constance. The critics didn't like either the performance, the production or the play. Kean did not have the physique for the role. The 'I banish you' speech was delivered with the rage of impotent despair.

JANUARY 25. John Liston and William Blanchard in Daniel Tayler's **The Antiquary** at Covent Garden Theatre. Musical drama based on Sir Walter Scott's novel. High spot was the escape across the sands with the tide coming in.

> The character of Oldbuck is one of the least entertaining we have ever seen Liston perform; his peculiar form of humour is thrown away upon it. *Observer*

FEBRUARY 22. Madame Vestris as Macheath in John Gay's **The Beggar's Opera** at Haymarket Theatre. One of Vestris's most successful roles.

> In a word we never remember an instance of an actress who contrived to be at once so very much a gentleman and yet so entire and unaltered a woman. *Examiner*

Charles Kemble as Hotspur in Shakespeare's Henry IV Part 1. The picture was engraved for The Theatrical Inquisitor in 1820. Charles was the youngest brother of Sarah Siddons and father of Fanny Kemble.

Painted by J.Boaden.   Engraved by Chas P..

Mr Kemble as Hotspur. In Henry the Fourth.

LEFT

William Charles Macready in Shakespeare's Macbeth. It was in this role that he took his farewell of the stage in 1851.

APRIL 27. Edmund Kean in Shakespeare's **King Lear** at Drury Lane Theatre. Out of respect for King George III, Lear had not been performed during his madness. 'I shall make the audience as mad as I shall be,' promised Kean. He had visited an asylum in preparation for the role. In the event he was upstaged by the storm; such was the din, he complained that he, let alone the audience, couldn't hear a word of what was being said.

> It will be quoted as the chef-d'oeuvre of the English drama, and must be handed down to the emulation of future actors. *The Times*

MAY 20. William Charles Macready in James Sheridan Knowles's **Virginius** at Covent Garden Theatre. 'The last act is an excrescence,' wrote Charles Crabb Robinson in his *Diary*. 'Macready's insanity is commonplace, his mode of murdering the tyrant by strangulation raised a laugh.'

> Austere, tender, familiar, elevated, mingling at once terror and pathos, he ran over the scale of dramatic expression with the highest degree of power. *Morning Herald*

> He has all that nature can give, with all that taste and talent can acquire. His person is tall and commanding – his carriage noble – his face, though not technically a first rate face, is wonderfully expressive, and his voice is peculiarly fine, deep and mellow. *Mirror*

JUNE 12. Madame Vestris in William Thomas Moncrieff's **The Shipwreck of the Medusa or The Fatal Raft!** at Royal Coburg Theatre. Mutiny, sharks and cannibalism: the play was based on Theodore Gericault's iconic painting of the nineteenth-century's most famous sea disaster. The narrative came from two survivors. The subject inspired two more spectacular productions: one a panorama, the other an exhibition at Bullock's Egyptian Hall, which attracted just under 50,000 spectators.

JUNE 20. Madame Vestris in James Cobb's **The Siege of Belgrade** at Drury Lane Theatre. Comic operetta with an elaborate battle scene. Music by Stephen Storace.

> [Madame Vestris] will become, I have no doubt, the darling of the public – she is by birth English and her articulation is not that of a foreigner, but she looks, walks and gesticulates so very French that I almost thought myself in the Theatre Feydeau.
> CHARLES CRABB ROBINSON, *Diary*

AUGUST 9. T. P. Cooke and Mrs W. H. Chatterley in J. R. Planché's **Vampyre or The Bride of the Isles** at English Opera House. The romantic melodrama was an adaptation of John Polidori's novel. The production introduced a new form of stage trap, the vamp trap, an opening with spring leaves, which was used to give an impression of an actor walking through a solid wall. Cooke was a huge success.

NOVEMBER 8. William Farren as Malvolio and Miss Greene as Olivia in Shakespeare's **Twelfth Night** at Covent Garden Theatre. Staged as an opera.

1820

Births	Deaths	History
Dion Boucicault, Irish-born dramatist, actor, theatre manager	King George III (b. 1738)	The Prince Regent accedes to the throne as George IV
Jenny Lind, Swedish singer	*Literature*	Bill of Pains and Penalties leads to trial of Queen Caroline for 'licentious behaviour'
Westland Marston, British dramatist, critic	*The Songs of Robert Burns* John Clare's *Poems Descriptive of Rural Life and Scenery*	
Florence Nightingale, British nurse		Cato Street Conspiracy to kill the Cabinet is exposed

1821

MARCH 12. William Charles Macready in Colley Cibber's version of Shakespeare's **Richard III** at Covent Garden Theatre. The production was spectacular, but it failed. Macready didn't like his performance.

APRIL 8. Miss Cubitt, Joseph Munden, John Pritt Harley and Madame Vestris in Colley's Cibber's **She Would and She Would Not** at Drury Lane Theatre. *The Drama* thought that by staging the play as an opera the production had destroyed much of its comic effect.

This person [Harley] absolutely overflows with fun and the sound of his voice is an alarm to gravity … Madame Vestris is a charming actress. Where did she hide her comic spirit so long? She is a treasure to Drury Lane and ought to be the pride of the manager. There is no actress at that theatre at all equal to her, excepting of course Miss Kelly; but then she has notes Miss Kelly cannot reach, and so the matter is even between them.   *London Magazine*

Theatre Royal, Haymarket, was built adjacent to the old theatre at a cost of £20,000. The architect was John Nash. The theatre opened in 1821 with a revival of Richard Brinsley Sheridan's The Rivals.

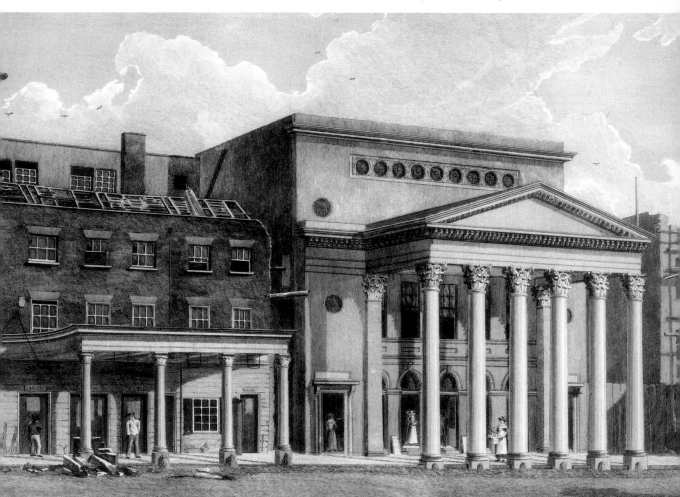

T. LANE delt.

London Pubd. by G. Humphrey 27 St. James's St. Novr. 26. 1821

Contending for a Seat.

Theatrical Pleasures: 'Contending for a seat'. This cartoon was published by G. Humphrey on 26 November 1821. The identity of the artist is not known.

APRIL 23. Mrs West and William Cooper in Nicholas Rowe's **The Tragedy of Jane Shore** at Drury Lane Theatre. William Wallack as Richard III. Pastiche Shakespeare: Edward IV's mistress is accused of sorcery by Richard.

> William Wallack is always a respectable actor, and sometimes a very good one; but the vein does not run through an entire character. William Cooper never offends, and, it must be owned, seldom pleases us. *London Magazine*

APRIL 25. John Cooper as Doge in Lord Byron's **Marino Faliero** at Drury Lane Theatre. 'The tragedy has been shorn of most of its poetical beauties,' said *The Drama*. 'A drawling story, stagnating through five boggy acts,' said *The Literary Gazette*. The play was performed without the licence of the author and the publisher and in defiance of an injunction of the Lord Chamberlain. 'It is not an acting play,' complained Byron to John Murray, his publisher.

❛ Were I capable of writing a play, which could be deemed stage-worthy, success would give me no pleasure, and failure great pain. ❜

LORD BYRON, Preface to *Marino Faliero*

MAY 15. William Charles Macready in Frederick Reynolds's musical version of Shakespeare's **The Tempest** at Covent Garden Theatre. 'Prospero is a mere conjuror of very doubtful worth,' wrote Charles Crabb Robinson in his *Diary*. 'Macready laboured through his part monotonously.'

JUNE 25. William Charles Macready as King Henry, John Fawcett as Falstaff and Charles Kemble as Hal in Shakespeare's **Henry IV Part 2** at Covent Garden Theatre. Staged primarily so that Macready could introduce a lavish coronation scene to anticipate the real-life coronation of George IV on 19 July 1821. 'No piece has ever been brought forth in this costly manner,' said *Drama*.

JULY 15. Master Betty decided to cut his throat when an engagement to perform at Covent Garden Theatre fell through; he failed to kill himself.

JULY. Henry Kemble in **Napoleon Bonaparte, General!, Consul!! and Emperor!!!** at Coburg Theatre. Kemble made his entrance on horseback. The coronation scene was particularly impressive. 'Had there been a little more plot,' said *The Drama*, 'it would have greatly improved the interest.'

AUGUST 1. A replica of King George IV's coronation at Drury Lane Theatre. A sumptuously costumed spectacular pageant. Robert Elliston played King George and was so convincing that the audience stood up on his entrance.

Births	Deaths	Literature
Junius Brutus Booth, Anglo-American actor	Elizabeth Inchbald, British dramatist, novelist (b. 1753)	Lord Byron's *Cain*
Charles Baudelaire, French poet	John Keats, British poet (b. 1795)	Thomas de Quincey's *Confessions of an English Opium Eater*
Feodor Dostoevsky, Russian novelist	Napoleon Bonaparte (b. 1769)	
Gustave Flaubert, French novelist	Queen Caroline	*History*
Rachel, French actress	*Notes*	Start of National Uprising in Greece
	Haymarket Theatre re-opens	*Manchester Guardian* founded

1821

SEPTEMBER 12. William De Camp as Figaro and Miss R. Corri as Susanna in Mozart's ***The Marriage of Figaro*** at Haymarket Theatre.

He [De Camp] was very warmly applauded in the military air, best known by the Italian title of 'Non piu andrai' which he sang from beginning to end with great dexterity.   *Drama*

SEPTEMBER 20. William Terry and Mrs Chatterly in James Kenney's ***Matchbreaking or The Prince's Present*** at Haymarket Theatre. There were angry letters in the press from French critics about Kenney not acknowledging his French source and passing the play off as his own.

NOVEMBER. Edmund Kean was charged by a female with indiscreet familiarities. *The Drama* penned the following epigram:

Kean is accused – and that is certain –
Of acting ill – behind the curtain;
But let's forgive him – I implore it –
He never acted ill before it.

Kean was notorious for copulating in his dressing-room back-stage, and did not mind keeping his audience waiting.

NOVEMBER 26. Benjamin Wrench and John Reeve in William Thomas Moncrieff's ***Tom and Jerry*** at Adelphi Theatre. This adaptation of the hugely popular *The Day and Night Scenes of Jerry Hawthorn Esq. and his Elegant Friend Corinthian Tom* was the first play to be performed for 100 consecutive performances. Tom and Jerry – the two Regency bucks – became a synonym for fighting, drinking and behaving badly. At one point ten theatres were playing Moncrieff's comedy at the same time.

In our opinion no drama should be run night after night beyond a ninth time.   *Observer*

MISS KELLY.

Fanny Kelly, the Anglo-Irish actress, established a theatre school in the Strand.

RIGHT

The cast of Richard Brinsley Sheridan's The Rivals at Theatre Royal, Haymarket, on the opening night, 4 July 1821. The layout of the theatre is clearly displayed at the bottom of this illustration.

Schabbelie del.   J. Stow sculp.

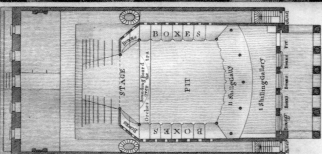

INTERIOR OF THE   NEW THEATRE
ROYAL   HAY MARKET,
it appeared on the Night   of its opening 4th July, 1821

London, Published 1st January 1823 by R. Wilkinson, No. 125 Fenchurch Street.

1822

JANUARY 14. Julia Glover and Mr Finn in Thomas Dibdin's *The Pirate or The Wild Woman of Zetland* at Surrey Theatre.

Mrs Glover gave a most admirable personation of the wild woman, Norma of the Fitful Head, and displayed uncommon skill and discrimination by the vigorous and effective manner in which she poured forth the sybillisms. *Drama*

MARCH 14. *The Youthful Days of Mr Mathews* at English Opera House. Virtuoso solo performances of character sketches.

MAY 20. Edmund Kean as Cardinal Wolsey in Shakespeare's *Henry VIII* at Drury Lane Theatre. John Cooper as King Henry. Mrs W. Watts as Queen Katharine.

MAY 21. Edmund Kean as Don Felix in Susannah Centlivre's *The Wonder! A Woman Keep a Secret* at Drury Lane Theatre. First produced in 1714. The women argue that they have just as much right to follow their inclinations as do men. Their fathers disagree and pack them off either to convents or into loveless marriages.

MAY 23. Joseph Munden as Sir Francis Gripe in Susannah Centlivre's *Busy Body* at Drury Lane Theatre. John Pritt Marley as Marplot. Julia Glover as Miranda.

AUGUST 12. William Charles Macready in Nathaniel Lee's *Alexander the Great* at Royal Amphitheatre.

Of Macready's Alexander we can say nothing whatever in praise. He appeared totally unmindful of the business of the scene and marred in almost every place the interest otherwise attendant on it, with the most perfect nonchalance. *Drama*

Helen Faucit (1817–98), starred in Sheridan Knowles's The Hunchback (1837) and three plays by Edward Bulwer-Lytton: The Lady of Lyons (1838), Richelieu (1839) and Money (1840).

yours very Sincerely
Helen Faucit

' *Melodramas are things which almost everybody abuses, and yet almost everybody goes to see them, and sees them with pleasure.* **'**

Drama, 1822

Births

Dion Boucicault, Irish
dramatist, actor

César Franck, Belgian
composer

Matthew Arnold, English poet

Notes

Royal Academy of Music,
London, founded

Deaths

Lord Castlereagh commits
suicide (b. 1769)

Fanny Kelly, Anglo-Irish
actress (b. 1790)

Percy Bysshe Shelley, British
poet drowns (b. 1792)

History

Brazil declares independence
from Portugal

George IV visits Scotland;
Scottish identity re-defined
by Walter Scott

Jean-François Champollion
uses the Rosetta Stone to
decipher ancient Egyptian
hieroglyphs

AUGUST 12. Sarah Egerton in Edward Fitzball's *Joan of Arc or The Maid of Orleans* at Sadler's Wells Theatre. 120 performances.

> [Mrs Egerton] gave a romance and almost an awful dignity to the character ... Her upcast eyes, inspired as it were, with unearthly light, seemed to commune with beings of another world, seen only by herself.
> EDWARD FITZBALL, *Thirty-Five Years of a Dramatic Author's Life*

NOVEMBER 11. Charles William Macready and Helen Faucit in Richard Lalor Shiel's **The Huguenot** at Covent Garden Theatre. 'The dialogue,' said *The Drama*, 'is a mere tissue of turgid rant, absurd conceits and dull metaphors of the description commonly called nonsense.' Shiel gave up play-writing.

DECEMBER 26. Joseph Grimaldi in **Harlequin and the Ogress or The Sleeping Beauty of the Wood** at Covent Garden Theatre. The crude liberties which were taken at the expense of the recently unveiled statue of Achilles in Hyde Park were much appreciated. (Such indeed was the public outrage at Achilles' nudity, the authorities had to add a fig leaf.) Grimaldi's contribution to the pantomime was a patent safety-coach which he had made characteristically from the most extraordinary and disparate materials. The loudest applause, however, was for the representation of a treadmill with some dozen gamblers on it.

> Grimaldi is the most intellectual and irresistible of clowns ... what a sentiment there is in his action! What interesting pathos in his countenance ... what an encyclopaedia of wit is his face! What a magazine of merriment! *News*

William Charles Macready (1793–1873), the actor-manager, never really enjoyed being an actor. His greatest role was generally considered to be King Lear.

John Reeve in Bachelor Torments or The Sweets of a Family at Adelphi Theatre in 1823.

MR. JOHN REEVE,
in the Whole of his Characters in
Bachelors Torments.

1823

JANUARY 22. Edmund Kean as Posthumus in Shakespeare's **Cymbeline** at Drury Lane Theatre. Miss Williams as Imogen. Charles Mayne Young as Iachimo.

FEBRUARY 15. John Liston in John Poole's **Deaf as a Post** at Drury Lane Theatre. In his diary Liston wrote: 'First act successful, second act very bad, third decidedly damned.'

MARCH 3. William Charles Macready as John and Helena Faucit as Constance in Shakespeare's **King John** at Covent Garden Theatre. J. R. Planché's historically accurate designs were based on costumes and scenery found in monumental effigies, seals and illuminated manuscripts of the thirteenth century. Macready's was dressed exactly as King John's effigy was in Worcester Cathedral. The barons were sheathed in mail and wore cylindrical helmets. Charles Kemble had a great success as Faulconbridge. *The Daily News* said, 'His first and second dress were particularly graceful and picturesque.'

MARCH 6. John Reeve as Cupid in **Cupid and the Nymph** at Adelphi Theatre.

MARCH 10. Edmund Kean in Shakespeare's **King Lear** at Drury Lane Theatre. Kean kept much more of the original text and restored the tragic ending.

MARCH 15. William Charles Macready in Mary Russell Mitford's **Julian** at Covent Garden Theatre. 'The play,' said *The Drama*, 'is the avowed production of a female pen and therefore entitled to a much larger indulgence from the rigid test of the strict rules of criticism.'

APRIL 24. John Reeve in **Bachelor Torments or The Sweets of a Family** at Adelphi Theatre. Reeve played all the characters, including a 50-year-old maiden aunt and an 18-year-old romantic girl. His impersonation of a French singing master and a naughty, spoilt boy were particularly popular.

MAY 8. Howard Payne and Henry Bishop's **Clari or The Maid of Milan** at Covent Garden Theatre. Operetta based on a French ballet. The Maid manages to keep her chastity despite the overtures of the Duke in whose castle she worked. Bishop's 'Home Sweet Home' was sung for the first time and became a popular parlour song.

Charles Kean (1811–68), actor-manager, son of Edmund Kean, was appointed Director of Queen Victoria's private theatricals at Windsor. His productions were famous for their historical accuracy, and he was elected a Fellow of the Society of Antiquaries in 1857.

John Reeve as Cupid in Cupid and the Nymph at Adelphi Theatre in 1823.

MR. JOHN REEVE AS CUPID.

MAY 19. Mrs Pope in **Dick Whittington and His Cat or London in 1370** at Royal Coburg Theatre. The cat was a real cat, unlike the production at Covent Garden Theatre, where a dog was dressed up as a cat.

JULY 7. Madame Vestris and John Liston in James Kenney's **Sweethearts and Wives** at Haymarket Theatre. One of Kenney's most popular successes.

JULY 28. James Wallack as Frankenstein and T. P. Cooke as ✱✱✱✱✱✱✱ [sic] in Richard Brinsley Peake's **Presumption or The Fate of Frankenstein** at English Opera House. The first of many adaptations of Mary Shelley's novel. Cook's monster was mute. He wore a wig of wild hair, and his make-up was charnel-green. In this version the monster kills Frankenstein in front of a glacier. As Frankenstein falls, he fires his pistol, which starts an avalanche, which also kills the monster.

> Others played ghosts and demons with unquestionable success; but how mechanically and solidly … it was he [Cooke] who first infused them with a true poetic element – gave them breath a dreamy indistinctiveness – a vague suggestive shadow which while it chained the sense, set the imagination free.
> *Illustrated London News*

Births
Isabella Glyn, British actor
Aleksandr Ostrovsky, Russian
dramatist

Deaths
John Philip Kemble British
actor-manager, brother of
Sarah Siddons (b. 1757)

Literature
Charles Lamb's *Essays of Elia*
Walter Scott's *Quentin Durward*

1823

OCTOBER 27. James Wallack and William Barrymore in Thomas Moncrieff's **The Cataract of the Ganges** at Drury Lane Theatre. Romantic melodrama, with military bands, dancing girls and a massacre. A British officer promises to help the Rajah to defeat his enemies and rescue his daughter, but only if the Rajah promises to give up female infanticide. The attraction of the production was the scenery painted by Clarkson Stanfield. The spectacle included a Grand Hindu Temple and a coach drawn by six horses. The cataract poured down from a cistern in the flies. The heroine made her escape on horseback riding up the cataract with fires blazing all around her. *The London Magazine* was unimpressed by the cataract, describing it as 'something like a pouring of a good tea-pot, only flatter'.

Welcome noise and nonsense, all the tinsel and trumpery, with their splendid delusions, to gratify the grown children of the metropolis. *Morning Chronicle*

NOVEMBER 18. William Charles Macready in James Sheridan Knowles's **Caius Gracchus** at Drury Lane Theatre.

For all the tragedies that we have witnessed this is incomparably the most boisterous. Every speech is followed by a shout that rings though the house … melodrame [sic] may like it and thrive best under its patronage, but it is beneath the intellect of the legitimate stage to sacrifice sense for unmeaning thunders. *Observer*

1824

MAY 3. Joseph Munden in Thomas Dibdin's **Past Ten O'Clock or A Rainy Night** at Drury Lane Theatre. Munden was very drunk and abusive to his fellow actors.

At the finish of the farce he advanced but he instantly, from the firm and manly way he had the whole night deported himself, dwindled into a decrepit whining little old man. He attempted to speak what he had proposed but was soon at a loss. He put on his spectacles and referred to a paper but they seemed to afford a very temporary aid.
JAMES WINSTON, *Diary*

MAY 22. Joseph Munden's last performance as Old Dornton in Thomas Holcroft's **The Road to Ruin** at Drury Lane Theatre. Robert William Elliston as Young Dornton. Sarah Harlowe as Widow Warren.

His [Munden] performance proves that for pathos (we would even call it sublimity) he need not yield the palm as the best tragedian of the day. *John Bull*

MAY 27. Charles Kemble as the King in **Charles the Second or The Merry Monarch** at Covent Garden Theatre. The king loses his purse in a public house in Wapping. He disguises himself as a sailor. John Fawcett played the landlord.

MAY 31. Joseph Munden's retirement is honoured at Drury Lane Theatre.

Ladies and Gentlemen, The Moment is now arrived when I have to perform the painful duty of bidding you farewell. When I call to remembrance that five and thirty years have elapsed since I first had the honour of appearing before you, I am forcibly reminded that I ought to leave the scene for younger and gayer spirits to mingle in. But it is not easy to shake off in a moment the habit of years and you will know, pardon me if I am tedious, since it is for the last time. I carry with me into private life, ladies and gentlemen, the deep and indelible remembrance of that kind , that liberal indulgence which you have at all times regarded my humble efforts to amuse. I feel that I am 'poor in thanks' but your kindness is registered here - and will never be forgotten: and should the recurrence of early association occasionally bring back the veteran comedian to your recollection – he will ask no higher fame. JOSEPH MUNDEN

It was the versatility of talent which ranked William Munden so high in the profession. Other men may succeed in a particular department, but he excelled in all. The humorous, good-natured as well as the testy and quarrelsome old gentlemen; – the ancient lover; – the dupe of antiquarian credulity; – the feeling and affectionate father; – the drunken son of William Crispin – all these characters, various and dissimilar as they are – found in him an admirable representative. He ran through the whole compass of comedy, and every-where successful. *The Times*

Joseph Munden in a role which was immortalised by Charles Lamb in his Essays: Autolycus in Shakespeare's The Winter's Tale. Munden was notorious for his mugging and up-staging.

JUNE 10. **The Revolt of the Greeks or The Maid of Athens** at Drury Lane Theatre. Inspired by the Greek war of independence against the Ottoman Empire.

JUNE 17. The advertisement for Davis's Royal Amphitheatre read: 'The Carnival of Venice or The Masquerade on a Horse at full Gallop. Monsieur Ducrow, without quitting the horse's back, acted Polichinel, Pierrot, Harlequin, Columbine, Bacchus and Adonis. This was followed by W. Barrymore's **Agamemnon, the Faithful Negro** during which there was a **Grand Ballet of Cocoa-nut Dancers**.'

JUNE 17. Triple bill at Aquatic Theatre, Sadler's Wells. First, a broad farce, **Love, Law and Pugilism or The Latin Scholar**; then a burletta, **The Heart of Oak**; and finally a melodrama, **The Brazen Water Tower or The Doubtful Child**.

JUNE 18. **The Battle of Waterloo** at Royal Garden, Vauxhall was billed as 'A Grand Military Fete, Ballets, minuets, gavottes, quadrilles, fireworks and an American aerialist enveloped in fire magnificently lit by 12,000 additional lamps.'

JULY 7. William Robert Goldsmith in Shakespeare's **Richard III** at Royal Coburg Theatre. Goldsmith was six years old. *The Morning Chronicle* was 'surprised and astonished'. *The Times* thought he had 'the most wonderful theatrical talent'. *The Weekly Dispatch* said they 'never recollected seeing a better piece of performance, even from old stagers'. *The Morning Post* 'listened to him with delight, but the house was so crowded that at times he could not be heard'.

JULY 22. Miss Noel and John Braham in Carl Maria von Weber's **Der Freischutz or The Seventh Ballet** at Covent Garden Theatre. *The Drama* claimed: 'A production composed of incidents so extraordinary and so improbable was never, perhaps, brought out at this or any other theatre, except a German one.'

AUGUST 10. Madame Vestris as Don Felix in James Kenney's **Alcaid or The Secrets of Office** at Haymarket Theatre.

Madame Vestris enacted Don Felix in a good, loose, dashing, rakehelly fashion. She is the best bad young man about town, and can stamp a smart leg in white tights with the air of a fellow who has an easy heart and a good tailor. *London Magazine*

AUGUST 16. Henry Kemble in Edward Fitzball's **The Burning Bridge or The Spectre of the Lake** at Surrey Theatre. Chinese melodrama.

OCTOBER 7. William Farren and Eliza Chester as Sir Peter and Lady Teazle in Richard Brinsley Sheridan's **The School for Scandal** at Haymarket Theatre. Charles Kemble as Charles Surface.

OCTOBER 12. Edward Fitzball's **The Floating Beacon or the Norwegian Wreckers** at Surrey Theatre. Nautical drama based on fact. 140 performances.

DECEMBER 10. Maria Tree as Rosalind, Charles Kemble as Orlando and Charles Mayne Young as Jaques in Shakespeare's **As You Like It** at Covent Garden Theatre. The production drew on songs from Shakespeare's other plays, and there were solos for Rosalind, Celia, Silvius and Touchstone, plus a duet for Rosalind and Celia.

1825

JANUARY 7. William Charles Macready and James Wallack in Philip Massinger's **Fatal Dowry** at Drury Lane Theatre. The run was cut short when Macready fell seriously ill, suffering from the inflammation of the diaphragm.

JANUARY 24. Edmund Kean in Shakespeare's **Richard III** at Drury Lane Theatre. Kean, who had been having an affair with Charlotte Cox, was taken to court by her husband, Alderman Cox, who was awarded £800 pounds. His wife left him, and many people felt Kean should abandon the stage. The uproar on his appearance was so great that not a word of the play was heard. Beer bottles, rotten fruit and vegetables were hurled at him. *The Times* described him as 'that obscene little personage'. Those who supported Kean, and they were equally vociferous, argued he offered no outrage to decency 'because decent people do not go to the theatre.'

JANUARY 24. Jean Henri, Tambour-Major to Napoleon, at Lyceum Theatre. Henri was accompanied by a full military band. One of his feats was to let fly 28 drumsticks in all directions and catch them under his arms and between his legs.

JANUARY 28. Edmund Kean in Shakespeare's **Othello** at Drury Lane Theatre. There was more uproar between the two factions. Those who supported him waved placards: 'Kean for ever! No cant! No hypocrisy!' Kean asked the audience whether it was the newspapers or the public who should decide whether he acted or retired. The majority of the audience wanted him to continue acting.

APRIL 4. J. Amherst's **Napoleon Bonaparte's Invasion of Russia or The Conflagration of Moscow** at Astley's Amphitheatre. Military and equestrian spectacle.

MAY 11. Charles William Macready in James Sheridan Knowles's **William Tell** at Drury Lane Theatre. Avona Bunn as Emma. Macready's performance was notable for its power and pathos.

We do think him [Macready] a man of genius, but a man of genius totally and irretrievably spoiled. We think he might have been the first actor of his day; he will now never be a good actor at all. He has been spoiled by a monstrous egregious and intolerable affectation, by misplaced praise and over-weaning self-estimation. Some years ago, he was, indeed of high promise – for his merits were many and great, and his faults, it was to be hoped, would wear out with time. He had taken, as we think, a just medium between the too great coldness of the Kemble school and the wildness and extravagance of Kean. He was gifted with a magnificent voice and he was a man of education and accomplishment. But all these advantages has he wasted. His voice he has injured intrinsically, besides the hideousness of the trick itself, by the constant use of that pumping oar with which he interlards all passages of passion; and in a similar way he has heightened and increased every one of his faults, and insisting upon their being beauties, has substituted them for what were his merits in truth. *Athenæum*

MAY 23. Madame Vestris as Rosalind in Shakespeare's **As You Like It** at Haymarket Theatre.

JUNE 7. Maria Malibran, a 17-year-old mezzo-soprano, made her highly successful debut as Rosina in Gioachino Rossini's **The Barber of Seville** at King's Theatre. Giuditta Pasta, who should have sung, was indisposed, and Malibran had taken over the role.

June 25. T. P. Cooke in Edward Fitzball's ***The Flying Dutchman or The Phantom Ship*** at Adelphi Theatre. The play was billed as 'a piece of diablerie.' Fitzball complained that Cooke 'walked through the rehearsals like a person who submits with noble resolution to martyrdom'. It wasn't until Cooke was in front of an audience that he realised what a good role he had been given and apologised to Fitzball.

September 13. John Liston in John Poole's ***Paul Pry*** at Haymarket Theatre. Paul Pry, an idle busybody, was Liston's most famous character and his image, in striped pants, hessian boots, top hat and tailcoat, was reproduced everywhere. 'I hope I don't intrude' became a popular catchphrase. Madame Vestris sang 'Cherry Ripe'. She had a rich contralto voice, and her ravishing singing was the talk of the town.

October 8. Junius Brutus Booth in Howard Payne's ***Brutus or The Fall of Tarquin*** at Drury Lane Theatre. Booth gave his usual imitation of Kean.

William Booth has returned to London, as might be expected quite unimproved in the histrionic art. America is the very last place where a player is likely to throw aside a vicious propensity to rant (that propensity being the most striking feature of William Booth's performance).
The Times

October 10. Ira Aldridge's debut in ***London in Revolt of Surinam or A Slave's Revenge*** at Royal Coburg Theatre. West Indian melodrama. An adaptation of Southerne's *Oronooko*. Aldridge was variously billed as the Celebrated American tragedian, A Man of Colour, Mr Keene Tragedian of Colour, The Black Roscius, and a Genuine Nigger.

The gentleman is in complexion of the colour of a new halfpenny, barring the brightness; his hair is woolly and his features, although they possess much of the African character, are considerably humanized. His figure is baker knee'd and narrow chested and owing to the shape of his lips, it is utterly impossible for him to pronounce English in such a manner as to satisfy even the unfastidious ears of the gallery. It appears in the playbills (and who can doubt them?) that this gentleman is one of the ornaments of the African Theatre in New York and for his own sake we regret that he did not stay there.
The Times

The first instance in which one of that complexion has displayed a striking degree of theatrical talent and which has secured him the rapturous approbation of an enlightened public on either side of the Atlantic.   *Playbill*

The disadvantage of colour which excluded him from all chances of success in America was not entirely overcome in England among a prejudicial, wanton and unthinking few, who could not let an opportunity pass for sneering at and ridiculing the 'presumptuous nigger'.   *Era*

October 20. William Wallack as Valentine and Mrs Devison as Angelica in William Congreve's ***Love for Love*** at Drury Lane Theatre. Mrs Kelly as Miss Prue. William Downton as Sir Sampson Legend. The play, which hadn't been acted for nine years, was heavily cut. The audience was notable by its absence; and, even after the half-price hour, the pit, galleries and boxes were thinly attended.

Births	*Literature*	*History*
Johann Strauss, junior, Austrian composer	Aleksandr Pushkin's *Boris Godunov*	John Nash begins conversion of Buckingham House into Buckingham Palace
Deaths	William Hazlitt's *The Spirit of the Age: Or, Contemporary Portraits*	Stockton to Darlington Railway opens, the first to carry goods and passengers
Jacques-Louis David, French painter (b. 1748)		

1825

The delicacy of sentiment which now prevails – the strict attention which is in our day paid to the decencies of life – would of course prevent the performance of any of Congreve's comedies in its original state. It is necessary the rotten parts should be cut away and that that only which would improve pleasure without offending morality. *Morning Chronicle*

OCTOBER 31. Edward Terry in Edward Fitzball's ***The Pilot*** at Adelphi Theatre. The nautical burletta was very loosely based on James Fenimore Cooper's novel of 1824, *The Pilot: A Tale of the Sea*. Fitzball changed the plot because he was frightened of giving offence to the Americans. T. P. Cooke played Long Tom Coffin and went on to specialise in playing sailor roles. He had served in the Royal Navy during his teens, and his performances were considered very convincing. Fitzball described Terry's performance as a masterpiece of acting, and declared a speech in Act 3 Scene 5 to be 'perhaps the most impressive effect ever produced by plain speaking in a melodrama'. On the 100th performance the management gave a great dinner on the Adelphi stage to 100 persons. Through an oversight the playwright was not invited, but he went along anyway and found that he was expected.

BELOW AND RIGHT

Scenes and characters from Edward Fitzball's
The Flying Dutchman, 1825.

Marks fec. Mr T. P. COOKE, as Vanderdecken. Mr ELLIOT, as Mowdry.
London, Pub.d by J. L. Marks,
17 Artillery St.r Bishopsgate.
Combat in the Flying Dutchman. Price 1.d Plain.

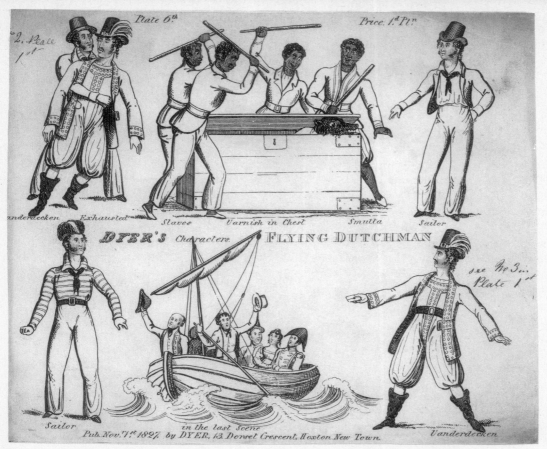

DYER'S *Characters.* FLYING DUTCHMAN

Vanderdecken Exhausted Slaves Varnish in Chest Smutta Sailor

Sailor *in the last Scene* Vanderdecken

see N⁰ 3 in Plate 1ˢᵗ

Pub. Nov. 1ˢᵗ 1827 by DYER, 13. Dorset Crescent, Hoxton New Town.

Flying Dutchman. Plate III

Thisbatea Vanderdecken Lucy Varnish as the Bear Sidia

Published Jan⁸ 8.. 1827 by H. anarow 13. Inkes C⁺ Row S⁺

Sentinel Peter Von Trammell L. astello 2..d Dress Cap⁺ⁿ Pepperonil Tom Willis

1826

JANUARY 16. Charles Kemble in Shakespeare's *Othello* at Covent Garden Theatre.

> There is nothing to condemn; much to praise; but the whole is insufficient. It wants the fierceness, the tenderness, the rage and the despair ... He was very ill supported by Frederick Warde as Iago and still worse by John Cooper as Cassio. Avonia Jones is a pretty girl but she is not equal to Desdemona. *The Times*

FEBRUARY 18. Madame Vestris in Thomas Arne's *Artaxerxes* at Covent Garden Theatre. Opera in the Italian manner.

MARCH 16. William Farren as Nathaniel Croaker in Oliver Goldsmith's *The Good Natur'd Man* at Covent Garden Theatre. The lugubrious Croaker has such a pessimistic view of life that he can read a love letter and mistake it for a description of a gunpowder plot.

> William Farren's Croaker is one of the finest pieces of acting ever beheld – one of the most laughable, and yet the furthest from mummery and caricature. This gentleman's powers – as he becomes more and more familiar with his audiences – seems to increase almost every day. When he first came to London he was an eminent, but limited, actor: this is not the case any longer. *The Times*

APRIL 12. Carl Maria von Weber's *Oberon or The Elf-King's Oath* conducted by Weber at Covent Garden Theatre. Libretto by J. R. Planché. Charles Bland as Oberon. John Braham as Sir Huon. William Austin as Charlemagne. Madame Vestris as Fatima. The spectacle included Oberon's bower (with a view of Baghdad), the Tigris, a ravine, and the ocean in a storm. The opera was a big success. Less than two months later Weber was dead from tuberculosis.

> The intermixing of so many principal actors who do not sing, the omission of the music in the most important moments – all these things deprive our Oberon the title of an Opera, and will make him unfit for all other Theatres in Europe; which is a very bad thing for me, but passons la dessus. CARL MARIA VON WEBER in a letter to J. R. Planché

JUNE 11. Robert William Elliston as Falstaff in Shakespeare's *Henry IV* at Drury Lane Theatre. 'What a combination of the wit, the humorist, the sensual feeder, the worldly philosopher and the gentleman!' said *The New Monthly Magazine*. *The Dramatic Register* thought Elliston was 'the most Shakespearian comic personation' he ever beheld. Macready (who was playing King Henry) thought in rehearsal he had been the best he had seen but that the performance didn't work for the audience.

Births
A. E. Sothern, American actor
Gustave Moreau, French painter

Deaths
Sophie Hagman, Swedish ballerina (b. 1758)
Carl Maria von Weber, German composer (b. 1786)

Literature
Burke's Peerage
Mary Shelley's *The Last Man*
James Fenimore Cooper's *The Last of the Mohicans*
Walter Scott's *Woodstock*
Benjamin Disraeli's *Vivian Grey*

History
Telford's Menai Suspension Bridge is opened
Invention of photography by Frenchman Joseph Niépce
First railway tunnel (on Liverpool to Manchester line)
University College London is founded

1826

The Mathew -orama or 1827 or Cockney Gleanings – Aint that a good un now.
Charles Mathews was one of the most popular comic actors of the day; his special
skill was that he was able to transform himself at incredible speed. The print, by
August Herview and A Ducôté, shows him in a variety of his caricatures.

AUGUST 28. E. L. Lewis as Louis XVI, Miss
Watson as Marie Antoinette and Henry Kemble
as Robespierre in **Reign of Terror or The Horrors
of the French Revolution** at Coburg Theatre.

OCTOBER 25. Daniel Terry in John Baldwin
Buckstone's **Luke, The Labourer or The Lost
Son** at Adelphi Theatre. Melodrama in a humble
contemporary rustic setting without any spectacle
and relying on simple emotions and pathos. Luke
is dismissed for habitual drunkenness. His wife
dies of starvation. T. P. Cooke played the lost
son, a sailor, who saves his father from being
murdered.

NOVEMBER 4. Charles Mayne Young, Charles
Kemble, Frederick Warde and Mrs Sloman in
Mary Russell Mitford's **Foscari** at Covent Garden
Theatre. The plot had nothing to with Byron's
version. *The Times* praised Mitford for having
'produced a tragedy of the legitimate drama – not a
pantomime of moonlight, procession and tinsel'.

NOVEMBER 25. Madame Vestris took legal
action against John Ducombe for publishing the
unauthorised *Memoirs of the Life, Public and Private
Adventures of Madame Vestris* and was awarded £100
damages; despite this, she was unable to stop
publication.

1827

FEBRUARY 19. Mr Terry, John Reeve and T. P. Cooke in Edward Fitzball's **The Flying Dutchman or The Phantom Ship** at Adelphi Theatre followed by T. P. Cooke in **The Pirate Doomed**.

APRIL 6. James Henry Hackett as Falstaff in **Henry IV Part 1** at Covent Garden Theatre. For many theatre-goers in the United States and England Hackett *was* Falstaff.

JUNE 8. Mlle Georges in Racine's **Phèdre** at French Theatre. 'She is very powerful,' said *The Literary Gazette*, 'but very coarse.' Georges was the former mistress of Napoleon.

> The loud declamatory addresses, and want of incident which distinguish the style of French tragedy, render most even of the boldest characters which belong to it, something monotonous … Every admirer should see this lady as there is no actress upon the English stage now, nor has been since the time of Mrs Siddons, which can be named in competition with her. *The Times*

JUNE 8. Royal Amphitheatre Astley's advertisement read as follows: 'National panoramic spectacle of Spain and Portugal or Rebels and Guerillas. After which a splendid hypo dramatic action called The British Artist or The Hundred Arabian Steeds. In the circle Mr Ducrow will perform the paramount feats of riding 4 and 5 horses at one time on the Courier of St Petersburg. To conclude with an entirely new comic pantomime called **The Flying Dutchwoman or Harlequin and The Enchanted Bay**.'

JUNE 20. Mlle Georges in Racine's **Iphigenie** at King's Theatre.

> An entire want of truth and nature. Her sudden changes of tone, mere artificial tricks, never inspired by the sentiment of the moment or that instinctive tact which goes at once to the heart. CHARLES CRABB ROBINSON, *Diary*.

JUNE 28. Mlle Georges and Eric Bernard in Voltaire's **Semanaris** at King's Theatre. 'We never saw a more able representation,' said *The Times*. 'Dignity, affection, horror, pathos were all expressed with power and truth.'

OCTOBER 1. Charles Kean, son of Edmund Kean, made his London debut as Young Norval in John Home's **Douglas** at Drury Lane Theatre. The audience was indulgent; the critics were damning.

1827

World premieres
Heinrich von Kleist's *The Prince of Homburg*

Literature
Victor Hugo's *Cromwell*

History
Battle of Navarino in Greek War of Independence

Deaths
Ludwig von Beethoven, German composer (b. 1770)
William Blake, British poet, painter, engraver, mystic (b. 1757)
Thomas Rowlandson, British caricaturist (b. 1756)

Notes
Dr Arnold is appointed Head of Rugby School
John Baldwin Buckstone becomes manager of Adelphi Theatre
William Corder murders Maria Martin in the Red Barn at Corder Farm in Polstead

OCTOBER 11. Charles Kean in Elizabeth Inchbald's **Lover's Vows** at Covent Garden Theatre.

The papers gave no quarter but went in unanimously to burn, sink and destroy – an overwhelming fleet gainst a little light-armed gunboat. JOHN WILLIAM COLE, *The Life and Theatrical Times of Charles Kean*

NOVEMBER 25. Miss Hughes, Antonio Sapio, Frederick Warde and Madame Vestris in the first performance in English of Mozart's **Entfuhrung**, in London, at Covent Garden Theatre. Additional airs by J. B. Cramer.

DECEMBER 3. William Richards in William Bayle Bernard's **Casco Bay or The Mutineers of 1727** at Olympic Theatre. Billed as 'Melo aqua-dramatic burletta spectacle'. The high spot was the ship in the storm. 140 performances.

It is worth a laughter-loving wight to go 10 miles to see Richards make the most singularly ludicrous grimaces imaginable when singing his celebrated burlesque song Ri-fum, Ti-fum. Our jaws are still aching from the effect of it. *The Times*

DECEMBER 26. William Howell and Miss Ryan in **Harlequin and Cock Robin and The Babes in the Wood** at Drury Lane Theatre. The pantomime kept the Brothers Grimm tragic ending. There had been an intention to include Mother Hubbard but the dog refused to perform.

A full house received this Christmas present very coldly during its progress and at its conclusion strong hissing proclaimed that its birth and death cannot be far removed from each other. *The Times*

'*Our theatres are fit for nothing – they are too large for acting and too small for a bull fight.*'

SAMUEL TAYLOR COLERIDGE, *Theatrical Observer*, 1828

1828

JANUARY 5. Mdlle Cardori and Madame Branbilla in London premiere of Giacomo Meyerbeer's **Margherita d'Anjou** at King's Theatre. Operatic melodrama.

MARCH 17. Benefit for Joseph Grimaldi on his retirement at Sadler's Wells Theatre. Grimaldi was ill and bankrupt.

MAY 26. Edward Elston, David Osbaldiston and Joseph Rayner in Edward Fitzball's **The Inchcape Bell or The Dumb Sailor** at Surrey Theatre. A nautical burletta. The first time Fitzball read the play to Elston, Elston had fallen asleep, but he pretended he had been wide awake and suggested he gave it to another management. Later, when Fitzball sent him the script again, Elston had no recollection of it all and accepted it immediately. Miss Scott played the dumb boy.

JUNE 28. Joseph Grimaldi had a second farewell benefit as Harlequin in **Harlequin Hoax** at Drury Lane Theatre. Miss Kelly and Tim Pritt Harley were Columbine and Harlequin. The stage was crowded with clowns, columbines, pantaloons and harlequins who had all come to say goodbye to Joey. Grimaldi, very frail, performed just one scene. In his final curtain call he said:

I thank you for the benevolence which has brought you here to assist your old and faithful servant in his premature decllne. Eight-and-forty years have not yet passed over my head, and I am sinking fast. I now stand worse on

JULY 6. John Baldwin Buckstone in Douglas William Jerrold's ***Vidocq, The French Police Spy***, at Surrey Theatre. An adaptation of Vidocq's recently published memoirs. Vidocq, a former convict and a master of disguise, had risen to the rank of chief of police.

JULY 7. Mr O. Smith as the Imp in ***The Bottle Imp*** at English Opera House. German legend. Music by G. H. Rodwell. 'The characters,' said *The Times*, 'are excessively insipid and uninteresting.'

JULY. ***Maria Marten or Murder in the Red Barn***, one of the most popular melodramas of the nineteenth century, was based on a notorious murder that had taken place in Polstead, Suffolk, in 1827. Maria was shot dead by her lover, William Corder, who was arrested, brought to trial, and hanged at Bury St Edmunds. Broadsheets, songs, penny-dreadfuls and anonymous plays cashed in on the story, even before he had come to trial.

JULY 11. John Cooper and William Farrell in R. Lacy's ***The Two Friends*** at Haymarket Theatre. Comedy and pathos.

OCTOBER 11. Charles Mayne Young and Miss Phillips in Mary Russell Mitford's ***Rienzi*** at Drury Lane Theatre. 'We are much mistaken,' said *The Times*, 'if the tragedy will not long continue to be admired and appreciated.'

my legs than I used to on my head. (*A laugh*) But I suppose I am paying the penalty of the course I have pursued all my life. In my desire and anxiety to merit your favour has excited me to more exertion than my constitution would bear, and lie vaulting ambition I have overleaped myself. JOSEPH GRIMALDI

I never saw any one equal to him. There was so much *mind* in everything that he did. CHARLES DIBDIN

1828

World premieres	Births	History
Gioachino Rossini's *Le Comte d'Ory* in Paris	Gabriel Charles Dante (Gabriel Rossetti), British painter, poet	Regent's Park is opened to the public
Literature	Henrik Ibsen, Norwegian dramatist	Royalty Theatre destroyed by fire
Noah Webster's 70,000 word *American Dictionary of the English Language*	Leo Tolstoy, Russian novelist, dramatist	Duke of Wellington becomes Prime Minister
		Horse-drawn buses in London

DECEMBER 2. William Cobham in Douglas William Jerrold's *Fifteen Years of a Drunkard's Life* at Royal Coburg Theatre. Domestic melodrama.

DECEMBER 8. *The Earthquake or The Spectre of the Nile* at Adelphi Theatre. 'The earthquake,' said *The Times*, 'is about as effective as an imitation of a sea-fight in a washing-tub.'

1829

FEBRUARY 9. Frederick Yates and T. P. Cooke Edward Fitzball's *The Red Rover or The Mutiny of the Dolphin* at Adelphi Theatre. Nautical burletta adapted from James Fenimore Cooper's novel *The Red Rover* of the same year. The high spot was the sinking of the ship.

JUNE 8. T. P. Cooke, William Baldwin Buckstone and Sarah Scott in Douglas William Jerrold's *Black Eye'd Susan or All in the Downs* at Surrey Theatre. Nautical melodrama: press gangs and corruption. Jerrold had served in the Napoleonic Wars as a midshipman and knew what he was writing about. 'The best thing I know between France and England,' he said, 'is the sea.' 150 performances.

> His [Cooke] acting in this character is unquestionably one of the finest things now to be seen on the English stage … Mr Cooke is confessedly the best sailor on stage; perhaps, that has ever been. *Athenæum*

> So thickly were marine simile and metaphor crowded into the dialogue that the very air of the theatre smelt of tar, and on coming out it jarred upon one to find the people without pigtails. But everyone went to see T. P. Cooke speak his piece to the court martial and dance the hornpipe. BERNARD H. BAKER, *Theatre*

JULY 15. N. Perkins in Ferdinand Ries's *The Robber's Bride* at English Opera House.

OCTOBER 5. Nineteen-year-old Fanny Kemble, John Philip Kemble's daughter, made her reluctant debut as Juliet in Shakespeare's *Romeo and Juliet* at Covent Garden. She wore a simple white ball

FANNY KEMBLE.

Fanny Kemble, actress (1809–93) in 1829. Her most famous roles were Shakespeare's Juliet, Portia and Beatrice, Richard Brinsley Sheridan's Lady Teazle in The School for Scandal and Julia in James Sheridan Knowles's The Hunchback.

gown. Her father would normally have been cast as Romeo; but it was felt that audiences might find the casting incestuous, and so William Abbott played Romeo. Kemble played Mercutio, his first appearance in the part. Fanny's mother, Maria Kemble, came out of retirement to play Lady Capulet. Mary Davenport was the Nurse.

> On the whole we do not remember to have seen a more triumphant debut.   *The Times*

> The illusion that she [Fanny Kemble] was Shakespeare's Juliet came so speedily as to suspend power of specific criticism.   *New Monthly Magazine*

> As for my success, there was, I believe, a genuine element in it; but there was also a great feeling of personal sympathy for my father and mother, of kindly indulgence for my youth; and a very general desire that the fine theatre which they exercised their powers should be rescued if possible from its difficulties. All this went to make up a result of which I had the credit.   FANNY KEMBLE, *Diary*

NOVEMBER 18. James Wallack, William Farren and Helen Faucit in J. R. Planché's **The Brigand** at Drury Lane Theatre. Designer: Charles Eastlake. The Brigand, an Italian Robin Hood, takes two students from the French Academy of Painting hostage and discovers he is the long-lost son of a Prince. Wallack was so successful in the role that the public didn't want to see him in anything else. 'Damn your Brigand,' he said to Planché. 'It has been the ruin of me.'

> We rather wish that Miss Faucit would restrain the energy of her action a little, she would then be more graceful and ladylike.   *Observer*

NOVEMBER 30. Mr Rumball in Douglas William Jerrold's **Thomas A' Becket** at Surrey Theatre.

DECEMBER 26. Elizabeth Poole in **Hop O' My Thumb** at Drury Lane Theatre.

DECEMBER 28. **The Elephant of Siam and The Fire Fiend** at Adelphi Theatre. The elephant came from Paris and was a great success, delivering letters to the harem, ringing bells, drawing a cork from a bottle, and drinking wine. The critics praised his docility and sagacity.

Walter Lacy as Narcissus Boss in John Baldwin Buckstone's Single Life, at Haymarket Theatre in 1839.

1829

World premieres
Johann Wolfgang von Goethe's *Faust Part 1* in Brunswick
Gioacchino Rossini's *William Tell* in Paris

Births
T. W. Robertson, British dramatist
Tommaso Salvini, Italian actor-manager

Notes
Madame Vestris becomes manager of Olympic Theatre
Lyceum Theatre is destroyed by fire
Pavilion Theatre opens
First Oxford/Cambridge University boat race: Oxford wins

History
Catholic Relief Act
Greece wins independence from Ottoman Empire
Perth in Western Austrialia is founded, and colonisation begins
Stephenson's locomotive 'Rocket' wins the Rainhill Trials

The
1830s

THE ELEPHANT AT THE ADELPHI.

London, Published by Orlando Hodgson, 22 Macclesfield Street North City.

1830

'A New Terrific interesting Nondescript translated from nothing and founded on undoubtedly questionable Facts which never took place in the Burman Wars, or any other, with Horrid Music, Dreadful scenery and Dilapidated Ruins – the Incidents perfectly unnatural – the Combatants unlike any thing ever attempted in this life and the spectres resembling nothing in the other, their appearance being most tremendously ridiculous than the worse attempted at any Contemporary Theatre, whether Major, Medium or Minor, covering all the necessary requisites for Ghostly Equestrian, Assinian, Monkeyam, Pedestrian, Vocal, Rhetorical, Allegorical, Pantomimical Tissue of Nonsense equal to anything that graced or disgraced a Theatre Royal or a mélange of Banditti, Soldiery, Peasantry, Nobles, Princes, Monks and MURDER *under the unassuming Denomination of Siamoraindianaboo, Princess of Siam; or the Royal Elephant!'*

ADELPHI THEATRE PLAYBILL FOR THE ELEPHANT OF SIAM

LEFT

The Elephant of Siam was a huge success at the Adelphi Theatre and ran until February 1830.

MARCH 8. Edmund Kean in Shakespeare's **Henry V** at Covent Garden Theatre. The costumes were magnificent, but Kean didn't know his lines and was booed. He appealed directly to the audience, who constantly interrupted him while he was speaking: 'I have worked hard, ladies and gentlemen, for your entertainment [*you have been well paid for it*]. That very labour, and the lapse of time and other circumstances had their effect upon my mind [*why do you drink so hard?*] I must plead my apology. I feel that stand here in the most degraded situation [*No, no! – why do you put yourself into it?*] and call upon you, as my countrymen, to show me that liberality, which has always distinguished English gentlemen.'

MAY 1. English premiere of Gioachino Rossini's **William Tell** at Drury Lane Theatre. Sung in English and performed under the title of **Hofer or The Tell of the Tyrol**. Adapted by J. R. Planché. Arranged by Henry Bishop. *The Times* thought 'the opera would have been far more effective than it is had Mr Planché introduced some good characters and comic situations.'

OCTOBER 25. John Reeve and John Baldwin Buckstone in John Baldwin Buckstone's **The Wreck Ashore or A Bridegroom from the Sea** at Adelphi Theatre. Buckstone was a popular comedian; the moment his voice was heard off-stage the audience started laughing. The programme also included **Scheming and Seeming** and a romantic burletta spectacle called **The Black Vulture or The Wheel of Death**.

World premieres	Deaths	History
Victor Hugo's *Hernani* in Paris. Riots	King George IV (b.1762) William Hazlitt, British essayist, critic (b.1778)	William IV accedes to throne on death of George IV Manchester to Liverpool railway opens
Births Jolly John Nash, British music hall artist J L Toole, British actor, comedian	**Literature** Stendhal's *Le Rouge and Le Noir* Alfred Lord Tennyson's *Poems*	**Notes** English Opera House is destroyed by fire

1830

Poster for Edmund Kean
in Shakespeare's King
Lear at Theatre Royal,
Haymarket, in 1830.

Theatre Royal Hay-Market.

Mr. KEAN

will perform KING LEAR THIS EVENING; being POSITIVELY the LAST NIGHT of his Engagement in London, previous to his departure for America.

This Evening, MONDAY July 12, 1830.

Will be performed, Shakspeare's Tragedy of

KING LEAR.

King Lear,   Mr. KEAN,
(Being POSITIVELY the LAST NIGHT of his ENGAGEMENT.)
Duke of Burgundy, Mr. CATHIE,   Duke of Cornwall, Mr. GALLOT,
Duke of Albany, Mr. W. JOHNSON, Earl of Gloucester, Mr. THOMPSON,
Earl of Kent,   Mr. WILLIAMS,
Edmund, Mr. BRINDAL,   Oswald, Mr. WEBSTER,
Edgar,   Mr. COOPER,
Physician, Mr. COOKE,   Captain of Guard, Mr. C. MORRIS,
Herald, Mr. FENTON, Edward, Mr. COVENEY, Old Man, Mr. M. BARNETT
First Ruffian, Mr. LODGE,   Second Ruffian, Mr. MOORE,
Regan,   Mrs. W. CLIFFORD,
Goneril,   Mrs. T. HILL,   Aranthe, Mrs. NEWCOMBE,
Cordelia,   Miss F. H. KELLY.
After which, a Comic Piece (in One Act) called

Popping the Question!

Mr. Primrose,   Mr. W. FARREN,
Henry Thornton,   Mr. COOKE,
Miss Biffin,   Mrs. GLOVER,
Ellen Murray, Mrs. NEWCOMBE, Miss Winterblossom, Mrs. TAYLEURE,
Bobbin,   Mrs. HUMBY.
To conclude with the Farce of

Modern Antiques.

Mr. Cockletop,   Mr. W. FARREN,
Frank,   Mr. VINING,   Joey,   Mr. WEBSTER,
Napkin,   Mr. COVENEY,   Hearty,   Mr. W. JOHNSON.
Thomas,   Mr. C. MORRIS,   John,   Mr. BISHOP,
Mrs. Cockletop, Mrs. W. CLIFFORD,   Belinda, Mrs. ASHTON,
Mrs. Cammomile, Mrs. COVENEY,   Nan,   Mrs. T. HILL,
Flounce,   Miss BARNETT,   Betty, Mrs. W. JOHNSON.
STAGE MANAGER MR. P. FARREN.   *VIVANT REX ET REGINA!*

BOXES 5s.—PIT 3s.—FIRST GALLERY 2s.—SECOND GALLERY 1s.
Doors to be opened at Six o'Clock, and the Performances to begin at Seven.
☞ Places for the Boxes to be taken of Mr. MASSINGHAM, at the Theatre, Daily, from Ten till Five.
N. B. PRIVATE BOXES may be had Nightly, and Free Admissions for the Season, on application at the Box-Office.

NO ORDERS WHATEVER WILL BE ADMITTED.

A New Drama, (in Two Acts,) called

THE FORCE of NATURE.

will be produced on FRIDAY July 16:
THE PRINCIPAL CHARACTERS:
Philip,   Mr. W. FARREN,
Frederick, Mr. COOPER,   Count de Beauvais, Mr. VINING,
Countess D'Harville,   Mrs. FAUCIT.
Matilda,   Miss MORDAUNT.

†*† On Wednesday and Thursday Evenings next, there will be no Performance.

†*† The New Petite Comedy, called

SEPARATION & REPARATION,

encreasing nightly in attraction, will be repeated Every Evening till further notice,
(This Evening excepted.)

DECEMBER 15. William Charles Macready and Helen Faucit in Lord Byron's **Werner or The Inheritance** at Drury Lane Theatre. Gothic verse drama with a sensational denouement involving a secret door. Byron had said in the published text that the play wasn't intended or shaped for the stage. Macready pruned and lopped the text but it was still heavy-going.

Mr Macready can be the ideal wretchedness. Misery in its abject form, finds in him a most willing and accomplished representative. The heroic frequently proved beyond his aim or scope, but the human, in its utmost weakness, he could realize to perfection.
Illustrated London News

It is true his Werner is not altogether free from those mannerisms in which he will indulge – but by far the greater part of it is marked by deep judgment, intense feeling and masterly delineation. *Athenæum*

DECEMBER 16. James Vining as Lord Splashton in Lord Glengall's **Follies of Fashion** at Drury Lane Theatre.

1831

JANUARY 3. James Wallack and Helen Faucit in Richard Brinsley Sheridan's **Pizarro** at Drury Lane Theatre. Faucit's Elvira, said *The Athenæum*, 'had not a single good point to recommend it. Coarseness and vulgarity were its only features.'

JANUARY 3. Maria Foote as Mary in Frederick Reynolds's **Mary Queen of Scots or The Escape from Loch Leven** at Olympic Theatre. Burletta. The setting, the furniture and even the cutlery were all historically accurate. The drama was followed by J. R. Planché's burlesque extravaganza, **Olympic Revels or Prometheus and Pandora**. Madame Vestris made her entrance through a trap-door. John Coleman said that she sang like an angel and danced like a sylphid. The production was spectacular. In the finale the branch of a huge palm opened to reveal fairies supporting a coronet of jewels. Doors opened 6.30. Performance began at 7.00. Boxes cost 4 shillings; pit 2 shillings; gallery 1 shilling. Seats were half-price at 9.00.

Her [Vestris] youth, her beauty, her superbly symmetrical proportions displayed to the utmost advantage by the classic costume, and possibly by the novelty of her position, procured her a reception so enthusiastic and overwhelming that she fairly broke down under it and had to wipe away her tears before she could utter a single word. JOHN COLEMAN, *Players and Playwrights*

JUNE 1. Charles Kean in Shakespeare's **Hamlet** at Covent Garden Theatre.

JUNE 3. Nicolo Paganini's London debut at King's Theatre.

'*If she [FANNY KEMBLE] means to act as she did on Thursday night, we have only to say, that it is of very little use for the papers to assert that she is about to be married and to leave the stage – for we shall certainly attend on behalf of the public, and forbid the bans.*'

Athenæum

Marie Taglioni (1804–84), one of the greatest dancers of the nineteenth century, is forever identified with Sylphide.

MADEMOISELLE TAGLIONI.

It was said that he [Paganini] had killed his wife in a fit of jealousy, and made the fiddle strings of her intestines, and the devil had composed a sonata for him in a dream … When you looked at him you thought all this was very likely to be true. His talent was almost supernatural.
JOHN WILLIAM COLE, *The Life and Times of Charles Kean*

Every tour de force and striking passage was not only applauded but cheered by the whole audience, and some of the variations were encored. At the end of every performance, and especially after the last, the applause, cheers and waving of handkerchiefs and hat, altogether presented a most extraordinary scene.
The Times

JULY 8. Giuditta Pasta and Giovan Rubin in London premiere of Gaetano Donizetti's **Anna Bolena** at King's Theatre. Donizetti had created the roles especially for them. Anna does not commit adultery, but she still gets the chop.

Of Madame Pasta's acting, it is hardly possible to speak in adequate terms. The energy of Medea, the dignity of Semiramide, the tender pathos of Desdemona, the profound affliction of Mary Stuart and that fascinating listlessness which forms the charm of her mad scene in Norma, were all displayed by turns, in situations which the author of the libretto appears to have formed expressly for her. Her vocal powers were less called into requisition than her histrionic talents. *The Times*

1831

World premieres
Vincenzo Bellini's *La Sonnambula* in Milan
Vincenzo Bellini's *Norma* in Milan
Giacomo Meyerbeer's *Robert le Diable* in Paris

Literature
Edgar Allan Poe's *Poems*

Births
Victorien Sardou, French dramatist

Deaths
Robert William Elliston, British actor, theatre manager (b. 1774)
Sarah Siddons, British actress, sister of John Philip Kemble (b. 1757)

Notes
Garrick Club, King Street, Covent Garden, founded

History
Coronation of William IV
HMS *Beagle*, with Charles Darwin aboard, sets sail
John Rennie's new London Bridge is completed; medieval bridge demolished

JULY 28. Giuditta Pasta and Giovan Rubin in London premiere of Vincenzo Bellini's **La Sonnambula** at King's Theatre. The heroine is a sleepwalker and is discovered asleep in a count's bedroom.

OCTOBER. Edmund Kean in a two-week season of plays by Shakespeare at Royal Coburg Theatre: **Richard III**, **Othello**, **Macbeth** and **King Lear**, for which he was paid £50 a performance. He told the badly behaved audience exactly what he thought of them: 'In my life I have never acted to such a set of ignorant, unmitigated brutes as I have before me.' Charles Kingsley described the Royal Coburg Theatre as 'a licensed pit of darkness, a trap of temptation, prolificacy and ruin.'

NOVEMBER 3. John Braham in Daniel Auber's **Fra Diavalo** at Covent Garden Theatre. A notorious bandit passes himself off as a marquis and compromises an innkeeper's daughter.

DECEMBER 26. **Harlequin and Little Thumb** at Drury Lane Theatre. Notable for the panoramic sights of Venice, which were based on Clarkson Stanfield's sketches, which had been drawn in situ.

DECEMBER 26. Madame Vestris in J. R. Planché's **Olympic Devils** at Olympic Theatre. Spectacular.

1832

JANUARY 25. Douglas William Jerrold's **The Rent Day** at Drury Lane Theatre. Rural poverty. The hero smashes the new machinery. This topical melodrama was based on two genre paintings by David Wilkie: *The Rent Day* and *Distraining for Rent*. Wilkie was moved to tears by the accuracy with which they had been recreated on stage.

FEBRUARY 8. Edward Elton in Thomas Moncrieff's **Eugene Aram or Saint Robert's Cave** at Surrey Theatre. Based on Bulwer-Lytton's novel published in 1831. Aram is arrested, tried and found guilty of a murder he had committed fourteen years previously and is hanged in Newgate Prison. The play was very popular.

FEBRUARY 20. Mr Wood, Mr Phillips, Mrs Wood and Mr Templeton in London premiere of Giacomo Meyerbeer's **Robert le Diable** at Drury Lane Theatre. The adaptation was called **The Daemon or The Mystic Branch**, and was so unlike the original that Meyerbeer was outraged.

MARCH 15. Fanny Kemble in Fanny Kemble's **Francis I** at Covent Garden Theatre.

A sad disappointment it would have been had I expected anything from a girl of nineteen who aspired to write a Shakespearian historical play … Miss Kemble wants for tragedy, figure and voice.
CHARLES CRABB ROBINSON, *Diary*

MARCH 15. Fanny Kemble in James Sheridan Knowles's **The Hunchback** at Covent Garden Theatre.

Her Julia has outstripped my most sanguine hopes. Can I say more? Yes – the soul of Siddons breathes its inspiration upon us again.
JAMES SHERIDAN KNOWLES, Preface to *The Hunchbank*

The Hunchback is the most delightful production: good in plot, dramatic in composition, elegant, vigorous, and poetical in language, deep in knowledge of human nature, varied in display of the passions and affections which adorn or disfigure it, and admirable in their developments … Of Miss Fanny Kemble it gives us real gratification to speak in terms

Engraved by Ridley from a Miniature by Smith.

His want of musical ear made his delivery of Shakespeare's blank verse defective, and painful to persons better endowed in that respect. It may have been his consciousness of his imperfect declamation of blank verse that induced him to adopt what his admirers called his natural style of speaking it; which was simply chopping it up into prose. FANNY KEMBLE

MAY 18. Wilhelmina Schroeder Devrient as Marcellina in London premiere of Ludwig Beethoven's **Fidelio** at King's Theatre. Sung in German.

Madame Devrient, as Leonora, sings and acts with a fervour and intensity of expression that positively thrills through one's veins – no words can convey the effect which she produces when she rushes forward to shield her husband from the dagger of Pizarro. *Athenæum*

MAY 30. Charles Mayne Young made his farewell in Shakespeare's **Hamlet** at Covent Garden Theatre.

JULY 7. Antonio Tamburini, Carlotta Grisi and Domenico Donzelli in Vincenzo Bellini's **La Straniera** at King's Theatre. The stranger is thought to be a witch. Tamburini sang and acted magnificently but Donzelli evidently roared a little too much in his effort to be heard above Grisi.

JULY 13. John Reeve in Richard Brinsley Peake's **The Climbing Boy** at Olympic Theatre. The boy, separated from his family, lost in a maze of chimneys, ends up in his own bedroom. Sentimental burletta. Miss Henderson played the boy.

JULY 16. Marie Taglioni in **La Sylphide** at Covent Garden Theatre. The role was created for her by her father, Filippo Taglioni.

of unqualified commendation. She has never appeared to better advantage. *Athenæum*

APRIL 14. William Charles Macready and Fanny Kemble in Shakespeare's **Macbeth** at Covent Garden Theatre. G. H. Lewes said that Macready stole into the murder chamber 'like a man going to purloin a purse, not like a warrior going to snatch a crown'. Kemble did not enjoy acting with Macready, who hadn't bothered to turn up to the first rehearsals. 'He growls and prowls and roams and foams about the stage in every direction, like a tiger in a cage, so that I never knew what side of me he means to be.'

I have never seen anyone so bad, so unnatural, so affected, so conceited. She [Fanny Kemble] alters the stage arrangements without any ceremony.
WILLIAM CHARLES MACREADY, *Journal*

World premieres

Gaetano Donizetti's *L'Elisir d'Amore* in Milan

Victor Hugo's *Le Roi s'Amuse* in Paris

Filippo Taglioni's *La Sylphide*

Literature

Johann Wolfgagn von Goethe's *Faust II*

Alfred Lord Tennyson's *Poems* (including The Lady of Shalott)

Births

Lewis Carroll, British novelist

Gustave Doré, French artist

Louisa May Alcott, American author

Deaths

Johann Wolfgang Goethe German poet, dramatist, novelist (b. 1749)

Joseph Munden, British actor (b. 1758)

Sir Walter Scott, Scottish novelist (b. 1771)

Notes

Madame Vestris introduces the box set

Edward Bulwer-Lytton chairs Select Committee of Inquiry into the state of theatre

Marylebone Theatre is opened

History

Great Reform Act: 'rotten boroughs' are abolished

Cholera epidemic breaks out in East End of London; some 3,000 die

Taglioni was a snowy cloud in a human shape … We have never seen a more numerous and brilliant audience. Paganini was in a box above the stage and never took his eyes off the stage whilst Mademoiselles Mars and Taglioni were on it. *Observer*

OCTOBER 1. Frederick Yates, John Reeve, John Baldwin Buckstone, George Bennett and Mr O. Smith in W Bayle Bernard's **Rip Van Winkle** at Adelphi Theatre. Melodramatic burletta based on a story in Washington Irving's *Sketch Book*. Rip was 55 years old, a good-for-nothing, aboriginal Dutchman who fell asleep and woke twenty years later to find the world had changed completely. The play ran for nearly 200 uninterrupted nights.

OCTOBER 6. Miss Phillips in Douglas William Jerrold's **The Factory Girl** at Drury Lane Theatre. The play coincided with the hearings of the Sadler Committee into factory conditions where girls were working 14 hours a day and dying of exhaustion. 'A more ticklish subject could not have been selected for scenic representation,' said *The Times*. The Press thought the play was bad, the incidents improbable,

the horrors of the workplace overstated, and that the theatre was an inappropriate place for a political tract.

There were disturbances in the Dress Circle.

Writers like Mr Jerrold deserve our gratitude as well as our admiration for their aim is not merely to amuse but to plead through the medium of the stage the case of the poor and oppressed classes of society. *Figaro in London*

OCTOBER 15. John Walker's **The Factory Lad** at Surrey Theatre. A political tract. A poacher, spokesperson for the factory boys, incites them to burn down the factory. 'The time has come,' he says, 'when the sky shall be like blood, proclaiming this shall be the reward of the avaricious, the greedy, the flint-hearted.' Six days after the play had opened governmental pressure forced the Surrey Theatre to withdraw it.

DECEMBER 26. Elizabeth Poole in **Puss in Boots or Harlequin and the Miller's Son** at Covent Garden Theatre. Poole was thought to have been the first principal boy to slap her thigh.

1833

JANUARY 26. William Farren in William Bayle Bernard's ***The Nervous Man and The Man of Nerves*** at Drury Lane Theatre. Farce.

MARCH 7. London debut of the Austrian dancer and choreographer Fanny Elssler and her sister, Theresa Elssler, in a shortened version of ***Faust*** at King's Theatre. Fanny got the most applause.

MARCH 25. Edmund Kean in Shakespeare's ***Othello*** at Covent Garden Theatre. Charles Kean as Iago. Ellen Tree as Desdemona. Father and son had never acted together before. Kean, aware that he was not feeling well, said to Charles: 'I don't know if I shall be able to kneel but if I do be sure to lift me up.' He collapsed into his son's arms during Othello's 'Farewell!' speech. 'O God I'm dying. Speak to them for me.' Kean was carried off stage. He died a few months later.

APRIL 10. Ira Aldridge in Shakespeare's ***Othello*** at Covent Garden Theatre. Frederick Warde as Iago. Ellen Tree as Desdemona. It was the first time that Aldridge had acted at a major theatre in London. *The Standard* thought he was a singularly gifted actor. *The Morning Advertiser* thought he was excellent. Most newspapers were hostile. *The Athenæum* thought it was an outrage that Ellen Tree should have to suffer the indignity of being pawed by a black man and that the production should not be repeated. The pro-slavery lobby agreed, and prevented Aldridge from appearing for more than two performances. *The Times* thought it was all right for him to perform at either Sadler's Wells Theatre or Bartholomew Fair, but didn't think it was right for him to perform at a great national establishment. One newspaper asserted that 'English audiences have a prejudice in favour of European features, which more than counter-balance the recommendations of a flat nose and thick lips.'

His declamation is not only ineffectual but very faulty; it is marked by numerous instances of false emphasis, incorrect readings and interpolations of the text, even, and by a few vulgarisms of pronunciation. It was however free from rant. It was upon a whole a failure. *Spectator*

His enunciation is distinct and sonorous, though his voice is efficient in modulation and flexibility; his features appear too hard and firm to admit of outwardly exhibiting the darker passions and most embittered sufferings of the heart. But he looks the character. *Globe*

He has a habit of thrusting out his chin and throwing back his brow which makes him look silly. He gabbles apace, but has no particular brogue – his action is not ungraceful but altogether unmeaning – his voice is weak, so is his conception. Theatricals we suspect will never be profitable to him. *Drama*

'*The wretched upstart is about to defile the stage, by a foul butchery of Shakespeare, and Othello is actually the part chosen for this sacrilege … we have before jammed this man into atoms by the relentless power of our critical battery ram but unless this notice causes the immediate withdrawal of his name from the bills, we must again inflict on him such chastisement as must drive him from the stage he has dishonoured, and force him to find in the capacity of footman or street-sweeper, that level for which his colour appears to have rendered him peculiarly qualified.*'

Figaro in London on Ira Aldridge

APRIL 24. Charles Kean as Leonardo Gonzaga, James Sheridan Knowles as Julian St Pierre and Ellen Tree as Mariana in James Sheridan Knowles's *Wife, A Tale of Mantua* at Covent Garden Theatre.

JUNE 12. David Obaldiston and Henry Wallack in Edward Fitzball's *Jonathan Bradford or The Murder at the Roadside Inn* at Surrey Theatre. A landlord is found guilty of murder and hanged. He was, in fact, totally innocent. The play was based on a recent crime. 161 performances.

> Nothing injures an author, especially a dramatic author, so materially, as lukewarm praise. For my own part, I should prefer the most extravagant abuse. EDWARD FITZBALL, *Thirty Five Years of a Dramatic Author's Life*

NOVEMBER 2. Ellen Tree as Rosalind in Shakespeare's *As You Like It* at Drury Lane Theatre. John Cooper as Orlando. William Charles Macready as Jaques. *The Observer* complained about Macready's delivery of the 'Seven Ages' speech: 'It was neither imitation nor description, but a little of both, and not enough of either.'

NOVEMBER 14. Julia Glover as Falstaff in Shakespeare's *The Merry Wives of Windsor* at Haymarket Theatre. She was not a success.

> Is it fitting employment for one of the beaux sexe to gloat over and describe the vices of such a character? It must assuredly be a depraved taste – or rather an absence of taste – that can delight in performances of this nature. *The Times*

NOVEMBER 21. William Charles Macready and Louisa Anne Phillips in Shakespeare's *Antony and Cleopatra* at Drury Lane Theatre. John Cooper as Enobarbus. Macready had read Plutarch's *Life of Marc Antony*, but he was physically miscast and uncertain of his lines. All grossness in the text had been removed, and only Clarkson Stanfield's designs had any grandeur.

> It was not that Mr Macready did not appreciate the character, or that he lacked any perception of its beauties, but he had not the power to execute the conception. *Morning Post*

> She [Phillips] carried passion to an extremity that rendered it ludicrous, and tossed and flaunted until Egypt's Queen – the haughty, the loving, the beautiful – was quite sunk in an actress who had literally got out of her depth. *Atlas*

DECEMBER 9. William Charles Macready in Shakespeare's *King John* at Covent Garden Theatre. In his diary Macready wrote: 'I am ashamed, grieved and distressed to acknowledge the trick. I acted disgracefully, worse than I have done for years. I shall shrink from looking into a newspaper tomorrow, for I deserve all that can be said in censure of me.'

World premieres
Victor Hugo's *Lucrèce Borgia* in Milan
Victor Hugo's *Marie Tudor* in Paris

Births
Edwin Booth, American actor-manager

Deaths
Edmund Kean, British actor (b. 1789)
John O'Keefe, Irish dramatist (b. 1747)
William Wilberforce, British campaigner for abolition of slave trade (b. 1759)

Notes
Dramatic Copyright Act

History
Abolition of slavery in British Empire
Falkland Islands annexed
Factory Act forbids employment of children for longer than 8 hours without a lunch break
Oxford Movement is established to oppose 'liberalisation' in theology

1833

Published by Tregear 123 Cheapside London.

Published by Tregear 123 Cheapside London.

TAGLIONI.

PAGANINI.

Silhouettes of Marie Taglioni (1804–84), the great dancer, and Niccolo Paganini (1782–1840), who was considered in the nineteenth century to be the greatest virtuoso violinist in the world.

'I am not handsome, but when women hear me play they come crawling to my feet.'

NICCOLO PAGANINI

1834

JANUARY 2. Douglas William Jerrold's *The Wedding Gown* at Drury Lane Theatre. The play was followed by *Mr and Mrs Pringle*, which was followed by *St George and the Dragon or The Seven Champions of Christendom* in a production by Andrew Ducrow that included numerous horses.

MAY 23. William Charles Macready in Shakespeare's *King Lear* at Covent Garden Theatre.

'I do not feel I have yet succeeded,' Macready wrote in his journal, 'but it is consoling to me to believe I have not failed.'

Mr Macready's chief peculiarity is that he altogether disdains to moderate his 'big manly voice' so as to make it appropriate to the 'childish treble' usually supposed to be characteristic of a man upwards of eighty years of age. *Athenæum*

Mr Macready's Lear was remarkable for its minuteness, the imbecility and irritability of age – the failings and feelings of the father – the remote and increasing encroachment of insanity – these things, with a psychological nicety almost unparalleled, were carefully set in strong relief, so that the individual Lear – choleric, mad and unforgiving – was exactly portrayed – the Lear of fact but not the Lear in its ideal and purely poetic truth. *Illustrated London News*

JUNE 10. William Charles Macready, Ellen Tree and John Cooper in Lord Byron's *Sardanapulus King of Assyria* at Drury Lane Theatre. The spectacular tragedy was dull and poorly performed; the earthquake was particularly disappointing.

I cannot work myself into reality in this part … I have not freedom enough to satisfy myself. I feel myself relapsing into my old habitual sin of striving for effect by dint of muscular exertion, and not restraining my body while my face and voice alone are allowed to act.
WILLIAM CHARLES MACREADY, *Journal*

JULY 2. William Abbott as King Charles and Mrs Fisher as Queen Henrietta Maria in Mary Russell's Mitford's *Charles I* at Victoria Theatre.

The royalist thoughts on the whole more applauded than the republican – Indeed great injustice done to the Roundheads in their histrionic representations. Cromwell was performed by Cathcart an imitator of Kean – his hypocrisy was coarse and could deceive no one. CHARLES CRABB ROBINSON, *Diary*

AUGUST 21. Double-bill at Haymarket Theatre: Signor Rubini in *Rural Felicity*, an opera, and William Farren, Mr Power and Julia Glover in John Baldwin Buckstone's *Married Life!*, a comedy.

OCTOBER 29. Henry Denvil and Ellen Tree in Lord Byron's *Manfred* at Covent Garden Theatre. Byron said that he had written the play 'with a horror of the stage and with a view to render the thought of it impracticable'. The acting, the music of Henry Bishop, and the scenery of Thomas Grieve contributed enormously to its surprising success.

A kind of poem in dialogue in three acts, but of a very wild, metaphysical and inexplicable kind … The first two acts are the best; the third is so-so; but I was blown with the first and second heats.
LORD BYRON in a letter to Mr MURRAY

There must be some merit in this piece since Goethe admired it – but as drama nothing could be worse – The invocations in lyric verse sounded like doggerel though great pains were taken by the declaimer to throw dignity and

1834

Births
Henry James Byron. British
  dramatist
William Morris, British artist
James Whistler, American
  painter

Deaths
Samuel Taylor Coleridge,
  British poet (b.1772)
Charles Lamb, British essayist
  (b.1775)

Notes
English Opera House re-opens
  and renamed the Lyceum
  Theatre
J. R. Planché's *History of British
  Costume* is published
A statute of Edmund Kean
  is proposed but many
  distinguished people refuse
  to contribute on account of
  his 'immorality'

Literature
Alfred De Musset's *Lorenzaccio*

History
Tolpuddle martyrs sentenced
  to 7 years' transportation to
  Australia for swearing an
  oath to join a trade union
Poor Law Amendment Act sets
  up workhouses for poor
Houses of Parliament burn
  down

> ' *He [Byron] is deplorable, has not the slightest feeling,
> nor one physical or mental qualification for the stage.* '
>
> BENJAMIN DISRAELI

tragic effect into the recitation. Action there is
not. It is a sort of Don Juan without wit or fun
or character – no relief – no variety.

CHARLES CRABB ROBINSON, *Diary*

I composed it actually with a *horror* of the stage,
and with a view to render even the thought of it
impractible, knowing the zeal of my friends that
I should try that for which I have an invincible
repugnance, viz a representation.

LORD BYRON in a letter to JOHN MURRAY

DECEMBER 13. Maria Ann Kelley as Nydia in
John Baldwin Buckstone's adaptation of Edward
Bulwer-Lytton's **The Last Days of Pompeii or
Seventeen Hundred Years Ago** at Adelphi Theatre.
Mount Vesuvius had only a minor eruption. Kelley
went to an asylum for the blind to study for
her role. Her vacant stare always got a round of
applause.

The most trying moment was when I had to
go down to the footlights and sing two songs.
I could never stop the tears rolling down my
cheek and the effort to maintain the rigid look
of the eyes was very painful.

MARIA ANN KELLY

DECEMBER 15. William Charles Macready in
Lord Byron's **Werner** at Drury Lane Theatre. Helen
Faucit as Josephine.

I acted Werner really well – almost too well
for some part of the house to which I make no
doubt the grinding and roaring and grimacing of
my hard-working colleague Stuart in Ulric must
have seemed much more like acting than my
more quiet mode of speaking.

WILLIAM CHARLES MACREADY, *Journal*

DECEMBER 15. Edward Fitzball's adaptation of
Lord Lytton's novel **The Last Days of Pompeii** at
Victoria Theatre. The eruption of Vesuvius here
at the Victoria had more impact than the one at
the Adelphi.

DECEMBER 26. T. P. Cooke as Sir Roland in
Isaac Pocock's **King Arthur and the Knights of
the Round Table** at Drury Lane Theatre. Based
on Walter Scott's poem, *The Bridal of Triermian*.
'It is as spectacle alone and not as drama, that
this piece must be considered,' said *The Times*,
'and considering it thus it deserves unqualified
praise.' Clarkson Stanfield and Pocock designed the
scenery and costumes. Andrew Ducrow's docile
stud won the most applause.

1835

JANUARY 24. Frederick Lemaître as Robert Macaire in Honoré-Victorien Daumier's *L'Auberge des Adrets* at English Opera House. A thief escapes from prison and gets shot by his side-kick. Lemaître had acted the role 500 times in France. *The Observer* described him as 'a man of extraordinary natural powers'. Not everyone agreed.

> I cannot acknowledge the great merit of Lemaître. He actually makes faces to make some barren spectators laugh – His acting is often mere buffoonery.
> CHARLES CRABB ROBINSON, *Diary*

FEBRUARY 17. James Wallack, Benjamin Webster and Helen Faucit in Douglas William Jerrold's *The Hazard of the Die* at Drury Lane Theatre. French Revolution melodrama: the lovers are released as they wait at the foot of the guillotine.

MARCH 12. J. R. Planché's *The Court Beauties* at Olympic Theatre. Hampton Court and St James's Park were recreated on stage. King Charles was accompanied by 12 spaniels. The beauties were Nell Gwynne, Duchess of Portsmouth, Castlemaine, Lucy Waters and La Belle Stuart, and they all looked as if they had stepped out of the paintings at Hampton Court.

Frederick Lemaître (1800–76), the great French actor, came to London in 1835 and was entertained by the leading London actors of the day. His most famous roles were Othello, Robert Macaire and Ruy Blas.

MAY 7. Maria Malibran in Vincenzo Bellini's *La Sonnambula* at Covent Garden Theatre. Malibran's final performance. Shortly afterwards she was thrown from a horse and died from her injuries. She was 29 years old.

The purity of her voice, the accuracy and felicity of execution, the profusion of gracefulness, and the intensity of feeling, which she displays, gives charm to the whole representation which seems to reach, as nearly as human genius can reach, the highest point of excellence. *The Times*

Malibran may be pronounced one of the greatest artists the world has ever produced. It is difficult to say whether she excelled most in acting or singing, in tragedy or comedy.
JOHN WILLIAM COLE, *The Life and Times of Charles Kean*

SEPTEMBER 7. T. P. Cooke, Jenny McCarthy and Charles Dillon in Thomas Haines's *Mr Poll and My Partner Joe* at Surrey Theatre. Nautical drama. Such was its popularity that 16,723 people came to see it in one week.

We witnessed the finest delineation of the character of the British sailor; the noble integrity and candour which direct his actions – the glorious enthusiasm which rouses him in his defence of his country – and the wanted courage which inspires him in the hour of danger. *Court Journal*

OCTOBER 1. William Charles Macready and Ellen Tree in Shakespeare's *Macbeth* at Drury Lane Theatre. Macready pursued the dagger round the stage. The critics thought his death scene was

superb, but he felt that he had acted badly. He wrote in his journal: 'I scarcely recollect when my feelings have been so wrought up to a state of agonizing bitterness as tonight; I feel almost desperate.'

Mr Macready's broken and terrifying whispers fell with a cold and death-like abruptness on the hearts of all – in the nearest and remotest corners of the theatre.
JOHN FORSTER, *Examiner*

OCTOBER 7. William Charles Macready in *Hamlet* at Drury Lane Theatre. Macready thought that this was his best Hamlet yet. Some members of the audience, including the American actor Edwin Forrest, didn't like the way he waved a handkerchief during the play scene and hissed. Forrest blamed Macready for his poor reception in London. Their rivalry would explode very nastily when Macready was in New York and they both elected to play Macbeth on the same night. In the riots that followed Macready's life was in serious danger.

OCTOBER 13. George Vanderhoff as Burley and Frederick Warde as Bothwell in *Cavaliers and Roundheads* at Drury Lane Theatre. Isaac Pocock's adaptation of Sir Walter Scott's novel, *Old Mortality*. *The Observer* said 'the incidents were neither probable nor coherent', but that 'they were extremely well acted'.

OCTOBER 28. Edward Bulwer-Lytton's *Paul Clifford* at Covent Garden Theatre. The burletta was so successful that it revived the theatre's financial fortunes. It was the stage coach and the six horses on the stage which brought in the much-needed audiences in large numbers.

1835

World premieres	Births	Notes
Gaetano Donizetti's *Lucia di Lammermoor* in Naples	Mark Twain, American author	St James's Theatre opens Buchner's *Danton's Death* (written; not produced until 1903)
	Deaths	
Literature	Charles Mathews, British actor (b. 1776)	
Théophile Gautier's *Mademoiselle de Maupin*	Isaac Pocock, British dramatist (b. 1762)	*History*
Nikolai Gogol's *Taras Bulba*	John Nash, architect (b. 1752)	Boers in Great Trek to South Africa

October 29. Miss Shirreff and Mr Phillips in William Balfe's **The Siege of Rochelle** at Drury Lane Theatre. Opera. Music by William Balfe. Libretto by Edward Fitzball. Balfe had a huge success, but his attempt to establish English opera in London failed, and he went to Paris.

November 16. Jacques-Fromental Halevy's **The Jewess** adapted by J. R. Planché at Drury Lane

Theatre. Opera based on Eugène Scribe's *La Juive*, and arranged for the English stage by T. P. Cooke. The Jewess did not die in a cauldron of boiling oil, a martyr to Christian bigotry, as she had done on the Paris stage. In London her life was saved. Planché apologised to Scribe for the rewrite.

French authors and French composers have furnished the whole material of our drama and we make ourselves the contempt of the arrogant Parisian, as all travellers can witness, in our slavish imitation. When will this degrading situation end?   *Observer*

John Liston (1776–1846) and Charles Mathews (1776–1835). Liston's most famous role was Paul Pry. The theatrical profession considered Mathews to be the comedy heir to Liston. Mathews was famous for the extraordinary range of characters he created in his 'At Home' solos.

LISTON.   C. MATHEWS.

1836

JANUARY 5. Helen Faucit made her debut as Julia in Sheridan Knowles's **The Hunchback** at Covent Garden Theatre.

IT IS OVER, IT IS OVER, this, as yet the most important day of my life, and, *I thank God, well over* – at least and I hope and trust so. It seems even now like a dream to me. I can remember nothing, think of nothing, but that it is over. Oh, happy, happy girl! And most of all happy in making those I love happy ... I will now bless the Almighty for having supported me through my (I must say it, because I felt it so) *fearful trial* and try to go calmly to sleep. *Again and again, thank God it is over!*
HELEN FAUCIT, *Diary*

Energy, pathos and grace are the essential of a tragic actress and we can safely say we never saw them more happily combined than in the person of the fair debutante ... Her enunciation is remarkably distinct, her carriage graceful and her action, though sometimes bordering on extravagant, is generally 'well suited to the word'.
Morning Chronicle

JANUARY 27. Charles Kemble as Jaffeir, David Osbaldiston as Pierre and Helen Faucit as Belvidira in Thomas Otway's **Venice Preserv'd** at Covent Garden Theatre. The whole house – pit, boxes and galleries – rose and cheered. 'She acted,' said one critic, 'as if she were not acting.' Not everybody was so favourable.

No doubt there was a great deal of truth on what was said against me, but I think it rather hard critics should see and judge you so severely on a *first appearance*.   HELEN FAUCIT, *Diary*

What we mainly and most of all like about Miss Helen Faucit is the fearlessness with

which she throws herself into the passion of the part.   *Morning Chronicle*

FEBRUARY 8. Helen Faucit in Benjamin Thompson's **The Stranger** at Covent Garden Theatre. 'Nauseous trash,' said *The Times*.

MARCH 10. George Bennett and Helen Faucit in **Romeo and Juliet** at Covent Garden Theatre. Bennett ranted and roared.

Oh! If I had not had a very different Romeo in my imagination, it would have been hard indeed to make one out of such an unromantic lover.   HELEN FAUCIT, *Diary*

Of all the characters hers [Juliet] is the one which I have found the greatest difficulty but also the greatest delight in acting.
HELEN FAUCIT, *On Shakespeare's Characters*

APRIL 12. Carlotta Grisi and Jules Perrot made their London debut in Andre Deshayes's ballet, **Le Rossignol**, at King's Theatre.

MAY 26. William Charles Macready and Helen Faucit in Thomas Noon Talfourd's **Ion** at Covent Garden Theatre. The critics found Faucit uninteresting. Macready thought she lacked heart. The play, nevertheless, proved highly fashionable.

There is something about Mr Macready that is quite august. I wonder if I shall ever get over the silly feeling? I fear not; for I think, if I may judge from the freezing and proud coldness of his manner, he dislikes me.
HELEN FAUCIT, *Diary*

JUNE 1. Pauline Duvernay as Florinda in Jean Coralli's **Le diable boiteux** at Drury Lane Theatre. Known in English as *The Devil on Two Sticks*. The bottle contains three beautiful women, one rich, one penniless, and the third, a dancer. The piece is famous for an exotic solo: the voluptuous and intoxicating cacucha. Duvernay had a big success in the role created by Fanny Essler in Paris.

AUGUST 9. Ellen Tree and George Vandenhoff in Thomas Noon Talfourd's adaption of Euripides's **Ion** at Haymarket Theatre. Tree's Ion became more and more effeminate. 'Her performance,' said *The Dramatic Register*, 'taken generally was miserably tame and ineffective … totally disagreeable.'

> Miss Tree's performance is a very pretty effort and a very creditable effort, but it is no more like a young man than a coat and waistcoat are. WILLIAM CHARLES MACREADY, *Journal*

> Miss Tree looked and acted most sweetly. *It is a very bad part*, but she made a great deal more of it than I shall be able to do.
> HELEN FAUCIT, Diary

AUGUST 19. William Charles Macready in Shakespeare's **Othello** at Haymarket Theatre. George Vandenhoff as Iago. Helen Faucit as Desdemona. Macready liked her performance very much.

> The Desdemonas that I have seen on the English stage have always appeared to me to acquiesce with wonderful equanimity in their assassination. On the Italian stage they run for their lives. I shall make a fight of it … My friends used to say, as Mr Macready did, that in Desdemona I was very hard to kill. How could

it be otherwise? I would not be dishonoured in Othello's esteem.
HELEN FAUCIT, *On Shakespeare's Characters*

DECEMBER 10. Madame Blasis, Signor Catoni and Signor Torri in London premiere of Gaetano Donizetti's **L'Elisir D'Amore** at English Opera House. The most frequently performed of all Donizetti's works.

DECEMBER 23. John Philip Kemble made his farewell as Benedict in Shakespeare's **Much Ado about Nothing** at Covent Garden Theatre. Helen Faucit played Beatrice.

DECEMBER 26. Charles Mathews, Madame Vestris and James Bland in J. R. Planché's **Riquet with the Tuft** at Olympic Theatre. Extravaganza. Planché had preferred the performance he had seen the French actor Potier give in Paris. He thought Mathews lacked tenderness in the love scenes. 'I also missed,' he said, 'the indefinable air of courtly breeding which reminded the spectator that the hideous, limping grotesque hunchback was a prince by birth and a gallant gentleman by nature.'

> James Bland established his reputation as the monarch of extravaganza … He made no effort to be funny but so judiciously exaggerated the expression of passion indicated by the mock-heroic language he had to deliver that while it became irresistibly comic, it never degenerated to mere buffoonery.
> JAMES ROBINSON PLANCHÉ

World premieres
Nikolai Gogol's *The Government Inspector* in St Petersburg
Mikhail Lermontov's *The Masquerade* in St Petersburg
Giacomo Meyerbeer's *Les Huguenots* in Paris

Births
W. S. Gilbert, British dramatist

Deaths
Jack Bannister, British actor (b. 1760)
George Colman the Younger, British dramatist (b. 1762)

Literature
Georg Buchner's *Woyzeck* (not performed until 1903)
Charles Dickens' *Pickwick Papers*

Notes
Charles Kemble appointed Examiner of Plays

History
London and Greenwich Railway is first to have a railway terminus in London
University of London created
Battle of the Alàmo, Texas
Mexico gains independence

1836

1837

JANUARY 4. William Charles Macready and Helen Faucit in Edward Bulwer-Lytton's **The Duchess de la Valliere** at Covent Garden Theatre. An adaptation of the novel by the Comtesse de Genelis. The Duchess falls in love with King Louis XIV and becomes his mistress. Her former lover is not pleased. She becomes a nun. Macready said the play was shamefully performed. The critics found it blasphemous, boring and totally unfit for stage representation.

JANUARY 19. William Farren in Charles Dance's **The Country Squire or Two Days at the Hall** at Covent Garden Theatre.

JANUARY 29. A troupe of Bedouin Arab tumblers performed at Adelphi Theatre. 'They are,' said *The Times*, 'the most active and elegant tumblers that ever exhibited before an English audience.'

APRIL 17. *The Peregrinations of Pickwick or Boz-la-la* at Adelphi Theatre. The Burletta was staged after Dickens had published only six instalments.

'*As long as splendid scenery and gay costumes are made more important than poetry, so shall poetry be kept in the background, and our national drama necessarily be in a depressed condition. Splendid scenery and gay costumes are unavoidable in a large theatre and hence we are opposed to them because they are opposed to poetry.*'

Observer, 1837

MAY 1. William Charles Macready as Strafford in Robert Browning's **Strafford** at Covent Garden Theatre. Helen Faucit as Lucy Carlisle. George Vanderholf as Pym. Benjamin Webster as Young Vane. Mr Dale as King Charles I. Strafford expects the king, his friend, to save him from the scaffold.

Macready looked as if he had stepped out of a portrait by Van Dyck. He had invited Browning to write him a play, but when he read it, he thought it was awful and didn't want to stage it, convinced it would fail; however, he couldn't see how to get out of doing it without offending Browning.

Macready acted very finely, as did Miss Faucit. Pym received tolerable treatment. The rest – for the sake of whose incompetence the play had to be reduced by at least one third of its dialogue – non ragionam di lor! ROBERT BROWNING

MAY 18. Helen Faucit as Imogen and William Charles Macready as Posthumus in Shakespeare's **Cymbeline** at Covent Garden Theatre.

Acted Posthumus in a most discreditable manner, undigested, unstudied. Oh, it was most culpable to hazard so my reputation! I was ashamed of myself. WILLIAM CHARLES MACREADY, *Journal*

I hear a great many talk of his faults of declamation, pauses, and so on, but I don't know it is; he never gives me time to see them … his overpowering earnestness makes amends for all. HELEN FAUCIT, *Diary*

JUNE 24. Wilhelmina Schroeder Devrient in Vincenzo Bellini's **Norma** at Her Majesty's Theatre. Schroeder, according to *The Times*, 'evidently acted on the principle of the Greek sculptors who never allowed passion to exhibit itself.'

JUNE 27. Eighteen-year-old Victoria succeeded to the throne on the death of King William IV.

AUGUST 15. John Baldwin Buckstone, William Farren, Louisa Nisbett and Julia Glover in John Baldwin Buckstone's **Love and Murder or The School of Sympathy** at Haymarket Theatre. Farce. The ladies have a passion for criminals, and they loved reading police reports and attending murder trials.

AUGUST 28. Samuel Phelps as Shylock and Mary Huddart as Portia in Shakespeare's **The Merchant of Venice** at Haymarket Theatre. Phelps's London debut. *The Observer* said there wasn't 'a spark of wily villainy in his style'.

SEPTEMBER 5. Samuel Phelps, William Farren and Fanny Fitzwilliam in George Colman the Younger's **The Iron Chest** at Haymarket Theatre. The chest contains documents which reveal that a man who had been tried and acquitted of murder had in fact committed it.

SEPTEMBER 30. William Charles Macready as Leontes in Shakespeare's **The Winter's Tale** at Covent Garden Theatre. Helen Faucit as Hermione. Mary Huddart as Paulina. George Bartley as Autolycus.

'We do wish,' said *The Observer*, 'that Macready would be sometime a little more distinct and slow in his delivery.' Macready didn't think he was an effective Leontes until the last act.

It is impossible to describe Macready here [the statue coming to life]. He was Leontes' very self. His passionate joy at finding Hermione really alive seemed beyond control … The whole change was so sudden, so overwhelming that I suppose I cried out hysterically, for he whispered to me, Don't be frightened, my child! Don't be frightened! Control yourself! … The intensity of Mr Macready's passion was so real, that I never could help being moved by it and feel much exhausted afterwards. HELEN FAUCIT

OCTOBER 9. Louisa Nisbett, Mr Elton, Benjamin Webster, Edward Strickland, Charlotte Vandenhoff and Julia Glover in J Sheridan Knowles's **The Love Chase** at Haymarket Theatre. Hero wins the love of his childhood sweetheart by pretending that he is loved by another.

T. P. Cooke in his most famous role, Long Tom Coffin in Edward Fitzball's The Pilot, at Haymarket Theatre in 1837. Cooke, who had been to sea as a young man, was always at his best when he was acting nautical characters.

MR T.P. COOKE AS LONG TOM COFFIN.

OCTOBER 31. T. P. Cooke as Long Tom Coffin in Edward Fitzball's **The Pilot** at Haymarket Theatre. The performance was attended by a drunken sailor who had never been in a theatre before. He took what he saw on stage for reality, and when the characters started fighting he leaped on stage and offered to help Cooke. The other actors fled to the wings.

NOVEMBER 6. William Charles Macready and Mary Huddart in Shakespeare's **Macbeth** at Covent Garden Theatre. Samuel Phelps as Macduff. *The Theatrical Observer* said the play 'had never been so well represented'. Macready thought he was at his best in the scene before the banquet. The play was acted every Monday for fourteen weeks.

NOVEMBER 28. Mary Huddart in Thomas James Serle's **Joan of Arc, The Maid of Orleans** at Covent Garden Theatre. Serle as King of France.

As a spectacle this piece equals anything ever produced on our stage. The storming of the city of Orleans, the coronation of the king, the capture of Joan, her death, are, each and all of them, highly effective and beautiful, and were hailed with enthusiastic shouts of applause. *Theatrical Observer*

Miss Huddart took the part with great force and energy. Refined judges would call her acting prodigiously extravagant, but what can a lady do when she has to act against drums, trumpets, cannon, huzzas, etc., unless she employ one physical force in opposition to another? *The Times*

NOVEMBER 30. Anne Romer in William Balfe's **Joan of Arc** at Drury Lane Theatre. The opera did not end with Joan's death. French soldiers rescue her from the stake and she was re-united with her lover. Romer's 'singing was remarkably powerful,' said *The Observer*, 'but not always in tune.'

DECEMBER 26. Helen Faucit in Nicholas Rowe's **Jane Shore** at Covent Garden Theatre. William Charles Macready as Lord Hastings. Not a word of the text was heard. The audience had come to see the pantomime, **Harlequin and Peeping Tom of Coventry**, which followed, and they didn't want to listen to a play.

'*Somewhat too sensitive for his own happiness, and much too impulsive for invariable consistency with his nobler moods.*'

ROBERT BROWNING on WILLIAM CHARLES MACREADY

1837

Births
Henri Becque, French dramatist
Henry Irving, British actor
Algernon Charles Swinburne, British poet, critic
Charles Wyndham, British actor-manager

Deaths
Georg Büchner, German dramatist (b.1813)
John Constable, British painter (b.1776)

Joseph Grimaldi, British-born clown (b.1778)
Alexander Pushkin Russian poet (b.1799)

Literature
Charles Dickens' *Oliver Twist*

Notes
City of London Theatre opens in Norton Folgate
Isaac Pitman invents his system of shorthand

Madame Vestris is declared bankrupt

History
Queen Victoria succeeds to the throne on death of King William IV
London Working Men's Association presents reform proposals; beginning of 'Chartism'
Euston Station opens

1838

JANUARY 8. Charles Kean in Shakespeare's **Hamlet** at Drury Lane Theatre. Anne Romer as Ophelia.

We learned after we had left the theatre – we own to our great astonishment – that Mr Kean had certainly never seen his father play Hamlet. We should have concluded from the performance of last night at Drury Lane, in technical phrase, so decided a hit, that we apprehend few who ever go to the theatre at all will be satisfied without seeing it. *Morning Post*

JANUARY 25. William Charles Macready in Shakespeare's **King Lear** at Covent Garden Theatre. Helen Faucit as Cordelia. The production was notable for restoring the original text and for getting rid of many of Nahum Tate's additions. There was no longer a love story between Cordelia and Edgar, and there was no happy ending. The Fool was restored and played by Priscilla Horton, who had a big success.

FEBRUARY 15. William Charles Macready as Claude Melnotte and Helen Faucit as Pauline in Edward Bulwer-Lytton's **Lady of Lyons or Love and Pride** at Covent Garden Theatre. Macready played the romantic imposter, a gardener's son, who pretends to be a prince and persuades the lady to marry him. Audiences were moved to tears by Faucit's performance. Such was her emotion on the first night that she ripped her handkerchief, without realising she had done it, only to find the critics accusing her of a cheap sensational bit of business. The play was a major turning point in her career. Queen Victoria liked the play so much that she saw it twice. 'Republican claptrap,' said *The Times*. 'No other school could nor would produce such morbid sentimentality, such turned sans-culottism.' Lytton 'makes his peasants talk sad stuff such as a manly peasant would never talk,' said *The Morning Post*.

It was curious to see a man of Bulwer's great mind evidently so much delighted by the praise and compliment of a little girl – because a queen!
WILLIAM CHARLES MACREADY, *Diary*

The effect [of Faucit's hysterical laughter] upon the audience was electrical because the impulse was genuine. But well do I remember Mr Macready's remonstrance with me for yielding to it. It was too daring, he said; to have failed it might have ruined the scene (which was true.) No one, moreover should ever, he said, hazard an unrehearsed effect. I could only answer that I could not help it. HELEN FAUCIT

MARCH 12. William Charles Macready in Shakespeare's **Coriolanus** at Covent Garden Theatre. Mary Warner as Volumnia. James Anderson as Aufidius. Pictorially stunning.

Every attempt at a stage triumph we happen to have seen before, compared with this, was as gilt gingerbread of a Lord Mayor's show – the gorgeous tinsel of an ill-imitated grandeur. This was the grandeur itself, the rudeness and simplicity, the lorry and the truth of Life. JOHN FORSTER, *Examiner*

MARCH 18. Helen Faucit as Rosalind in Shakespeare's **As You Like It** at Covent Garden Theatre. Faucit's first attempt at the role. 'I was too young at the time to value her,' she said, 'and could not enter fully into her rich complex nature as to do justice to it.'

APRIL 5. Fanny Persiani in the London premiere of Gaetano Donizetti's **Lucia di Lammermoor** at Her Majesty's Theatre. 'The material on which she had to work,' said *The Times*, 'was poor and spiritless.'

APRIL 7. William Charles Macready as Francis, James Anderson as Jacopo and Helen Faucit as Marina in Lord Byron's **The Two Foscari** at Covent Garden Theatre. 'Lord Byron has always seemed to us singularly deficient in the simplest requisites of dramatic writing,' said *The Examiner*. 'His tragedies are poems in dialogue.'

> Read the newspapers, excepting always the eloquent writer in the Morning Chronicle, found additional cause to regret that I had devoted myself to the ungrateful task of striving to win the opinion of such profligate, ignorant and bad men.
> WILLIAM CHARLES MACREADY, *Journal*

APRIL 18. Charles Kean in Shakespeare's **Hamlet** at Drury Lane Theatre. Anne Romer as Ophelia. Kean got rid of the traditional rolled-down stocking, a device which actors in the past had used to convey Hamlet's madness. *The Athenæum* thought he was the best Hamlet he had seen.

APRIL 30. James Anderson and Helen Faucit in Shakespeare's **Romeo and Juliet** at Covent Garden Theatre. William Charles Macready as Friar Laurence. James Vining as Mercutio.

> ' *What a scene is this [the potion scene in Romeo and Juliet] – so simple, so grand, so terrible! What it is to act I need not tell you. What power it demands and yet what restraint.* '
> HELEN FAUCIT, *On Some of Shakespeare's Female Characters*

JUNE 5. Marie Taglioni in Filippo Taglioni's **La Sylphide** at Her Majesty's Theatre. The season also included **La Parisienne**, **Mirande**, **Le Revolte au Serail**, **La Fille du Danube** and **La Fille de L'air**. Such was Taglioni's success that seats were sold at treble the price. A carriage which travelled from Windsor to London was named after her.

JUNE 10. Charles William Macready in Shakespeare's **Henry V** at Covent Garden Theatre.

Miss Vandenhoff as Katharine. James Vining as Dauphin. Priscilla Norton as Boy. The Chorus was played by John Vandenhoff as Time with scythe and hour glass. The music was selected from the work of Purcell, Handel and Weber. The most elaborate production Covent Garden had known. A cast of over 70 were lavishly costumed. Macready wore a Roman tunic and a hat with enormous ostrich feathers. The chorus' speeches were accompanied by Clarkson Stanfield's paintings and tableaux of the fleet setting sail, the siege of Harfleur, the English and French camps at Agincourt, and Henry's triumphant return to London. One of the many stunning effects was when the troops painted on the backcloth transformed into live soldiers.

> To impress more strongly on the auditor, and render more palpable those portions of the story which have not the advantage of action, and still are requisite to the Drama's completeness, the narrative and descriptive poetry spoken by the Chorus is accompanied with Pictorial Impressions from the pencil of Mr Stanfield. *Playbill*

> The melting away of the pictorial into the real siege was truly wonderful; and the transition was managed with such consummate skill, that it was utterly impossible for any one to detect the precise moment at which either the one ended, or the other commenced. *Oddfellows*

> The scenic effects, instead of being kept subordinate to the dialogue and action, as the accessories of a picture, are made principal, and divert the attention too much from the poetry and the personation and moreover the attempt physically to realize what can only be suggested to the mind, sometimes defeats itself. *Spectator*

> I went before the curtain, and amidst shoutings and wavings of hats and handkerchiefs by the whole audience the stage was literally covered with wreaths, bouquets and branches of laurels.
> WILLIAM CHARLES MACREADY, *Journal*

MR O. SMITH, as Newman Noggs.   MRS KEELEY, as Smike   MR J. WEBSTER, as Nicholas Nickleby

in MR E. Stirlings popular Barletta of Nicholas Nickleby from the much admired Work by MR Dickens.
Newman Noggs. "Is this the boy of desperate character? Poor fellow! Poor fellow!"

O. Smith as Newman Noggs, Maria Ann Kelly as Smike, and J. Webster as Nicholas in an adaptation of Charles Dickens' novel, Nicholas Nickleby, at Adelphi Theatre in November 1838. One of the remarkable features of Victorian theatre was the speed with which new works by popular authors were dramatised for the stage. Dickens' novel was being serialised, and only eight out of twenty parts of Nickleby had appeared when this adaptation was staged.

SEPTEMBER 26. Helen Faucit as Imogen, Samuel Phelps as Posthumus and George Vandenhoff as Iachimo in Shakespeare's **Cymbeline** at Covent Garden Theatre. 'We have never seen this young lady act a serious part with such true and delicate feeling,' said *The Athenæum*. 'Her smile and tears seemed spontaneous.' Faucit, however, regarded her first attempt at Imogen as no more than 'an experiment'. Later, Imogen would prove to be one of her greatest roles.

OCTOBER 13. William Charles Macready as Prospero in Shakespeare's **The Tempest** at Covent Garden Theatre. Samuel Phelps as Antonio. Helen Faucit as Miranda. James Anderson as Ferdinand. Priscilla Horton as Ariel. Music selected from the works of Henry Purcell, Thomas Linley and Dr Thomas Arne and arranged by T. P. Cooke. The production opened with Carl Mario von Weber's Overture to *The Ruler of Spirits* and the ship floundering on the rocks.

> I look back on the production with satisfaction, for it has given to the public a play of Shakespeare's which has never been seen before, and it has proved the charm of simplicity and poetry.
> WILLIAM CHARLES MACREADY, *Diary*

> Mr Macready excels in passages of tender emotion, but he absolutely transcends himself in those of high and impetuous feeling. You see the passion flashing in his eye and flaming on his cheek and you hear it in the thunder of his voice – the finest voice upon the stage. Here he never thinks of his delivery, but gives utterance the rein, and lets it bound along with all the freedom of wild and headlong nature.
> JAMES SHERIDAN KNOWLES

the Late
JOHN REEVE.

World premieres
Hector Berlioz's *Benvenuto Cellini* in Paris
Victor Hugo's *Ruy Blas* in Paris

Births
James Albery, British dramatist
John Wilkes Booth, Anglo-American actor
Henry Irving, British actor
Genevieve Ward, American-born actress

Deaths
Thomas Maddison Morton, British playwright (b. 1764)
Thomas Attwood, British composer (b. 1765)

Notes
National Gallery opens in Trafalgar Square
Era newspaper begins publication

History
The People's Charter published
'Tolpuddle martyrs', having been pardoned, return to England
Grace Darling, young daughter of lighthouse-keeper, helps rescue sailors and becomes national heroine; she dies of tuberculosis four years later
Anti-Corn Law League founded in Manchester
Coronation of Queen Victoria

OCTOBER 25. Miss Rainforth in William Dimond's **The Royal Oak** at Covent Garden Theatre. Superannuated melodrama. Rainforth sang 'Rest, Warrior, Rest!' 'What audiences have done to deserve such an affliction we know not,' said *The Athenaeum*.

NOVEMBER 19. J. Webster as Nicholas in Edward Stirling's adaptation of Charles Dickens' **Nicholas Nickleby** at Adelphi Theatre. Mr Wilkinson as Squeers. Maria Ann Kelly as Smike. O. Smith as Newman Noggs. The actors looked like their counterparts in George Cruickshank's drawings. Dickens, who was only half-way through the story, hated the adaptation. The first night audience couldn't make up its mind whether to sympathise with Smike or whether to roar with laughter. Kelly wasn't ideal casting for an overgrown boy of nineteen, but her performance, nevertheless, was heart-rending. Edward Stirling's adaption, which was staged when only eight parts of the novel had

been published, ended with Smike alive and coming into a fortune. Dickens thought the production excellent, but he object to a stage versions of his novels before he had finished writing them. Keeley was universally praised by the critics. The *Literary Gazette* thought she was perfection: 'She is Smike.'

DECEMBER 11. E. F. Saville as Bill Sikes, Master Owen as Oliver. Mr Heslop as Bill Sikes and Miss Martin as Nancy in **Oliver Twist** at Surrey Theatre. This serio-comic burletta in three acts by George Almar was staged one month after the final instalment had been published. Ira Aldridge played Fang, the Police Magistrate (London's first black police magistrate?). W. Smith as Bumble. Charles Dickens was so appalled by what he saw that he lay down on the floor in his box and did not get up until the final curtain fell. The actors looked as if they had stepped out of the caricatures of Boz.

'*It is a hopeless endeavour to attract people to a theatre unless they can be first brought to believe they will never get in.*'

CHARLES DICKENS

1839

JANUARY 7. Van Amburgh's lions and tigers appeared at Drury Lane Theatre. Queen Victoria was so thrilled by the experience that she went four times, much preferring their roaring performance to Helen Faucit's roaring performance in Edward Bulwer-Lytton's *The Lady of Lyons*.

FEBRUARY 25. Maria Ann Kelley as Oliver, Frederick Yates as Fagin, Mrs Frederick Yates as Nancy and O. Smith as Sykes in Edward Stirling's adaptation of Charles Dickens' **Oliver Twist** at Adelphi Theatre. 'Smith raises the brutality of the character almost to the low sublime of tragedy,' said *The Athenæum*. *The Times* thought the play was better than the novel. *The Theatrical Observer* said Yates' Fagin was 'a most faithful and appalling picture of the heartless sordid villain', and that he had 'never seen a finer histrionic portrait'. Dickens thought that if Oliver were to be played by an actress, it should have been played by a very sharp girl of thirteen or fourteen.

MARCH 18. Helen Faucit as Rosalind in Shakespeare's **As You Like It** at Covent Garden Theatre. James Anderson as Orlando. William Charles Macready as Jaques. John Pritt Harley as Touchstone. Those who expected Faucit's Rosalind to be hearty and voluble – in the tradition of Mrs Jordan's Rosalind – were disappointed. 'She walked about,' said *The Examiner*, 'with so continued and uneasy a sense of the exposure of her legs, that we thought her anxious at every step, to conceal the one behind the other.'

JULY 23. Walter Lacy in John Baldwin Buckstone's **Single Life** at Haymarket Theatre. A humorous cross-section of unmarried people. Lacy played an elegant, self-loving fop.

OCTOBER 4. William Charles Macready as Shylock in Shakespeare's **The Merchant of Venice** at Haymarket Theatre. Macready in his journal described his performance as an utter failure: 'I felt it and suffered much for it.'

OCTOBER 28. Maria Ann Keeley as Jack in John Baldwin Buckstone's **Jack Sheppard** at Adelphi Theatre. Based on William Harrison Ainsworth's novel. Jack wasn't hanged; he died in the flames after his house was set on fire. The scenery was based on George Cruickshank's drawings. *The Times* said the play was better than the novel. 'Nothing could be more exquisite than Mrs Keeley's acting,' said *The Observer*. Keeley looked as if she had stepped out of William Hogarth's painting, *The Apprentice*. There were seven other plays about Jack Sheppard, in London in 1839. Buckstone's version was accused of having been directly responsible for the murder of a member of the aristocracy by his valet. The Lord Chamberlain, worried about the effect the plays were having on everyday crime, decided to ban them all. A fourteen-year-old boy, sent to prison for picking a pocket of £25, had confessed he liked the play very much and had seen it many times.

Births
Marie Wilton, British actress
Modest Mussorgsky, Russian composer
Ouida (Maria Louise Ramé), British novelist

Notes
Royal General Theatrical Fund is established

Literature
Charles Dickens' *Nicholas Nickleby* (dedicated to William Charles Macready)
William Harrison Ainsworth's *Jack Sheppard*
Edgar Allan Poe's *The Fall of the House of Usher*
Stendhal's The Charterhouse of Parma

History
William Fox Talbot shows his calotype photographic process to the Royal Institution
The Opium War with China starts
House of Commons rejects Chartist petition

1839

The
1840s

The Mirror
OF
LITERATURE, AMUSEMENT, AND INSTRUCTION.

| No. 1031.] | SATURDAY, NOVEMBER 7, 1840. | [PRICE 2d. |

NEW FRONTAGE OF THE ADELPHI THEATRE.

The new frontage of Adelphi Theatre as pictured in 1840. The new façade was by Samuel Beazley.

PREVIOUS PAGE

Helen Faucit (1817–98) created Clara in Edward Bulwer Lytton's Money at Haymarket Theatre in 1840. Faucit would become William Charles Macready's leading lady, and played such Shakespearian roles as Imogen in Cymbeline, Desdemona in Othello, Lady Macbeth, and Constance in King John.

1840

JANUARY 23. William Charles Macready as Ruthven and Miss Montague as Mary and E. W. Elton as Rizzo in J. Haynes' *Mary Stuart* at Drury Lane Theatre. Ruthven plots to murder Rizzio. The role didn't offer Macready many opportunities since Haynes was more interested in ideas than in drama. Samuel Phelps played the jealous, irascible Darnley.

> The part [Rizzio] was acted with a great zeal and much pain by Elton; he should, however, avoid the crouching behind the Queen to avoid his murderers, as though this expression of personal fear is historically true, it mars the beauty of his ideals. Could he sing a trifle more in tune? *The Times*

FEBRUARY 7. Ellen Tree, Mr Moore and James Anderson in Leigh Hunt's *A Legend of Florence* at Covent Garden Theatre. A wife, who was presumed to be dead, returns home. Her husband thinks she is a ghost and refuses her entry to his house. She goes to her lover who realises she is not a ghost.

FEBRUARY 21. *The Fortunate Isles or The Triumph of Britannia* at the Olympic Theatre. A grand allegorical and national masque staged in honour of Queen Victoria's marriage to Albert of Saxe-Coburg.

MARCH 9. Mr Hicks in *Presumption or The Fate of Frankenstein* at Victoria Theatre. O. Smith as ★★★★★★ [sic].

MARCH 18. Thomas Verny and Filippo Coletti in Gaetano Donizetti's *Torquato Tasso* at Her Majesty's Theatre. Tasso, a totally sane poet, is confined in a lunatic asylum for seven years by a jealous rival.

> The third act is, perhaps, as good as anything Gaetano Donizetti has composed, which,

> *' Nearly all that has happened in the last twenty years has tended more or less to degrade the profession: what is wanted is something to elevate it and then we should have an abundant supply of actors, as of painters, lawyers or apothecaries. '*
>
> *Observer Dramatic Intelligence*, 1840

however, will not be thought great praise by those who look upon him as about a fifth-rate composer of a second or third-rate school. *Observer*

> It is in his usual style – a mere string of reminiscences without a single spark of invention, variety of expression, and dramatic character. *Herald*

APRIL 20. J. R. Planché's *The Sleeping Beauty in the Wood* at Covent Garden Theatre. Gorgeous and picturesque. Madame Vestris sang the popular 'Nix My Dolly'.

MAY 23. William Charles Macready, Helen Faucit and Samuel Phelps in Sergeant Talfourd's *Glencoe or The Fate of the Macdonalds* at Haymarket Theatre. The massacre was incidental. The author's name was kept secret until the curtain call. Talfourd was a Member of Parliament.

JULY 6. Charles Kean in Shakespeare's *Macbeth* at Haymarket Theatre.

> Mr Kean's success last evening was one of the most brilliant which has ever been recorded in the annals of the drama. Of Mr Kean, as the actor, we saw or thought nothing. It was Macbeth, Macbeth, Macbeth, Ever and anon, who appeared before us. *Morning Post*

Cromwell's son wants to lead a quiet life and doesn't want to follow in his father's footsteps and lead a rebellion.

NOVEMBER 16. Madame Vestris as Oberon In Shakespeare's *A Midsummer Night's Dream* at Covent Garden Theatre. Music by Felix Mendelssohn. Much of the text was restored. In the final scene the fairies, fitted with twinkling coloured lights, flitted through the auditorium. The production was aimed at an audience who had enjoyed *La Sylphide*. Vestris appeared in full armour.

DECEMBER 8. William Charles Macready as Alfred Evelyn and Helen Faucit as Clara in Edward Bulwer-Lytton's *Money* at Haymarket Theatre. Evelyn had proposed to Clara, who had turned him down because she was poor and didn't want to be a burden and drag him down still further. He presumed she had turned him down because he was not rich. Once he comes into the money, he, stupidly, proposes to the daughter of his employer for whom he works as an unpaid secretary. The plot concerns Evelyn's machinations to get out of his moral obligation. The quickest way is to lose his fortune at the gaming tables. His employer (who has no money himself) was interested in Evelyn as a son-in-law only as long as he was rich. The

SEPTEMBER 19. Mr Moore as John di Procida in James Sheridan Knowles's *Bride of Messina* at Covent Garden Theatre. A partly factual, partly fictional, account of the emancipation of Sicily from France. The scenery was superb.

SEPTEMBER 26. William Charles Macready, Helen Faucit and Edward Strickland in James Serle's *Master Clarke* at Haymarket Theatre. Oliver

1840

World premieres
Gaetano Donizetti's *La fille du régiment* in Paris

Births
Thomas Hardy, British novelist, poet, dramatist
Helena Modjeska, Polish-born actress
Emile Zola, French novelist, critic

Deaths
Beau Brummel, British dandy (b. 1778)
Fanny Burney, British dramatist, diarist (b. 1752)

Notes
Royalty Theatre opened
Diorama in Oxford Street named Princess's Theatre

History
Queen Victoria marries her cousin Prince Albert of Saxe-Coburg-Gotha
First adhesive postage stamps: 'Penny Black' and 'Twopence Blue'
Chimney Sweeps Act attempts to outlaw 'climbing boys'
Bradshaw publishes world's first railway timetables

play was a big success, and was regularly revived throughout the century.

> With a little more care for the means and a regard to truth and nature, Sir Edward Bulwer might have produced a genuine comedy reflecting the manners and spirit of the day. *Athenæum*

> The satire is not remarkably pungent, the sentimental language seldom rises above the commonplace … there was no brilliancy, though sometimes it seemed to be attempted. The merit of the piece really lay in the constructions of some of the scenes when a great number of persons could be combined with effect. *The Times*

> Acted the part of Eveleyn – not satisfied. I wanted lightness, self-possession, and in the serious scenes, truth. I was not good. I feel it. WILLIAM CHARLES MACREADY, *Journal*

1841

MARCH 4. William Farrell as Sir Harcourt Courtley, James Anderson as Charles Courtley, Charles Mathews as Sir William Dazzle, Madame Vestris as Grace Harkaway and Louisa Nisbett as Lady Gay Spanker in Dion Boucicault's **London Assurance** at Covent Garden Theatre. Boucicault was twenty years old, and the play was presented under the pseudonym of Lee Morton. The story-line owed something to Sheridan's *The Rivals* and Goldsmith's *She Stoops to Conquer*. The 63-year-old Sir Harcourt Courtly, pretending to be a very unconvincing 40-year-old, thinks he is the index of fashion and the pattern of the beau monde. His joint-creaking morning toilette is a straight crib of Lord Ogleby in Colman and Garrick's *The Clandestine Marriage*. He goes to Gloucestershire to marry a young heiress and finds his son is there before him. He flirts with Lady Gay Spanker whose metaphors are drawn entirely from the saddle and who is already married. The use of real carpets, chandeliers, ottomans, windows and mirrors drew rounds of applause and established a style which predated the realistic plays of Tom Robertson. 59 performances.

> It will not bear analysis as a literary production. In fact my sole object was to throw together a few scenes of a dramatic nature; and therefore I studied the stage rather than the moral effect. DION BOUCICAULT

> Imperturbable, full of resource, and prepared for all contingencies, he [Charles Mathews] was the very ideal of the part. JOHN WESTLAND MARSTON, *Our Recent Actors*

> There were some good bits in it, but if it were not for the excellent actors, I hardly think it would do well. QUEEN VICTORIA, *Journal*

APRIL 12. J. R. Planché's **Beauty and the Beast** at Covent Garden Theatre. Extravaganza.

MAY. Rachel, the great French tragic actress, made her London debut at Her Majesty's Theatre and was hailed as the French Siddons. Her repertoire included Racine's **Andromaque** and **Bajazet**, Corneille's **Horace** and **Ariane**, and Schiller's **Maria Stuart**. Of the last *The Times* said, 'the situation of two queens coarsely insulting each other is by no means dignified and was unworthy of Schiller.'

> To dwell upon Rachel's excellence in the various aspects of Phèdre would be to quote the tragedy almost entire … she could express the tortures of unhappy love and of remorse, and the transports of indignation with the fervour, the minuteness and variety of the romantic school, and also with the noble and imposing outlines of classic art. In her, beauty and grandeur of utterance and attitude entered into the expression of the

The Mirror

OF

LITERATURE, AMUSEMENT, AND INSTRUCTION.

No. 1042.]   SATURDAY, JANUARY 16, 1841.   [Price 2d.

INTERIOR OF

THE PRINCESS'S THEATRE,

OXFORD STREET.

The interior of The Princess's Theatre, Oxford Street, in 1841. The architect was Marsh Nelson. The theatre, which had opened in 1840, was up for sale by auction. Part of the advertisement read as follows: 'This truly beautiful coup d'oeil of the interior is unquestionably superior to anything of the kind on the continent and far exceeds in brilliance, harmony and effect the celebrated theatre at Versailles.'

strongest passion. There was grace in her fury, majesty in her despair.

JOHN WESTLAND MARTSON, *Our Recent Actors*

MAY 29. Madame Celeste in William Bayle Bernard's **Marie Ducange** at Haymarket Theatre. Marie goes mad when she is told her marriage is not legal and her husband deserts her. She regains her sanity three months later when he comes back and pretends that time has stood still and that he has never been away. The melodrama had been specially written for Celeste. *The Observer* said she 'was in the highest degree natural and effective'.

JULY 8. Marie Taglioni and Guy Stephen in **L'élève d'Amour** at Her Majesty's Theatre. The divertissement offered a mixture of soft voluptuousness and quiet elegance. *The Times* said Taglioni had never been more brilliant.

JULY 18. Charles Kean and Ellen Tree in Shakespeare's **Romeo and Juliet** at Haymarket Theatre. James William Wallack played Mercutio.

Kean invests it with passion rather than emotion, with manliness than sentimentality. The voice of the actor seemed too tragic for the gushing happiness of what he saw and heard and felt. *Observer*

AUGUST 23. William Thomas Moncrieff's **Giselle or The Phantom Night Dancers** at Sadler's Wells Theatre. Aquatic spectacle billed as 'A Domestic, Melodramatic, Choreographic, Fantastique, Traditional Tale of Superstition'.

NOVEMBER 2. Adelaide Kemble made her London debut in Vincenzo Bellini's **Norma** at Covent Garden Theatre.

Miss Kemble stands alone as the English prima donna. The same cultivation, the same command over the voice, the same thorough knowledge does not exist in any of our other vocalists, and not only could they not arrive at, but they could not challenge a comparison. *The Times*

NOVEMBER 17. **City and Country** at Covent Garden Theatre was two separate plays: **Discovery** written by Richard Brinsley Sheridan's mother and **Tender Heart** written by Richard Steele. The adaptor had attempted to remove all that was dull from the former and all that was offensive from the latter, but evidently without success.

DECEMBER 27. William Charles Macready as Shylock in Shakespeare's **The Merchant of Venice** at Drury Lane Theatre. Mrs Warner as Portia. Samuel Phelps as Antonio. Spectacular production. Macready wrote in his diary that he had acted very nervously.

DECEMBER 29. Charles Macready as Valentine and James Anderson as Proteus in Shakespeare's **The Two Gentlemen of Verona** at Drury Lane Theatre. Robert Keeley as Launce. Miss Fortescue as Julia. Miss Ellis as Silvia. Samuel Phelps as Duke of Milan. The production was praised for the scenery. Fortescue apologised to Macready for not doing justice either to him or to the play.

World premieres
Jean Coralli and Jules Perrot's *Giselle* in Paris

Births
Squire Bancroft, British actor-manager
Constant Coquelin, French actor
Jean Mounet-Sully, French actor
Clement Scott, British critic

Deaths
Lermontov, Russian novelist (b. 1814)
Tyrone Power, American actor (b. 1795)
Frederick Reynolds, British dramatist (b. 1764)

Literature
Charles Dickens' *The Old Curiosity Shop*
First edition of *Punch*

History
Thomas Cook starts his travel agency
New Zealand becomes a British colony
Thomas Carlyle and others open the London Library in the Travellers' Club on Pall Mall
Kew Gardens opens to the public for the first time

1841

1842

William Charles Macready in Shakespeare's King John in 1842.

JANUARY 1. George Vandenhoff as Prospero in Shakespeare's **The Tempest** at Covent Garden Theatre. Miss Vandenhoff as Miranda.

[Vandenhoff] has adhered more strictly to the original text, the only exception being the omission of indelicate passages, for which all lovers of the stage ought to be thankful. *Dramatic and Musical Review.*

FEBRUARY 5. Priscilla Horton and Anne Romer in George Friederic Handel's **Acis and Galatea** at Drury Lane Theatre. Scenery by Clarkson Stanfield.

FEBRUARY 7. William Farren, Madame Vestris and Charles Mathews in Dion Boucicault's **The Irish Heiress** at Covent Garden Theatre. Boucicault's eagerly awaited second play disappointed critics and public alike. The premiere was not helped by Farren forgetting his lines and having to rely on the prompter throughout the performance.

FEBRUARY 25. Douglas William Jerrold's **Bubbles of the Day** at Covent Garden Theatre. John Westland Marston thought it was the most brilliant of all Jerrold's comedies. 'It abounds in caustic irony and brilliant wit,' said *The Theatrical Observer.*

MARCH 12. Carlotta Grisi in Giovanni Coralli and Jules Perrot's **Giselle** at Her Majesty's Theatre. Lucien Petipa as Albrecht. The most famous of romantic ballets. The great French poet and novelist, Theophile Gautier, who had lauded Grisi's performance in Paris, accompanied her to London. She danced with a perfection, a lightness, a boldness and a chaste voluptuousness that put her in the first rank between Fanny Elssler and Marie Taglioni. The name of Carlotta Grisi would become inseparable from Giselle.

APRIL 11. Charles Kean and Ellen Kean in Edward Moore's **The Gamester** at Haymarket Theatre. Morbid sentimentality and feeble dialogue, but touching performances.

APRIL 30. Madame Vestris and Charles Mathews relinquished management of Covent Garden Theatre, finding it financially unviable. Ten days later Mathews declared himself bankrupt. The farewell programme included Adelaide Kemble in **La Sonnambula**, Matthews in **Patter versus Clatter** and Vestris as Prince Paragon in J. R. Planché's extravaganza, **The White Cat**.

> What has Mme Vestris done for the stage? She has banished vulgarity, coarse manners, double entendre, and impertinence, from the boards over which she presided, and in their place, has evoked the benefits that flow from a dramatic representation of polished manners, refinement, and politeness. Her green-room was the resort of the learned, witty, and the wise, a miniature picture of polite and well-bred society, whence a wholesome example spread on all within its influence. *Morning Post*

MAY 20. William Charles Macready, James Anderson and Samuel Phelps in Lord Byron's **Marino Faliero** at Drury Lane Theatre. Faliero, the Doge of Venice, feeling that the office is nothing more than a pageant, joins a conspiracy to overthrow the junta. The conspiracy is betrayed, and he is executed. Byron lifted many familiar phrases and lines from Shakespeare.

JUNE 4. Ellen Kean in Frederick Knowles' **The Rose of Arragon** at Haymarket Theatre. Kean's performance was praised for its purity and pathos.

JUNE 8. Robert Kelley in Charles Selby's **The Boots of the Swan** at New Strand Theatre. Billed as an original bit of fun. Boots, who is completely deaf, disguises himself as a detective and, while pretending to be drunk, he actually does get drunk.

JUNE 10. Rachel in a season of plays at her Majesty's Theatre. Her repertoire included Corneille's **Le Cid** and **Ariane**, Voltaire's **Tancrede**, Racine's **Bajazet** and Schiller's **Maria Stuart**.

> Charming as was the Rachel of 1841, she was not to be compared for energy, for passion – in a word for completeness, with the Rachel of 1842. *The Times*

OCTOBER 1. Louisa Nisbett as Rosalind in Shakespeare's **As You Like It** at Drury Lane Theatre. James Anderson as Orlando and William Charles Macready as Jaques and Adam. Music included the Overture from the first movement of Beethoven's *Pastoral Symphony*. Macready restored much of Shakespeare's text, but he rejected any dialogue which the audience might find offensive. The production was spectacular. The wrestling match had no fewer than 74 actors on stage. In the forest there were leashed hounds and falconers with their birds. Shepherds and shepherdesses created a temple of flowers for Hymen. Queen Victoria

---

World premieres
August Bournonville's *Napoli* in Copenhagen
Giuseppe Verdi's *Nabucco* in Milan
Richard Wagner's *Rienzi* in Dresden

Births
Arthur Sullivan, British composer

Literature
Alfred Lord Tennyson's *Morte d'Arthur*
Robert Browning's *Dramatic Lyrics*
Charles Dickens' *American Notes*
Nikolai Gogol's *Dead Souls*

Notes
Marylebone Theatre opened
Charles Mathews imprisoned for debt

History
First Anglo-Afghan War
Alfred John Francis attempts to shoot Queen Victoria
First peace-time income tax introduced: 7d. in pound for those earning more than £150 per annum
'Rebecca Riots' in Wales against high charges of turnpikes
'Plug Riots' amid continuing protest for reform

1842

liked Kean's performance, especially his delivery of the Ages of Man speech. The *Spectator* thought Nisbett was 'utterly devoid of sentiment'. *The Times* thought she was 'unrestrained with no hint of underlying seriousness'. Certain critics felt that Nisbett and Mrs Sterling (who was playing Celia) should have swapped roles.

> Not having seen her [Nisbett], ye don't know what beauty is. Her voice was liquid music – her laugh – there never was such a laugh! – her eyes living crystals – lamps lit with the light diving! – her grace, her taste, her nameless but irresistible charm. SAMUEL PHELPS

> We had neither the caustic humour nor the poetical melancholy of Jaques, nor the brilliant wit and despotical fancifulness of the princess shepherd boy, duly given, we had warbling of birds, and sheep-bells tinkling in the distance to comfort us. FANNY KEMBLE

OCTOBER 20. William Charles Macready in Shakespeare's **Othello** at Drury Lane Theatre. Samuel Phelps as Iago. James William Wallack in his Memoirs said that Macready in his woolly wig 'looked like an elderly negress of evil repute going to a fancy ball'.

OCTOBER 24. William Charles Macready as John and Helen Faucit as Constance in Shakespeare's **King John** at Drury Lane Theatre. James Anderson as Faulconbridge. Samuel Phelps as Hubert. Miss Newcome as Arthur. A spectacular production which opened with Beethoven's *Symphony in C.*

Faucit was compared to Siddons, and found wanting. Macready thought that *The Morning Post's* criticism was malignant, and that *The Morning Herald's* criticism was very ignorant and vulgar. The public rated John as one of his best performances.

> Macready's eye was as sensitive and cultivated as his ear was the reverse. HELEN FAUCIT

> I admit Miss Faucit's ability is great and unquestionable, but so is her affectations. The truth is she gives herself airs – and a little of that went a long way with me. We didn't get on well together, and I fear we have never been just to each other. Still she is a great actress, and a woman whose character and conduct do honour to her profession. SAMUEL PHELPS

NOVEMBER 19. James Anderson as Valentine and Helen Faucit as Angelica in William Congreve's **Love for Love** at Drury Lane Theatre. Samuel Phelps as Scandal. Robert Keeley as Ben. Maria Ann Keeley as Miss Prue. Louisa Nisbett as Mrs Frail. The play had not been revived since the Restoration era.

> The knife was not spared on this occasion and the piece was of a most unexceptionable morality. It was, in short, emasculated. The objectionable parts were all omitted. Everything prurient was cut out, and the grave and fastidious were satisfied. But was that an improvement? *Observer*

> **'** *Woman's words coming from a man's lips, a man's heart – it is monstrous to think of! One quite pities Shakespeare, who has to put up with seeing his brightest creations thus marred, misrepresented, spoiled.* **'**
> HELEN FAUCIT, *On Some of Shakespeare's Female Characters by One Who Has Personated Them*

1843

JANUARY 21. Helen Faucit as Imogen in Shakespeare's **Cymbeline** at Drury Lane Theatre. William Charles Macready as Iachimo. James Anderson as Posthumus.

> Miss Faucit was a pathetic Imogen; but her mannerisms, which have now become confirmed, greatly marred the picture that Shakespeare drew. *Dramatic and Musical Review*

FEBRUARY 11. Samuel Phelps, Helen Faucit and Fanny Stirling in Robert Browning's **A Blot in the 'Scutcheon** at Drury Lane Theatre. 'Genuine genius,' said *The Morning Post*. Browning had written the play for Macready, but Macready was too ill to act it. Macready curtailed the run because he was jealous of Phelps' success in the role.

> The plot is plain enough but the acts and feelings of the characters are inscrutable and abhorrent and their language is as strange as their proceedings … A few of the audience laughed, others were shocked, and many applauded; but it is impossible that such a drama shall live, even if it were artfully constructed which this is not. *Athenæum*

> Pride raged in him [Phelps] like a demon; his features were convulsed, his gestures wild, his voice charged with sardonic hatred and scorn; while his despair after slaying the betrayer of his sister, was strangely moving by its heart-broken quietude. JOHN WESTLAND MARSTON, *Our Recent Actors*

FEBRUARY 24. William Charles Macready as Benedict and Louisa Nisbett as Beatrice in Shakespeare's **Much Ado About Nothing** at Drury Lane Theatre was followed by William Charles Macready and Helen Faucit in John Milton's **Comus**.

His friends were pleased with him, and he with himself; but the general public said he [Macready as Benedict] was as melancholy as a mourning-coach in a snowstorm. JAMES ANDERSON

> It was the most perfect representation of the poem ever produced for the entertainment of the public. Macready's impersonation of Comus was perhaps a little too mannered; but it was on the whole a very effective performance. *Observer*

FEBRUARY 28. Fanny Elssler in Giovanni Coralli and Jules Perrot's **Giselle** at Her Majesty's Theatre. Her mad scene was highly acclaimed. 'This Giselle is a work of the greatest genius,' said *The Times*.

MAY 12. William Charles Macready in Sheridan Knowles' **Virginius** at Drury Lane Theatre. 'His unrivalled portrait of Virginius defies criticism – it is perfect,' said *The Dramatic and Musical Review*.

JUNE 14. Queen Victoria made a state visit to Drury Lane Theatre to see Shakespeare's **As You Like It** and **A Thumping Legacy**. 'What surprised us most of all,' she wrote in her diary, 'was the really beautiful acting of Miss H. Faucit as Rosalind. She looked quite pretty in male attire & was so lively & naïve.'

JUNE 29. Luigi Lablache as Don Pasquale and Carlotta Grisi as Norina in the London premiere of Gaetano Donizetti's **Don Pasquale** at Her Majesty's Theatre. The last opera buffa of the first half of the nineteenth century to remain in the international repertoire.

> Donizetti is a master of varied and prodigious powers. If he would but deliberate a little more, write one quarter of what he does he would produce things more likely to make lasting impressions. *Illustrated London News*

SEPTEMBER 30. Miss Rainforth, Mr Borrani and Mr Harrison in Michael Balfe's opera **The Siege of La Rochelle** and Carlotta Grisi in Giovanni Coralli's ballet, **La Peri**, at Drury Lane Theatre. The Sultan falls in love with the Queen of Fairies.

Her [Grisi] grand achievement is the pas de deux with Petipa in the first act. She introduces several evolutions totally unlike anything that has been seen before; such as a flying movement from one stage to the other in which she is supported by Petipa; but seems as if supported by air alone; such a spring she takes from an eminence at the back of the stage which she continues by a brilliant advance to the lamps.

The applause of the audience at these feats was a perfect storm that has rarely been equalled.
The Times

NOVEMBER 27. Premiere of William Balfe's opera **The Bohemian Girl** at Drury Lane Theatre. Libretto by Alfred Bunn after Saint-George and based on a ballet. The most successful English opera of the first half of the nineteenth century. A Gypsy queen is thwarted in her efforts to kill her lover and imprison the girl who loves him. Two ballads – 'I Dreamt that I Dwelt in Marble Halls' and 'When Other Lips and Other Hearts' – proved enormously popular.

1844

FEBRUARY 6. Charles Mathews as Sir Charles Coldstream in Dion Boucicault's **Used Up** at Haymarket Theatre. Coldstream retires to the country and pretends to be a plough-boy. Mathews had a big success and it became one of his favourite roles.

As the languorous man of fashion Charles Mathews is faultless. There is an exquisite moderation in his performance which shows a nice perception of nature. The coolness is never overdone. The languor is never obtruded … From first to last we have a character the integrity of which is never sacrificed for isolated effects. But in the second act where the man of fashion appears as a plough-boy, all sense of artistic truth is wanting … He is not at all like a plough-boy, nor like Sir Charles acting the ploughboy. G. H. LEWES, *On Actors and the Art of Acting.*

MARCH 4. Jullien's **Bal Masque** at Covent Garden Theatre. An evening of musical entertainment. The audience could dance or watch or both.

RIGHT

Jullien's Bal Masque at Covent Garden on 4 March 1844.

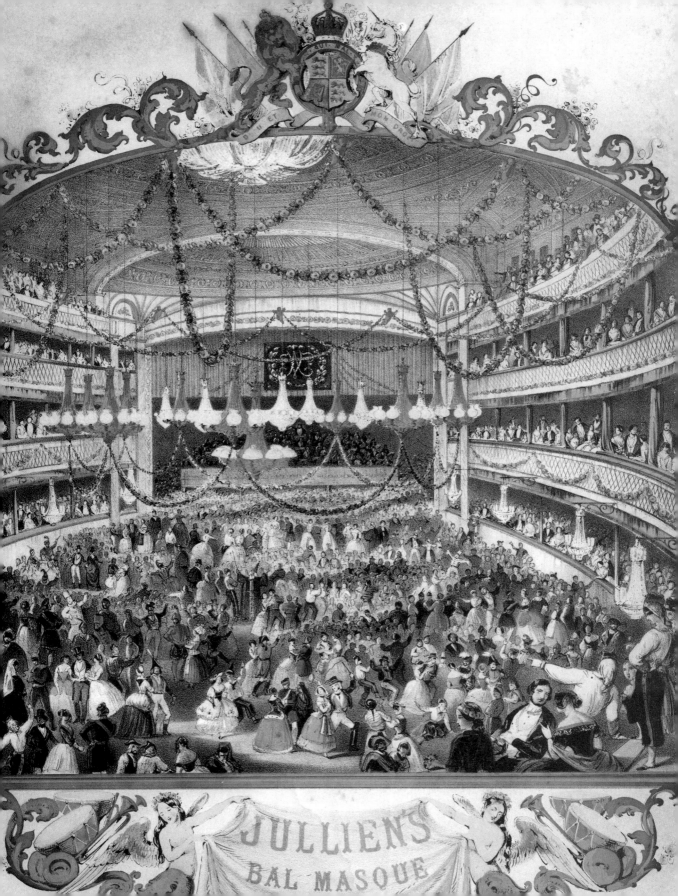

JULLIENS
BAL·MASQUE

SADLER'S WELLS THEATRE

' *Without, the Theatre by night was like the worst kind of Fair, in the worst kind of town. Within, it was like a bear-garden, resounding with foul language, oaths, catcalls, shrieks, yells, blasphemy, obscenity, a truly diabolical clamour. Fights took place any where at any period of the performance … Phelps conceived the desperate idea of changing the character of the dramatic entertainments presented at this den from the lowest to the highest, and utterly changing with it the character of the audience.* '

CHARLES DICKENS

MARCH 16. Benjamin Webster and Louisa Nisbett in Shakespeare's **The Taming of the Shrew** directed by Benjamin Webster and J. R. Planché at King's House. Acted in neo-Elizabethan fashion, without scenery, but with placards to denote where the action was taking place. Webster impersonated Shakespeare in the Induction, which didn't go down well with the critics. Nisbett got all the praise.

MARCH 9. Carlotta Grisi in Jules Perrot's **Esmeralda** at Her Majesty's Theatre. Ballet based on Victor Hugo's *Notre Dame du Paris*. Quasamado is in love with Esmeralda. 'Abundant evidence,' said *The Observer*, 'that Grisi is one of the best mimes of the age … wonderful … perfection.'

MARCH 24. General Tom Thumb, the American dwarf, was 6 years old, 25 inches tall and weighed 15 pounds. He sang, danced and gave imitations of Napoleon at the Egyptian Hall, and performed for Queen Victoria at Buckingham Palace. P. T. Barnum, the American impresario, toured Tom Thumb in Britain and Ireland. His real name was Sherwood Edward Stratton, and he lived until 1883.

APRIL 11. Carlotta Grisi and Jules Perrot danced their version of the polka at Her Majesty's Theatre. Lola Montes had just made a sensational debut in Paris in **The Polka**. The critics didn't think ballet dancers should be ballroom dancers.

MAY 27. Samuel Phelps and Mrs Warner in Shakespeare's **Macbeth** at Sadler's Wells Theatre.

Since Edmund Kean's we have seen nothing better for vigour and effect. It is essentially distinct from and stands in contrast with Mr Macready's, which, however, fine and classical in its conception, is but too obviously open to the Scottish sneer of presenting 'a very respectable gentleman in considerable difficulties … The straightforward and right energy of Mr Phelps's acting, on the contrary, made all present contemplate the business as one of seriousness

1844

World premieres
Giuseppe Verdi's *Ernani* in Venice
Giuseppe Verdi's *I Due Foscari* in Rome

Births
Sarah Bernhardt, French actress
Richard D'Oyly Carte, British manager
John Hare, British actor, manager

Friedrich Neitzsche, German ethical writer
Kate Terry, British actress

Literature
Charles Dickens' *Martin Chuzzlewit*
Alexander Dumas's *The Count of Monte Cristo* (1844–46)
William Makepeace Thackeray's *The Luck of Barry Lyndon*

Notes
Samuel Phelps began his 15 year management of Sadler's Wells Theatre

History
Co-operative movement begins with Pioneers' first shop in Toad Lane, Rochdale
Royal Commission on the Health of Towns is set up
Opening in USA of Samuel Morse's first telegraph line

Samuel Phelps (1804–78), actor-manager, staged all but four of Shakespeare's plays when he was lessee of Sadler's Wells Theatre. His most famous roles were Hamlet, Othello and Richard III.

> ❛The distinguished characteristic of SADLER'S WELLS productions were clearness and intellectual vigour – the plain straightforward meaning of the text was put over before you without any supercilious veneer of subtlety; the decoration was sufficient but not superfluous; above all there was nothing amphigamous about the acting.❜
>
> JOHN COLEMAN, Memoirs of Samuel Phelps

and reality, while the occasional pathos of his declamation thrilled the heart of many a rude bosom with delight. *Athenæum*

JUNE 24. Samuel Phelps and Mrs Warner in Shakespeare's **The Merchant of Venice** at Sadler's Wells Theatre.

SEPTEMBER 3. Frank Matthews as Pecksniff, Frederick Vining as young Martin, Richard Younge as old Martin, Mrs Keeley as Mrs Gamp and Mrs Frank Matthews as Mrs Tidgers in Edward Stirling's adaptation of Charles Dickens' recently completed **Martin Chuzzlewit** at Lyceum Theatre. Hugely successful.

OCTOBER 14. Benjamin Webster and Dion Boucicault's adaptation of Dumanoir and D'Ennery's **Don Caesar de Bazan** at Adelphi Theatre. King Charles of Spain falls in love with a ballad singer. 'A monstrous piece of sentimentality,' wrote Charles Crabb Robinson in his diary, '... an outrage in common sense and yet popular at Paris.' It was, in fact, so popular there were productions at the same time at the Haymarket, Queen's, Princess's and Surrey Theatres.

NOVEMBER 14. Robert Keeley and Alfred Wigan in Tom Taylor's **A Trip to Kissingen** at Lyceum Theatre. A cockney gives his passport to a forger and lands in trouble. Taylor, just down from Trinity College, dashed off his farce in one day. It ran for 50 performances.

NOVEMBER 18. Charles Mathews and Madame Vestris in Dion Boucicault's **Old Heads and Young Hearts** at Haymarket Theatre. Romantic comedy. Roebuck wants to marry Kate. His parents want him to marry a rich widow. Roebuck asks his friend Coke to court the widow, but Coke's elder brother is already courting her. A kindly cleric tries to sort things out and is blissfully unaware that he is only making things worse.

DECEMBER 28. Henry Betty (Master Betty's son) made his debut in Shakespeare's **Hamlet** at Covent Garden Theatre. Hoarse and inarticulate, he was not helped by some unruly members in the Pit.

1845

JANUARY 27. Madame Celeste in John Baldwin Buckstone's **The Green Bushes** at Adelphi Theatre. Drama set in the American colonies. Love, hate and revenge. A wild, passionate and half-savage woman of the woods, half-Indian, half-French, shoots her English lover, a married man, dead. 'Plenty extravagance and improbability,' said *The Morning Chronicle*. The role established Madame Celeste's popularity as an actress.

FEBRUARY 13. Charlotte Cushman, the American actress, made her London debut as Bianca in W. T. Moncrieff's **Fazio** at Princess's Theatre. 'Her triumph,' said John Westland Marston in *Our Recent Actors*, 'was merely an exhibition of passion so intense and impetuous that one forgot its monotony.'

FEBRUARY 21. Edwin Forrest and Charlotte Cushman in Shakespeare's **Macbeth** at Princess's Theatre. Coming out of the murder chamber, Macbeth – a novelty, this – very nearly murdered Lady Macbeth, not realising who she was.

> There was an exuberance of power, a plenitude of New World energy, much of which must be subdued – some of it utterly destroyed – before the actress [Charlotte Cushman] is consummated. *Athenæum*

FEBRUARY 27. Charlotte Cushman as Rosalind and Walter Lacy as Orlando in Shakespeare's **As You Like It** at Princess's Theatre. Cushman in disguise looked every inch a man and spoke like one, too. 'Miss Cushman's Rosalind is inferior to none; in force and depth it is perhaps without rival,' said The *Athenæum*. James William Wallack played Jaques as if Jaques were a member of a Greek tragedy chorus.

MARCH 6. Edwin Forrest in Shakespeare's **King Lear** at Princess's Theatre. 'There were,' said *The Athenæum*, 'no fits, nor starts, nor spasmodic convulsions, no violent heavings, no mannerisms, no affectation to mar the uniform grandeur of the scene.'

APRIL 19. Charlotte Cushman, Henry Wallack and Leigh Murray in Sheridan Knowles' **The Hunchback** at Princess's Theatre. Her [Cushman] passion is painfully gasping and spasmodic,' said *The Observer*, 'but her lighter and more subdued scenes were excellent.'

MAY 2. Charlotte Cushman in James Kenney's **Infatuation** at Princess's Theatre. A Duchess, who had been forced into a marriage with a Jacobin by Napoleon, falls in love with a German conspirator who turns out to be a cold-hearted swindler. Cushman, said *The Observer*, 'acted with her usual intensity and energy.'

MAY 23. Charlotte Cushman in John Tobin's **Honey Moon** at Princess's Theatre.

> She did not play ill but never did an actress realise a more disagreeable impression – her face all but disgusting so that I could have no pleasure looking at her.
> CHARLES CRABB ROBINSON, *Diary*

	World premieres	*Literature*	*History*
1845	Giuseppe Verdi's *Giovanna d'Arco* in Milan	Benjamin Disraeli publishes Sybil	Beginning of Potato Famine in Ireland
	Giuseppe Verdi's *Alzira* in Naples	Charles Dickens' *The Cricket on the Hearth*	First cricket match at Kennington Oval
	Richard Wagner's *Tannhäuser* in Dresden		First university boat race is held on the river Thames

JULY 12. Marie Taglioni, Carlotta Grisi, Fanny Cerrito and Lucile Graham in Jules Perrot's **Pas de Quatre** at Her Majesty's Theatre. Divertissement. Music by Cesare Pugini. 'Matchless for taste and elegance,' said *The Times*.

NOVEMBER 1. Samuel Phelps in Shakespeare's **King Lear** at Sadler's Wells. The play Shakespeare wrote. The Observer thought his performance could stand with the best. Some critics thought Phelps excited only compassion, never awe, and that there was a lack of masculine strength; but for many he was the finest Lear of his generation.

> Mr Phelps's performance of Lear may easily be excelled in royal dignity, and in physical vigour; but, as a pathetic piece of acting, is unrivalled. *Observer*

NOVEMBER 6. Helen Faucit as Rosalind in Shakespeare's **As You Like It** at Haymarket Theatre. Faucit concentrated on sentiment rather than comedy. She never allowed the woman to disappear behind the boy. *The Athenæum* was charmed by 'the simplicity, the delicacy, the purity of the delineation'.

> I could never speak these words [in the mock-marriage] without a trembling of the voice and the involuntary rushing of happy tears to the eyes, which made it necessary for me to turn my head away from Orlando. HELEN FAUCIT on acting Rosalind in *As You Like It*

NOVEMBER 15. Miss Romer, Miss Poole, William Harrison and Mr Borrani in William Vincent Wallace's **Maritana** at Drury Lane Theatre. Book by Edward Fitzball based on Dumanoir and D'Ennery's **Don Caesar de Brazen**. Maritana is a street singer who marries a man on the eve of his execution. The opera was popular for the next 50 years.

> No opera brought out for many years past has created a greater sensation.
> *Illustrated London News*

DECEMBER 29. Charlotte Cushman as Romeo in Shakespeare's **Romeo and Juliet** at Haymarket Theatre. 'As a Shakespearian actress she appears to be on the railroad to fame, but, we fear, it is only in the second class,' said *Era*. Her sister, Susan Cushman, played Juliet. Cushman was the most acclaimed Romeo of the nineteenth century – male or female. 'She has,' said one critic, 'suddenly placed a living, breathing, burning Italian upon boards, where we have hitherto had an unfortunate and somewhat energetic Englishman.'

> Of Charlotte Cushman's Romeo, it may at once be said that it was a signal triumph. It gave full scope to her impetuosity in emotion and to the virile force of her style. As a lover the ardour of her devotion exceeded that of any male actor I have ever seen in the part.
> JOHN WESTLAND MARTSON, *Our Recent Actors*

❛For a long time Romeo has been a convention. Miss Cushman's Romeo is a creative, living, breathing, animated, ardent human being.❜

The Times

> Miss Cushman took the part of Romeo, and no one would ever have imagined she was a woman, her figure and voice being so masculine, but her face was very plain. Her acting is not pleasing, though clever, and she entered well into the character, bringing out forcibly its impetuosity. QUEEN VICTORIA, *Journal*

> Few Romeos in London's memory had looked young enough and passionately agile enough to be convincing, but watching this fiery young gallant, one witness was soon exclaiming that this Miss Cushman seemed 'just man enough to be a boy!'
> JOSEP LEACH, *Bright Particular Stars*

1846

JANUARY 5. Benjamin Webster as John the Carrier and William Farren as Caleb in Benjamin Webster's adaptation of Charles Dickens' **The Cricket on the Hearth or A Fairy Tale of Home** at Haymarket Theatre.

MARCH 3. Luciano Fornasari and Madame Bellini in London premiere of Giuseppe Verdi's **Nabucco** at Her Majesty's Theatre. Verdi said it was with this opera that his career had truly begun.

> It will be in vain for the lover of great music to look in this opera for that sustained grandeur of conception which should characterize such a subject. The composer has it not in him; at least he has not as yet developed the loftiest attribute of musical genius. *Observer*

APRIL 13. J. R. Planché's **The Birds** at Haymarket Theatre. An adaptation of Aristophanes' comedy. There were topical jokes at the expense of house-building and rail-speculation.

> It was a succès d'estime, I am proud to say, with many whose opinion I value highly, but not d'argent as far as the treasury was concerned. J. R. Planché

JUNE 3. Carlotta Grisi and James Silvain in Joseph Mazilliere's ballet, **Paquita**, at Drury Lane Theatre. *The Observer* reported that 'the thermometer was almost at the "boiling-point" within the theatre and the mental temperature of the crowd who follows it was in a constant ebullition of delight.'

JUNE 25. Charlotte Cushman as Viola and Susan Cushman as Olivia in Shakespeare's **Twelfth Night** at Haymarket Theatre. William Farren as Malvolio. John Baldwin Buckstone as Sir Andrew Aguecheek. Benjamin Webster as Feste.

> There is a deficiency of interest about the character [Viola], arising from the utter want of purpose in the heroine's career, so that the performance requires an actress of no ordinary taste to render it in any way tolerable … wanting a proper conception of that she [Charlotte Cushman] has to express, her fluency sinks into a mere histrionic 'gift of the gab' instead of arising by the power of her imagination into true dramatic oratory. *Era*

William Charles Macready (1793–1873) in the 1840s. Macready's finest role was generally considered to be Macbeth.

World premieres

Vincenzo Berlioz's *La Damnation de Faust* in Paris (concert)

Felix Mendelssohn's *Elijah* at Birmingham Festival

Giuseppe Verdi's *Attila* in Venice

Births

Wilson Barrett, English actor, manager and playwright

Deaths

Jean-Gaspard Deburau, French mime (b. 1796)

John Liston, British comic actor (b. 1776)

Literature

Benjamin Disraeli's *Sybil*

Edward Lear's *Book of Nonsense*

Prosper Merimée's *Carmen*

Charles Dickens founds the Liberal *Daily News*

History

Corn Laws are repealed

Koh-i-Noor diamond is surrendered to Queen Victoria

Potato famine in Ireland continues

US declares war on Mexico

At height of 'railway mania' a total of 272 railway constructions bills are enacted in 1846

Waterloo Station opens

JULY 25. Samuel Phelps as Falstaff in **Henry IV Part 1** at Sadler's Well's Theatre. Phelps didn't look fat enough.

In this theatre the great dramatists of our Augustan age have found a humble but not an unworldly home; and the middle and lower classes of people throng to hear and admire plays originally written specially for their ears. *Observer*

JULY 30. Ira Aldridge in Ira Aldridge's **The Black Doctor** at City of London Theatre. Adaptation of a French play. A mulatto doctor heals, loves and marries the daughter of a French aristocrat.

AUGUST 3. Helen Faucit in Sophocles' **Antigone** at Haymarket Theatre. 'Her attitudes were studiously classical and statuesque,' said *The Times*. 'Mendelssohn's music by the chorus was wonderfully queer.'

SEPTEMBER 28. Robert Keeley as a mischievous pupil and Maria Ann Keeley as his fag in Tom Taylor's **To Parents and Guardians** at Lyceum Theatre. Farce set in a boarding school run by Mr Swish, a tyrant in the Wackford Squeers mould. Alfred Wigan had a big success as a French count.

OCTOBER 19. William Charles Macready in Lord Byron's **Werner** at Sadler's Wells Theatre.

Werner himself is a character which nobody living can personate so well as Macready and we doubt whether any who are dead could have equalled him in it. His very mannerisms – singularities entirely his own – become him in Werner, by turns a fitful, passionate, gloomy and miserable noble. *Era*

NOVEMBER 3. Garrick Theatre burned down after a performance of **The Battle of Waterloo**.

DECEMBER 26. Mr Johnson as Ali Baba in N. Lee's **The Forty Thieves or Harlequin Ali Baba and the Robbers' Cave** at Astley's Amphitheatre. The high spot was a staging of the inauguration of the Wellington Statue drawn by real dray horses.

1847

JANUARY 13. Samuel Phelps in Francis Beaumont and John Fletcher's *A King and No King* at Sadler's Wells Theatre. The revival was hailed as the most important step which had been taken in the serious task of restoring the poetic drama to the English stage.

FEBRUARY 23. Two elephants performing at Astley's Amphitheatre were presented with lots of bouquets. The elephants, we are told, had rather hoped for carrots and turnips.

Samuel Phelps in Shakespeare's Macbeth at Sadler's Wells Theatre in 1847.

MARCH 1. Mark Howard in George Dibdin-Pitt's *The String of Pearls or The Fiend of Fleet Street* at Britannia Theatre. Billed as fact and based on the original Sweeney Todd story by Thomas Prest, which had appeared in *The People's Periodical*, a penny dreadful, in 1846. The Britannia in Hoxton was one of London's 'blood-tubs', theatres specialising in sensational melodramas.

MARCH 11. Madame Celeste and Fanny Elizabeth Fitzwilliam in John Baldwin Buckstone's *The Flowers of the Forest*. Melodrama. Two women are in love with a man who is on trial for a murder, which had been committed by a gypsy boy, who had murdered because he had been severely whipped. Miss Woolgar played the boy,

MARCH 17. Grand English Opera Company at Drury Lane Theatre. Sims Reeves and Charlotte Birch in William Balfe's *The Maid of Honour* conducted by Hector Berlioz. The season was a financial disaster.

APRIL 5. J. R. Planché's *New Planet or Harlequin Out of Place* at Haymarket Theatre. Priscilla Norton as Neptune. James Bland as Mars. Julia Bennett as Venus. John Baldwin Buckstone as Mercury and Harlequin. 'There is no playwright,' said *The Observer*, 'to equal to Mr Planché in the production of a burlesque allusive and domestic travesty.'

APRIL 7. Samuel Phelps as Prospero in Shakespeare's *The Tempest* at Sadler's Wells Theatre. 'No player in existence could surpass him in his illustration of the character,' said *The Observer*. The production was on a magnificent scale. *The Athenæum* thought the play had never been better staged. Thirteen-year-old Ellen Terry played Ariel. George Bennett had a big success as Caliban.

PRINCESS'S THEATRE

Mr J. M. MADDOX, Sole Lessee and Manager, Duchess Street, Portland Place.

THE EMINENT TRAGEDIAN

Mr. MACREADY

(Who is engaged for a limited period) will perform CARDINAL WOLSEY, for the Sixth Time for many Years. *This Evening.*

This Evening, WEDNESDAY, October 27th, 1847

Will be presented, Sixth Time for many Years,

SHAKSPERE's HISTORICAL PLAY of

KING HENRY VIIIth

With appropriate Scenery, Dresses, and Appointments.

King Henry the Eighth,	Mr. COOPER
Cardinal Wolsey,	**Mr. MACREADY**
Cardinal Campeius,	Mr. WYNN
Archbishop Cranmer,	Mr. GILBERT
Duke of Buckingham,	Mr. RYDER

Duke of Norfolk, Mr. C. FISHER, Duke of Suffolk, Mr. HOWARD
Earl of Surrey, Mr. CONWAY Lord Chamberlain, Mr. PALMER
Lord Sands, — Mr. COMPTON
Sir Thomas Lovel, Mr. BARKER Sir Henry Guildford, Mr. A. HARRIS
Gardiner Bishop of Winchester — Mr. NEVILLE,
Cromwell, — Mr. JAMES VINING
Surveyor to the Duke of Buckingham, Mr. COURTNEY
Capucius, Mr. TAYLOR Clerk of the Court, Mr. BOLOGNA
Keeper of the Council Chamber, Mr. T. HILL, Brandon, Mr PAUL
Sergeant at Arms, Mr. WATSON King at Arms, Mr. BURTON

NOBLES OF THE COURT.

Messrs. STACY, KNIGHT, BOWTALL, YOUNG, FRANKS, HENRY, WILSON, FOREST, CARTER, WOODBRIDGE, JOHNSON, HARTNELL, GREEN, ELLIS, THOMPSON, &c.

LORDS, BISHOPS, JUDGES, OFFICERS, GUARDS & ATTENDANTS.

Queen Katherine, Miss CUSHMAN

Anne Boleyn,	Miss SUSAN CUSHMAN.
Lady Denny,	Mrs. SELBY
Patience,	Miss A. ROMER

Duchess of Norfolk, Miss HODSON Duchess of Dorset, Miss WEBBER

Notice will be given of the First Appearance of the Distinguished Vocalist, E. BRADY, BOW... Madame

ANNA THILLON

MACREADY's Nights are MONDAYS, WEDNESDAYS & FRIDAYS.

VARIOUS NOVELTIES ARE IN PREPARATION.

Musical Director, Mr. LODER. Leader, Mr. F. EAMES. Stage Director, Mr. EMDEN.

Dress Circle 5s. Boxes 4s. Pit 2s. Gallery 1s. Half-price—Dress Circle 2s. 6d. Boxes 2s. Pit 1s. Gallery 6d.
Private Boxes, £2. 2s. and £1. 11s. 6d. Proscenium Boxes, £2. 12s. 6d.

ORCHESTRA STALLS, (which may be retained the entire evening) 6s.

Doors to be opened at half-past Six and the Performance to commence at 7. Half Price at the End of the Third Act.

Private Boxes, Stalls and Places, may be had at the Box-Office, of Mr. W. MASSINGHAM; of Messrs. MITCHELL, ANDREWS, EBERS, and OLIVIERA, Bond Street; Mr SAMS, St. James's Street; and at the Carlton Library, Regent Street.

W. G. Ross, concert and supper-room singer, made his debut at Cider Cellars and appeared at Vauxhall Gardens in 1847. Ross was famous for a gruesome ballad that told the story of a chimney-sweep who was hanged at Tyburn for his criminal activities.

APRIL 10. The Royal Italian Opera was established at Covent Garden Theatre, opening with two operas by Giuseppe Verdi: **Ernani** and **I Due Foscari**.

MAY 4. Jenny Lind in Giacomo Meyerbeer's **Roberto Il Diavelo** at Her Majesty's Theatre.

> Never did any theatrical event within living memory create such a sensation without and within the walls of a theatre as the debut of last night of Mddle Jenny Lind. But the most important fact is that never was expectation so gloriously realised. *Morning Post*

MAY 13. Jenny Lind in Vincenzo Bellini's **La Sonnambula** at Her Majesty's Theatre.

> Nothing could exceed those fine full rich notes which are peculiar to the Swedish nightingale and which exercise a fascination over an audience, almost magical. Those notes of Jenny Lind so spontaneous, so melodious, so touching must be heard before a notion of them can be formed; there is nothing to which they can be compared. *The Times*

JUNE 26. Carlotta Grisi as Water, Carolina Rosati as Fire and Fanny Cerrito as Air in **The Elements** at Drury Lane Theatre. All three dancers were featured as Earth. Libretto and choreography by Jules Perrot. Music by Bajetti.

JULY 27. Edward Wright, Sarah Woolgar and Emma Harding in J. Sterling Coyne's **How to Settle Accounts with Your Laundress** at Adelphi Theatre. One of the most popular farces of the century. A lady pretends to commit suicide and then seeks refuge at her faithless lover's establishment.

SEPTEMBER 27. Samuel Phelps and Isabella Glyn in Shakespeare's **Macbeth** at Sadler's Wells Theatre

> Mr Phelps's performance was conceived in the highest poetry, with no 'false starts', no spouting, no pointed ranting, no misdirected energy that fires the unreflecting many into sudden admiration. It was all deep, genuine, well-uttered passion and emotion. *News*

NOVEMBER 1. John Baldwin Buckstone and John Pritt Harley in John Maddison Morton's **Box and Cox** at Lyceum Theatre. Adapted from *Une chambre a deux lits* by E. F. Prieur and A. Letorzec. Billed as 'a romance of real life', it was one of the most popular farces of the century. Cox is a journeyman hatter. Box is a journeyman printer. Cox is genteel and sarcastic. Box is furious and vulgar. They occupy the same room: one occupies it by day, the other by night. Neither is aware of the other's existence and thinks he is the sole tenant, and so when they finally meet they both presume the other is an intruder. They then

---

1847

World premieres	Literature	Notes
Alfred De Musset's *Un Caprice* in Paris	Anne Brontë's *Agnes Grey*	Covent Garden Theatre becomes Royal Italian Opera
Giuseppe Verdi's *Macbeth* in Florence	Charlotte Brontë's *Jane Eyre*	Madame Vestris and Charles Matthews manage Lyceum Theatre 1847–55
	Emily Brontë's *Wuthering Heights*	
Births	Charles Dickens' *Dombey and Son* (1847–48)	
George Grossmith, British actor	William Makepeace Thackeray's *Vanity Fair* (1847–48)	**History**
William Terriss, British actor		Factory Act introduces 10-hour day
Ellen Terry, British actress		Mormons found Salt Lake City

discover that they are both engaged to the same widow. Mrs Macnamara played Mrs Bouncer, the housekeeper.

NOVEMBER 29. Ellen Tree as Rosalind in Shakespeare's *As You Like It* at Sadler's Wells Theatre. Tree was praised for her buoyancy, vivacity and sweetness. Her success in New York established the play as a favourite in America.

DECEMBER 7. A special performance of scenes from Shakespeare's plays by the leading actors of the day to raise money to purchase Shakespeare's house in Stratford upon Avon. The three-hour production began with Macready in Henry VI's death scene and closed with Mrs Warner in the statue scene from *The Winter's Tale.*

DECEMBER 27. Madame Vestris in J. R. Planché's *The Golden Branch* at Lyceum Theatre. Extravaganza based on a fairy tale, *Le rameau d'or,* by Madame d'Anois. 'It merits approbation,' said *The Observer,* 'not only on account of its pleasantness but also because a certain vein of didactic morality runs through it, and which will benefit the present season.' Vestris sang 'Poor Joe Miller'.

1848

The legend of a ghost at Drury Lane Theatre began in 1848 when a skeleton with a dagger in its ribs was found behind a walled-in cubby hole.

JANUARY 3. G. V. Brooke in Shakespeare's *Othello* at Olympic Theatre. Macready was surprised at the praise Brooke got. 'He has,' he wrote in his diary, 'no pretensions to genius, judgement, taste or any artistic quality. He has physical advantages but a most common mind, and no real passion.'

It is a pity he should prefer to act Shakespeare, for which he is as little qualified as the company engaged to support him – rather than a good ranting, roaring melodrama which he would play admirably. This would be infinitely better than making a melodrama of Othello.
HENRY MORLEY

JANUARY 17. Charles Kean and Ellen Kean in George W. Lowell's *The Wife's Secret* at Haymarket Theatre. The play was specially commissioned by the Keans for their return to London after a long absence. *The Observer* was not impressed with the play, which was dismissed as a mere vehicle, neither ingenious nor novel.

JANUARY 20. Mr Stuart and Isabella Glyn in Shakespeare's *Macbeth* at Olympic Theatre. Glyn's London debut; she was extremely nervous. *The Athenæum* found her very natural and unaffected and free from rant. The witches played a key part, appearing throughout the production.

FEBRUARY 21. William Charles Macready and Fanny Kemble in Shakespeare's *Macbeth* at Princess's Theatre. Macready was no fan of Kemble's:

Acted Macbeth, I think, with peculiar strength, care and effect, was occasionally disconcerted by the monstrous pretender to theatrical art, who to me, is most unnatural and bad. I don't know her effect on the audience, but cannot think it good.
WILLIAM CHARLES MACREADY, *Diary*

In every one of his characters there is an intense personality of his own that, while one is under the influence, defies all criticism – moments of such overpowering passion, accents of such tremendous power, looks and gestures of such thrilling, piercing meaning, that the excellence of those parts of his performance more than atones for the want of greater unity in conception and smoothness in the entire execution of them. FANNY KEMBLE

World premieres
Alfred de Musset's *Il faut qu'une porte soit ouverte ou fermé* in Paris
Alexandr Ostrovosky's *The Bankrupt* in Moscow

Births
Sydney Grundy, British dramatist
Madge Kendal, British actress, mother of T. W. Robertson
Adelaide Neilson, British actress

Deaths
Emily Brontë, British novelist (b. 1818)
Andrew Ducrow, Belgian-born manager, mime, equestrian, acrobat (b. 1793)

Literature
Mrs Gaskell's *Mary Barton*
Karl Marx and Friedrich Engels' *Communist Manifesto*

Notes
Queen Victoria appoints Charles Kean as director of royal theatricals at Windsor

History
Foundation of the Pre-Raphaelite Brotherhood
Wellington organises defence of London against Chartists amid background of revolution in Paris
Start of Californian gold rush
Boards of Health set up

MARCH 20. Ira Aldridge as Zanga in Dr Young's *The Revenge* and as Mungo in Thomas Dibdin and Isaac Bickerstaffs's *The Padlock* at Surrey Theatre. Aldridge was equally adept in tragedy and farce. *The Morning Advertiser* thought he was excellent. *The Daily Telegraph* thought his performance was a treat of high order.

JUNE 13. Fanny Cerrito as Spring, Carlotta Grisi as Summer, Caroliona Rosati as Autumn and Marie Taglioni as Winter in Jules Perrot's *Quatre Saisons* at Her Majesty's Theatre. The ballerinas could not agree among themselves as to which of them should have the honour of entering last. The ballet master appealed to the theatre manager to decide. His solution was elegantly simple: let the oldest have the honour of coming on last. The dancers were then only too willing to defer to each other.

SEPTEMBER 27. Samuel Phelps as Coriolanus and Isabella Glyn as Volumnia in Shakespeare's *Coriolanus* at Sadler's Wells Theatre. Phelps, worried about his performance, had delayed the opening, but he was still very nervous on the first night, and not at his best.

NOVEMBER 11. Ellen Kean as Viola in Shakespeare's *Twelfth Night* at Haymarket Theatre.

Ellen Kean's Viola is one of those charming impersonations which silence criticism. Skilful distribution of light and shade, mixed gaiety with sadness, naïveté and poetry are the attributes which in this part present her to us as an inimitable actress. *Athenæum*

NOVEMBER 20. Robert and William Brough's *The Enchanted Island* at Adelphi Theatre. Based on Shakespeare's *The Tempest* it burlesqued the revolution in Italy. Trinculo and Stephano were cast as incompetent rebels.

DECEMBER 14. Charles Kean as Valentine and William Creswick as Proteus in Shakespeare's *The Two Gentlemen of Verona* at Haymarket Theatre. Julia Bennett as Sylvia. Robert Keeley as Launce. The text was cut and re-arranged.

DECEMBER 26. Miss Howard and Kathleen Fitzwilliam in J. R. Planché's *The King of the Peacocks* at Lyceum Theatre. Fairy extravaganza based on the Countess D'Anois's *La Princesse Rosette*.

DECEMBER 26. Drury Lane Theatre was converted into a Hippodrome in order to accommodate M. Dejeans's Equestrian Troupe from the Cirque National de Paris.

LEFT

Gustavus V. Brooke in Shakespeare's Othello at Olympic Theatre in 1848. His Shakespearian roles also included Hamlet, Shylock and Richard III. He was imprisoned for debt. Upon his release he set sail on the SS London in 1866 for a second visit to Australia, but the badly overloaded ship sank in the Bay of Biscay, and Brooke was drowned.

1849

JUNE 5. Charles Kean and Ellen Kean in Shakespeare's **Macbeth** at Haymarket Theatre.

It is in presenting Lady Macbeth as a woman composed of good and evil, like all humanity, not an incarnate fiend, that Mrs Kean's performance is entitled to the highest degree of commendation. *Observer*

JUNE 29. Charles Kean and Ellen Kean in John Westland Marston's **Stratmore** at Haymarket Theatre. The government determines to enforce religious conformity in Scotland. Blood is shed.

In the closing scene Mr Kean exhibited a depth of earnestness and a degree of passion indicating art of a very high order. Mrs Kean was one of those exquisite and touching delineations of female character to which she alone can give full effect. *Observer*

JULY 12. John Baldwin Buckstone and Mrs Fitzwilliam in John Baldwin Buckstone's **An Alarming Sacrifice** at Haymarket Theatre. Farce. A country servant wants to discover if she is loved for herself or for the money she has unexpectedly inherited from her former employer.

To carry drollery to its furthest point seemed the height of Buckstone's ambition … To see him in Sir Benjamin Backbite in *The School for Scandal* was a rare treat for those who were not nice as to the boundary-line between comedy and farce … It is true that in almost every part he was Buckstone; it is equally so that the public did not wish him to be anyone else … He knew he was the pet of the audience, and never lost a chance of taking it into his confidence by a sort of advertising look, which seemed to say, 'Attention! Something droll is about to happen.' JOHN WESTLAND MARSTON, *Our Recent Actors*

JULY 25. Benefit for James Kenney at Drury Lane Theatre. Kenney was unable to attend: he had died that very morning.

OCTOBER 22. Samuel Phelps and Isabella Glyn in Shakespeare's **Antony and Cleopatra** at Sadler's Wells Theatre. Phelps played the original text with great success for a record 22 performances. *The Illustrated London News* said Glyn's classical statuesque poses were 'the most superb thing ever witnessed on the modern stage. Antony might well lose the world for such a woman.'

The interest of this magnificent play is decidedly of an epic character. It requires an audience specially educated to appreciate its sublimity and beauty. *Athenæum*

1849

World premieres
Eugène Scribe's *Adrienne Lecouvreur* in Paris
Giuseppe Verdi's *Luisa Miller* in Naples

Births
August Strindberg, Swedish dramatist
Frances Hodgson Burnett, Anglo-American playwright and author

Deaths
James Kenney, British dramatist (b. 1780)
Edgar Allan Poe, American novelist, poet (b. 1809)
Anne Brontë, author (b. 1820)

Literature
Charles Dickens' *David Copperfield* (1849–50)

Notes
A riot at Astor Place Theatre in New York prevents Macready from performing

History
Major cholera epidemic kills 14,000 in London
Rome proclaimed a republic
The Punjab is annexed to the British Empire

Ellen and Charles Kean in Shakespeare's Macbeth at Haymarket Theatre in 1849. Kean was a stickler for historical accuracy; his wife was a stickler for Victorian propriety, and, as we can see, she dressed accordingly.

The harmony which Miss Glyn effected between so many lighter moods and the imperial dignity of her more tragic passages, especially that of her death, was surprisingly fine. In coquetry, in anger, in cunning, in subjugation, and in her royal end, she was still the same Cleopatra.
JOHN WESTLAND MARSTON, *Our Recent Actors*

DECEMBER 26. J. R. Planché's *The Island of Jewels* at Lyceum Theatre. Extravaganza designed by William Beverley: fantasy, farce, songs, dances, ballets, puns, transformation scenes, operatic parodies, Shakespearian parodies. The finale was magical: the leaves of a palm tree opened to discover six fairies, each supporting a coronet of jewels. 111 performances.

The 1850s

DUET,
SUNG IN THE GRAND SPECTACLE OF THE
"**PRINCE OF HAPPY LAND**,"
BY MADAME VESTRIS & MISS S?. GEORGE.

1850

MARCH 20. Samuel Phelps and Isabella Glyn in Shakespeare's **Macbeth** at Sadler's Wells Theatre. The witches were cut to three. 'Mr Phelps's Macbeth,' said *The Illustrated London News*, 'is entitled to take rank with the most artistic assumptions of the day … In the murder and banquet scenes she [Glyn] was self-possessed, appalling, sustained, triumphant – the very heroine of crime.'

APRIL 11. Benjamin Webster as Dr Primrose and Maria Ann Keeley as Mrs Primrose in J. Stirling Coyne's adaptation of Oliver Goldsmith's **The Vicar of Wakefield** at Strand Theatre. Coyne's version was more farcical than Tom Taylor's version.

JULY 12. Julia Glover at her Farewell Benefit Night at Drury Lane Theatre played Mrs Malaprop in Richard Brinsley Sheridan's **The Rivals**. William Farren as Sir Anthony Absolute. Louisa Nisbett as Lydia Languish. Helena Faucit as Julia. Farren issued the following circular in advance:

> She has devoted her earnings to the support of five generations: her grandfather, her parents, her husband, her children and grandchildren, have successively been mainly dependent on her exertions. The object of the proposed benefit is, in the first place, to offer testimony of public respect to merit so rare; and, in the second place, to secure the means of making comfortable the remaining years of a life worn by long toil, and already beginning to sink under the effects of natural decay.

SEPTEMBER 2. Samuel Phelps in Shakespeare's **Hamlet** at Sadler's Wells Theatre. *Tallis Dramatic Magazine* thought his performance 'elaboratively impressive, meditative, courtly and decidedly one of the best embodiments of the character.'

SEPTEMBER 28. Charles Kean began his management of the Princess's Theatre with Shakespeare's **Twelfth Night**. Ellen Kean as Viola. Mr Meadows as Malvolio. Mr Drinkwater as Orsino. Robert Keeley as Sir Andrew Aguecheek. Maria Ann Keeley as Maria. John Pritt Harley as Feste. Miss Phillips as Olivia. Joseph Addison as Sir Toby Belch. 'Never,' said *The Leader*, 'do we remember to have seen *Twelfth Night* so well played; never perhaps was it relished with such gusto. It showed how much could be done by casting a play well.'

> Malvolio though one of the principal characters in *Twelfth Night* is by no means a thankful part. There is apt to be a dry uncouthness about him, even when he is represented by an able artist, which wearies more than it amuses. Mr Meadows played Malvolio with greater ease than is usually shown and by a jaunty courtliness gave an animation to a character which relieved his formality.   *Observer*

NOVEMBER 5. C. V. Brooke and Helen Faucit in Westland Marston's **Philip of France and Marie de Melanie** at Olympic Theatre. Philip wants to divorce his wife to marry Marie. When the Pope refuses, Philip suggests Marie should become his mistress. She refuses.

> Miss Helen Faucit is a rich boon to the public, for since the days of Siddons and O'Neill she is the most worthy exponent of the lofty poetical drama. She is the Rachel of the English stage. Her fine appreciation of the poetry is equalled by her power of characterisation and the exquisite melody of her voice.   *Literary Gazette*

LEFT

J. R. Planche's The Prince of Happy Land was performed at Lyceum Theatre in 1851.

World premieres
Richard Wagner's *Lohengrin* in Weimar

Births
Robert Louis Stevenson, British novelist
Hamo Thornycroft, London-born sculptor

Deaths
William Wordsworth, British poet (b. 1770)

Notes
Charles Kean and Robert Keeley assume management of the Princess's Theatre
Crystal Palace is built in Hyde Park by Sir Joseph Paxton for the Great Exhibition

History
Sir Robert Peel dies after falling from a horse on Constitution Hill
Roman Catholic hierarchy is established in Britain
Alfred Tennyson becomes Poet Laureate
Lehman Brothers is set up, initially as cotton trading firm, in Alabama

NOVEMBER 21. Madame Celeste, Paul Bedford, George Honey and H Hughes in Robert Brough and Mr Bridgeman's **Jessie Gray** at Adelphi Theatre. Cruel aristocrat is determined that his nephew (who has disguised himself as a music master in order to go courting) shall not marry a plebeian.

NOVEMBER 20. Isabella Glyn in John Webster's **The Duchess of Malfi** at Sadler's Wells Theatre. George Bennett as Bosola. Samuel Phelps as Duke Ferdinand. Not performed since 1707, the posters carried lengthy tributes to the play's qualities from William Hazlitt and Charles Lamb. The horrors were severely curtailed; but *The Times* still thought that, 'the revolting nature of the story, and the anti-climax of the fifth act were beyond the reach of the reformer's skill.' Glyn, it was said, 'exhibited a figure of voluptuous majesty, a mingling of dazzling beauty and intellectual command.'

She [Miss Glyn] rises into the majesty and intensity of a Pasta or a Siddons. Greater acting is impossible – more thrilling, terrible, yet pathetic. *Illustrated London News*

Instead of holding the mirror up to nature, the drama holds the mirror to Madame Tussauds. GEORGE HENRY LEWIS

DECEMBER 4. Madame Vestris, Charles Mathews and George Vining in J. R. Planché's **Day of Reckoning** at Lyceum Theatre. The working man versus the aristocracy. The naturalness of the acting was much admired.

A noble, loving, suffering woman, she [Vestris] stands there, represented with a truth, a grace, a gentle pathos I have no epithets to characterise. GEORGE HENRY LEWES, *Leader*

‘ *The notion that the stage is a mere source of frivolous amusement never crossed the mind of Charles Kean, industriously promulgated, not only by the enemies of theatre, but by the great body of modern dramatists.* ’

The Times

1851

FEBRUARY 3. William Charles Macready in Shakespeare's ***King Lear*** at Haymarket Theatre.

> Most anxious to make my last performance one to be remembered. Nervous, anxious and uneasy. Went to the theatre and collected myself, preparing for a great effort. Acted Lear, certainly in a superior style to what I ever did before. Power, passion, discrimination, tenderness constantly kept in mind.
> WILLIAM CHARLES MACREADY, *Diary*

FEBRUARY 14. John Baldwin Buckstone's ***Good for Nothing*** at Haymarket Theatre. The programme also included Mr Stuart as Charles II and Mr Davenport as Rochester in ***Presented at Court***, and William Douglas Jerrold's ***Black Ey'd Susan***.

FEBRUARY 26. William Charles Macready took his farewell in Shakespeare's ***Macbeth*** at Haymarket Theatre. Mrs Warner as Lady Macbeth. Samuel Phelps as Macduff. Seats in a box cost £3. The audience, many in tears, stood, waved hats and handkerchiefs, thunder-stamped and shouted: 'Macready! Macready! Bravo!' A voice in the gallery yelled: 'The last of the Mohicans!' Macready was 57 years old. He was glad he would never act again. The last words in his journal were 'Thank God!'

> As I look back on my long, professional career I see in it but one continuous record of indulgence and support extended to me, cheering me in my onward progress and upholding me in mortifying circumstances. WILLIAM CHARLES MACREADY in his farewell speech.

BELOW

Child prodigies: 5-year-old Ellen and 6-year-old Kate Bateman in scenes from Shakespeare in 1851.

OVERLEAF

A caricature of the opera boxes at Her Majesty's Theatre during the time of the Great Exhibition in 1851.

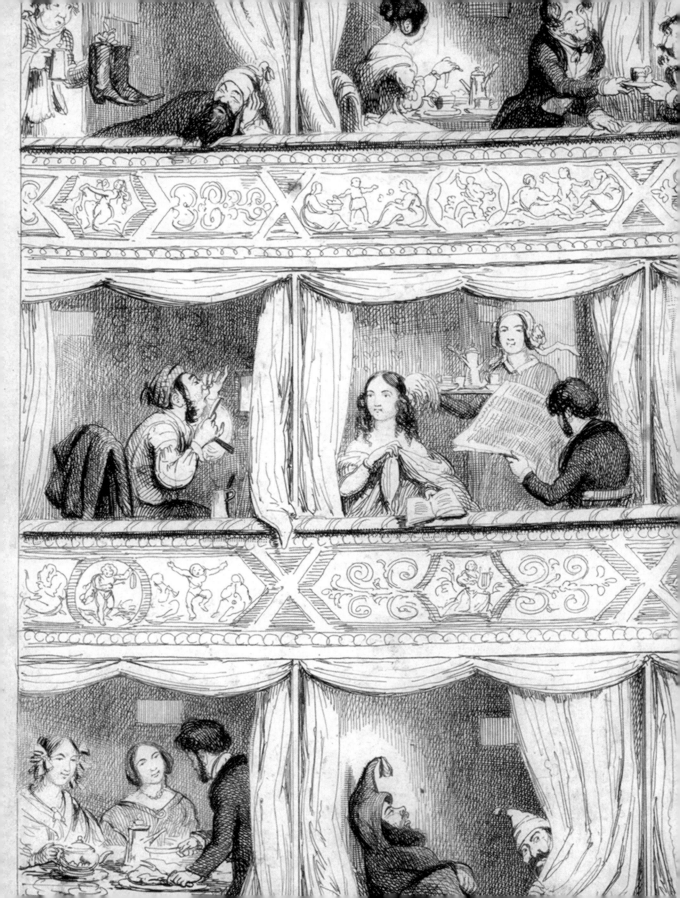

Red Rufus or Harlequin Fair, Fiction and Fantasy was the Christmas pantomime at Olympic Theatre in 1851.

MARCH 6. Charles Kean and Ellen Kean in Dion Boucicault's ***Love in a Maze*** at Princess's Theatre. Colonel on his wedding day leaves his bride at the church to go off to fight a duel with a Lord, who turns out to be the ex-lover of the bride.

> I never saw anything more exciting. The Keans acted beautifully and she acted really wonderfully in the most crucial and alarming moments, literally keeping one in a state of terror and suspense, so that one quite held one's breath, and was quite trembling when the play came to an end. QUEEN VICTORIA, *Journal*

MARCH 17. Charles Kean as the villain and Ellen Kean as the heroine in John Oxenford's adaptation of Alexandre Dumas' ***Pauline*** at Princess's Theatre. 'The evident object of this drama is to inspire a continuous feeling of terror,' said *The Observer*. Queen Victoria was seen clinging to the curtains of her box when the heroine fell into the clutches of the murderer.

JUNE 2. Rachel in Racine's ***Phèdre*** at St James's Theatre. 'With one exception on the English stage we have no actress capable of illustrating the heroic and pathetic,' said *The Illustrated London News*.

AUGUST 25. William Farren in T. W. Robertson's ***A Night's Adventure or Highways and Byways*** at Olympic Theatre. The play ran only four nights. 'It was a damn bad play,' said Farren. 'Not as bad as the acting,' said Robertson. The retort did not improve their relationship.

SEPTEMBER 15. Samuel Phelps in Shakespeare's ***Timon of Athens*** at Sadler's Wells Theatre. 'The intensity of such misanthropy is scarcely to be fully interpreted by the over-loud declamation used as a substitute for passion,' said *The Athenæum*. 'Thus whenever it occurred it was a mistake: – though on the whole the part was inoffensively acted.'

SEPTEMBER 29. Kate Bateman made her debut as the Infant Phenomenon in an adaptation of Charles Dickens' **Nicholas Nickleby** at Surrey Theatre.

AUGUST 30. Kate Bateman and her sister Ellen Bateman in scenes from Shakespeare at St James's Theatre. They acted Lady Macbeth, the fifth act of **Richard III** and the trial scene from **The Merchant of Venice**. They also acted in more suitable roles for their age in Eugène Scribe's **The Young Children**. The Bateman sisters were only eight and six years old. They performed under the auspices of P. T. Barnum, and many people were worried that they were being exploited.

> Nothing is left but the wearisome absurdity of such big words in such little mouths.
> HENRY MORLEY, *Journal of a London Playgoer*

OCTOBER 2. Charles Mathews as Affable Hawk in George Henry Lewis' **The Game of Speculation** at Lyceum Theatre. Hawk is willing to sacrifice his daughter to pay his creditors. The production did such good business that the actors were given an extra week's salary.

DECEMBER 26. W. Shalders in Nelson Lee's pantomime, **Red Rufus or Harlequin Fact, Fiction and Fancy** at Olympic Theatre. Miss Rawlings as Fiction. Mr Stubborn as Fact. Miss Adams as Fancy. Red Rufus was the nickname of King William II.

DECEMBER 30. Madame Vestris in J. R. Planché's **Prince of Happy Land or The Fawn of the Forest** at Lyceum Theatre. Fairy extravaganza based on Countess D'Anois' *Le biche au bois.*

> ‘ *I can spin out these rough and tumble dramas as a hen lays eggs. It's a degrading occupation but more money has been made out of a guano than out of poetry.* ’
> DION BOUCICAULT

THE

CORSICAN BROTHERS.

OR

LA

VENDETTA

1852

JANUARY 16. Isabella Glynn as Julia in Sheridan Knowles' *The Hunchback* at Drury Lane Theatre. 'We never knew her more impulsive or energetic,' said *The Illustrated London News*. 'In many parts the conception of the character is peculiar, but she justifies it by her admirable execution.'

FEBRUARY 9. Charles Kean as John and Ellen Kean as Constance in Shakespeare's **King John** at Princess's Theatre. Alfred Wigan as Faulconbridge. John Ryder as Hubert. Kate Terry as Arthur. The production was a series of beautiful pictures. The costumes, weapons, banners and decorations were historically accurate, and there were brilliant recreations of the Gate of Angiers, the battlefields, and the orchards of Swinstead Abbey. King John's rejection of Rome and the Papal Legate was greeted with cheers from boxes, pit and gallery.

We seldom see nowadays such a complete abandonment of the actress to the spirit of the scene as the torrent of woe with which she [Mrs Kean] bewailed the loss of her son. It was grief exulting in its own abundance, and claiming reverence from all who beheld it. *Spectator*

The scene between the young Prince (Kate Terry) and Hubert (Mr Ryder, the epitome of rough pity and manly devotedness) was an excellent example of really fine, natural and powerful pathetic acting. *Illustrated London News*

It is almost worth while to be past middle life in order to have seen Miss Kate Terry in Arthur. SIR GEORGE OTTO TREVELYAN, *Life of Lord Macaulay*

FEBRUARY 24. Charles Kean as Louis and Fabien dei Franchi in Dion Boucicault's **The Corsican Brothers** at Princess's Theatre. Alfred Wigan as Chateau Renaud. The production, one of the biggest successes of the year, famous for its gorgeous tableaux and supernatural effects, was genuinely scary. The ferocious duel in the Bois de Boulogne was particularly exciting. Queen Victoria enjoyed the production so much that she went to see it four times. Such was its popularity that there were versions of the story at six other London theatres.

The tableau of the Duel, which Fabien witnesses, almost immediately after the vanishing of the ghost, was beautifully grouped and quite touching. The whole, lit by blue light and dimmed with gauze, had an unearthly effect, and was most impressive and creepy.
QUEEN VICTORIA, *Journal*

She [Queen Victoria] might just as well go to the salons and witness blood and murder pieces as this silly, wild and impossible farrago. Good heavens! It seems incredible that in a Christian land such things can be. *News*

MARCH 6. Robert Keeley and Maria Ann Keeley in Tom Taylor's **Our Clerks** at Princess's Theatre. Farce. Two clerks, flirting with two nannies, have to hide nannies and their respective babies in a cupboard when their boss returns earlier than expected.

MARCH 15. Ira Aldridge as Aaron in Shakespeare's **Titus Andronicus** at Britannia Theatre. A radical re-write. The play had not been produced for 128 years. Aldridge made Aaron the hero. He deleted the rape of Lavinia, the cutting of her hands and tongue, all the decapitations, and the gross language. Titus was virtuous. Tamora was chaste. Her sons were well behaved. Only Saturninus remained true to Shakespeare. Aldridge 'rants less

LEFT

Dion Boucicault's The Corsican Brothers or La Vendetta at Princess's Theatre in 1852 was one of his greatest successes.

157

than almost any tragedian we know,' said one critic. 'He makes no vulgar appeal to the gallery. He is thoroughly natural, easy and sensible.'

Mr Aldridge's presentation of the Moor was exceedingly clever and effective; his performance was remarkable for energy, tempered by dignity and discretion. *Theatrical Journal*

APRIL 12. Charles Mathews in Henry Lewes and Charles Mathews' *A Chain of Events* at Lyceum Theatre. Drama, farce, spectacle and ballet. The shipwreck in the storm was the high spot.

APRIL 12. Benjamin Webster in Mark Lemon's *Mind Your Own Business* at Haymarket Theatre. Webster had a big success playing a drunkard.

JUNE 14. Dion Boucicault made his acting debut in London in his own melodrama, *The Vampire: A Phantasm* at Princess's Theatre. This spectacular and supernatural story was set in three acts and over three centuries. The vampire was crushed and buried beneath a falling tower. 'The accumulation of horrors becomes somewhat wearisome,' said *The Observer*.

The extreme point of inanity … tedious trash … Though it may be too dull to pervert the tastes of those who witness its vapid extravagancies, it has power to bring discredit on the most genial of arts. *Examiner*

JUNE 20. Emil Devrient in Goethe's *Faust* at St James's Theatre. Faust was upstaged by Herr Khun's Mephistopheles.

SEPTEMBER 1. Samuel Phelps as Parolles and Miss Cooper as Helena in Shakespeare's *All's Well That Ends Well* at Sadler's Wells Theatre. The production's success led to the play's critical reappraisal.

SEPTEMBER 13. George Frederick Cooke in Edward Fitzball's adaptation of Harriet Beecher Stowe's *Uncle Tom's Cabin or Negro Life in America* at Olympic Theatre.

It has been somewhat hastily concocted – and indeed is very roughly done. It is in two acts; and in the necessity of extreme compression, both characters and situations are condensed and blended, and so many modifications and adaptations are introduced that little besides the general colouring and bare outline remain of the original story. Even that is changed in its effect by the contrivance of a fortunate catastrophe. *Athenæum*

OCTOBER 18. An African opera troupe appeared in William Brough's adaptation of Harriet Beecher Stowe's *Uncle Tom's Crib or Negro life in London* at Strand Theatre.

OCTOBER 18. *Off to the Diggens or London Scheme in 1852* at Surrey Theatre. A slice of life: picturesque workers with spades, pick-axes, cradles and lynch-law weapons.

OCTOBER 25. Samuel Phelps in Shakespeare's *Henry V* at Sadler's Wells Theatre. It seemed as if the soldiers were marching three abreast. Madame Tussaud had provided dummies which were attached to either side of each actor.

1852

World premieres
Alexandre Dumas's *La Dame aux Camélias* in Paris

Births
George Edwardes, Irish-born English theatre manager
Lady Augusta Gregory, Irish dramatist, theatre manager
William Poel, British director, actor

Deaths
Junius Brutus Booth, Anglo-American actor (b. 1796)
Nikolai Gogol, Russian dramatist (b. 1809)
Duke of Wellington, British General and Prime Minister (b. 1769)

Literature
Charles Dickens' *Bleak House* (1852–53)

History
King's Cross Station, Europe's biggest, is completed
Louis Napoleon assumes title of Emperor of France
Great Ormond Street Hospital admits first patient

ROYAL PRINCESS'S THEATRE.

OXFORD STREET.

UNDER THE MANAGEMENT OF

Mr. CHARLES KEAN,

No. 3, TORRINGTON SQUARE.

SHAKESPEARE'S HISTORICAL PLAY OF

KING JOHN

Will be Repeated This Evening, on Friday and Monday Next.

THIS EVENING, WEDNESDAY, MARCH 3rd, 1852

Will be performed SHAKESPEARE's Historical Play of

KING JOHN

The DRESSES, WEAPONS, BANNERS and DECORATIONS are Selected from the following Authorities :—

MEYRICK's "Ancient Armour;" C. H. SMITH's "Ancient Costume of Great Britain;" PLANCHE's "Costume of King John;" STRUTT's "Dresses and Habits of the People of England;" FAIRHOLT's "Costume in England;" FOSBROKE's "Encyclopædia of Antiquities;" DUGDALE's "Monasticon Anglicanum;" SHAW's "Dresses and Decorations;" STOTHARD's "Monumental Effigies;" PUGIN's "Glossary of Ecclesiastical Ornament and Costume;" THE HERALD OFFICE; LECOMTE's "Costumes Civiles et Militaires de la Monarchie Francaise;" MONTFAUCON's "Monarchie Francaise;" HERBE's "Costumes Francais;" WILLEMIN's "Monumens Francais."

King John,	Mr. CHARLES KEAN,
Prince Henry, *(his Son, afterwards King Henry III.)*	Miss ROBERTSON,
Arthur, Duke of Bretagne, *(Son of Geoffrey, late Duke of Bretagne, Elder Brother of King John)*	Miss KATE TERRY,
William Mareshall, Earl of Pembroke,	Mr. G. EVERETT,
Geoffrey Fitzpeter, Earl of Essex, *(Chief Justiciary of England)*	Mr. STACEY,
William Longsword, Earl of Salisbury,	Mr. JAMES VINING,
Robert Bigot, Earl of Norfolk,	Mr. BRAZIER,
Hubert de Burgh, *(Chamberlain to the King)*	Mr. RYDER,
William Plantagenet, Earl de Warrenne,	Mr. CROMPTON,
William, Earl of Arundel, Mr. COLLIS, Robert, Baron Fitzwalter,	Mr. MARKS,
Bohun, Earl of Hereford, Mr. SANDFORD, Vere, Earl of Oxford,	Mr. MERCER,
Robert de Ros, Mr. BARNES, Richard de Percy, Mr. TURIN, Gilbert de Clare,	Mr. LYGO,
King John's Pages,	Miss J. LOVELL and Miss HASTINGS,
Sheriff of Northampton, Mr. LANE, 1st Knight,	Mr. PAULO,
2nd Knight, Mr. HARDING, English Herald,	Mr. ROLLESTON,
Robert Faulconbridge, *(Son to Sir Robert Faulconbridge)*	Mr. MEADOWS,
Philip Faulconbridge, *(his Half-Brother, Bastard Son to King Richard I.)*	Mr. ALFRED WIGAN,
Attendants on Hubert,	Mr. TRAVIS and Mr. BURDETT,
James Gurney, *(Servant to Lady Faulconbridge)* Mr. STOAKES, Peter of Pomfret, *(a Prophet)*	Mr. PARSLOE,
Archbishop, Bishops, Mitred Abbots, Monks, Esquires, Standard Bearers, Heralds, Attendants, &c. &c.	
Philip Augustus, King of France,	Mr. C. FISHER,
Lewis, the Dauphin,	Mr. STANTON,
Archduke of Austria, Mr. F. COOKE, Giles, Viscomte de Melun,	Mr. J. F. CATHCART,
Chatelain D'Arras, Mr. STRINGER, Thibaud, Count de Blois,	Mr. HAINES,
Eustache de Neuville, Mr. WARNER, Chatelain de St. Omer,	Mr. MORGAN,
Baldwin de Bretel, Mr. LEBRUN, Bartholomew de Roye,	Mr. PARKE,
Ralph de Beaumont, Mr. HUNTER, French Herald,	Mr. DALY,
Chatillon, Count de Nevers, *(Ambassador from France to King John)*	Mr. C. WHEATLEIGH,
Cardinal Pandulph, *(the Pope's Legate)*	Mr. GRAHAM,
Attendants on the Cardinal, Notarius Apostolicus, Cross Bearers, Bishops, Monks, Knights Templars, &c.	
Governor of Angiers,	Mr. ADDISON,
Citizens, Messrs. Daniels, M'Kemma, Stowell, Dalrymple, Coleburn, Perry, Jones, Shepherd, Wills, &c., &c.	
Knights Templars, Barons, Austrian Knights, Esquires, Trumpeters, Standard Bearers, Attendants, &c.	
Queen Elinor, *(Widow of King Henry the Second, and Mother to King John)*	Miss PHILLIPS,
The Lady Constance, *(Mother to Arthur)*	Mrs. CHARLES KEAN,
Blanche, *(Daughter to Alphonso, King of Castile, and Niece to King John)*	Miss MURRAY,
Lady Faulconbridge, *(Mother to the Bastard and Robert Faulconbridge)*	Mrs. W. DALY,
Ladies,	Misses BRADY, MAURICE, MIRE...

The audience at Sadler's Wells is not the most critical in the world but it has a firm belief in Shakespeare and it perfectly understands the strong and spirited in histrionic art. Mr Phelps touches his hearers in the right place and they wake up to the glories of St Crispin's Day as if the battle were to be fought over again.
The Times

Henry V is, however, not a good acting piece … Had it not been for the billing of the spectacle, and the extreme friendliness of the audience who were disposed to applaud everything to the echo, the revival might not have fared as well as it did.   *Observer*

NOVEMBER 16. Charles Mathews and Mr Suter in **Those Dear Blacks** at Lyceum Theatre. Farce. An emancipated slave employs a white man to be his servant, but the white man is so inefficient that he has to do all the work himself.

NOVEMBER 20. Fanny Stirling as Peg Woffington in Tom Taylor's **Masks and Faces** at Haymarket Theatre. An attempt to redeem Woffington's

reputation. Benjamin Webster played Triplet, the starving poet.

NOVEMBER 22. Equestrian production of Harriet Beecher Stowe's **Uncle Tom's Cabin** at Astley's Amphitheatre.

NOVEMBER 29. Alfred Wigan as George, Madame Celeste as Cassy and Mrs Woolgar as Eliza in Mark Lemon's **Slave Life**, an adaptation of Harriet Beecher Stowe's *Uncle Tom's Cabin*, at Adelphi Theatre. Lemon introduced new characters.

DECEMBER 27. Mme Vestris in J. R. Planché's **The Good Woman in the Wood** at Lyceum Theatre. Fairy extravaganza. Designer: William Beverley.

The fairies have had millions of worshippers, hundreds of poets, and one supreme artist, and that artist is William Beverley. Mme Vestris, to whose taste the public owes so much (and cheerfully acknowledges the debt!) was in wonderful voice.
GEORGE HENRY LEWES, *Leader*

1853

FEBRUARY 14. Charles Kean and Ellen Kean in Shakespeare's **Macbeth** at Princess's Theatre. The play was set in the Norman Conquest period. Kean played Macbeth as a Scottish warrior, and wore an eagle feather in his headdress. Banquo's ghost had a luminous face. Musicians played at the banquet. The décor was influenced by King's Cross railway station, which had opened in 1852.

Mr Kean's Macbeth is considerably reduced and mellowed in style. The level passages are many – and finely delivered in that low or whispering and thrilling tones by which he often reminds us of his great father.   *Athenaeum*

MARCH 28. J. R. Planché's **Mr Buckstone's Ascent of Mount Parnassus** at Haymarket Theatre. A panoramic extravaganza in one act.

APRIL 25. Helen Faucit in Robert Browning's **Colombe's Birthday** at Haymarket Theatre. A poem rather than a drama. 'Whether the taste of the public for so refined a creation on the stage is yet formed, remains to be seen,' said *The Athenæum*.

MAY 1. Frederick Robson in Francis Talfourd's burlesque: **Macbeth Somewhat Removed from the Text** at Olympic Theatre.

MAY 14. Giorgio Ronconi in the London premiere of Giuseppe Verdi's **Rigoletto** at Covent Garden Theatre. Mario Sammarco as Mantua. Angiolina Bosio as Gilda. Rossini recognised Verdi's genius. The London critics did not. 'His present work is rather worse than better,' said *The Morning Post*. 'The most feeble, the most uninspired, the barest and the most destitute of ingenious contrivance, with little likelihood of maintaining its place on the stage,' said *The Times*.

Rigoletto cannot be franked, however, as a masterpiece; it is full of plagiarisms and faults; and yet it abounds with the most captivating music. *Illustrated London News*

JUNE 13. Ellen Kean in Lord Byron's **Sardanapalus** at Princess's Theatre. A panorama of Assyria: the play became a vehicle for a series of costly and elaborate tableaux based on the recent excavations at Nineveh and the researches of Mr Layard.

JUNE 15. **The Battle of Waterloo** at Astley's Amphitheatre. 110 performances.

JUNE 20. Madame Celeste, Leigh Murray and Frederick Wigan in Dion Boucicault's **Genevieve or the Reign of Terror** at Adelphi Theatre. Can Marie Antoinette be saved from the guillotine? Adaptation of Alexandre Dumas' *Le chevalier de la maison rouge*. *The Examiner* said that Celeste 'acted with that high finish that elevates even melodramatic acting to the dignity of histrionic art'.

' *Every reader of Shakespeare is disposed to regard the Midsummer Night's Dream as the most essentially unactable of all his play.* '

Examiner

OCTOBER 8. Samuel Phelps as Bottom in Shakespeare's **A Midsummer Night's Dream** at Sadler's Wells Theatre. The scenes melted one into another. The dream-like effects were created by gaslight and green gauzes. Puck was played by a little boy. Phelps presented Bottom as a man in a dream from the very start of the play and even when he was playing Pyramus in the mock-tragedy.

OCTOBER 13. Charles Selby's **Hotel Charges or How to Cook a Biffin** at Adelphi Theatre. A captain deludes an hotelier into believing that he is a journalist working for *The Times*. The comedy was based on recent letters to *The Times* concerning the exorbitant charges hotels were asking.

OCTOBER 17. J. R. Planché's **The Camp at the Olympic** at Olympic Theatre. The gods argue over the merits of Tragedy, Comedy, Farce, Opera, Burlesque, Melodrama and Spectacle. The extravaganza was followed by Tom Taylor's **Plot and**

Passion, a spy story set in the Bonaparte era. A woman falls in love with the man she must betray. John Emery played Fauché, Napoleon's Minister of Police. Frederick Robson played Fauché's secretary.

Mr Robson embodied in his presentment by turns the most consummate villainy, the most artful duplicity, the deepest emotion, the truest love, the bitterest revenge and the most callous indifference. It may be said that of all our present actors, though one of the least in body, Mr Robson is one of the greatest in style, power, purity of expression, and perhaps, intelligence. *Athenæum*

1854

FEBRUARY 20. Charles Kean in Shakespeare's *Richard III* at Princess's Theatre. The playbill listed a formidable array of authorities for its historical research, but, unfortunately, the diminutive tents for Richard and Richmond on the Bosworth battlefield looked like shower baths.

MARCH 20. O. Smith, Robert Keeley, Benjamin Webster, Leigh Murray, Madame Celeste and Miss Woolgar in Tom Taylor and Charles Reade's *Two Loves and a Life* at Adelphi Theatre. The Jacobites plot rebellion. Meanwhile, two women fall in love with the same man.

We have here all the vulgar elements of an Adelphi drama, lifted far above the regions of vulgarity, the oldest tricks of the stage being made new and striking by some touch which sets the stamp of genius upon them.
HENRY MORLEY, *Journal of a London Playgoer*

MARCH 20. Walter Lacy and Maria Lacy in William Bayle Bernard's *A Storm in a Teacup* at Princess's Theatre. Husband presumes a letter comes from his wife's ex-lover. She presumes the letter comes from his ex-lover.

APRIL 19. David Fisher and Carlotta Leclercq in Dion Boucicault's *Faust and Marguerite* at Princess's Theatre. Charles Kean as Mephistopheles.

Mr Charles Kean is a born spectacle-maker … Faust and Marguerite will draw the eyes of the town; especially the eyes that have the least brains behind them. It is the very triumph of vulgar sensationalism, uninformed by a spark of genius. *Punch*

The tawdry nature of the piece in general was redeemed by his acting of Mephistopheles. The contempt of this personage for human failings and inconsistencies was blended with a sense of so much amusement at them, and the satirical comments were uttered with so much dry intelligence, that the sinister Mephistopheles became far more diverting than many characters in set comedy. Now and then, however, there was a revelation of something terrible in the grotesque individuality – like the gleam which suddenly comes into the eye of a playful cat at the sight of a bird – which made the entire effect unique. JOHN WESTLAND MARSTON, *Our Recent Actors*

MAY 20. Leigh Murray, Madame Celeste and Benjamin Webster in Charles Selby's *The Marble Heart* at Adelphi Theatre. Parisian femme fatale destroys young sculptor. Intellectual satire on fashionable society based on *Les filles de marbre* by M. M. Barrière and Thiboust. The drama was heavy-going and lasted as long as *Hamlet*.

AUGUST 14. Charles Dickens' *Hard Times* at Strand Theatre. The adaptation provided a happy ending.

World premieres

Victorien Sardou's *La Taverne* in Paris

Births

Oscar Wilde, Anglo-Irish dramatist

Leoš Janáček, Czech composer

Francis Wilson, American actor and comedian

Arthur Rimbeau, French poet

Deaths

Charles Kemble, British actor, younger brother of Sarah Siddons (b. 1775)

Literature

Mrs Gaskill's *North and South* (1854–55)

Charles Dickens' *Hard Times*

Walt Whitman's *Leaves of Grass*

Notes

Crystal Palace re-opens on new site at Sydenham

Alhambra Palace is built

History

Crimean War begins

The Charge of the Light Brigade in the Battle of Balaklava

OCTOBER 2. Thomas Mead and Isabella Glyn in Tom Taylor and Charles Reade's **The King's Rival** at St James's Theatre. George Vandenhoff as King Charles II.

This sort of drama is frequent on the French stage, but the English public has yet to learn its proprieties; and in the present instance, the difficulty was increased by the grossness of some of the incidents in which Nell Gwynne (Mrs Seymour) is introduced. *Illustrated London News*

OCTOBER 16. Frederick Robson in Tom Taylor's **A Blighted Being** at Olympic Theatre. One-act farce. It was Robson's ability to be both droll and pathetic at one and the same time that made him so popular with audiences.

OCTOBER 21. Samuel Phelps in Shakespeare's **Pericles** at Sadler's Wells Theatre. Edith Heraud as Marina. 'There's not much scope for acting,' said *The Theatrical Journal*. The play succeeded only because of the magnificent costumes and scenery. The production omitted Gower and bowdlerised the brothel scene.

An admirably painted panorama slides before our eyes and the whole theatre seems to be in the course of actual transportation to the triumph of Ephesus which is the crowning glory of the play. HENRY MORLEY, *Journal of a London Playgoer*

Mr Phelps is the best commentator of Shakespeare the people have ever had – a commentator that instead of obscuring the text, as commentators generally do, throws a new light upon it. *Lloyd's Weekly*

NOVEMBER 20. Miss Wyndham in Mark Lemon's **The Railway Belle** at Adelphi Theatre. Broad one-act farce set in a railway refreshment room. Charles Selby and Mr Rogers were cast as rival lovers.

DECEMBER 26. Frederick Robson in J. R. Planché's **The Yellow Dwarf and the Ring of the Gold Mines** at Olympic Theatre. Robson's greatest role. He and Planché raised the fairy extravaganza to tragedy.

The story has been chosen evidently with a view to providing a character which Mr Robson might display his rare power of combining tragic passion and real hints of the terrible with ludicrous burlesque, and seldom has that clever actor been so neatly to the part. *Examiner*

He [Robson] sings and dances delightfully, contriving to have the most extraordinary legs imaginable. QUEEN VICTORIA, *Journal*

1855

JANUARY 13. Charles Kean in Dion Boucicault's **Louis XI** at Princess's Theatre. A tragedy was turned into farce. The audience, unable to take seriously a French king with a thick Irish accent, roared with laughter. *The Daily News* dismissed Kean's acting as 'mere rant'.

JANUARY 29. Charlotte Cushman and Ada Swanborough in Shakespeare's **Romeo and Juliet** at Haymarket Theatre. 'For force and passion,' said *The Illustrated London News*, 'Cushman's Romeo 'exceeds that of any male performer.' Some theatre-goers thought if Cushman was playing Romeo then Charles Kean should play Juliet.

> We have seen Miss Cushman as Miss Romeo; and though the lady lover is full of flame, it is the flame of phosphor – it shines, but it does not burn. *Lloyd's Weekly Newspaper*

Charlotte Cushman and Ada Swanborough in Shakespeare's Romeo and Juliet at Haymarket Theatre in 1855. 'As a lover,' said Westland Marston, 'the ardour of her devotion exceeded that of any male actor I have seen in the part.'

FEBRUARY 5. Benjamin Webster in Dion Boucicault's *Janet Pride* at Adelphi Theatre. Madame Celeste played wife and daughter, both called Janet Pride. The mother dies. The daughter twenty years later is brought to the Old Bailey for a crime her father committed. She is convicted. He kills himself. The Old Bailey's entire Central Criminal Court was recreated on stage. 'The acting of Webster and Celeste,' said *The Theatrical Journal*, 'is beyond all praise.'

MARCH 3. Henry Marston and Isabella Glyn in Shakespeare's *Antony and Cleopatra* at Standard Theatre. The theatre was capable of holding 5,000. The citizens of Shoreditch turned out in great numbers.

' *The poetic drama rejected by the frivolous and the fashionable has yet a home in the heart of the working class; and can operate as an influence, even when not understood, on the imagination of the masses.* '

ATHENÆUM

The manner in which she played it on Saturday was exquisite – surprising, such dash, rapidity, force, dazzling effect we have seldom witnessed even in the greatest of Rachel's efforts … such is the vivid and ever-varying light and shade exhibited in Miss Glyn's Cleopatra, which must now be accepted as one of the most perfect impersonations on the stage of Europe. *Illustrated London News*

MARCH 26. Isabella Glyn in John Webster's *The Duchess of Malfi* at Standard Theatre.

In the range of the Elizabethan drama, it would, perhaps, be difficult to find a piece more

exactly suited to an unsophisticated audience with a strong stomach for melodramatic horror. Mrs Glyn, by giving the comedy tone to the early scenes deprives them of their offensive character. *Theatre Journal*

MAY 10. Queen Victoria attended the London premiere of Giuseppe Verdi's *Il Trovatore* at Covent Garden Theatre. Jenny Ney as Leonora. Giovanni Graziani as Conte de Luna. Enrico Tamberlik as Manrico. Pauline Viardot as Azucena.

While writers, learned in musical lore, have been labouring to prove that Verdi is a shallow pretender, his operas have been giving delight to thousands in every part of Europe. *Illustrated London News*

MAY 14. Alfred Wigan, George Vining and Samuel Emery in Tom Taylor's *Still Waters Run*

Deep at Olympic Theatre. Dramatisation of Charles Bernard's novelette, *Le Gendre*. A long-suffering North Countryman outwits a forger and saves the honour of his wife's aunt.

> Everything like commonplace exaggeration is shunned, and the language is made to approximate as much as possible to that of real life. Seldom do we see acting so rigidly truthful.   *The Times*

> I don't think I ever saw anything meant to be funny that struck me as so extraordinarily droll. I couldn't get over it all.   CHARLES DICKENS on Emery's performance.

MAY 16. Charles Kean as Cardinal Wolsey, Mrs Kean as Queen Katharine and Walter Lacey as King Henry in Shakespeare's **Henry VIII** at Princess's Theatre. The production ran for 100 consecutive performances. The text, 'assiduously purified from all objectionable passages and expressions' was made available: 6,000 copies were sold.

> The appearance of the Angels in the dream of Queen Katharine if not coming too near to spiritual manifestation is full of ethereal grandeur, and has a most impressive effect upon the audience who while the scene is enacted sit like statues, as though divinity indeed were arranged before them.   *Theatrical Journal*

> We will run the risk of being charged with exaggeration by declaring in the most unequivocal terms that the play of Henry VIII

as produced last night at the Princess's Theatre is the most wonderful spectacle that has ever been seen on the London stage.   *Examiner*

> Nothing more delicate in conception or execution was, perhaps, ever seen on the stage. The sentiment of it as delicious as the delineation is exquisite.   *Athenæum*

> We would prefer to have Shakespeare acted than Shakespeare merely furnished.
> *Lloyd's Weekly Newspaper*

JULY 21. William Farren took his farewell at Haymarket Theatre in his favourite role: Lord Ogleby in George Colman the Elder's **The Clandestine Marriage**. The acting profession turned up in force to pay tribute to him.

> It was only to the wonderful talent of Mr Farren that The Clandestine Marriage owed its lengthened existence. His finished portrait of a luxurious, decrepit noble-hearted old lord, in which every detail was finished to the highest degree of perfection, retained a potent charm long after the character had ceased to have a living significance.   *The Times*

DECEMBER 26. Frederick Robson and Samuel Emery in J. R. Planché's **The Discreet Princess** at Olympic Theatre. Based on *The Stories of Mother Goose*. Robson was highly praised for the way in which he was able to combine comedy and tragedy in one performance.

1856

MARCH 4. *A Grand Ball Masque* took place at Covent Garden Theatre. The event was described by certain newspapers as a 'sickening picture on a large scale of human degradation and vice'. At the end of the evening, just after the National Anthem had been played, a fire was discovered. The roof collapsed. All the scenery, costumes, music library – which included Weber's score for *Oberon* and the original manuscripts for Sheridan's *The School for Scandal* – were burned. Four paintings from Hogarth's *Seasons* sequence were also destroyed. At great risk to his life, a bill-sticker managed to save some valuable books.

APRIL 21. Charles Dillon in his London debut in Charles Webb's **Belphegor** at Sadler's Wells Theatre made an immediate impact.

> He is no declaimer, but speaks naturally, and even in phrases of the highest passion, is never noisy, substituting intention for stormy vehemence. In these particulars he presents new points and differs from nearly all the English artists who have obtained reputation. His power over the feelings is extraordinary. In the first act of the present play he gradually melted his audience from scene to scene, and long ere the fall of the curtain every eye was moist with sympathetic tears. *Athenæum*

APRIL 26. Charles Kean as Leontes and Ellen Kean as Hermione in Shakespeare's **The Winter's Tale** at Princess's Theatre. 102 performances. The production took its inspiration from fourth-century BC and recreated Syracuse and Asia Minor in all their splendour. Nine-year-old Ellen Terry played Mamillius. *The Times* described her as vivacious and precocious. Terry never missed a performance.

> As for *The Winter's Tale* we never saw so much beautiful scenery with so much dreary acting. It was Shakespeare not illustrated but painted out. The whole thing was a moving panorama. We confess that we prefer a moving play.
> *Lloyd's Weekly Newspaper*

MAY 24. Marietta Piccolimini as Violetta, Enrico Calzolari as Alfredo and Benevento as Germont in London premiere of Guiseppe Verdi's **La Traviata** at Her Majesty's Theatre. A triumph for Piccolimini.

> The book is of far more consequence than the music, which, except as for it affords a vehicle for the utterance of the dialogue, is of no value whatsoever, and, moreover, because it is essentially as a dramatic vocalist that the brilliant success of Mademoiselle Piccolimini was achieved. *Illustrated London News*

Births	Deaths	History
William Archer, Scottish critic, dramatist, translator of Ibsen	Madame Vestris, British actress, singer, theatre manager (b. 1797)	Treaty of Paris brings Crimean War to an end
Sigmund Freud, Austrian psychiatrist		National Portrait Gallery in London opens
Réjane, French actor	*Notes*	Victoria Cross introduced for acts of conspicuous valour
George Bernard Shaw, Irish-born British dramatist	Covent Garden Theatre again destroyed by fire	London General Omnibus Company begins horse bus operations in London
Brandon Thomas, British dramatist, actor	Pavilion Theatre destroyed by fire	

AUGUST 4. James Holloway in Shakespeare's ***Richard III or The Death of White Surrey*** at Astley's Theatre. The play was cut to three acts and the horse was the star. 90 performances.

OCTOBER 15. John Pritt Harley as Bottom, Caroline Heath as Helena and Miss Bufton as Hermia in Shakespeare's ***A Midsummer Night's Dream*** at Princess's Theatre. Music by Felix Mendelssohn. Designed by Frederick Lloyds. The production was a series of dazzling *tableaux vivants* on a monumental scale. The opening scene showed Ancient Athens in all its classical grandeur. Kean had recreated it with archaeological accuracy, even to the tools and furniture in Peter Quince's workshop, which were all copied from recent discoveries in Herculaneum. There were over 90 fairies and a maypole dance. Inevitably Shakespeare's text suffered. Ellen Terry, who was playing Puck, made her entrance through a trap-door seated on a mushroom.

He [Kean] does not indulge in decorative magnificence for the mere sake of dazzling by show or to baffle competition. His purposes are

'Ill met by moonlight, Titania.' Oberon and Titania in a scene from Shakespeare's A Midsummer Night's Dream at Princess's Theatre in 1856.

Marietta Picolimini in Guiseppe Verdi's La Traviata *at Her Majesty's Theatre in 1856. Verdi had wanted the opera, which was based on Alexandre Dumas'* La Dame aux camélias, *to be staged in modern dress, but the action was put back to the seventeenth century in order to appease Victorian susceptibilities. Marguerite Gautier was based on the real-life Parisian courtesan, Marie Duplessis, Dumas' mistress.*

more lofty and intellectual; they aim at truth, propriety and instruction … [Ellen Terry] played Puck better than I have ever yet seen the trying part filled; there was a clearness of voice, a gracefulness of pose, and a hearty appreciation of the mischief she was causing.
Illustrated London News

SEPTEMBER 5. Marie Wilton in William Brough's **Perdita, The Royal Milkmaid** at Lyceum Theatre. A musical version of Shakespeare's *The Winter's Tale.* Wilton 'is a charming debutante,' said *The Morning Post*, 'sings prettily, acts archly, dances gracefully and is withal a most bewitching presence.'

SEPTEMBER 8. William Creswick as a Guadaloupe slave in E. Plouvier's **The Half-Caste** at Surrey Theatre. The half-caste arrives in Paris, posing as an English nobleman, and takes revenge for the wrongs he has suffered in the past. The audience was apathetic.

DECEMBER 1. Charles Dillon in Shakespeare's **Othello** at Lyceum Theatre. Dillon was 'natural, not at all declamatory, sometimes familiar, always dramatic, and rather intensely passionate than vehemently demonstrative,' said *The Athenæum*. 'Sometimes his pathos in its intensity became sublime.'

LAST NIGHT
OF KING
RICHARD THE SECOND.

This Evening, MONDAY, JUNE 29th, 1857,
The Performances will commence with a Farce, in One Act, by Mr. DAVID FISHER, entitled

MUSIC HATH CHARMS

Mr. Alfred Poppleton Pertinax, — — Mr. DAVID FISHER
Captain Bremont, — Mr. RAYMOND
Adrien de Beauval, Mr. BARSBY — M. Rabinel, Mr. BRAZIER
Madame Mathilde de La Roche, — Miss CARLOTTA LECLERCQ
Lucille, Miss KATE TERRY

After which, for the 85th and

LAST TIME,
SHAKESPEARE's Tragedy of

KING RICHARD
THE SECOND.

King Richard the Second, — — Mr. CHARLES KEAN
Edmund of Langley, Duke of York, (Uncles to the King) Mr. COOPER
John of Gaunt, Duke of Lancaster. Mr. WALTER LACY
Henry, surnamed (Duke of Hereford, Son to John of Gaunt, afterwards Mr. RYDER
Bolingbroke, King Henry the Fourth)
Duke of Aumerle, (Son to the Duke of York) Mr. BRAZIER
Mowbray, Duke of Norfolk, Mr. J. F. CATHCART
Duke of Surrey, Mr. RAYMOND — Earl of Salisbury, Mr. G. EVERETT
Lord Berkley, Mr. J. COLLETT
Sir John Bushy, Mr. ROLLESTON
Sir William Bagot, (Creatures to King Richard) Mr. WARREN
Sir Thomas Green, Mr. BARSBY
Earl of Northumberland, — Mr. H. MELLON
Beary Percy, (his Son) Miss BUFTON
Lord Ross, Mr. TERRY — Lord Willoughby, Mr. F. COOKE
Lord Fitzwater, Mr. WILSON — Bishop of Carlisle, Mr. H. BUTLER
Sir Pierce of Exton, Mr. PAULO — Sir Stephen Scroop, Mr. GRAHAM
Two Gardeners, Mr. MEADOWS and Mr. MORRIS
Keeper of the Prison, Mr. COLLIER — Groom, Mr. CORMACK
Queen to King Richard, — Mrs. CHARLES KEAN
Duchess of Gloster, — Mrs. DALY
Duchess of York, — Miss DESBOROUGH
Ladies attending on the Queen, — Miss DALY and Miss J. LOVELL
Boy, in the Episode, — Miss KATE TERRY

SCENE---DISPERSEDLY IN ENGLAND & WALES.
ACT 1.—Scene 1.
London---Privy Council Chamber
IN THE PALACE OF WESTMINSTER.
The Walls and Roof are Decorated with the Badges and Cognizances of Richard the Second.
Scene 2.
A ROOM IN THE DUKE OF LANCASTER'S PALACE
Scene 3
GOSFORD GREEN near COVENTRY
Lists set out for the Com at between Bolingbroke and Norfolk. The Royal
Pavilion with King Richard seated on a Throne, & many Noblemen with him
ACT 2.—Scene 1.
A BED-ROOM in ELY HOUSE
Scene 2.
Entrance to ST. STEPHEN'S CHAPEL (Restored)
Scene 3.
The WILDS in GLO'STERSHIRE
ADVANCE OF BOLINGBROKE'S ARMY.
ACT 3.—Scene 1
Milford Harbour, in Wales,
WITH PEMBROKE CASTLE (Restored.)
RICHARD'S FLEET AT ANCHOR
Scene 2.
WALES IN THE NEIGHBOURHOOD OF FLINT CASTLE.

1857

MARCH 12. Charles Kean in Shakespeare's ***Richard II*** at Princess's Theatre. Several cuts were needed to accommodate the costly spectacle. The production was notable for the visuals of the horseback riders, the trumpeters, sword-bearers and the colourful banners. There was a moment of pure fiction when an old soldier attempted to pay homage to the king and was prevented by a contemptuous mob. 'We consider it to be the greatest hit of modern times,' said *Theatre Journal*. 85 performances.

An increasing taste for recreation wherein instruction is blended with amusement, has for some time been conspicuous in the English public; and surely, an attempt to render dramatic representations conducive to the diffusion of knowledge – to surround the glowing imagery the great Poet describes – exhibiting men as they once lived – can scarcely detract from the enduring influence of his genius. Repeated success justifies the conviction that I am acting in accordance with the general feeling. When plays, which formerly commanded but occasional repetition, are enabled, by no derogatory means, to attract audiences for successive months, I cannot be wrong in presuming that the course I have adopted is supported by the irresistible force of public opinion, expressed in the suffrages of an overwhelming majority.
EDMUND KEAN, *Playbill*

A display of too minute correctness in armorial bearings, weapons and household vessels, made the Stage an auxiliary to the Museum and forced it to combine lessons on archaeology with the display of character and passion.
JOHN WESTLAND MARSTON, *Our Recent Actors*

As a well-known connoisseur of dramatic art remarked in the stalls on the first night of performance, the whole work is more like the production of a society of antiquaries than the result of a single manager's energy and genius. *The Times*

JULY 1. Charles Kean as Prospero in Shakespeare's **The Tempest** at Princess's Theatre. Kate Terry as Ariel. A. Ryder as Caliban. Rose Leclercq as Miranda. Eleanor Buffton as Ferdinand. Charles Mathews as Stephano. John Pritt Harley as Trinculo. The striking scenery was by William Telbin. There were 20 minutes of storm and the ship tossing on the sea before the shipwreck – and the play – could begin. To operate the machinery 140 operatives were needed. The trees, waterfalls, wood nymphs and satyrs were magical. The descent of Juno from the flies was accompanied by floating Hours, Graces and Spirits. Ariel became the leading role. The daintiest of spirits, she descended in a ball of fire, rose from a tuft of flowers, sailed on water on the back of a dolphin, rode a bat, and flew through the air. The only thing she didn't do was sing. Elizabeth Poole, who played Juno, sang Ariel's songs.

So with Shakespeare, so it has been with Charles Kean, it was the grandest, the most sublime effect of England's immortal bard – it has been the crowning point of all the manager of the Princess's has done. *Theatre Journal*

He has reformed, nay he has even regenerated the national drama of the country. He has revived a pure taste, which seemed verging to extinction. Mr Charles Kean has made the Princess's Theatre the acknowledged home of Shakespeare. *Theatre*

Prospero bids farewell to Ariel in Shakespeare's The Tempest at Princess's Theatre in 1857.

SHAKSPEARE'S PLAY OF "THE TEMPEST," AT THE PRINCESS' THEATRE: SCENE THE LAST.—(SEE NEXT PAGE.)

Births

Joseph Conrad, Polish-born
  novelist
Richard Masefield, British
  dramatist
Hermann Sudermann, German
  playwright

Deaths

Alfred de Musset, French
  poet, dramatist (b. 1810)
Douglas William Jerrold,
  British dramatist (b. 1803)
W. T. Moncrieff, British
  dramatist (b. 1794)

Literature

Charles Baudelaire's *Les Fleurs
  du Mal*
George Eliot's *Scenes of Clerical
  Life*
Thomas Hughes' *Tom Brown's
  Schooldays*
Anthony Trollope's *Barchester
  Towers*

Notes

Charles Kean is elected fellow
  of the Society of Antiquaries
  of London

History

Indian Mutiny begins
Albert created Prince Consort
Siege and capture of Delhi
  from the East India Co.
Matrimonial Causes Act
  updates divorce laws and
  moves legal proceedings
  from ecclesiastical to civil
  courts for the first time
British Museum Reading
  Room opens in Bloomsbury
World's oldest surviving
  football club, Sheffield FC,
  is set up

JULY 8. William Farren and John Baldwin Buckstone in Tom Taylor's **Victims** at Haymarket Theatre. Comedy of marriage. Painter Angus Leopold Egg would include a poster for *Victims* in his narrative triptych, *Past and Present*, a tragedy of marriage, which was exhibited at the Royal Academy in 1858.

JULY 11. Vitaliani and Adelaide Ristori in Shakespeare's **Macbeth** at Lyceum Theatre. Acted in Italian. Macbeth was presented as a weak man dominated by his wife. According to one critic his nervousness was so exaggerated as to make him ridiculous.

> When she [Ristori] came on the stage she seemed to fill the stage with her majestic presence ... One can understand why, in her own lifetime, she was called 'the Siddons of modern Italy'. *Daily News*

SEPTEMBER 30. Henry Marston as Biron in Shakespeare's **Love's Labour's Lost** at Sadler's Wells Theatre. The medieval court setting was worthy of Sir Philip Sydney's Arcadia. Samuel Phelps as Don Armado was, said *The Times*, 'one of his choicest comic impersonations – an entirely fresh creation, totally distinct from the fops of stage convention.'

OCTOBER 27. Louisa Payne and Mr Harrison in premiere of William Balfe's **The Rose of Castile** at Lyceum Theatre. Libretto by Augustus Glossop Harris and Edmund Falconer. Conductor was Mark Mellon. Comic opera. Husband-to-be disguises himself as a muleteer to discover what his bride-to-be is really like. She disguises herself as a peasant girl to find out what he is really like. 100 performances.

OCTOBER 5. Henry Howe and Amy Sedgwick in her triumphant London debut in Edward Bulwer-Lytton's **The Lady of Lyons** at Haymarket Theatre.

OCTOBER 31. T. P. Cooke came out of retirement for one performance of William Douglas Jerrold's **Black Ey'd Susan** at Adelphi Theatre to honour the remembrance of Jerrold who had died recently. Cooke was such a success he was asked to stay on for an extra week.

> He [Cooke] was regarded as a living symbol of the British sailor ... Bright, jovial, active and hearty, this veteran of the footlights could have played anything that smelt of the sea. *Theatre Journal*

The last appearances have been the happiest of my career. I feel so juvenile that I find it difficult to persuade myself that I am on the shady side of seventy. (Cheers) I have been on the stage fifty-three years. (Cheers) I never did take a final farewell and I do not feel inclined to take that suicidal act, so retire this evening in the hope that I may again re-appear.
T. P. COOKE in his address to the audience.

NOVEMBER 7. William Farren and Amy Sedgwick in Tom Taylor's *An Unequal Match* at Haymarket Theatre. Baronet marries blacksmith's daughter. The girl is taunted by society, but, in the end, triumphs over his former mistress.

There is not, we think, any very great promise in her [Sedgwick] performance; she will not console veteran playgoers for the loss of their old favourites; but she is a very useful accession to the strength of the London stage.
Saturday Review

DECEMBER 14. Samuel Phelps in Shakespeare's *Hamlet* at Sadler's Wells Theatre.

He [Phelps] does not, like Kean, seize upon some remarkable passage or striking incident to depict with extravagant colour an unusual force, but throws a proportionate strength of tint into every single beauty and individual part, distributing through in his whole performance an evenness of effect, a perfect contrast of light and shade. *Theatre Journal*

BELOW

The elopement of Jessica in Shakespeare's Merchant of Venice at Princess's Theatre in 1858.

RIGHT

The Great American Circus at Royal Alhambra Palace in 1858.

1858

APRIL 3. The Alhambra Palace opened with a spectacular production: Howes and Cushing's **Great United States Circus**.

APRIL 17. Charles Kean in Shakespeare's **King Lear** at Princess's Theatre. Miss Poole as Fool. (Garrick, Kemble and Edmund Kean had always cut the Fool.) The action was set firmly in Anglo-Saxon times. The opening scene was adorned with spears, shields, the triumphs of battle, and a blazing Yule-log. All repulsive and coarse passages were removed, including the blinding of Gloucester. The storm was terrific. 32 consecutive performances.

The triumphant development of genius displayed by Mr Kean in his embodiment of Shakespeare's sublime creation places beyond doubt his supremacy as a histrionic artist.
Illustrated London News

As a physical and an intellectual performance it is unexampled, and his [Charles Kean] embodiment there is a perfectness, a consummation of minutest detail no other actor of the present day could attain, yet there is not the smallest aim of exaggeration, but all nature in what he does. *Theatre Journal*

THE NEW ROYAL ITALIAN OPERA-HOUSE, COVENT GARDEN.—(EDMUND BARRY, ARCHITECT.)

APRIL 29. Charles Dickens gave his first public reading at St Martin's Hall. He read **The Cricket on the Hearth**. As a reader for charity he had gained a large following. Two weeks earlier he had read **A Christmas Carol** as a charity performance in aid of The Hospital for Sick Children.

MAY 15. The new Royal Italian Opera opened with Giulia Grisi and Enrico Mario in Giacomo Meyerbeer's **The Huguenots**. The scene changes took so long that by midnight the opera had not even reached the end of the third act. The management decided to stop there and played the National Anthem. Audiences sitting in the upper regions became abusive and yelled and hissed and demanded the fourth act all through the anthem. They had to go home without seeing it.

JUNE 12. Charles Kean as Shylock in Shakespeare's **The Merchant of Venice** at Princess's Theatre. 'There are no tears in his pathos; there is no terror in his wrath,' said *The Leader*.

> It has been my object to combine with the poet's art a faithful representation of the picturesque city; to render it again palpable to the traveller who has actually gazed upon the seat of its departed glory; and at the same time, to exhibit it to the student, who has never visited this once … The famed place of St Mark's Square, with the ancient Church the Rialto, its Bridge, the Canals and Gondolas, the Historic Columns, the Ducal Palace and the Council Chamber, are successively presented to the spectator. Venice is re-peopled with the past, affording truth to the eye, and reflection to the mind.
>
> CHARLES KEAN, *Playbill*

IRA ALDRIDGE, THE AFRICAN TRAGEDIAN, AS "OTHELLO."

LEFT

The new Royal Italian Opera House opened in 1858 with Meyerbeer's opera, Les Huguenots.

RIGHT

Ira Aldridge in Shakespeare's Othello at Lyceum Theatre in 1858.

Charles Kean has now stepped into the place vacated by his father to complete the quintumvirate of great Shylocks and satisfy the world that the modern stage has not degenerated. JOHN WILLIAM COLE, *The Life and Theatrical Times of Charles Kean*

JULY 31. Ira Aldridge in Shakespeare's **Othello** at Lyceum Theatre. 'His appearance,' said *Era*, 'is a great moral lesson in favour of anti-slavery.' *The Theatrical Times* said it would be better if Mr Elphinstone, who was cast as Iago, restricted himself to ultra melodramatic parts.

In tragedy he [Aldridge] has a solemn intensity of style, bursting occasionally into a blaze of fierce invective or passionate declamation: while the dark shades of his face become doubly sombre in their thoughtful aspect: a nihilistic gloom spread over them and an expression more terrible than paler lineaments can readily assume. *Illustrated London News*

World premieres
Jacques Offenbach's *Orphée aux Enfers* in Paris

Births
André Antoine, French director
George Alexander, British actor-manager
Frank Benson, British actor-manager
Eleanora Duse, Italian actor

Charles Hawtrey, British actor
Giacomo Puccini, Italian composer

Deaths
Rachel, French actor (b.1820)

Literature
R. M. Ballantyne's *Coral Island*
Anthony Trollope's *Doctor Thorne*

Notes
Royal Opera House re-built; it re-opens on 15 May
Alhambra Theatre opens as a music hall

History
'Great Stink' as hot weather exacerbates the effects of river pollution on Thames
Indian Mutiny ends; East India Co. cedes power to Crown

1858

1859

FEBRUARY 4. Charles Kean in Dion Boucicault's version of Casimir Delavigne's **Louis XI** at Princess's Theatre. Kean perfected an absolute triumph,' said *Theatre Journal*. 'We say it without hesitation, that in that character he stands by himself – that he is irreproachable – that no other actor in England could rival him.'

He will undoubtedly be best remembered by his Louis the Eleventh, which, in its fusion with passion of the extreme realism previously almost confined to comedy, formed a new type of acting on the English stage.

JOHN WESTLAND MARSTON, *Our Recent Actors*

MARCH 28. Charles Kean in Shakespeare's **Henry V** at Princess's Theatre. Ellen Kean as Chorus (renamed Clio, Muse of History) and presented as a classical statue, and acted in the grand manner,

Shakespeare's Henry V at Princess's Theatre in 1859. Henry enters London after his victory at Agincourt, a scene not to be found in Shakespeare.

accompanied by tableaux to illustrate the narrative. The assault on Harfleur was brilliantly realised. The Crispin Day speech was particularly admired. Henry's return to London after Agincourt received the full spectacle: Kean on horseback was greeted by 200 highly disciplined cheering supernumeraries. Kate Terry played the Boy. ('The gem of the performance,' said *The Athenæum*.) The production lasted four hours. Twice during the course of the production Mr and Mrs Kean had to appear before the drop curtain to acknowledge the applause. They lost a great deal of money on the venture.

We may say without exaggeration that all London flocks to see it and all England crowded to London for the same purpose. When the curtain fell on the last night of its performance, every one felt it would never rise again on a Shakespearian exhibition of similar excellence. The entire outlay exceeded £300. The bill for the rehearsals of the supernumeraries alone amounted to £160, including their refreshment.
JOHN WILLIAM COLE, *The Life and Theatrical Times of Charles Kean*

The only way of making the Shakespeare drama attractive in an age frivolous beyond precedent in its amusements was the way adopted by Mr Charles Kean.   *The Times* in response to criticism of Kean's scenic wonders

APRIL 11. Edith Heraud in Sophocles' **Antigone** at Crystal Palace Concert Room. A reading. Music by Felix Mendelssohn. The effect was immense,' reported *The Daily News*. 'Her clear mellow voice reached the ears of the vast audience.'

APRIL 19. There was a riot at Sadler's Wells Theatre when the production of the opera **Martha** stopped in mid-performance because nobody had been paid for two weeks. The singers tried to continue, but the noise the people backstage were making made it impossible.

MAY 29. Samuel Phelps and Isabella Glyn in Shakespeare's **Antony and Cleopatra** at Standard Theatre.

Mr Phelps should seek to speak more quickly; Miss Glyn more slowly. Both would benefit by the mutual accommodation and the audience would be better satisfied. The violent contrast between the natural and the artificial would be diminished, and we would no longer be puzzled with the cross-purposes of two antagonistic schools in one and the same picture.
Illustrated London News

JUNE 10. Frederick Robson in Tom Taylor's **Payable on Demand** at Olympic Theatre. Hero succumbs to temptation and is saved in the nick of

---

World premieres
Charles Gounod's *Faust* in Paris
Alexander Ostrovsky's *The Storm* in Moscow
Giuseppe Verdi's *Un ballo in maschera* in Rome
Richard Wagner's *Tristan und Isolde* in Prague

Births
Mary Anderson, American actor
Arthur Conan Doyle, British novelist
Jerome K. Jerome, British novelist

Deaths
Thomas De Quincey, British writer, opium-eater (b. 1785)
Leigh Hunt, British critic, essayist, poet (b. 1784)
Thomas Babington Macaulay, British essayist, historian (b. 1800)

Literature
Charles Darwin's *On the Origin of Species by Natural Selection*
Charles Dickens' *A Tale of Two Cities*
George Eliot's *Adam Bede*
Omar Khayyam translated by Edward Fitzgerald

Notes
Charles Kean terminates his management of Princess's Theatre
Vauxhall Gardens closes amid financial difficulties and changing tastes

History
War of Italian Liberation
First overseas cricket tour, to Canada and USA
'Big Ben' at Westminster works for the first time
Blondin crosses Niagara Falls on a tightrope
Building of Suez Canal begins

1859

time by the arrival of a carrier pigeon with vital information.

JULY 30. *The Mountain Cataract or The Poor Slave* at Pavilion Theatre. The climax involved cascading water. The cascade was so successful that it swept the musicians out of the orchestra pit.

The interior of New Adelphi Theatre was completed in 1859 to accommodate 1,500. Adelphi Dramas became synonymous with strong melodramas.

AUGUST 1. Charles Kean in Dion Boucicault's *The Corsican Brothers* at Princess's Theatre.

The most effective melodrama ever produced on any stage. A ghost story that has almost found credence in the nineteenth century, thanks to the completeness of the scenic contrivances and acting of Mr Kean.   *The Times*

A scene from Asmodeus or The Devil of Two Sticks at New Adelphi Theatre. Grand extravaganza.

AUGUST 29. Charles Kean took his farewell of the stage as Wolsey in Shakespeare's **Henry VIII** at Princess's Theatre. In his curtain call speech he said:

> I have always entertained the conviction that in illustrating the great plays of the grandest poet who ever wrote, historical accuracy might be blended with pictorial effect, that instruction and amusement would go hand in hand. I find it impossible that because every detail is studied with an eye to truth, such a plan can in the most remote degree detract from the beauties of the Poet ... But to carry out my system of pictorial illustration, the cost has been enormous, far too great for the limited arena in which it was incurred. As a single proof I may state that in this little Theatre where £200 is considered a large receipt and £250 an extraordinary one, I expended in one season along a sum little short of £50,000. During the run of some of the great revivals as they are called, I have given employment and consequently weekly payment to nearly 500 persons. CHARLES KEAN

OCTOBER 18. Samuel Phelps in Tom Taylor's **The Fool's Revenge** at Sadler's Wells Theatre. Adaptation of Victor Hugo's *Le roi s'amuse*.

> This drama is in no sense a translation, and ought not, I think, in fairness, to be called even an adaptation ... I found so much in it that seemed to me inadmissible to our stage – so much, besides, that was wanting in dramatic motive and cohesion, and – I say in all humility – so much that was defective in that central secret of stage effect, climax, that I determined to take the situation of the jester and his daughter, and to recast it in my own way. TOM TAYLOR in his Preface to the play.

NOVEMBER 10. Benjamin Webster, David Fisher and Sarah Woolgar in Watts Phillips's **The Dead Heart** at Adelphi Theatre. Melodrama set during the French Revolution: the heart is dead and vengeance is alive. The hero takes another's place on the scaffold. Sounds like a straight crib of *A Tale of Two Cities*, but Phillips actually wrote his play three years before Charles Dickens published his novel.

STRAND ⚜ THEATRE.
Sole Lessee. Miss SWANBOROUGH.
UNDER THE MANAGEMENT OF
Miss SWANBOROUGH

☞ TREMENDOUS HIT of the New Grand Comic
OPERATIC EXTRAVAGANZA,
By ANDREW HALLIDAY, Esq., Joint Author of "KENILWORTH," entitled
ROMEO and JULIET;
OR, THE
CUP OF COLD POISON!
With entirely New and Elegant Scenery, Costumes, and Appointments.

☞ The Free List is entirely suspended, the Public Press excepted.

This Evening, MONDAY, November 7th, and during the Week.
The performances will commence at Seven, with the laughable Farce, by W. BROUGH, Esq.,

TRYING IT ON!

Mr. Walsingham Potts, -	Mr. W. H. SWANBOROUGH,
Mr. Jobstock, Mr H. J. TURNER	Mr. Tittlebat, Mr. W. MOWBRAY,
Mrs. Jobstock,	Mrs. C. SELBY,
Fanny,	Miss BUFTON,
Lucy, (her Niece) (her Maid)	Miss LAVINE.

After which, at Eight o'clock, a New Grand Comic Operatic Extravaganza, by
ANDREW HALLIDAY, Esq., Author (jointly) of KENILWORTH, entitled

ROMEO
AND
JULIET;
OR,
THE CUP
OF
COLD POISON!

The Overture and the whole of the Music Composed and Arranged by Herr FERDINAND WALLERSTEIN.
The Elegant Costumes by Mr. S. MAY, Mrs. RICHARDSON, and Numerous Assistants.
Properties, and Stage Appointments, by Mr. SCARBORO'.   Machinery by Mr. RATTY.   Ballet Arranged by Mr. J. LAURI.
And the Extensive Scenery, by Messrs. ALBERT CALLCOTT, and W. BROADFOOT.

Capulet, (a rich Nobleman, who in Verona did dwell—a stern Parent with one Daughter	**Mr. H. J. TURNER**
Romeo, (a nice Young Man—supposed to have been the Original Villikins—addicted to Walking in the Back Garding)	**Miss CHARLOTTE SAUNDERS**
Juliet, (an uncommon nice Young Gal—the "One Daughter" of Capulet—a belle whom all the Young Fellows in Verona are anxious to ring)	**Miss MARIE WILTON**
Tybalt, (a Fighting Man—	

The
1860s

1860

JANUARY 30. Charles Forrester as Darnay and Sydney Carton in Tom Taylor's adaptation of Charles Dickens' *A Tale of Two Cities* at Lyceum Theatre. Madame Celeste as Colette and Madame Lefarge. James Vining as Manette. Dickens had only just completed the novel.

In these days when most dramas of the English stage are adapted from French sources it is gratifying to witness a piece which is indebted for its origins to English genius.
Illustrated London News

FEBRUARY 23. Mr and Mrs Charles Mathews in John Baldwin Buckstone and Tom Taylor's *The Overland Route* at Haymarket Theatre. Farce. Husband leaves his shrewish wife. The first two acts were set aboard a homeward-bound steamer. The audience groaned out loud when a set of lost teeth were picked up off the floor and replaced in the mouth of their toothless owner.

The cave scene from Dion Boucicault's The Colleen Bawn at Adelphi Theatre in 1860.

MARCH 12. John Emery and Charles Verner in Edward Fitzball's **Christmas Eve or The Duel in the Snow** at Drury Lane Theatre. The final scene in the Bois de Boulogne was based on Jean-Léon Gérome painting, *Duel after the Masked Ball*, which depicted the death of a pierrot, killed by a man masquerading as an Indian. The painting, which had caused a sensation when it was exhibited in the Salon in 1857, inspired a number of theatrical productions in Paris and London.

MAY 15. Samuel Phelps in Shakespeare's **Othello** at Sadler's Wells Theatre.

One of the chief merits of Mr Phelps as an actor of Shakespeare is that he studies each play as a poem, avoids all temptation to mere personal display, and directs attention to the poet whom he is illustrating rather than to himself as the illustrator. *Examiner*

AUGUST. A hippopotamus performed at Alhambra Palace. 'The animal,' said *The Illustrated London News*, 'is remarkable for its laziness yet shows signs of intelligence.'

SEPTEMBER 10. Dion Boucicault as Myles Na-Coppaleen and Agnes Robertson as Eily in Dion Boucicault's **The Colleen Bawn or The Brides of Garryown** at Adelphi Theatre. Based on Gerard Griffin's novel, *The Collegians*, which in turn was based on a famous murder trial. Written

John Baldwin Buckstone (1802–79), actor and dramatist, was the author of The Green Bushes *(1845) and no fewer than 160 farces, operettas and burlettas. He was also the theatre manager of Theatre Royal, Haymarket, and his ghost is said still to haunt the building to this day.*

drama. Myles, the comic hero, makes a spectacular running dive from a rock into a lake to save the heroine from drowning. The lake was created by 20 small boys shaking yards of blue cloth. With his charm, songs, jigs and gift of the gab, Myles would become Boucicault's most famous role and he would be still playing him well into his sixties.

One of the best constructed and most striking dramas of domestic life that had ever been put upon the stage … The attempted drowning of Eily O'Connor, in a very picturesque lake, is, perhaps, too really horrible. *The Times*

Nothing could be more simple and artless than her [Agnes Robertson] manner as the charming peasant girl, nothing more touching than her unrepining sorrow when she feels that her husband no longer loves her. *Daily Telegraph*

in nine days, rehearsed while it was still being written, it premiered in New York, and was one of Boucicault's greatest successes. It ran for 296 performances in London, at that time the longest run in the history of the English stage. Queen Victoria saw it three times. It was the first sensation

1860

World premieres
Eugène Labiche's *The Voyage of Monsieur Perrichon* in Paris
Victorien Sardou's *Les Pattes de mouche*

Births
J. M. Barrie, Scottish dramatist, novelist
Anton Chekhov, Russian dramatist
Charles Froham, American producer
Miss A. E. F. Horniman, British theatre manager
Dan Leno, music hall artist

Ada Rehan, Irish-American actress

Deaths
Alfred Bunn, British actor, theatre manager (b. 1798)

Literature
Wilkie Collins' *The Woman in White*
Serialisation of Charles Dickens' *Great Expectations* begins
George Eliot's *The Mill on the Floss*

History
Abraham Lincoln is elected President of USA
The Palace of Westminster, including the Houses of Parliament are completed
First known sound recording is made – a patented 'phonautogram' by French printer and inventor Édouard-Léon Scott de Martinville
First Open Championship is played at Prestwick, Ayrshire
First National Eisteddfod of Wales is held in Denbigh

OCTOBER 27. Charles Fechter, Miss Heath and Walter Lacy in Victor Hugo's **Ruy Blas** at Princess's Theatre. Fechter's English-speaking debut in London.

His accent and his gesticulations are French but his articulation is perfectly clear and there is music in his voice which would sound equally well through the medium of any language.
The Times

In melodrama Mr Fechter acts effectively without extravagance. He suits action to word with a nicety not usual upon the English stage and without obtrusion of his art.
HENRY MORLEY, *Journal of a London Playgoer*

NOVEMBER 3. William Creswick as Count Fosco in J. R. Ware's adaptation of Wilkie Collins's **The Woman in White** at Surrey Theatre. Miss Page played Anne Catherick and Lady Clyde. A pirated version coincided with the last instalment of the novel, which was being published in Charles Dickens' magazine *All the Year Round*, and had increased the magazine's circulation to 100,000 copies. *The Illustrated London News* said the novel had been 'adapted to the presumed low taste of the audience and not intended to educate them in a better'.

DECEMBER. Jolly John Nash made his debut in London at the South London Music Hall. Nash, who would later be billed as The Merry Son of Momus of Side-Slitting, was the original laughing comedian.

1861

MARCH 20. Charles Fechter in Shakespeare's **Hamlet** at Princess's Theatre. 'The whole of the third act sparkles with genius,' said *The Daily News*. Fechter had suggested to Samuel Phelps that he might like to play the Ghost. Phelps was insulted: 'Damn your impudence!' he exclaimed. 115 performances.

The performance is worth seeing as a curiosity ... Probably Shakespeare never has been, or will be, played so well by a foreign artist as Mr Fechter has played Hamlet and it would be wholly incorrect to measure it by an English standard.   *The Times*

He made a deep impression upon the most intellectual of playgoers – and moreover upon a class of person who look upon theatrical exhibitions with a feeling nearly akin to contempt. *Morning Herald*

Mr Fechter does not act. He is Hamlet. What we principally liked in the first act was

an intense and unmistakable sorrow that it displayed, which exceeded every demonstration of the kind that we have ever witnessed in this character ... He managed to slay the king, not only without raising the usual laugh in the audience but producing the excitement of terror in the audience by the reality of the combat. *Athenæum*

'*A French Hamlet – um! Mr Fechter's; the best I ever saw was German, Emil Devrient's; but then German and English as far as Hamlet is concerned are one; but a 'parlez-vous!' I may like it prodigiously if I ever see it; but I do not feel as if I should.*'
FANNY KEMBLE in a letter quoted in
John Philip Kemble's further records

MAY 14. Adelina Patti's London debut as Amina in Vincenzo Bellini's **La Sonnambula** at Royal Italian Opera. Patti was 18 years old.

> Is Mademoiselle Adelina Patti a phenomenon? – Decidedly yes. Is she a perfect artist? Decidedly no. How could a girl of scarcely 18 summers have realised perfection in an art so difficult?   *The Times*

MAY 25. Adelina Patti in Gaetano Donizetti's **Lucia di Lammermoor** at Royal Italian Opera.

> One of the greatest attractions of this powerfully worked up scene [mad scene] in the hands of Mademoiselle Patti – who imitates no preceding model (being too young, indeed to have profited by it) – is its entire and abiding freshness. The conception is original and the execution is brilliant, and the one is as strikingly picturesque as the other is surprising.   *The Times*

MAY 26. Jules Leotard, the French aerialist, made his London debut at the Alhambra. Leotard was billed as the greatest living flying trapeze artist, and was the inspiration for George Leybourne's song *The Daring Young Man on the Flying Trapeze*, which Leybourne sang for the first time at Alhambra Palace in 1868.

> He [Leotard] performs the most outstanding feats on a rope 150 feet high. On it he wheels a barrow, runs backwards and forwards in a sack blindfold, also when his feet in shackles and baskets. The Public Press pronounce him to be one of the Marvels of Creation.   *Playbill*

JUNE 1. Charles Blondin, the French tightrope walker, made his first appearance in England at Crystal Palace. Blondin was billed as 'The Hero of Niagara'. He had won fame from crossing Niagara Falls on a tightrope in 1859. He then repeated the same feat blindfolded, then he did it with a wheelbarrow, then carrying his manager on his back, and finally he walked on the tightrope on stilts.

JUNE 15. Antonio Giuglini as Ricardo and Thérèse Tietjens as Amelia in London premiere of Giuseppe Verdi's **Un Ballo in Maschera** at Lyceum Theatre.

> Verdi, like the generality of the Italian composers, writes 'with ease' – that is, he manufactures with an expectation that knows neither fatigue nor limit. In music of this class, thought, ingenuity and contrivance are the things consulted, and the quality of the produce is naturally thin and valueless in proportion. That Verdi is popular is, however, a fact, not to be gainsaid.   *Observer*

SEPTEMBER 21. Samuel Phelps in Dion Boucicault's **Louis XI** at Sadler's Wells Theatre.

> Mr Phelps's performance as Louis cannot fail to be looked upon as one of the most remarkable of his numerous successful personations, and

1861

Premieres
De Musset's *On ne badine avec l'amour* in Paris

Births
Albert Chevalier, British music hall artiste

Deaths
Prince Albert, Consort to Queen Victoria (b.1819)
Eugène Scribe, French dramatist (b.1791)

Literature
Publication of Dickens' *Great Expectations* is completed
George Eliot's *Silas Marner*
Mrs Henry Wood's *East Lynne*

Notes
London Pavilion opens
Royalty Theatre opens
Jolly John Nash at New Oxford Music Hall sings 'I Couldn't Help Laughing It Tickled Me So.'

History
Serfdom is abolished in Russia
Tooley Street fire in Southwark rages for two days, prompting creation of Metropolitan Fire Brigade
American Civil War begins with Confederate attack on Fort Sumter, SC
Victor Emmanuel proclaimed King of Italy
Post Office Savings Bank opens

as another proof of his conscientious devotion to his art, at a time when finished acting is certainly not the rule upon the stage. *Standard*

OCTOBER 4. American actor Edwin Booth's debut in London as Shylock in Shakespeare's ***The Merchant of Venice*** at Haymarket Theatre. Mrs Charles Young as Portia. Audiences, who expected Booth to have the fiery passion of his father Junius, were disappointed.

The performance must be allowed to possess merits which raise it above the level of mere mediocrity, but which still fall short of the standard that would enable it to rank as an effort of genius. *Observer*

OCTOBER 5. Edwin Booth as Sir Giles Overreach in Philip Massinger's ***A New Way to Pay Old Debts*** at Haymarket Theatre. Booth could not compete with the audience's memories of Edmund Kean in the role. 'He did not,' said *Era*, 'startle the audience into one of those outbursts of enthusiasm that indicate the advent of a new tragedian whose genius will enforce admiration.'

OCTOBER 23. Charles Fechter as Othello and John Ryder as Iago in Shakespeare's ***Othello*** at Princess's Theatre. In 1862 they reversed roles. 'Mr Fechter's acting of Othello is the triumph of intellect over many disadvantages,' said *The Illustrated London News*, 'namely an imperfect pronunciation and deficient physical force.'

The effects in some respects belong rather to English melodrama than to English tragedy. And Mr Fechter even closes his Othello with a melodramatic, false reading, by half-throttling Iago. (It looked as if he was going to stab Iago, not himself.)
HENRY MORLEY, *Journal of a London Playgoer*

An intelligent innovator like M. Fechter gives people something to talk about. *Saturday Review*

He then played Hamlet and gave a new and charming representation to a part in which no actor has been known to fail; and the uncritical

concluded that he was a great actor. But when he came to a part like Othello which calls upon the greatest capabilities of an actor, the public then remembered he was a foreigner and discovered he was not a tragedian.
Cornhill Magazine

OCTOBER 28. Edwin Booth in the Colley Cibber version of Shakespeare's ***Richard III*** at Haymarket Theatre. Booth was compared with his father and found wanting.

OCTOBER 31. Edwin Booth in Edward Bulwer-Lytton's ***Richelieu*** at Haymarket Theatre. 'The finest piece of acting I ever saw in my life,' said Charles Kean.

NOVEMBER 5. Edwin Booth in Shakespeare's ***Hamlet*** at Haymarket Theatre. The critical consensus was that the days of the old classical school of acting were dead and buried.

NOVEMBER 9. Herman Vezin, Walter Lacy and Mrs D. P. Bowers in Edmund Falconer's ***Peep o' Day or Savoureen Deelish*** at Lyceum Theatre. Sensational drama of Irish peasant life based on one of John Banim's *Tales by the O'Hara Family* and billed as 'illustrative of the transition of Ireland 50 years ago'. A jig turns into a nasty fight. There's a brutal murder and the heroine is very nearly buried alive. The production was notable for a beautiful panorama of the Lake of Killarney and a sensation scene in a quarry. The scenery was by Thomas Grieve and William Telbin. 'The effect of light, shade and perspective,' said *The Morning Paper*, 'are literally magical.' 346 performances.

NOVEMBER 11. Edward Askew Sothern and John Baldwin Buckstone in Tom Taylor's ***Our American Cousin*** at Haymarket Theatre. 477 performances. The comedy was inspired by the Americans coming to the Great Exhibition of 1851 at Crystal Place. It had played 800 times in the United States. Sothern's performance as Dundreary, an asinine, simpering, lisping, indolent peer, was one of the great comic performances of the nineteenth century. The high spot was his reading of his brother Sam's letter. At every performance he had to do an encore. Sothern

transformed a mediocre play and spawned a whole industry. There were Dundreary shoes, hats, ankle-length coats, dressing-gowns, plaid trousers, long whiskers and monocles. Dundrearyisms became all the rage. His walk included a Negro minstrel hop. 'The funniest thing in the world,' said *The Athenæum*. Buckstone was cast as an outrageous Yankee. The play was constantly revived in England until 1879. *Our American Cousin* was the play which President Abraham Lincoln was watching at the Ford Theatre in Washington, DC, in 1865 when he was assassinated by John Wilkes Booth.

You analyze his [Dundreary] oddities in vain for there is no single epithet in the English language in which they can be concentrated or defined. Nouns such as noodle, fool, lunatic, dandy equally with such adjectives as queer, old, eccentric, idiotic utterly fail to describe his character or person.
Illustrated Sporting and Dramatic News

A weaker, worse constructed or more worthless play, it is scarcely possible to imagine … The sense of enjoyment derived from it [Sothern's Dundreary] is so great as to render the spectator comparatively indifferent to the general worthlessness of the play.   *Observer*

To test him [Sothern's Dundreary] by anything in the actual world would be to ignore his special merit, which consists in giving to a conventional notion the most novel and fantastic expression that can be imagined.   *The Times*

NOVEMBER 18. Dion Boucicault as Salem Scudder and Mrs Boucicault as Zoe in Dion Boucicault's **The Octoroon or Life in Louisiana** at the New Adelphi Theatre. This anti-slavery drama had had its premiere in New York in 1860. Zoe, the octoroon, had one-eighth Negro blood. The production had two sensation scenes: a public slave sale and the firing of a Mississippi river boat. An

The slave market scene in Dion Boucicault's The Octoroon at Adelphi Theatre in 1861.

attempt to introduce humour was made when an old Negro started boasting of his qualities in order to fetch a better price. A camera was used for the first time on stage to unmask a villain. The London audience didn't like it when the heroine was killed in the last act and they booed. Boucicault instantly rewrote the last act and announced that he had done so in his playbill:

> Mr Boucicault begs to acknowledge the hourly receipt of many letters, entreating that the termination of *The Octoroon* should be modified and the Slave Heroine saved from an unhappy end. He cannot resist the kind feeling expressed throughout this correspondence, nor refuse compliance with a request so easily granted. A New Last Act of the Drama, composed by the Public, and edited by the Author, will be represented on Monday night. He trusts the Audience will accept it as a very grateful tribute to their judgement and taste, which he should be the last to dispute.

1862

JANUARY 18. George Vining and Miss Herbert in George Vining's **Self-Made** at Adelphi Theatre. The plot was based on a story by Chevalier de St Georges: a mulatto slave escapes from St Domingo to become a chevalier and a leader of fashion in Paris.

FEBRUARY 10. **The Lily of Killarney** at Covent Garden Theatre. Operatic version of Dion Boucicault's *The Colleen Bawn*. Book by John Oxenford and Dion Boucicault. Music by Julius Benedict.

FEBRUARY 10. Mrs Boucicault in Dion Boucicault's **The Dublin Boy** at Adelphi Theatre. The adaptation of Vanderburch's *Le Gamin de Paris* transferred the action to Ireland. For many critics Mrs Boucicault was the prettiest little Irish boy they had ever seen.

> The character of the reckless hero – the mischievous but good-hearted boy – exactly suits the mingled dash and delicacy of Mrs Boucicault's style. *Athenæum*

MARCH 1. Mrs Boucicault as Violet and Dion Boucicault as Grimaldi in Dion Boucicault's **Life of an Actress** at Adelphi Theatre. Violet, a poor street singer, ends up so educated and so refined that she acts in the plays of Corneille. The story owed something to the incidents in the life of the French tragedienne, Rachel.

> When Violet is falling under the influence of the opiate, Mrs Boucicault's gentle demeanour robs an unpleasing situation of more than half its repulsiveness. *Daily Telegraph*

> Mr Boucicault's portraiture of the, by turns obsequious, courteous and indignant Grimaldi was in all respects a masterpiece of histrionic ability … we are not quite sure that the drama itself (which is partly compilation and partly adaptation) will add much to his reputation as a dramatist; but his reputation as an actor must be augmented by the skill and tact with which he has embodied and supported the part of the hero. *Athenæum*

MARCH 3. John Ryder as Othello and Charles Fechter as Iago in Shakespeare's **Othello** at Princess's Theatre. Fechter wasn't an obvious villain. It wasn't what he said but when he was silent that he revealed his true character.

MARCH 27. **The Rajah of Nagpore or The Sacred Elephant of the Pagoda** at Astley's Amphitheatre featured colossal performing elephants. Billed as brilliant horsemanship, it was followed by a comic ballet.

THE STRAND MUSIC HALL.—Mr. E. BASSETT KEELING, ARCHITECT.

SECTIONAL VIEW OF THE INTERIOR OF

THE STRAND MUSIC HALL, LONDON.

195

Marie Wilton (1839–1921), actress and theatre manager, established The Prince of Wales's Theatre as a theatre of quality to which the respectable middle classes were happy to come. She was married to Squire Bancroft.

MARCH 8. Kate Terry as Mrs Union in Horace Wigan's **Friends or Foes** at St James's Theatre. Adaptation of *Nos intimes*. Terry stood in at short notice for Miss Herbert, who was ill, and immediately established herself as an actress of the first rank. *The Daily News* raved: 'It is altogether a most charming delineation and we believe could not be surpassed on any stage.'

APRIL 14. John Emery and Louise Keeley as Mr and Mrs Perrybingle in Dion Boucicault's **Dot**,

a dramatisation of Charles Dickens' *The Cricket on the Hearth*, at Adelphi Theatre. Sarah Woolgar as Tilly Slowby. J. L. Toole had a big success as Caleb Plummer. Boucicault gave the story a fairy framework and introduced a sensation scene.

APRIL 21. Dion Boucicault in a shorter version of his play **The Phantom** at Adelphi Theatre was made up to look like a melancholy Byron. The supernatural horrors were increased by W. Telbin's recreation of the heights of Ben Nevis.

MAY 10. Margaret Cooper in R. W. Taylor's **The Lady in a Lake** at New Royalty Theatre. Burlesque: puns, parodies and dances.

JULY 29. Marie Wilton and Mr Rogers in J. P. Wooler's **Marriage at Any Price** at Strand Theatre. Farce. Reversal of roles: Wilton was dressed as a man and Rogers was dressed as a woman.

SEPTEMBER 15. Dion Boucicault and Mrs Boucicault in Dion Boucicault's **The Relief of Lucknow** at Drury Lane Theatre. This grand

1862

Births
Adolphe Appia, Swiss stage
   designer
Georges Feydeau, French
   playwright
Gerhart Hauptmann, German
   playwright
Maurice Maeterlinck, Belgian
   poet, dramatist, essayist,
   Nobel prize winner
Elizabeth Robins, British
   actress
Arthur Schnitzler, Austrian
   dramatist

Deaths
James Sheridan Knowles,
   Anglo-Irish dramatist
   (b. 1874)
Johann Nestroy, Austrian
   actor, dramatist (b. 1801)

Literature
Mary Braddon's *Lady Audley's Secret*
Victor Hugo's *Les Miserables*

History
World's first underground
   rail journey takes place
   on Metropolitan Railway
   between Paddington and
   Farringdon Street
204 miners die in Hartley
   Colliery Disaster
Riots in Stalybridge over
   recession in cotton industry
Robbery with violence made
   punishable by flogging
Construction of Thames
   Embankment begins

military spectacle was originally produced in New York in 1858 under the title of *Jessie Brown*. The curtain fell on a mêlée of Hindoos and the 78th Highlanders. (Lucknow had been relieved on 25 September 1857.)

> As a literary composition it has nothing whatever to command it, but as an animated military spectacle it will be sure to gain applause. Nothing, perhaps, can be more feeble in dialogue and more lax in construction; but a lively and incessant detonation of gunpowder supplies the place of language. *Observer*

OCTOBER 2. Dion Boucicault wrote a letter to *The Times* advocating improvements to theatre buildings and offered to be a subscriber to the extent of £5,000.

NOVEMBER 3. Louise Payne in William Vincent Wallace's **Love's Triumph** at Covent Garden Theatre. Libretto by J. R. Planché.

NOVEMBER 6. Samuel Phelps took his farewell as manager of Sadler's Wells Theatre in Shakespeare's *Julius Caesar*. He played Brutus. In his curtain call speech he said:

> The production of thirty-four plays by Shakespeare, some of which have been considered unactable, is a feat, I believe, never before attempted by any manager in modern times. It has been to me a labour of love – an object of pride, rather than a source of profit, for when I tell you that a single play of Pericles cost in its production £1,000 and the expense lavished upon the others being very great, you will easily perceive how impossible it was in such a theatre as this that my labour should be rewarded by large pecuniary profit … Dramatic representations have, and, I believe, in some form or other always will stand in the foremost rank of those amusements; and it is surely better that the young who are so easily and strongly impressed by them, should receive those impressions from the plays of Shakespeare, rather than the sensational dramas and translations from the French of questionable morality.
> SAMUEL PHELPS

1863

FEBRUARY 28. Louisa Herbert in C. H. Hazelwood's adaptation of Miss Braddon's novel, **Lady Audley's Secret**, at St James's Theatre. Robert Audley, having deserted his wife and child, returns from Australia after three years, to find that she is married to a besotted knight, old enough to be her grandfather. Lady Audley, the arch villainess, goes mad. Between February and April there were productions in three other theatres: Queen's, Princess's and Britannia.

> It is only in two acts, and the putting of the superfluous husband into the well followed so closely on the bigamy, the glow of the arson, again, so closely on the stain of murder, and the interesting heroine goes mad so immediately, with the glow of the house she had burnt still on her face, and the man she has burnt in it dying on a stretcher by her side, that the audience has a pudding all plums.
> HENRY MORLEY, *Journal of a London Playgoer*

MARCH 10. The Adelphi Theatre celebrated the marriage of the Prince of Wales and Princess Alexandria of Denmark with free tickets for a bill which included: J. L. Toole and Paul Bedford in **A Grey Mare**, a comedietta; **A Valentine** recited by Avonia Jones; Benjamin Webster and Henrietta Simms in **One Touch of Nature**; and J. L. Toole, Paul Bedford, Sarah Woolgar and Miss Kelly in H. J. Byron's **George De Barnwell**, a burlesque pantomime.

Tom Taylor (1817–80) was the author of some seventy plays, including Still Waters Run Deep (1855), Our American Cousin (1858), The Ticket-of-Leave Man (1863), The Contested Election (1859), The Overland Route (1860), 'Twixt Axe and Crown (1870) and Anne Boleyn (1876).

Tom Taylor's The Ticket-of-Leave-Man was premiered at Olympic Theatre in 1863, and became one of the most famous melodramas of the nineteenth century.

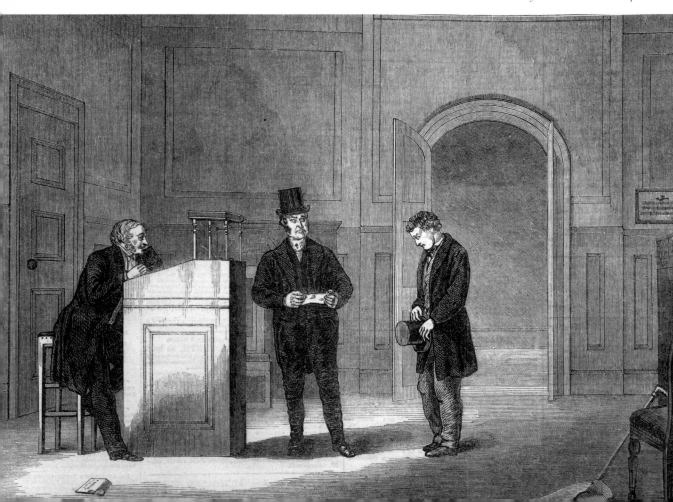

The Adelphi Theatre was sold out on 21 March 1863, the night it celebrated the marriage of Prince Edward, Queen Victoria's eldest son, and Princess Alexandra.

MAY 27. Henry Neville and Kate Smith in Tom Taylor's ***Ticket-of-Leave-Man*** at Olympic Theatre. Horace Wigan as Detective Hawkshaw. A Lancashire lad, wrongfully convicted of passing forged notes, goes to Pentonville for four years, where he is an exemplary prisoner. He returns to society, wanting to be honest, but is barred from earning an honest living the moment people know he is an ex-convict. Unexpectedly, it is the policeman who shows more mercy than the employer, who sacks him on his wedding day. Hawkshaw, the very first stage detective, reminded audiences of Buckett in *Bleak House*. Some of the other characters also seemed to have stepped out of Dickens: the gossiping granny, her mischievous grandson, the down-and-out actor and his singer wife. Taylor provided a mixture of sentiment, sensation and direct appeals to the audience's collective social conscience. The acting and the settings, particularly the graveyard, were praised for their reality. *The Ticket of Leave Man* was the most popular melodrama of its time, originally running for 407 performances. Neville would still be playing the leading role in 1910.

> Though of necessity many of his personages utter a great deal of vulgar talk it is obvious throughout that the dialogue has been written by no vulgar hand. Above all he has avoided the maudlin sentimentality that inflated bombast which really vulgar writers often employ to elevate a homely subject. *The Times*

Kate Bateman, the American actress, as Leah, the role she had already created in New York. Solomon von Mosenthal's Leah had its London premiere at Adelphi Theatre in 1863.

1863

It is to be feared that people go to the Theatre to enjoy themselves and it may be feared that such was the object of a certain absconding Clerk in going to the Olympic Theatre with £2,500 of his employers money in his pocket, with which, in the ease of his heart, as Wordsworth says, he had taken himself off from Liverpool. But the ease of his heart could not withstand the pressure of Mr Tom Taylor's play. *The Ticket-of-Leave-Man* awakened three-fifths of a conscience in this Clerk's breast – he was so affected that he went out of the theatre, got three envelopes, and sent £1,500 back to his employers. This Clerk took his place in the Pit of the Olympic, if not a hardened, yet certainly an unsoftened and unchastened offender against social law and right. He went to the theatre a striking example of instantaneous conversion from the error of his way. RICHARD BRINSLEY SHERIDAN printed in the programme:

JUNE 11. Antonio Giuglini as Faust and Thérèse Tietjens as Marguerite in London premiere of Charles Gounod's **Faust** at Her Majesty's Theatre. Edouard Gassier as Mephistopheles. Sung in French.

It is original, vigorous and dramatic; but it shows a disregard or defiance of the existing laws of musical composition which often render it harsh, rugged and unpleasing. In this respect it may be regarded as 'music of the future'.
Illustrated London News

JULY 2. Enrico Tamberlik as Faust and Marie Miolan-Carvalho as Marguerite in Charles Gounod's **Faust** at Covent Garden Theatre. Jean-Baptiste Faure as Mephistopheles. Gounod created the role for Miolan-Carvalho. *The Times* was not impressed: '[she] walks the stage with a placid composure and muscular rigidity of a somnambulist – scarcely ever keeps her eyes on Faust.'

SEPTEMBER 21. Mr Belmore in F. C. Burnand's **The Deal Boatman** at Sadler's Wells Theatre. This adaptation of Charles Dickens' *David Copperfield*, based on the Peggoty episodes, didn't feel as if it were a work by Dickens.

OCTOBER 1. Kate Bateman's debut on the London stage in **Leah** at Adelphi Theatre. Jewish maiden is deserted by her lover. An adaptation of Solomon von Mosenthal's *Deborah*.

Miss Bateman hurls down the great solemn curse with aplomb, and everybody shrinks. She reappears in enfeebled condition and murmurs forth forgiveness, whereupon everybody weeps. The means to the end are broad rather than subtle, but they are forcibly and skilfully employed, and when the curtain falls the actress has fairly subjected her audience.
Saturday Review

OCTOBER 14. Samuel Phelps in Lord Byron's **Manfred** at Drury Lane Theatre. The high spot was the spectacle of the Hall of Arimanes.

The dialogue began to suffer from the declamatory monotone to which Mr Phelps had set it and the exuberant action of his right arm became excessively troublesome to those who were naturally annoyed by its perpetual action. *Illustrated London News*

There must be some merit in this piece since Goethe admired it – but as a drama nothing could be worse – The invocation in lyric verse sounds like doggerel though great pains were taken by the declaimer to throw dignity and tragic effect into the recitation. Action there is not. It is a sort of Don Juan without wit or fun or character.
HENRY CRABB ROBINSON, *Journal*

On the whole Lord Byron never did much good, and he did some evil. His genius was morbid and he died before he could emerge into purer air. *Theatre Journal*

1864

FEBRUARY 27. The Irish identical twins Charles and Henry Webb got top billing as the two Dromios in Shakespeare's **The Comedy of Errors** at Princess's Theatre.

APRIL 30. Edward Askew Sothern in T. W. Robertson's **David Garrick** at Haymarket Theatre. Garrick acts the drunken boor in order to stop the infatuation of a young lady. Certain critics didn't think it was acceptable to put a real person in a play and then give him an entirely fictitious setting.

Mr Sothern's acting, remarkable for its ease and polished finish, was most warmly appreciated. The drunken scene in the second act was marvellously well executed and for grace as well as characteristic vigour could scarcely have been better done. The audience here seemed quite wild with excitement.   *Theatre Journal*

AUGUST 5. George Vining in Dion Boucicault's **The Streets of London** at Princess's Theatre. When Boucicault was in New York in 1857 he adapted a French drama, *Les pauvres de Paris* and called it *The Streets of New York*. It was a great success. When he returned to Liverpool he revived it and called it *The Streets of Liverpool*. He then changed the title according to the city he was playing in. Finally, it arrived in London. The play mixed melodramatic spectacle and social observation to become a Christian sermon in which the audience was encouraged to give to the poor on their way home. The sensation scene was the burning of a house. There was a real fire-engine and real horses on stage.

It is the most depressing instance, without exception, of an utterly degrading and debasing theatrical taste that has ever come under my notice. For not only do the audiences – all classes – go, but are unquestionably delighted.
CHARLES DICKENS in a letter to John Forster

*Edward Askew Sothern in
T. W. Robertson's Garrick at
Haymarket Theatre in 1864.*

The burning house in Dion Boucicault's Streets of London at Princess's Theatre in 1864. Boucicault's plays were famous for their 'sensation' scenes.

OCTOBER 17. Helen Faucit as Imogen in Shakespeare's **Cymbeline** at Drury Lane Theatre. Faucit's 'representation is truly remarkable,' said *Theatre Journal*, 'and in pathos and natural beauty leaves her without any rival in proud possession of the tragic throne.'

It [Imogen] is, perhaps, on the whole her cleverest assumption, marked by extreme refinement and a large amount of study, extending almost to every word. Her motions are guided and regulated by the most exquisite taste and present to the eyes a series of sculpturesque attitudes.   *Athenæum*

NOVEMBER 19. Helen Faucit as Rosalind in Shakespeare's **As You Like It** at Drury Lane Theatre. Walter Montgomery as Orlando. James Anderson as Jaques. Walter Lacy as Touchstone.

Miss Faucit acting is a delight. If she has not the art to conceal art, the art she does not conceal, is founded on quick and refined perception of the poetry she is interpreting.
HENRY MORLEY, *Journal of a London Playgoer*

World premieres
Jacques Offenbach's *La Belle Hélène* in Paris

Births
Vesta Tilley, British male impersonator
Frank Wedekind, German dramatist

Deaths
T. P. Cooke, British actor (b. 1786)
Frederick Robson, died of stage fright (b. 1822)

Notes
The Great Vance, music hall artist, singer of broad cockney songs, makes his debut at the South London Palace; his most popular song was 'Cliquot'.
George Leybourne sings 'Champagne Charlie Is My Name' for the first time at Gilbert Music Hall. The prototype Charlie was the notorious gambler, the fourth Marquis of Hastings.

Literature
Charles Dickens' last novel *Our Mutual Friend* (1864–65)
Elizabeth Gaskell's *Wives and Daughters*
Anthony Trollope's *The Small House at Allington*
Jules Verne's *Journey to the Centre of the Earth*

History
Charing Cross station opens
Public debate in Oxford about Darwinian evolution

1864

1865

JANUARY 30. Kate Bateman as Julia in James Sheridan Knowles' **The Hunchback** at Adelphi Theatre.

> Now that I have seen her in two plays, I do not hesitate to rank Miss Bateman among the clever actresses whose special excellence is bounded within limits so narrow as that although, once carefully and exclusively presented, it may win for a short time a deserved success, it does not enable them permanently to hold their own among performers of the highest class.
> HENRY MORLEY, *Journal of a London Playgoer*

MARCH 6. Helen Faucit began a season of plays at Haymarket Theatre: Imogen in Shakespeare's **Cymbeline**, Rosalind in Shakespeare's **As You Like It** and Lady Teazle in Richard Brinsley Sheridan's **The School for Scandal**. 'It is certain,' said *The Pall Mall Gazette*, 'that no one can read *As You Like It*, after seeing such a Rosalind as Helen Faucit without reading it illuminated.'

MARCH 22. H Vandenhoff, Dion Boucicault and Mrs Boucicault in Dion Boucicault's **Arrah-na-Pogue or The Wicklow Wedding** at Princess's Theatre. Based on events that took place during the Fenian rebellion in 1798. The anti-British lyric, 'The Wearing of the Green', became the unofficial anthem of the Irish Freedom Movement. The play's title means Arrah-of-the-Kiss. The heroine had hidden a plan of escape in her mouth. She delivered the plan with a kiss. The trial scene in Bernard Shaw's *The Devil's Disciple* owed much to this play.

> Of the acting in this excellent drama it is impossible to speak in words of too glowing eulogy. Mr Boucicault so thoroughly understands the Irish character that it is no marvel he should so well portray it … His Hibernian humour is so natural and expressed with so much truthfulness in both the tone of his words, and the changes of his countenance, that the illusion of reality is never broken for a moment and the idea of acting passes away for the time from the mind of the absorbed spectator.   *Era*

APRIL 14. John Wilkes Booth assassinated President Abraham Lincoln at Ford's Theatre, Washington, DC, during a performance of Tom Taylor's **Our American Cousin**.

Births
Mrs Patrick Campbell, British actress
Rudyard Kipling, British writer
Konstantin Stanislavsky, Russian actor, director, teacher
W. B. Yeats, Irish dramatist

Deaths
John Wilkes Booth, American actor (b. 1839)
Elizabeth Gaskell, British novelist (b. 1810)

Literature
Lewis Carroll's *Alice's Adventures in Wonderland*
John Henry Newman's *The Dream of Gerontius*
Lev Tolstoy's *War and Peace* (1865–69)

Notes
Mr and Mrs Bancroft began management of Prince of Wales's Theatre, known locally as The Dust Hole, and transformed it into middle-class respectability.

History
William and Catherine Booth set up The Christian Mission in Whitechapel, later named the Salvation Army
Elizabeth Garrett Anderson graduates as first woman doctor in UK
American Civil War ends
Abraham Lincoln assassinated
Paul Bogle is executed after leading Murant Bay rebellion in Jamaica
Ku Klux Klan is formed in Tennessee

1865

JUNE 23, 26, 28, 30. *Handel Festival* at Crystal Palace.

JUNE 30. Edward Terry and Kate Terry in Tom Taylor's ***The Serf or Love Levels All*** at Olympic Theatre. A Russian serf is sent by his master to Paris and is transformed into a gentleman. He falls in love with a countess who is not pleased when she discovers he had been a serf.

JULY. Frederick Hazelton's ***Sweeney Todd or The Barber of Fleet Street or The String of Pearls*** at Bower Saloon.

JULY 19. Adelaide Neilson made her debut in Shakespeare's ***Romeo and Juliet*** at Royalty Theatre. Shortly before her debut she had been working as a Shakespearian-reciting barmaid in the Haymarket area.

AUGUST 21. Ira Aldridge in Shakespeare's ***Othello*** at Haymarket Theatre. Walter Montgomery as Iago. Madge Robertson as Desdemona. Aldridge returned to London from Europe and Asia, laden with honours and titles conferred upon him by crowned heads and literary and scientific and musical bodies.

SEPTEMBER 4. Joseph Jefferson, the American actor, in his London debut as Rip in Dion Boucicault's ***Rip van Winkle*** at Adelphi Theatre. An adaptation of Washington Irving's novel. Boucicault reconstructed the play at Jefferson's request. 'In Mr Jefferson's hands,' said *The Times*, 'the character of Rip becomes the vehicle for an extremely refined psychological exhibition.'

OCTOBER 4. George Vining and Louisa Moore in Charles Reade's ***It's Never Too Late to Mend*** at Princess's Theatre. Adaptation of Reade's novel. The purpose of the novel – subtitled *A Matter of Fact Romance* – was to reform abuse in prison. The production was praised for its 'glaring realism'.

Whether the abuses belong to the past or to the present is of little moment, neither is mere truth a sufficient reason for stage presentation.
The Times

Gangs of convicts passed by the spectator while the treadmill with all its horrors was exhibited. Next came the representation of the Silent

Joseph Jefferson, the American actor, in his most famous role: Rip van Winkle in Dion Boucicault's version of Washington Irving's novel at Adelphi Theatre in 1865. Jefferson played Rip no fewer than 2,500 times. Audiences did not want to see him in anything else.

system with a melodramatic accompaniment of human passion and agony. At this point the audience began to show signs of repugnance. They were somewhat conciliated by the extreme beauty of the scenes in Australia. *Athenæum*

NOVEMBER 4. Samuel Phelps in Shakespeare's **King John** at Lyceum Theatre. James Anderson as Faulconbridge. The production was notable for its lavish recreations of Angiers, Northampton Castle and Swinstead Abbey.

NOVEMBER 11. Squire Bancroft, Mrs Bancroft, John Clarke, Frederick Dewar, John Hare and Sophie Larkin in Tom Robertson's **Society** at Prince of Wales's Theatre. This satire on club-life among modern literary men had been originally rejected because of its recognisable sketches of well-known people. 150 performances.

I don't suppose that before the curtain drew up on Robertson's *Society* any one had heard a word about, and knew there was such an actor as John Hare. Before the curtain fell the young actor was famous and everyone who had social and newspaper influence was talking about him. CLEMENT SCOTT, *Sunday Times*

DECEMBER 22. Kate Bateman as Juliet in Shakespeare's **Romeo and Juliet** at Her Majesty's Theatre. Her last appearance prior to her departure for America and retirement from the stage. 'A performance of this nature is beyond the pale of criticism,' said *The Daily News*; 'it would be useless to praise it and ungracious to condemn it.' (Bateman's Romeo in America had been Wilkes Booth, the assassin of President Abraham Lincoln.)

DECEMBER 26. David Fisher and Louise Kelley in J. R. Planché's adaptation of Jacques Offenbach's **Orpheus in the Underworld** at Her Majesty's Theatre. It repeated the success that it had enjoyed in Paris.

Mr David Fisher played Orpheus with intelligence and the fiddle like an angel. Miss Louise Kelley was a charming Eurydice and sang like a nightingale. So with the addition of pretty scenery, pretty dresses and some pretty faces, we pulled through pretty well. It was not Offenbach's opera; but the piece went merrily with the audience and ran from Christmas to Easter. J. R. PLANCHÉ, *Autobiography*

1866

SEPTEMBER 15. Dion Boucicault, John Emery and John Cooper in Dion Boucicault's **The Long Strike** at Lyceum Theatre. The debt to Mrs Gaskell's *Mary Barton* was acknowledged on the playbills. A factory boss attempts to seduce the daughter of a Chartist. The Chartist shoots him and then goes mad. The most exciting moment was when the villain was apprehended with the aid of the recently invented electric telegraph, the first time it had ever been used on a stage.

SEPTEMBER 15. Mary Wilton, Louisa Moore and John Hare in T. W. Robertson's **Ours** at Prince of Wales's Theatre. The comedy, set during the

Crimean War, was inspired by Sir John Everett Millais' painting *The Black Brunswicker*. Robertson admitted that war, wealth and matrimony could brutalise, but he was quick to reassure his audience that they could at the same time elevate and ennoble. The heroine, faced with a choice between a rich Russian Prince (with 400,000 serfs), and a poor English cadet, naturally chooses the Englishman. In the last act all the ladies arrive in the Crimea and go off (so we presume) to watch the Charge of the Light Brigade and see their men-folk die before their very eyes. A roly-poly pudding was made on stage with improvised culinary utensils. 'Mr Robertson,' said *The Daily*

ABOVE

The third act in Tom Robertson's Ours at Prince of Wales's Theatre in 1866. The third act, which took place in the Crimea, was admired for its realism: first there was the snow, which came into the hut every time the door was opened, and then there was the joy of watching two actors actually making a roly-poly pudding on the stage.

LEFT

Thomas William Robertson (1829–71) the 'cup-and-saucer' playwright, was the author of Ours (1864), Society (1865), Caste (1867), Play (1868), School (1869) and MP (1870).

‘ I do not want actors, but men and women who will do as I tell them. ’

TOM ROBERTSON

'*My opinion of Robertson as a stage-manager is of the very highest. He had a gift peculiar to himself, and which I have never seen in any other author, of conveying by some rapid and almost electrical suggestion to the actor an insight into the character assigned to him. As nature was the basis of his own work, so he sought to make actors understand it should be theirs. He thus founded a school of natural acting which completely revolutionized the then existing methods, and by so doing did incalculable good to the stage.*'

JOHN HARE

Robertson invented stage-management. It was an unknown art before his time. Formerly, in a conversation scene, for instance, you simply brought down two or three chairs from the flat and placed them in a row in the middle of the stage, and then people sat down and talked, and when the conversation was ended the chairs were replaced. Robertson showed how to give life and variety and nature to the scene by breaking it up with all sorts of little incidents and delicate by-play. I have been at many of his rehearsals and learnt a great deal from them.

W. S. GILBERT

News, 'evidently relies more upon the brilliancy of his dialogue and the originality of his situations, than upon any subtleties of plot … The acting was very near perfection.' The play and its production firmly established the reputation of the theatre, the Bancrofts and Robertson. (Stalls cost 6*s*.; dress circle 3*s*.; pit and amphitheatre 1*s*. 6*d*. Gallery 6*d*. Private boxes £2 2*s*.)

The Russian prince [John Hare] simply lived. It was no stage figure of tradition or convention but an interesting personality whose every look, word, gesture and even feature, seemed indispensable parts of a perfect whole.

ARTHUR GODDARD, *Players of the Period*

An epigrammatic tendency, which not only shows itself in dialogue, but points the entire fable; a predilection for domestic pathos which is ever kept in check by a native abhorrence of twaddling sentimentality; a firm steady hand and a freedom from convention in the delineation of character; an eye for picturesque effects that arise less from the employment of accessories than from the arrangement of group that are the natural result of the action and a connexion with the realities, which, perhaps, must not be too closely scrutinized, but which, to a certain extent makes the stage reflect the world with more than usual accuracy – these are the characteristics which distinguish the best work of Mr T. W. Robertson and which have made each of them [*Society* and *Ours*] one off the leading pieces of the season. *The Times*

OCTOBER 6. Dion Boucicault's ***The Flying Scud or Four-Legged Fortune*** at Holborn Theatre. Turf melodrama. The jockey was drugged and so the hero had to take his place and ride Flying Scud to victory. The production, with its crowds, carriages and pickpockets, brought William Powell Frith's painting, The Derby Day (1857–58), vividly to life. The horses were made out of cardboard, except for Scud. 'There are many things in it,' said *The Observer*, 'that cannot fail to please at least uneducated audiences.' 207 performances.

OCTOBER 27. Lydia Foote and Dominic Murray in Wilkie Collins' ***The Frozen Deep*** at Olympic Theatre. Two rivals are in love, and one is determined to kill the other. Gloomy drama in picturesque scenery. 'The story is perhaps over-melodramatic,' said *The Athenæum*, 'and a happy ending might have made it more popular.'

DECEMBER 29. Miss McDonnell, Miss Addison and Mr Charles in W. S. Gilbert's ***Dulcamara or The Little Duck and The Great Quack*** at St James's Theatre. Burlesque of Gaetano Donizetti's *The Elixir of Love*. 'A mass of puns, some unequivocally good, some admirably bad, and all comic in the extreme,' said *The Times*. 'Mr Gilbert takes the most outrageous liberties with the story.'

The New Amphitheatre, Holborn, opened in 1867. The architect was Thomas Smith.

1867

JANUARY 9. Charles Fechter as Maurice D'Arbel in Henry Leslie's adaptation of Stendhal's **Rouge et Noir** at Lyceum Theatre. The life of a gambler: the transformation of a happy, sinful member of fashionable society to a tattered, miserable, starving mendicant. 'There are playgoers who prefer such themes,' said *The Illustrated London News*, 'but they are not of the highest class.'

MARCH 16. Henry Neville, Mrs Alfred Mellon and J. L. Toole in Watts Phillips' **Lost in London** at Adelphi Theatre. A poor miner demands redress of a fair duel from the rich man who has seduced his wife. The rich man refuses because they are not of the same class.

APRIL 6. Lydia Foote, Marie Wilton, Squire Bancroft, George Honey and John Hare in T. W. Robertson's **Caste! or The Soldier's Return** at Prince of Wales's Theatre. A charming and senti-mental comedy about class distinctions. Robertson wrote miniature realistic dramas of contemporary domestic life, so miniature and domestic that they came to be known as 'the cup-and-saucer plays of the bread-and-butter school'. A fine, rich lord marries beneath him. His best friend and his mama are horrified, feeling that a poor, humble ballet dancer might do for a liaison, but certainly never for a wife. Robertson's satire on snobbery and his caricature of the working man were very gentle. The play approves of the social system: 'Oh, Caste's all right. Caste is a good thing if it's not carried too far. It shuts the door to the pretentious and the vulgar: but it should open the door very wide for exceptional merit. Let brains break through its barriers, and what brains can break through love may leap over.'

The Times said that Tom Robertson 'combined the geniality of Mr Dickens with the cynicism of Mr Thackeray'. Shorthand experts were placed, for several successive nights, in different parts of the theatre to take down the text so as to enable the play to be acted throughout the United States without paying one cent of royalties.

> The play had that hearty human interest that springs from the vigorous portraiture of character and the truthful representation of life and manners as they really are.
> THE BANCROFTS, *Recollections of Sixty Years*

Marie Wilton and John Hare in Tom Robertson's Caste at Prince of Wales's Theatre in 1867. Caste was Robertson's most famous cup-and-saucer drama and much admired in its day for its new naturalism, both in acting and setting.

Sir Arthur Sullivan (1842–1900) was the composer of Cox and Box. His partnership with W. S. Gilbert did not begin until Trial by Jury, which was composed in 1865.

Mr Hare is so refined and perfect an actor, so true an observer of life that we are not surprised to find him made up as a sharp, wiry, veritable working-man who might have stepped out of any carpenter shop in England. The scene in which he reads to his intended the trade circular he has just composed is the most exquisite and unforced bit of comedy we have seen for years. *Daily News*

APRIL 21. Dion Boucicault as Sir Alan Ruthven in Dion Boucicault's **The Phantom** at Holborn Theatre. 'We doubt however if the British public will ever cordially accept the subject,' said *The Illustrated London News*. 'The superstition on which it is founded is deficient in beauty and not redeemed by morality.'

APRIL 22. F. C. Burnard's **Olympic Games** at Olympic Theatre. Burlesque. Mars and Venus are in love, and Vulcan can't get a divorce. *The Illustrated London News* said 'Author, actor and artist revelled in the nonsense, which proper enough to burlesque, rather bewildered than enlightened the audience.'

APRIL 22. Madge Robertson in Andrew Halliday's **The Great City** at Drury Lane Theatre. A slice of middle-class London life: romantic and vulgar. There were recreations of Charing Cross Hotel, St Paul's Cathedral, Westminster Bridge by moonlight, and a railway station. The latter was based on William Powell Frith's painting.

MAY 11. Mr Quintin and George Du Maurier in Arthur Sullivan's **Cox and Box or The Long Lost Brothers** conducted by Arthur Sullivan at Adelphi Theatre. Libretto by Francis Cowley Burnand based on John Maddison Morton's *Box and Cox*. 'Quite as striking and as lively as anything by M. Offenbach,' said *The Times*. Du Maurier was best known as a cartoonist, illustrator and novelist.

Mr Sullivan's music is, in many places, of too high a class for the grotesquely absurd plot, to which it is wedded. It is very funny here and there, and grand and graceful when it is not funny; but the grand and graceful have, we think, too large a share of the honours to themselves. W. S. GILBERT, *Fun Magazine*

MAY 15. Henry Loraine and Isabella Glyn in Shakespeare's **Antony and Cleopatra** at Princess's Theatre. Glyn was 44 years old. An Egyptian ballet heralded the entrance of the lovers. The splendid scenic effects were by Thomas Grieve and Frederick Reynolds.

The witchery of the blandishments, the Asiatic undulations of the form, the variety of the enchantments, the changes of mood, the impetuous passion, and in the end the noble resignation all these points are brought out with

A scene from Shakespeare's Antony and
Cleopatra at Princess's Theatre in 1867.

' How unlike the life of our own dear Queen! '
VICTORIAN THEATERGOER

an accuracy of elocution and with a force of
genius which leave no doubt in the mind that
Miss Glyn is as great an actress as ever adorned
the English stage.   *Athenæum*

JULY 30. Charles Mathews appeared twice
in Douglas William Jerrold's farce, **Cool as a
Cucumber**. First, acting it in French at St James's
Theatre for the Benefit of M. Ravel, and then
acting it in English at Olympic Theatre.

Take all the flattering adjectives I have applied to
his other successful creations, put them together,
even then they would not do justice to that

matchless impersonation which was altogether
the most delightful comedy performance I have
ever witnessed.   JOHN COLEMAN

AUGUST 31. Kate Terry made her farewell as
Juliet in Shakespeare's **Romeo and Juliet** at Adelphi
Theatre. Henry Neville was Romeo.

The widespread feeling that that the stage is
losing one of its chosen ornaments had been
manifest by the full houses, more and more
crowded on each successive night … She has
done nothing in her range of Shakespearian
parts, to our thinking, so full of charm,

World premieres

Giuseppe Verdi's *Don Carlos* in Paris

Births

Arnold Bennett, British novelist

John Galsworthy, British dramatist, novelist

Luigi Pirandello, Italian dramatist

Harry Relph (Little Tich), British music hall artist

Florenz Ziegfeld, American impresario

Deaths

Ira Aldridge, African-American actor (b. 1807)

Literature

Karl Marx's *Das Kapital*, vol. 1

Anthony Trollope's *The Last Chronicle of Barset*

Emile Zola's *Thérèse Raquin*

Notes

Queen's Theatre opens

His Majesty's Theatre is destroyed by fire

History

Fenian risings in Ireland and attempted capture of Chester

John Stuart Mill tries to introduce women's suffrage: House of Commons votes 196:73 against.

Russia sells Alaska to the US for 2 cents per acre

Benjamin Disraeli's Reform Act doubles franchise

Barnardo's children's shelter in Stepney opens

Last convict ship sails for Australia

---

sweetness and power of passion as her Juliet … In the interests of art we deeply regret her retirement. *The Times*

She has been accepted by intelligent audiences as one of the most graceful of the exponents of the domestic drama that ever trod the boards, and the remarkable intelligence she brought to bear upon these subjects of modern invention doubtless gave to the many indifferent dramas in which she appeared a temporary reputation far beyond their deserts. *Illustrated London News*

OCTOBER 5. Ada Swanborough as William Tell in H. B. Byron's **William Tell with a Vengeance** at Strand Theatre. Burlesque. Mrs Tell (played by actor in drag) teaches her son how to shoot. His arrow hits her. 'This,' said *The Illustrated London News*, 'is not caricature, but desecration.'

OCTOBER 9. Charles Reade's adaptation of his novel, **Griffith Gaunt or Jealousy**, at Drury Lane Theatre. A campaign against sexual hypocrisy: Reade thought it was his best novel; nobody thought it was his best play.

DECEMBER 26. Henry Irving and Ellen Terry in **Katherine and Petruchio**, Garrick's adaptation of Shakespeare's *The Taming of the Shrew*, at Queen's Theatre. They were not a success.

DECEMBER 26. Charles Fechter, Benjamin Webster, Henry Neville and Carlotta Leclercq in Charles Dickens' and Wilkie Collins' **No Thoroughfare** at Adelphi Theatre. There are two separate stories – one is about a Foundling Hospital, the other is about a murder in Switzerland. The play lasted four hours, and the two stories never came together.

OVERLEAF, LEFT

Faw Fee Fo Fum or Harlequin Jack and the Giant Killer was the pantomime at Drury Lane Theatre in 1867

Valentine and Orson or Harlequin, The Big Bear and the Little Fairy, was the pantomime at Holborn Theatre in 1867.

OVERLEAF, RIGHT

The Goose with the Golden Eggs, The Babes in the Wood or Harlequin Robin Hood and His Merry Men was the pantomime at Covent Garden Theatre in 1867.

Cock Robin and Jenny Wren or the Little Man Who Wooed the Little Maid was the pantomime at Lyceum Theatre in 1867.

DRURY LANE

HOLBORN

COVENT GARDEN

LYCEUM

1868

FEBRUARY 1. Samuel Phelps in **The Hypocrite**, John Oxenford's version of Moliere's *Tartuffe* at Drury Lane Theatre. It seemed unlikely that Phelps' cleric would ever have been allowed into Orgon's house in the first place.

FEBRUARY 15. Squire Bancroft, Mrs Bancroft, Lydia Foote, Mrs Leigh Murray, John Hare and William Blakely in T. W. Robertson's **Play** at Prince of Wales's Theatre. The least successful of Robertson's plays. There were two sorts of 'play': the husband was a gambler, his wife was an actress. The husband contemplates bigamy while his wife is in America. 'The dialogue is remarkably brilliant,' said *The Athenæum*, 'and compensates for the manifest defects of the story.'

FEBRUARY 17. Mrs Stirling in J. S. Coyne's **The Woman of the World** at Olympic Theatre. The woman of the world proved to be not worldly enough.

FEBRUARY 24. Barry Sullivan in Colley Cibber's version of Shakespeare's **Richard III** at Drury Lane Theatre.

His voice is a little deficient in compass, and his declamation is apt consequently to become somewhat monotonous, but on the whole he supports the part heroically. Hoarseness in the last act must have befallen all Richard's time out of mind for the part is terribly taxing to the lungs, and in the same way some degree of mouthing and ranting can hardly ever have been wholly dispensed with.
DUTTON COOK, *Pall Mall Gazette*

APRIL 13. A Japanese troupe of acrobats and conjurors made their first appearance in London at Lyceum Theatre.

MAY 28. Dion Boucicault's **Foul Play** at Holborn Theatre. Based on Charles Reade's novel. The hero is a convict (falsely convicted, of course) who is deported to Australia. He escapes and falls in love with the villain's fiancée. They are shipwrecked on an island and lead an idyllic and chaste life until they return to London to expose the villain, who, when he is confronted with his forgeries and near-murders, goes mad.

JULY 28. Agnes Cameron and Charles Verner in premiere of Benjamin Disraeli's **The Tragedy of Count Alacros** at Astley's Amphitheatre. The story, based on a thirteenth-century ballad, was first published in 1839. 'With such interpreters,' said *The*

The apprentices fight in Fleet Street: a scene from an adaptation of Sir Walter Scott's The King of Scots at Drury Lane Theatre in 1868.

Illustrated London News, 'it is a wonder the tragedy survived its first two acts, which, we venture to say, were not understood by a single auditor.'

Mr Disraeli is constitutionally flowery and fluent to redundancy ... Many of the actors were so unskilled in their profession as to be wholly inaudible, while the majority of those who could be heard were but imperfectly acquainted with the words of their parts and talked nonsense to make out their scenes, as builders fill cavities by shooting in rubbish ... So courageous an exhibition of incapacity can hardly ever have been seen in a London theatre. The stage management was that of a strolling company in a barn. DUTTON COOK, *Pall Mall Gazette*

AUGUST 12. H. J. Montague, Walter Lacy, Dominic Murray and Rose Leclercq in Dion Boucicault's **After Dark** at Princess's Theatre. Brilliant recreations of Victoria Station, Blackfriars Bridge and the Music Hall. The sensation scene was the rescue of a drugged man, who is lying on a railway line. He is grabbed to safety at the last minute, just as the train approaches.

> In a little while playwrights, we may hope, will learn that the success of realism they affect means the ruin of all that is noblest in the drama, or may grasp a truth more likely to impress them; namely in the end the system they have adopted will prove fatal to their own interests. *Athenæum*

SEPTEMBER 26. Samuel Phelps in *King of the Scots*, Mr Halliday's adaptation of Sir Walter Scott's novel, *The Fortunes of Nigel*, at Drury Lane Theatre. 'It must be confessed that all that is good and effective in the drama is Sir Walter Scott's,' said *The Observer*, 'nearly all that is tedious and ineffective is Mr Halliday's.' Phelps played both the king and a miserly usurer, a striking double-act.

OCTOBER 17. Charles Fechter in *Monte Cristo* at Adelphi Theatre. Interminable and tedious adaptation of Alexandre Dumas' novel. The audience got so restive that they addressed each actor on his entrance with the question, 'Shall you be long, sir?' In Paris the production had wisely been spread over three nights.

1869

JANUARY 7. Charles Dickens read the murder of Nancy from his novel, **Oliver Twist**, at St James's Hall. He had given a private reading in December 1868 to ascertain whether audiences would be able to take the horror.

> He has always trembled on the boundary line that separates the reader from the actor; in this case he clears it in a leap … he entirely abandoned himself to the torrent of frightful events and even flings away the book long before he has reached the conclusion that he may be without apparent obstacle to his utterance. The savage nature of the Jew, always tempered by cowardice, the bold brutality of the housebreaker, the shrieking despair of Nancy, belong to the highest order of histrionic art. *The Times*

JANUARY 14. Edward Askew Sothern and Caroline Hill in T. W. Robertson's **Home** at Prince of Wales's Theatre. A son, in order to save his father from the snares of a woman of low birth, gets into disguise and is so convincing that even his father doesn't recognise him.

Charles Dickens gave the last of his highly dramatic readings in 1869. His readings were hugely popular on both sides of the Atlantic.

January 16. H. J. Montague, Carlotta Addison, Mr Bancroft and Marie Wilton in T. W. Robertson's *School* at Prince of Wales's Theatre. A lord falls in love with a teacher, and a cavalry officer falls in love with an heiress.

Their [*Home* and *School*] hold upon an audience is due to three gifts which Mr Robertson possesses in a remarkable degree – power of characterisation, smartness of dialogue and a cleverness in investing with romantic associations commonplace details of life. *Athenæum*

It may be noted that the limited size of the Prince of Wales's Theatre is of real advantage to the class of plays Mr Robertson is fond of producing; a story gains in strength and significance by being brought so closely to the view of the spectators; and the players are not constrained to unnatural shouting and grimaces in order that their speeches may be heard and the expression of their faces seen from distant portions of the house. Both author and actors are thus enabled to avoid exaggeration of language and manner which has long been a prominent failing in dramatic writing and representation. DUTTON COOK, *Pall Mall Gazette*

March 29. Charles Fechter and Carlotta Leclercq in Wilkie Collins' *Black and White* at Adelphi Theatre. Drama set in Trinidad forty years earlier before the passing of the Emancipation Act. A French gentleman discovers he is the son of a quadroon and a slave. An heiress decides to ignore the black blood in his veins and accept him as her lover, only to find he has been thrown into prison and put up for sale.

March 29. William Brough's *Joan of Arc* at Strand Theatre. Extravaganza: Joan survives, marries, and has three children.

April 10. Maggie Brennan and John Clarke in T. W. Robertson's *A Breach of Promise* at Globe Theatre. Based on *Les Amours de Cleopatre*. Irish dressmaker frightens her faithless fiancé into marriage when he tries to ditch her for somebody richer. She arrives at his wedding party pretending to be mad.

April 24. William Brough's *The Field of the Cloth of Gold* at Strand Theatre. Puns, parodies, dances and spectacle.

June 15. Handel Festival at Crystal Palace. *The Messiah* was performed to an audience of 19,217.

June 19. Charles Santley in Ambroise Thomas' *Amleto* at Covent Garden Theatre. Opera. Christine Nilsson as Ophelia. There are three kinds of music – the wags used to say – good, bad and Ambroise Thomas. At the Paris premiere in 1868 Hamlet didn't die. This was rectified for London. The Ghost turned up at Ophelia's funeral and ordered his son to kill Claudius, which he did there and then. There was no duel with Laertes.

World premieres
Henrik Ibsen's *The League of Youth* in Christiana (Oslo)
Richard Wagner's *Das Rheingold* in Munich

Births
George Robey, British comedian
Tyrone Power, American actor
Henry Wood, conductor
Lawrence Binyon, poet and scholar

Literature
R. D. Blackmore's *Lorna Doone*
W. S. Gilbert's *The Bab Ballads*
Mark Twain's *Phileas Finn*
John Stuart Mill's *The Subjection of Women*

Notes
Charing Cross Theatre opens
Folies Bergère opens in Paris (under the original name Folies Trévise)

History
Suez Canal opens
Girton College is founded for women
Hudson's Bay Co. cedes administrative control of Canada to Britain
Cutty Sark, tea clipper, is launched at Dumbarton
Diamond rush begins in South Africa
Holborn Viaduct and Blackfriars Bridge open

1869

Exquisite poetry turned into feeble, jingling rhymes; set to music which is not only devoid of dramatic tension, but is, merely considered as music, weak and ineffective. Probably, a French librettist could do justice to such a splendid theme and certainly Mr A. Thomas is unequal to the task of marrying music to the verse of Shakespeare. Christine Nillson is the best Ophelia to be found on the lyric stage. *Theatre*

JUNE 21. Kate Bateman in Tom Taylor's **Mary Warner** at Haymarket Theatre. Domestic tear-jerker, extreme sentimentality, rampant pathos and artificial suffering. A wife is convinced that her husband is guilty of theft. To save him from imprisonment and disgrace, she confesses to stealing a cash-box and goes to prison for five years. She comes out and is charged with robbing a gentleman. The production was notable for its vast steam engines and its recreation of Brixton Prison, a Police Court, a squalid Lambeth alley (lit with real gas lamps) and a grimy garret with a view of Westminster Clock Tower.

It should be said that Miss Bateman played with genuine force and feeling … whether the part was worth playing at all is another matter. *Athenæum*

BELOW

A scene from Wilkie Collins' Black and White at Adelphi Theatre in 1869.

RIGHT

A scene from Dion Boucicault and H. J. Byron's Lost at Sea at Adelphi Theatre in 1869.

It is with regret we have now to chronicle that the Haymarket Theatre hitherto devoted to better uses and distinguished for representations of a more refined class, has also fallen victim to the infection under mention: has, indeed, been seized with an attack of dramatic jail-fever of a most virulent kind. This remarkably unpleasant story is set forth at great length and presented on the stage with even more than the ordinary regard for realism of effect distinguishing the performance of works of the class.

DUTTON COOK, *Pall Mall Gazette*

AUGUST 5. Katherine Rogers in Dion Boucicault's **Formosa (The Most Beautiful), The Railroad to Ruin** at Drury Lane Theatre. A dastardly attempt by two scoundrels to stop Oxford winning the boat race – by getting their best oarsman into debt and arrested – is thwarted. The play caused a furore because the leading role was a high-class prostitute – a furore, fanned by the playwright, who, whenever the box office receipts took a fall, sent off letters to newspapers, under various pseudonyms, denouncing the play. The boat-race took place on stage. Henry Irving played the chief villain.

I am neither a literary missionary nor a martyr; I am simply a manager of a theatre, a vender of intellectual entertainment to the London public, and I found that Shakespeare spelt ruin and Byron bankruptcy. To the extremity to which I was led by my faith in the fine taste of the upper classes for the poetic drama, I turned to the dramatist who had made the fortunes of more than one manager in London.

FREDERICK CHATTERTON, theatre manager, in a letter to *The Times*

OCTOBER 2. Dion Boucicault and H. J. Byron's **Lost at Sea**, a London Story, at Adelphi Theatre. 'It has,' said *The Observer*, 'every fault that can be crowded into one piece and into 3 hours' representation.'

OCTOBER 25. John Baldwin Buckstone, Madge Robertson and Mr Howe in Tom Taylor and A. W. Douburg's **Old Men and New Acres** *or* **A Managing Mama** at Haymarket Theatre.

Madge Robertson would be a much better artist if she would learn to speak more plainly and to carry herself more gracefully. *Observer*

NOVEMBER 6. Mr Allerton, Brandon Ellis, Beatrix Shirley and Isabelle Armour in Dion Boucicault's **Forbidden Fruit** at Lyceum Theatre. A woman takes her revenge on her faithless lover by having sex with a total stranger.

The original is a powerful and subtle work, so daring and morbid in the analysis, both psychological and psychological that it incurred gross censure in Paris ... We can scarcely conceive a theme less fitted for art, and especially theatrical art. A plot like this cannot be manipulated as to be rendered suitable for the English stage. *Athenæum*

NOVEMBER 17. Mr Wybert and Clara Rousby in C. H. Hazelwood's **The Driven Snow** *or* **Tempted in Vain** at Britannia Theatre. Rustic heroine manages to preserve her virtue despite many temptations.

Henry Irving and Isabel Bateman in Edward Bulwer-Lytton's Richelieu at Lyceum Theatre in 1873.

The 1870s

1870

JANUARY 8. Matti Reinhardt in W. S. Gilbert's **The Princess** at Olympic Theatre. This elegant and arch mock-heroic extravaganza in blank verse was based on Alfred Lord Tennyson's poem. Gilbert admitted that three ladies dressed as gentlemen disguised as ladies, 'imparted an epicene character to the proceedings which rather interfered with the interest of the story'.

Henry Irving in the role that established him on the London stage: Digby Grant in James Albery's Two Roses at Vaudeville Theatre in 1870.

JANUARY 22. Clara Rousby as Elizabeth and Miss Pauncefort as Mary in Tom Taylor's **'Twixt Axe and Crown or The Lady Elizabeth** at Queen's Theatre. Sentimental historical drama in blank verse. Rousby was famous for her beauty, not her acting.

APRIL 23. John Hare and Mr Addison in T. W. Robertson's **M P** at Prince of Wales's Theatre. Election contest between a country gentleman and a *nouveau riche* vulgarian.

> The result is that we have at least one theatre in London to which we need not be ashamed to take an intelligent foreigner in order to convince them that the lighter comedy, at least, of our time, can still be written and acted in England with more finish and truth to nature, perhaps, than in that earlier time, when weightier stage work was better done than now.   TOM TAYLOR

> In a more spacious theatre, and by an audience more largely leavened with the usual pit and gallery public, these light and sparkling plays would probably be voted slow in movement, slight in texture and weak in interest, but in this pretty little bandbox of a house, with such artists as Marie Wilton, Hare, Bancroft, and their associates to interpret them, almost at arm's length of an audience who sits as in a drawing-room to hear drawing-room pleasantries, interchanged by drawing-room personages, nothing can be better fitted to amuse. Author, actors, and theatre seem perfectly fitted for each other. *The Times*

JUNE 4. Henry Irving as Digby Grant in James Albery's **Two Roses** at Vaudeville Theatre.

> The selfish arrogance, the stuck-up hauteur, the transparent hypocrisy, and the utter heartlessness of the character, made all the more odious from the assumption of sanctity, were depicted by Mr

Irving with exquisite truthfulness of detail, and admirable brilliancy and vigour of general effect. His make-up for the part was excellent, and his whole performance spirited, characteristic, and life-like. *Morning Post*

JUNE 14. Funeral of Charles Dickens at Westminster Abbey.

JULY 23. George Santley and Mille Murka in London premiere of Richard Wagner's **The Flying Dutchman** at Drury Lane Theatre. Conductor: Signor Arditti.

[Wagner] The best-abused man in Europe – deservedly abused for his arrogance, undeserved for his music … Mr Santley's superb voice and superber singing tell with full effect … much of the music allowed to him is cruel enough to make the sturdiest musicians waver. *Observer*

OCTOBER 24. William Kendal as Jack Absolute and Agnes Robertson as Lydia Languish in Richard Brinsley Sheridan's **The Rivals** at Haymarket Theatre.

The Haymarket still has a character enjoyed by few other theatres. It is looked up to by the public. Let us therefore encourage the Théâtre Française tone which the Haymarket enjoys, though in these days we can hardly hope for the Government grant. *Observer*

A scene from Oliver Goldsmith's The Vicar of Wakefield at The Standard Theatre in 1870.

World premieres

Modest Mussorgsky's *Boris Godunov* (three scenes) in St Petersburg

Arthur St Leon's *Coppelia* in Paris

Bedrich Smetana's *The Bartered Bride* (definitive three act version) in Prague

Richard Wagner's *Die Valkyrie* in Munich

Births

Harry Lauder, Scottish music hall artist

Hilaire Belloc, British writer

Marie Lloyd, British music hall artist

Nellie Wallace, Scottish comedian

Deaths

Charles Dickens, British novelist, dramatist, public reader (b. 1812)

Alexander Dumas père, French novelist, dramatist (b. 1802)

Literature

Charles Dickens' *The Mystery of Edwin Drood* (unfinished)

Notes

Opera Comique opens
Vaudeville Theatre opens

History

Franco-Prussian War begins

Married Women's Property Act acknowledges that wives may own property of their own

Competitive entry exams introduced for civil service

First Vatican Council

Rome becomes capital of a newly unified Italy

NOVEMBER 5. Samuel Emery as Dr Primrose and Emily Pitt as Olivia in **The Vicar of Wakefield** at Standard Theatre. John J. Douglas' version turned Oliver Goldsmith's novel into a melodrama. Emery was an unconvincing cleric. The raging fire was as sensational as the burning building in Dion Boucicault's *The Streets of London*.

NOVEMBER 19. John Baldwin Buckstone as the King and Mrs Chippendale as the Queen in W. S. Gilbert's **The Palace of Truth** at Haymarket Theatre. A fairy comedy in blank verse based on a story by Madame de Genlis. The characters unwittingly reveal their true natures.

DECEMBER 19. J. B. Howard and Adelaide Neilson in Shakespeare's **Romeo and Juliet** at Drury Lane Theatre.

There is perhaps no actress now on the stage who more perfectly understands the routine of the art and certainly there are none who can give greater force to the scenes which frequenters of the playhouse look for marked effects … In an age when tragedy is out of fashion the young and rising actress has determined to make Juliet her own and the applause of a crowded house bore witness to her success. *The Times*

1871

JANUARY 10. Fanny Brough and A. W. Young in T. W. Robertson's **War** at St James's Theatre. A German girl betrothed to a French officer marries him when he is dying. He doesn't die. Disappointing bathos.

FEBRUARY 3. Death of Tom Robertson. As a mark of respect, the Bancrofts closed The Prince of Wales's Theatre, where Robertson's plays had been performed.

The whole secret of his success was truth. Behind his work there lay not only a consummate knowledge of the stage, but a touch of inborn genius, and he achieved his success without pandering to the lower taste of humanity. There was not the slightest suspicion of vulgarity in his art. He never wrote a line or suggested a thought with a coarse or dubious intention. His aspirations were noble and his characters gentle; and, though there was much cynicism in his plays, it was never levelled at anything pure or good.

THE BANCROFTS, *Recollections of Sixty Years*

APRIL 18. Clara Rousby in Tom Taylor's **Joan of Arc** at Queen's Theatre. Five acts: The Maid Mystic, The Maid Missionary, The Maid Militant, The Maid Manifest and The Maid Martyr. Inferior to Schiller. This religious and warlike pageant was for a public which wanted spectacle and not drama.

SEPTEMBER 11. Isabel Bateman, Henry Irving and George Belmore in Sydney Bateman's **Fanchette or The Will of the Wisp** at Lyceum Theatre. Based on Georges Sand's prose-poem, *La Petite Fadette*. Wild Breton peasant girl is tamed by love. 'At best,' said Dutton Cooke in *The Pall Mall Gazette*, 'Fanchette only provides a showy part for a young actress whose possibilities of obtaining distinction are supposed to be enhanced by the fact that her play-fellows are denied any chance of shining.'

OCTOBER 9. George Vining and Ada Dyas in Wilkie Collins' own adaptation of his novel, **The Woman in White**, at Olympic Theatre. Dyas doubled as the mad Ann Catherick and the sane Lady Clyde. 'Collins,' said *The Daily Telegraph*, 'is a novelist whose every novel looks as if it were constructed with a view to dramatic representation.' The play ended with Count Fosco's death. Vining was much criticised, but Collins insisted he was very happy with the casting. The play ran for five months.

A scene from Wilkie Collins' The Woman in White at Olympic Theatre in 1871.

OCTOBER 23. Mr Addison as Mr Pickwick, Mr Belmore as Sam Weller and Henry Irving as Jingle in James Albery's **Pickwick** at Lyceum Theatre. Adaptation of Charles Dickens' *Pickwick Papers*. *The Athenæum* complained that 'no scene was effectual in representation and none was even moderately lively'.

NOVEMBER 11. William Congreve's **Love for Love** at Gaiety Theatre. Five acts were reduced to three by John Hollingshead who argued: 'There are many people – thankful for small mercies – who will perhaps accept even a mangled version of Congreve in preference to no Congreve at all.'

NOVEMBER 25. Henry Irving as Mathias in Leopold Lewis' **The Bells** at Royal Lyceum. The most famous of all Victorian melodramas was an adaptation of M. M. Erckmann-Chatrian's *The Polish Jew*. Mathias, the highly respected burgomaster of a village in Alsace, had killed a Polish Jew for his money and burned his body in a lime-kiln. Fifteen years later he is still haunted by the sound of the bells on the horses that drew the Jew's sledge. On the eve of his daughter's wedding he dreams that he is in the dock, convicted, and sentenced to death. The next morning he dies.

'The whole play was merely a series of variations on one theme – Irving!' wrote Edward Gordon Craig, who has left a vivid account of his first entrance, the unlacing of his boots, and the horror creeping up on him as he hears the bells. 'It was,' said Craig, 'the finest point that the craft of acting could reach.'

Etienne Singla's music played a key part, each character having his own motif. Equally crucial were the sound effects: the raging storm, the breaking crockery, the clock striking ten, the church bell, and, of course, the throbbing horse bells. Thirty-four years later, and only two days before he died, Irving was still playing Mathias. Even in the twenty-first century the agonised cry of 'The Bells! The Bells!' remains part of the theatre-goers' collective consciousness, a remarkable testimony to the mesmerism of his acting.

DECEMBER 9. William Kendal as Pygmalion and Madge Robertson as Galatea in W. S. Gilbert's **The Palace of Truth** at Haymarket Theatre. Written in blank verse, Gilbert's most profitable comedy led to a spate of Pygmalion plays.

> Mrs Kendal could do more with a flick of an eyelid than anyone else could suggest with a movement of the whole head. SIR GEORGE ARTHUR, *From Phelps to Gielgud*

DECEMBER 26. Master John Manly in E. L. Blanchard's **Tom Thumb or Harlequin King Arthur and the Knights of the Round Table** at Drury Lane Theatre. Pantomime. The performance began with traditional community singing. The audience patriotically sang 'God Bless the Prince of Wales' three times. Tom Thumb led an army of children against the Anglo-Saxons. The high spot of the harlequinade was a recreation of William Powell Frith's painting of Derby Day.

1871

World premieres
Giuseppe Verdi's *Aida* in Cairo

Births
Leonid Andreyev, Russian writer
Laurence Irving, British actor
Barry Jackson, British director, manager
Marcel Proust, French novelist
J. M. Synge, Irish dramatist

Deaths
T. W. Robertson, British dramatist (b. 1829)

Literature
Charles Darwin's *The Descent of Man*
George Eliot's *Middlemarch*

Notes
Alhambra Theatre opens as a music hall
Royal Albert Hall is opened

History
Paris Commune is established
Cricketer W. G. Grace scores 2,739 runs in the season
Bank Holidays introduced
Scotland defeat England in first rugby international
Stanley meets Dr Livingstone in Ujiji, Tanzania
Civil Rights Act in US gives legal remedy for blacks against abuses inflicted by Ku Klux Klan

Henry Irving in his most famous role: Mathias in Leopold Lewis's The Bells at Lyceum Theatre in 1871. 'The Bells! The Bells! The Bells!' were probably the most imitated words by theatre people well into the twentieth century.

DECEMBER 26. G. H. Macdermott in H. J. Byron's **Blue Beard** at Covent Garden Theatre. Pantomime. Twelve headless ladies, carrying their heads under their arms, sang 'Three Blind Mice' as a dirge.

'*Sensation is what the public wants and you can't give them too much of it.*'

DION BOUCICAULT

DECEMBER 26. J. L. Toole and Nellie Farren in Gilbert and Sullivan's **Thespis among the Olympians** or **The Gods Grow Old** at Gaiety Theatre. A theatrical company invites the gods to come and spend a year on earth. Operatic extravaganza, written, composed, rehearsed and produced within five weeks.

The first night I had a great reception, but the music went badly, and the singer sang half a tone sharp, so that the enthusiasm of the audience did not sustain towards me.   ARTHUR SULLIVAN

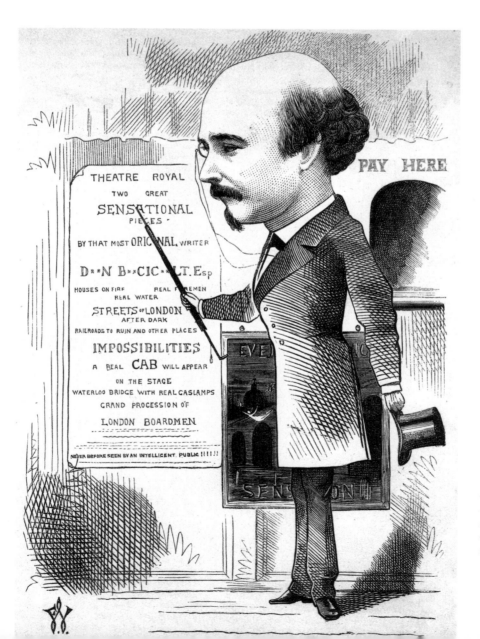

Dion Boucicault (1820–90), prolific Anglo-Irish playwright, was the author of some two hundred plays, including The Corsican Brothers (1852), The Vampire (1852), The Poor of New York (1857; the title was adapted to every city it visited), Jessie Brown (1858), The Coleen Bawn (1860, one of his best), Rip Van Winkle (1863), The Flying Scud (1866), Formosa (1869), Arrah-na-Pogue (1864), The Shaughraun (1874, the best).

Boucicault made a bigamous marriage to an American actress 44 years his junior, claiming that his common-law wedding to Agnes Robertson was not legally biding.

1872

JANUARY 8. George Rignold as Glaucus and Henrietta Hodson as a blind girl in John Oxenford's adaptation of Edward Bulwer-Lytton's **The Last Days of Pompeii** at Queen's Theatre. The eruption of Vesuvius was less than awesome.

FEBRUARY 13. Robert Reece's **The Very Last Days of Pompeii** at Vaudeville Theatre. Burlesque of Edward Bulwer-Lytton and the Queen's Theatre production.

MARCH 5. Charles Fechter in Victor Hugo's **Ruy Blas** at Adelphi Theatre. The supporting roles were poorly cast.

A comparison between the general presentation of the play in Paris and that in London will explain why in one city the drama is prized and studied as art, while in the other it can scarcely obtain the support of men of intellect as an amusement. *Observer*

MARCH 30. Lionel Brough and Mr Mervin in Jacques Offenbach's **La Vie Parisienne** at Holborn Theatre. The operetta was very freely adapted by Francis Cowley Burnard. The production relied on pretty scenery, pretty dresses and pretty faces, and was so poorly sung that many critics felt it was almost a libel upon Offenbach.

A scene from Bulwer Lytton's The Last Days of Pompeii at Queen's Theatre in 1872.

Isabel Bateman in Euripides' Medea in Corinth at the Lyceum Theatre in 1872.

A scene from Francis Albert Marshall's False Shame at The Globe Theatre in 1872.

MARCH 30. J. S. Clarke and Mrs Raymond in George Colman the Younger's **The Poor Gentleman** at Strand Theatre.

Among the dramatic writers whose work enriched our English literature during the past century those of George Colman the Younger seems to retain an evergreen quality. If we remove some sentimental homilies we find a genuine play as fresh in its diction, humour and character as if it had lately proceeded from a living brain. DION BOUCICAULT

JULY 8. Isabel Bateman in Euripides' **Medea at Corinth** at Lyceum Theatre. Adaptation by W. G. Wills. 'She is not Medea,' said Dutton Cook in *The Pall Mall Gazette*, 'she is, indeed, nothing like Medea. She fails to impress the spectators with a due feeling of awe.'

SEPTEMBER 28. Henry Irving as Charles, Isabel Bateman as Henrietta and George Belmore as Cromwell in William Gorman Wills' **Charles I** at Lyceum Theatre. Cromwell was a cipher and Belmore was mis-cast.

During the last act there was hardly a dry eye in the house. Women sobbed openly, and even men showed an emotion which comported ill with the habitual serenity of the stalls. Much of this uncomfortable gratification was due to the acting of Mr Irving, who has once more created a great role … he might be the incarnate portrait of Vandyke [sic]. *Daily News*

SEPTEMBER 21. Maria B. Jones and James Fernandez in Andrew Halliday's adaptation of Sir Walter Scott's **The Lady of the Lake** at Drury Lane Theatre. The Knight of Snowdon takes his vengeance on the treacherous Red Murdoch, who has just slain Blanche of Devon. The production – billed as 'a new grand romantic poetical spectacle and musical drama' – was a series of superb tableaux, and a complete triumph.

SEPTEMBER 28. George Ringold, Henrietta Hodson and Ellen Wallis in Sir Charles Young's **Montcalm** at Queen's Theatre. Montcalm was a chateau in the Pyrenees. A murdered aunt appeared as a ghost.

Varies between exaggerated sentiment and abject silliness; It is scarcely necessary to add that it was received with rapturous applause. *Observer*

NOVEMBER 4. H. J. Montague and Rose Massey in Francis Albert Marshall's **False Shame** at Globe Theatre. A comedy based on Bronson Howard's *Saratoga*. The hero is so successful in hiding his noble nature that he is mistaken for a villain.

ABOVE

Henry Irving as King Charles in W. G. Wills' Charles I at Lyceum Theatre in 1872.

RIGHT

A scene from Sir Walter Scott's The Lady of the Lake at The Drury Lane Theatre in 1872.

1872

World premieres
Ivan Turgenev's *A Month in the Country* in Moscow

Births
Aubrey Beardsley, British artist
Max Beerbohm, British critic, essayist, caricaturist
C. B. Cochran, British impresario
Edward Gordon Craig, British director, designer, theorist
Ralph Vaughan Williams, British composer

Deaths
Edwin Forrest, American actor (b. 1806)
Eliza O'Neill, Irish actress (b. 1791)
John Poole, British dramatist (b. 1786)

Literature
Samuel Butler's *Erewhon*
Thomas Hardy's *Under the Greenwood Tree*

History
Ballot Act introduces secrecy into voting
First English FA Cup final, held at Kennington Oval
Licensing Act introduces drinking hours and licences
Canadian brig *Mary Celeste* found totally abandoned
Fire destroys nearly 1,000 buildings in Boston, MA
Vesuvius erupts
Yellowstone becomes the world's first national park

'*The secret of what will and what will not be a theatrical success is as far from being discovered as ever. When my theatre was dirty and old and uncomfortable it was always crowded. The public made me rich and I tore down the old hovel and built an elegant theatre [the New Adelphi] to show my gratitude. Confound them! They won't come to it.*'

BENJAMIN WEBSTER, *The Same Only Different*

A scene from Leopold Lewis' The Wandering Jew at Adelphi Theatre in 1873.

DECEMBER 16. John Clayton in Campbell Clarke's **Awaking** at Gaiety Theatre. A father, driven mad by the death of his child, regains his senses when he is tricked into believing that time hasn't passed and that a newly born child is the child who died. Clayton modelled his performance entirely on the one that the French actor Febvre was giving in Paris. Audiences, who had seen both actors, apparently, couldn't tell the difference.

DECEMBER 23. Kate Santley in **The Black Crook** at Alhambra Theatre. Hugely successful in America. Libretto by Pouton Brothers. Music by Georges Jacobi and Frederic Clay. Santley sang the hit number: 'Nobody Knows As I Know'. 204 performances.

1873

JANUARY 4. Margaret Robertson and James Baldwin Buckstone in W. S. Gilbert's *The Wicked World* at Haymarket Theatre. Fairies fall in love with two rowdy Gothic knights. Moral: fairies should not fall in love with rowdy knights.

> At dress rehearsal he [Gilbert] was often in front when we didn't know he was there and he would suddenly shout out: 'What on earth do you think you are doing?'
> MADGE KENDAL (née Margaret Robertson)

APRIL 14. Benjamin Webster as Rodin in Leopold Lewis' *The Wandering Jew* at Adelphi Theatre. The play was difficult to follow for those who hadn't read the novel. The high spot was the spectacular scene in the Arctic regions when the Jew contemplates his descendents in a series of striking tableaux.

> The voice of the veteran actor and manager [Benjamin Webster] is no longer what it was, and occasionally his words are scarcely audible, but his by-play as Rodin is always eloquent, and many are his attitudes which would form an admirable study for a painter. *The Times*

APRIL 19. Henry Irving in W. G. Wills' *The Fate of Eugene Aram* at Lyceum Theatre. The afterlife of an undetected murderer.

> He [Irving] gave the world a representative of terror, remorse, bravado and despair which will not soon be forgotten.
> ARTHUR GODDARD, *Players of the Period*

> The acting of Mr Irving in this character is wonderfully fine, so deeply impressive that once only, by a bit of business with lights and a looking-glass, quite unworthy of the play and of him, does he remind one that he is acting and not living through that mortal struggle … Then comes the terror, abject indeed for a while, with desperate, breathless rally, thick incoherent speech, failing limbs, ghastly face, dry lips and choking throat, as dreadful as only fear can be and horribly true. *Spectator*

MAY 12. C. H. Macdermott and H. A. Major's *Ku Klux Klan or The Secret Deaths Union of South America* at Britannia Theatre. American sensational drama. The Negro, according to the playbill, gets his revenge, and England is described as 'The True Land of Liberty'.

World premieres
Emile Zola's Therese *Racquin* in Paris

Births
Gerald du Maurier, British actor-manager

Lady Ottoline Morrell, British patron of writers and artists

Alfred Jarry, French poet, dramatist

Max Reinhardt, Austrian director

Ford Maddox Ford, English novelist, poet, critic, editor

Deaths
Edward Fitzball, British dramatist (b. 1792)

Edward Bulwer-Lytton, British dramatist (b. 1803)

William Macready, British actor (b. 1793)

Notes
Alexandra Palace is destroyed by fire just 16 days after opening in May; it is rebuilt and re-opens in May 1875

Literature
Arthur Rimbaud's *Saisons en Enfers*

Jules Verne's Round the World in 80 Days

Anthony Trollope's *The Eustace Diamonds*

History
White Star line's RMS *Atlantic* hits rocks and sinks off Nova Scotia; 547 die

Beginning of long series of economic recessions in later nineteenth century

*Henry Irving in W. G. Wills' The Fate of
Eugene Aram at Lyceum Theatre in 1873.*

MAY 17. Pauline Luigini in Charles Lecoq's *La
Fille de Madame Angot* at St James's Theatre.
Angot's daughter was a flower-girl in France in
1793. One of the most successful French light
operas. The score had many high spots, including
'Je Vous Dit Tou', 'Marchande de Mare' and
'Jours Fortunées'. 'Pauline Luigini is a lively little
personage,' said *The Observer*, 'but her voice is thin
and shrill.'

MAY 19. Ada Cavendish and Frank Archer in
Wilkie Collins' *The New Magdalen* at Olympic
Theatre. Morbid sentimentalism. 'The moral,' said
Era, 'appears to be that a young woman may stray
from virtue's path and lie and steal and cheat, but
if she repents in the end she is sure not only to be
forgiven but to be glorified as a saint and married
to a clergyman of the Church of England.'

JUNE 20. Adelaide Ristori in Paolo Giacometti's
Marie Antoinette at Drury Lane Theatre. Wordy
and tedious historical drama.

SEPTEMBER 22. James Anderson and Ellen Wallis
in Shakespeare's *Antony and Cleopatra* at Drury
Lane Theatre. Shakespeare played a secondary role
to the spectacle. A pictorial illustration accompanied Enobarbus' description of Cleopatra's barge.

Antony's marriage was celebrated with thirty singing choirboys and a ballet called *The Path of Flowers*. The Battle of Actium was so realistic that the management had to reassure the public that they were in no danger. Anderson complained it was impossible to act because of the racket the stage-hands were making when changing the scenery. Financially the production was disastrous.

> During the first three acts, in which there is 'one halfpenny worth' of Shakespearean 'bread' to an intolerable deal of 'scenic' sack, the delight of the audience with everything set before it was unbounded. In the concluding act, which was wholly Shakespearean, there was a gradual cooling, and the verdict at the end, though favourable, was far less enthusiastic than it would have been could the play have ended with the fight at Actium. *Athenæum*

> These persons who insist that Shakespeare's plays should be represented in their entirety love Shakespeare 'not wisely but too well' – that is to say they love him to his great injury and the public loss, since they prevent the managers from presenting his plays in such an abridged form as would render them agreeable to modern audiences. Many of Shakespeare's Plays are never represented at all, simply because they are too long and managers, with the fear of Idolaters before their eyes, are afraid to curtail their dimensions. Thus playgoers have been robbed of much enjoyment of the highest kind. If half a loaf is better than no bread, surely it is better to have a little Shakespeare than none at all. ANDREW HALLIDAY, manager, in his printed edition of *Antony and Cleopatra*

SEPTEMBER 27. Henry Irving as Cardinal and John Clayton as King in Edward Bulwer-Lytton's ***Richelieu*** at Lyceum Theatre. The critics were divided. 120 performances.

> Here is tragic acting in the grandest style, and it will be borne in mind, that although Richelieu is not a tragedy, it belongs practically to the tragical category, as none can do justice

to it but a tragedian … The pit not only rose, but made its rising conspicuous by the waving of countless hats and handkerchiefs. Not bare approval but hearty sympathy was denoted by this extraordinary demonstration; and this sympathy nothing but genius and thoroughly self-abandonment on the part of the artist could have produced. *The Times*

> The house shook and rang with applause; but the excitement was unwholesome and the cheers forced. It was thee wild delirium of a revival meeting … a triumph of din, an apotheosis of incoherence … The delicacy and grace of the acting were lost in the whirlwind of noise. *Observer*

> The Lyceum company numbers few actors of any note, and occasionally the drama suffered gravely from the incompetence of its exponents.
> DUTTON COOK

OCTOBER 14. Edgar Bruce and W. J. Hill in Arthur A. Beckett's ***On Strike*** at Court Theatre. Billed as an entirely new and social problem.

> The British workman and his ways of settling knotty disputes connected with his trade do not afford a peculiarly attractive subject for a stage picture, since the nearer the delineation comes to realistic truth, the more repulsive and uninteresting it is apt to become. *Observer*

DECEMBER 18. Samuel Emery as Captain Cuttle in Andrew Halliday's ***Heart's Delight*** at Globe Theatre. Based on Charles Dickens' *Dombey and Son*. The high spot was Emery's delivery of the dirge over the drowned Walter.

> A struggle between joviality and grief which few who heard it are likely to forget. He [Emery] is laughing to the last even in his tears; but all at once the grief gets the mastery, and the half-gulp, half hysterical sob of the artist commands the attention of even of the dullest audience. *Daily Telegraph*

1874

MARCH 21. Fanny Holland in W. S. Gilbert's *Topsyturveydom* at Criterion Theatre. A comedy set in a society where insults are received as the highest compliment.

APRIL 4. John Hare as Sir Peter Teazle, Mary Wilton as Lady Teazle and Squire Bancroft as Joseph Surface in Richard Brinsley Sheridan's *The School for Scandal* at Prince of Wales's Theatre. This innovative production was set in its exact period and much admired for its beauty, truth and freshness. The actors rejected all the traditional stage business. A black page called Pompey was introduced. A minuet was danced.

My wife resolved that our Pompey should be a real one, but we had great difficulty finding him. The docks, workhouses, charitable institutions, and every likely place we could think of were searched in vain. At last a boy of the true type of African beauty, with large protruding lips, gleaming eyes, receding forehead, woolly hair, and a skin which shone like a well-coloured meerschaum pipe, was lent to us by an owner of sugar plantations. The boy was called 'Biafra' after the ship he came over in, and looked a picture in his laced scarlet coat, his white turban, and gilt dog-collar.

THE BANCROFTS, *Recollections of Sixty Years*

SEPTEMBER 26. James Anderson as Richard in Andrew Halliday's **Richard Coer de Lion** at Drury Lane Theatre. Adaptation of Sir Walter Scott's *The Talisman*. A whole act was devoted to juggling feats, acrobatics and ballet.

It is impossible to pronounce upon the play or the actors, except as participation in a pageant or a circus entertainment … all question of dramatic art must be dismissed from the mind … Perhaps the one grain of consolation to be gained from the style of acting more prominently asserting itself on our largest stage is that the days of burlesque must shortly come to an end, since human ingenuity can scarcely outsize, or human voice outrave the extravagancies of that which is put forth as a serious performance.   *Athenæum*

OCTOBER 31. Henry Irving in Shakespeare's **Hamlet** at Lyceum Theatre. A major turning point in his career. 200 performances.

Here is a Hamlet who is always zealous and thoughtful; often very adroit; who spares no pain to please; who has at command a certain feverish impetuosity, which, if it makes his passion sometimes too petulant, is yet surprisingly effective on the stage; and he is, in short, as complete a representative of the part as the modern theatre can furnish.
DUTTON COOK, *Pall Mall Gazette*

There could be no question of the success, for here was such a Hamlet as had never been seen before, and only vaguely dreamed of. In fact this act [the scene with Gertrude] was so exhausting and overpowering in its intensity that the audience was worn out by the absorbing passion of the actor.   CLEMENT SCOTT, *Theatre*

It is a moot point whether Mr Irving is the more successful when he appeals to the heads or the hearts of the audience.
ARTHUR GODDARD, *Players of the Period*

LEFT

Henry Irving in Shakespeare's Hamlet at Lyceum Theatre in 1874. He was for many people the finest Hamlet of his generation.

BELOW

A scene from Tom Taylor's Clancarty at The Olympic Theatre in 1874.

World premieres

Modest Mussorgsky's *Boris Godunov* (complete opera) in St Petersburg

Johann Strauss II's *Die Fledermaus* in Vienna

Births

Lilian Baylis, British theatre manager

G. K. Chesterton, British writer

Harry Houdini, American magician

Vsevoled Meyerhold, Russian actor, director

Nigel Playfair, British actor, dramatist, manager

Hugo von Hofmannsthal, Austrian poet, dramatist

William Somerset Maugham, British novelist, dramatist

Deaths

Master William Henry Betty, British actor (b. 1791)

Chang and Eng Bunker, 'Siamese twins' (b. 1811)

Literature

Thomas Hardy's *Far From the Madding Crowd*

Serialisation begins of Anthony Trollope's *The Way We Live Now*, a satire in London life

Notes

First Impressionist exhibition in Paris

Meiningen Players formed by the Duke of Saxe-Meiningen

Criterion Theatre opens

Vesta Tilley, the greatest music hall male impersonator, makes her debut at Canterbury Music Hall.

History

Agricultural workers strike for six months

Factory Act limits working hours and tries again to protect children from work as chimney sweeps

NOVEMBER 30. George Belmore in **Hamlet the Hysterical** at Princess's Theatre. Delusion in Five Spasms. Spoof of Henry Irving's performance. The Ghost turned out to be Shakespeare, and he and Hamlet discussed the prospects of drama and sang a song.

DECEMBER 14. Samuel Phelps as Falstaff in Shakespeare's **The Merry Wives of Windsor** at Gaiety Theatre. Mrs Wood and Rose Leclercq as the wives. Herman Vezin as Ford. Arthur Sullivan wrote music for the final scene at Herne's Oak.

Mr Phelps' Falstaff is wholly without unction and geniality. It is affecting, however, and it is a Falstaff, though scarcely the Falstaff we imagine. JOSEPH KNIGHT, *Theatrical Notes*

1875

JANUARY 16. William Farren and David James in H. J. Byron's **Our Boys** at Vaudeville Theatre. The boys are the respective sons of a baronet and a *nouveau riche* businessman. They come to London for some fun and meet two girls. 'A masterpiece in comic writing,' said *The Daily Telegraph*. 1,362 performances.

Mr Byron burnishes conventional and old-fashioned characters until they shine with all the gloss of novelty, and brighten commonplace situations and actions with dialogue no less amusing than extravagant and out of place. JOSEPH KNIGHT, *Theatrical Notes*

MARCH 25. Fred Sullivan as the Judge in Gilbert and Sullivan's **Trial by Jury** at Royalty Theatre. Breach of promise: whimsical burlesque of law courts. *Punch* thought it was 'the funniest bit of nonsense'. Fred was Arthur Sullivan's brother.

In whimsical invention and eccentric humour Mr W. S. Gilbert has no living rival among our dramatic writers and never has his peculiar vein of drollery or satire been more conspicuous … It would be difficult to conceive of Mr Gilbert's verses without Mr Sullivan's music or of Mr Sullivan's music without Mr Gilbert's verses. Each gives each a double charm.
Daily News

APRIL 1. Tomasso Salvini in Shakespeare's *Othello* at Drury Lane Theatre. In his London debut Salvini made as big an impact as Edmund Kean had done in his debut.

Nearing the end, he rises, and at the supreme moment cuts his throat with a short scimitar, hacking and hewing with savage energy and imitating the noise that escaping blood and air may together make when the wind pipe is severed. Nothing in art so terribly realistic as this death scene has been attempted. It is directly opposed to Shakespeare. JOSEPH KNIGHT, *Athenæum*

APRIL 17. Charles Coghlan as Shylock and Ellen Terry as Portia in Shakespeare's **The Merchant of Venice** at Prince of Wales's Theatre. Shakespeare was completely upstaged by the pictorial effects, which had been researched in Venice. The gallery jeered, and the press condemned. 'The venture was wrecked by Coghlan,' said Squire Bancroft. 'It was very clever, very natural, exactly the Jew you might meet in Whitechapel, but it was grey instead of being lurid and quite ineffective.'

So completely did he [Coghlan] fail, however, to grasp the part, or to render intelligible his conception, that during the trial scene the audience scarcely seemed conscious of his existence, and the proceedings might almost have continued without his presence. Against this regrettable miscarriage must be placed the triumph of Miss Terry, whose Portia revealed the gifts which are rarest on the English stage. More adequate expression has seldom been given to the light-heartedness of maidenhood. JOSEPH KNIGHT, *Theatrical Notes*

H. J. Byron (1834–84), playwright and manager, was the author of Our Boys *and some 40 pantomimes and burlesques.*

APRIL 23. Helen Faucit, for many the ideal Rosalind of the age, came out of retirement to play Rosalind in a benefit performance of Shakespeare's **As You Like It** at Drury Lane to raise money for the Shakespeare Memorial Theatre.

MAY 7. Tomasso Salvini in Soumet's **The Gladiator** at Drury Lane Theatre. The gladiator is ordered to slay his Christian daughter. 'So dignified and noble is the appearance of Signor Salvini,' said *The Athenaeum*, 'it is difficult to believe in his practice of a profession like a gladiator. A stronger expression of blood lust is necessary to the full development of the character.'

'*The custom of summoning actors before the curtain – which we believe sprung up in Paris about the middle of the last century, but was not adopted in this country until Edmund Kean played Brutus – is bad enough; the spectacle of a performer acknowledging applause when the action ought to be going on is worse … The fault lies with the audience than the actor, who would give much offence by declining to appear and not generally obey the call. How persons so deliberately sacrifice their own enjoyment is difficult to perceive.*'

The Times

SEPTEMBER 4. Dion Boucicault as Conn, William Terriss as Captain Molyneux, J. B. Howard as Robert Ffolliott and Mrs Boucicault as Moya in Dion Boucicault's **The Shaughraun** at Drury Lane Theatre. The play was premiered in New York in 1874. Conn, the Shaughraun, is the soul of every fair, the life of every funeral, the first fiddler at all weddings and patterns. 'Mr Boucicault is probably the best stage Irishman that has been seen,' said Joseph Knight in *Theatrical Notes*. 'It is impossible to make drollery more unctuous and blarney more attractive than they appear in his rendering.'

MAY 8. Christina Nilsson and Ernest Nicolini in the London premiere of Richard Wagner's **Lohengrin** at Covent Garden Theatre. Sung in Italian.

The novelty of his writing is found in the dreary and monotonous strains so often allotted to the solo singers, to whom he seems to say, 'I don't care what your emotions and passions may be; you will not express them, but my orchestra shall do so.' *Athenaeum*

MAY 24. Henry Neville in James Albery's **The Spendthrift** at Olympic Theatre. Neville played a Good Samaritan who befriends a drunkard. 'Mr Albery is the most original, witty and inventive of English dramatists,' said Joseph Knight in *Theatrical Notes*, 'and he is also the least able of giving a fitting shape to the quaint ideas with which his brain teems.'

MAY 31. Tommaso Salvini as **Amletto** at Drury Lane Theatre. A large contingent of actors was in the audience.

No actor of our day has brought to the part of Hamlet equal intelligence and mastery of art, equal ripeness of method. *Athenæum*

SEPTEMBER 25. Henry Irving and Kate Bateman in Shakespeare's **Macbeth** at Lyceum Theatre. Irving saw Macbeth as 'a bloody-minded, hypocritical villain' and over-emphasised his cowardice.

Success has come easily to Mr Irving, and he has remained, as the first tragic actor in England, decidedly incomplete and amateurish. His personal gifts – face, figure, voice, enunciation – are rather meager; his strong points are intellectual. He is ingenious, intelligent, and fanciful; imaginative he can hardly be called, for he signally fails to give their great imaginative value to many of the superb speeches he has to utter. In declamation he is decidedly flat; his voice is without charm, and his utterance without subtlety. HENRY JAMES, *Nation*

Mr Irving must learn, however, that his mannerisms have developed into evils so formidable, they will, if not checked, end by ruining his career. His slow pronunciation and his indescribable elongation of syllables bring the whole occasionally near burlesque … It is impossible to preserve the music of Shakespeare if words of one syllable are to be stretched out to the length of six. Mr Irving's future depends greatly on his mastery of this defect. *Athenæum*

THEATRE ROYAL

Drury  Lane.

Actual and Responsible Manager ... Mr F. B. CHATTERTON,
Russell Street, Covent Garden.

ENGAGEMENT OF

MR & MRS DION BOUCICAULT,

Who will appear as " Conn " and " Moya. "

A MORNING PERFORMANCE

OF

THE SHAUGHRAUN

On Wednesday, the 27th October, 1875.

SATURDAY, October 16th, MONDAY 18th, 1875, and every evening during
the week, the performances will commence with a Laughable Farce, entitled

THE WHITE HAT

Characters by Messrs J. R. JACKSON, S. CALHAEM and W. HOLMAN.
Miss CLARA JECKS, Mrs J. CARTER and Miss MACDONALD

After which will be performed, for the First Time in England, the New and
Original Irish Drama in Three Acts, entitled

THE SHAUGHRAUN

By DION BOUCICAULT.

With New and Romantic Scenery, by

Mr WILLIAM BEVERLY.

Captain Molineux (a young English Officer commanding a detachment
at Ballyragget) ... Mr W. TERRISS
Robert Ffolliott (a young Irish Gentleman, under sentence as a Fenian,
in love with Art O'Neale) Mr J. B. HOWARD
Father Dolan ... (the Parish Priest of Suilabeg, his Tutor and
Guardian) ... Mr DAVID FISHER
Corry Kinchela ... (a Squireen) ... Mr HENRY SINCLAIR
Harvey Duff (a Police Agent, in disguise of a Peasant, under the name
Keach) ... Mr SHIEL BARRY
Conn ... ... Mr DION BOUCICAULT
(the Shaughraun, the soul of every Fair, the Life of every Funeral, the First
Fiddle at all weddings and patterns)
Sergeant Jones, of the 41st ... ... Mr ERNEST TRAVERS

World premieres
Georges Bizet's *Carmen* at
Opéra Comique, Paris

Births
Mistinguette, French music
hall artiste
Edgar Wallace, British
novelist, dramatist

Deaths
William Bayle Bernard, British
dramatist (b. 1807)

Literature
George Henry Lewes' *On
Actors and the Art of Acting*

Notes
Richard D'Oyly Carte
premieres Gilbert and
Sullivan's *Trial by Jury*
at Royalty Theatre to
considerable acclaim

History
First Cross-Channel swim, by
Captain Matthew Webb,
takes almost 22 hours
Baazalgette's sewerage system
for London is completed
Artisans Dwellings Act
empowers local authorities
for first time to clear slums
Asia's first stock exchange is
established in Bombay
First Kentucky Derby is held

The secret of the spell which this extraordinary actor exercises over the imaginations of audiences is not difficult to discover. It lies in the imaginative power with which he is able to depict the most terrible passions of the human soul in a great crisis of action, and in the wonderful expressiveness of countenance which on these occasions never desert him. To the playgoer whose memory is haunted with the Macbeths of the past there is a peculiar pleasure in the total absence in all Mr Irving's performances of mere conventional details. *Daily News*

OCTOBER 2. Herman Vezin and Carlotta Atkinson in H. J. Byron's **Married in Haste** at Haymarket Theatre. The hero marries against his guardian's wishes. He is reduced to penury and his wife returns to her father.

Mr Byron has never acquired either perfect ease on the stage, nor that variety of tone, movement, and expression which are the triumph of the finished actor. But then he rarely takes to himself a part connected with the serious action of the pieces, and he is apparently ambitious of success chiefly in the art of quietly dropping those witty and whimsical observations in the invention of which his powers have certainly undergone no deterioration. *Daily News*

NOVEMBER 6. Mrs Bancroft, Squire Bancroft, Charles Coghlan and Miss Terry in Charles Reade and Tom Taylor's **Masks and Faces** at Prince of Wales's Theatre.

Dear, kind, unjust, generous, cautious, impulsive, passionate, gentle, Charles Reade! Who combined so many qualities, far asunder as the poles. He was placid and turbulent, yet always majestic. He was inexplicable and entirely lovable – a stupid old dear, and as wise as Solomon! He seemed guileless, and yet had moments of suspicion and craftiness worthy of the wisdom of the serpent. ELLEN TERRY quoted by SQUIRE BANCROFT, *Recollections of Sixty Years*

1876

FEBRUARY 1. Adelaide Nielson as Rosalind in Shakespeare's **As You Like It** at Haymarket Theatre. 'Miss Neilson is irresistible,' said Joseph Knight in *Theatrical Notes*. 'The archness and sauciness of the whole, dashed as they are at times with sadness and passion, are electrical.'

FEBRUARY 7. Adelaide Neilson in Tom Taylor's **Anne Boleyn** at Haymarket Theatre. Charles Harcourt as King Henry. Miss Carlisle as Jane Seymour.

> Not for a moment does the heroine touch our sympathies and get near our hearts … Miss Neilson is by no means a great or a very accomplished actress, and her art has not gained in refinement or discipline by her absence from the London stage. She is skilled, however, in a certain routine of theatrical artifice, and can duly accomplish the smiles and frowns, the stares and starts, the tricks of gesture and attitude, which are the main constituents of popular acting. Over pathos she has but a limited command, and she cannot enable the spectator ever to forget that she is acting, and acting in a very conventional fashion.
> DUTTON COOK, *World*

FEBRUARY 14. Henry Irving as Othello and Henry Forrester as Iago in Shakespeare's **Othello** at Lyceum Theatre. Isabel Bateman as Desdemona. Irving's performance was marred by excessive grimaces, frantic gesticulation, occasional lugubrious sentimentality, incoherence, and excessive luxuriousness.

> He [Irving] wearies the eye with his incessant changes of posture, his excessive and graceless movements of head and hands; while he offends the ear by too frequently permitting the fervour of his speech to degenerate into unintelligible and inarticulate rant. DUTTON COOK, *World*

Jennie Lee as Jo, an adaptation of Charles Dickens' Bleak House, at Globe Theatre in 1876.

> To ask one man [Irving] to represent night after night for many weeks or months such characters as Hamlet, Macbeth or Othello, is as to require of the English army to fight a battle of Waterloo every day … In his pathos he is monotonous without being tender, in his rage violent without being dignified, while his love for Desdemona has be taken on trust from the words that are put in his mouth. *The Times*

FEBRUARY 21. Jennie Lee as Jo, the Crossing-Sweeper, in J. P. Burnett's *Jo*, at Globe Theatre. The play was based on Charles Dickens' *Bleak House*. Lee, who was principally known for her work in burlesque, would go on playing Jo until 1921. Burnett, who also played Detective Bucket, was Lee's husband.

The part was acted with a realism and pathos difficult to surpass. A more striking revelation of talent has seldom been made. In get-up, and in acting, the character was thoroughly realized; and the hoarse voice, the slouching dejected gait, and the movement, as of some hunted animal, were admirably executed. *Athenæum*

APRIL 2. Adelaide Neilson as Isabella and Charles Harcourt in Shakespeare's *Measure for Measure* at Haymarket Theatre.

The scorn of her [Nielson] look, the invectives that rained from her lies were overwhelming. Passion seemed to give her bodily height and majesty; she towered in her denunciation. Rarely has an audience in the midst of a play been so taken by storm. She was thrice recalled amidst an agitation of delight rarely indeed paralleled. JOHN WESTLAND MARTSON, *Our Recent Actors*

APRIL 18. Isabel Bateman as Mary in Alfred Lord Tennyson's *Queen Mary* at Lyceum Theatre. The text and characters had been cut by half, losing much of the best poetry. Henry Irving had the small role of Philip. Clement Scott in *The Daily Telegraph* thought, 'The milkmaid's song and the long speech in which Elizabeth wishes she were a milkmaid so that she might escape the horrors and dangers surrounding her, might advantageously be omitted.'

The art of Miss Bateman has strict limitations. Her voice is hollow, her delivery is monotonous, her manner is conventional; her histrionic method altogether is wanting in variety and in light and shade. DUTTON COOK, *World*

APRIL. Ernesto Rossi's season of Shakespeare's plays in Italian at Haymarket Theatre included *Hamlet*, *King Lear* and *Macbeth*. Hamlet, spinning about with his legs and arms in the air and stamping and dancing on his mother's picture of Claudius, was thought to be somewhat excessive. 'So essentially Northern in conception is Hamlet,' said one critic, 'it may be doubted whether a true notion of it can win its way into Spanish or Italian brains.'

MAY 6. Emma Albani and Signor Carpi in the London premiere of Richard Wagner's *Tannhäuser* at Covent Garden Theatre. A brilliant success.

MAY 20. John Clayton as the strike leader in John Saunders' *Abel Drake* at Princess's Theatre.

The hero is a working man and working men on the stage, whatever they may be in real life, are never objects of over much sympathy or interest. But a working man with a grievance, an

---

1876

World premieres
Henrik Ibsen's *Peer Gynt* in Oslo
Richard Wagner's *Siegfried* in Bayreuth
Richard Wagner's *Gotterdammerung* (part of *Der Ring des Nibelungen* cycle) in Bayreuth

Births
Jack London, American author
Mata Hari, exotic dancer, spy

Deaths
Charlotte Cushman, American actress (b.1816)
Frederick Lemaitre, French actor (b.1800)
Samuel Phelps, British actor (b.1804)

Literature
George Eliot's *Daniel Deronda*
Alfred Lord Tennyson's *Harold*
Mark Twain's *Tom Sawyer*

Notes
James Abbott McNeill Whistler begins a libel action against John Ruskin: a farthing's damages awarded

History
Statue of Prince Albert finally placed in Albert Memorial
Plimsoll marks introduced
George Custer defeated in Battle of Little Big Horn

invention, and a Lancashire dialect – there really is no other word for him – is an intolerable bore. *The Times*

JUNE 22. Adelina Patti in the London premiere of Verdi's **Aida** at Covent Garden Theatre. Nicolini as Radames. Ernesta Gindele as Amneris.

In no previous part has the lady shown higher intelligence or more pathos and power; and her assumption places her in the first rank of lyric tragedians. The French tenor Signor Nicolini, although energetic as an actor, sang persistently with a palsied voice, and marred every bit of cantabile. *Athenæum*

SEPTEMBER 11. Hermann Vezin in W. S. Gilbert's **Dan'l Druce, Blacksmith** at Haymarket Theatre. Drama set in the seventeenth century. A blacksmith lives a lonely and miserly life in a cabin on the Norfolk coast. His character is transformed when he adopts an abandoned three-year-old girl. When she grows up he discovers she is his daughter. Marion Terry played the daughter. Forbes Robertson played the daughter's young lover.

SEPTEMBER 16. John Coleman in a rare revival of Shakespeare's **Henry V** at Queen's Theatre. Charlotte Leighton as Chorus. Lavish production: to make it more popular with audiences a masque for the wedding of the royal couple and a ballet for the French court were introduced.

To the majority of the audience the play is wholly spectacle and Shakespeare's words might almost be regarded as a species of music. The question, whether it is worth while to present him at all in the manner in which he is now seen, remains in abeyance.
JOSEPH KNIGHT, *Theatrical Notes*

SEPTEMBER 23. Barry Sullivan in Colley Cibber's version of Shakespeare's **Richard III** at Drury Lane Theatre. The audience treated the play as if it were a burlesque and greeted every murder with roars of laughter.

SEPTEMBER 30. Miss Heath in W. G. Wills' **Jane Shore** at Princess's Theatre. The production ran for five months.

Miss Heath is affected and stagey to a degree fatal to any possibility of interest. Her expression of grief, monotonous at first, grew irritating before the close and moved a portion of the audience to frequent outburst of derision. JOSEPH KNIGHT, *Theatrical Notes*

SEPTEMBER 30. Madge Kendal and Arthur Cecil in Saville Rowe and B. C. Stephenson's **Peril** at Prince of Wales's Theatre. French playwrights treated adultery far more lightly than their British counterparts did, and this adaptation of Victorien Sardou's *Nos Intimes* caused something of a scandal.

The personages and occurrences of *Nos Intimes* are repellent, but it must not be supposed that *Peril* fails to entertain. In truth it pleases greatly, if rather as a farce than as a portrayal of fact. DUTTON COOK, *World*

DECEMBER 18. Kate Munro in London premiere of Johann Strauss' **Die Fledermaus** at Alhambra Theatre. The high spot was the laughing song.

The music so far as it goes is very pleasing; but the dialogue is capable of considerable improvement … Its success is certain.
Illustrated London News

'*You've no idea what a poor opinion I have of myself and how little I deserve it.*'
WILLIAM SCHWENK GILBERT (1836–1911)

1877

JANUARY 29. Henry Irving in Shakespeare's *Richard III* at Lyceum Theatre. Irving was not Shakespeare's Richard but the historical Richard, the statesman and courtier, who was described by one contemporary as 'the most enchanting man'. 'No one,' said Clement Scott in *The Daily Telegraph*, 'can doubt it is his greatest triumph as an actor.' *The Morning Post* found him 'brilliant, energetic, impassioned and full of life and character'. Henry James thought he was 'an elegant grotesque'. The play ended on 'A horse! A horse! My kingdom for a horse!'

The desire of the actor appears to depict Richard not as the petulant, vapouring,

capering, detonating creature he has so long been represented in the theatre, but as an arch and polished dissembler, the grimmest of jesters, the most subtle and the most merciless of assassins and conspirators, aiming directly at the crown ... As an actor's first impersonation of a part entirely new to him, it is startling in its originality, its power and completeness. DUTTON COOK, *World*

MARCH 30. Arthur Cecil and Marie Bancroft in **The Vicarage** at Prince of Wales's Theatre. An adaptation of Octave Feuillet's one-act proverb by Clement Scott. A fireside story. Robert Kendal played the old friend who persuades the vicar that he should give up his dull routine and travel with him to Rome, Naples and Venice.

MARCH 31. Charles Wyndham, Fanny Joseph and Miss Eastlake in James Aubrey's **Pink Dominos** at Criterion Theatre. French marital farce. Two wives disguise themselves so successfully that they are able to trick their unfaithful husbands. *The Observer* thought Aubrey's adaptation was 'so suggestive as to be unhealthy'.

APRIL/MAY. C.H. Macdermott sang G.W. Hunt's immensely popular **War Song** at London Pavilion during the diplomatic crisis.

We don't want to fight, but, by Jingo, if we do
We've got the ships, we've got the men, we've
    got the money too
We've fought the Bear before and while we're
    Britons true
The Russians shall not have Constantinople.

LEFT

Arthur Cecil and Mrs Bancroft
in The Vicarage at Prince of
Wales's Theatre in 1877.

MAY 19. Henry Irving in Charles Reade's **The Lyons Mail** at Lyceum at Lyceum Theatre. This Napoleonic drama, inspired by a true story, was one of the most popular productions in Irving's repertoire. He played two roles: the saintly Lesurques and the villainous Dubosc, a monster of drunken devilry. Lesurques, mistaken for Dubosc, is accused of murder and sentenced to be guillotined. He is saved by the combined efforts of his wife, his children, and Dubosc's mistress. The performance was a masterpiece of macabre humour.

> Scarcely more than ten seconds after Dubosc has rushed behind the opening door Lesurques enters, calm and collected and utterly free from any excitement … The word marvellous is certainly not too strong to describe the command of feature and demeanour which enables him thus to change his identity to say nothing of his dress in such a space of time. *Standard*

OCTOBER 8. George Honey as Cheviot Hill, Lucy Buckstone as Minnie and Marion Terry as Belinda in W. S. Gilbert's **Engaged** at Haymarket Theatre. All the characters express the most noble and tender sentiments in the most flowery and high-faluting language, yet they always act from self-interest, and are willing to ditch their nearest and dearest instantly if there is a choice between love and money. Cheviot Hill, who falls in love, on sight, with any woman he meets, and finds himself engaged to three women at the same time, is thoroughly objectionable, a stingy and bad-tempered character, but (to the surprise of the audience) he gets the girl in the end. The nice guy loses out. *Engaged* didn't get a good press and was dismissed by *Figaro* as 'completely degrading to author, actors and spectators alike'.

> It is absolutely essential to the success of the piece that it should be played with the most perfect earnestness and gravity throughout. There should be no exaggeration in costume, make-up or demeanour. W. S. GILBERT

NOVEMBER 17. George Grossmith as J. Wellington Wells and Rutland Barrington as the Vicar in Gilbert and Sullivan's **The Sorcerer** at Opera Comique. 'Magnificent in its choral and orchestral combination,' said *The Daily News*. 'A gem of comic and original writing,' said *The Evening Standard*.

> Mr Gilbert is a perfect autocrat, insisting that his words shall be delivered, even to an inflection of the voice, as he dictates. He will stand on the stage and repeat the words with appropriate action, over and over again until they are delivered as he desires. GEORGE GROSSMITH

DECEMBER 22. Susie Vaughan as Robin in E. L. Blanchard's **Robin Hood and His Merry Men** at Adelphi Theatre. The pantomime was by acted entirely by children. Robin and Maid Marian were transformed and became Harlequin and Columbine.

OVERLEAF

The programme for James Albery's Pink Dominos at Criterion Theatre in 1877.

World premieres
Henrik Ibsen's *The Pillars of Society* in Copenhagen
Marius Petipa's *La Bayadere* in St Petersburg
Camille Saint-Saens' *Samson et Dalila* in Weimar
Victorien Sardou's *Dora* in Paris

Births
James Agate, British critic
Harley Granville Barker, British director, dramatist

Literature
Anna Sewell's *Black Beauty*
Emile Zola's *L'Assommoir*

Notes
Her Majesty's Theatre opens
New Grecian Theatre opens

History
Queen Victoria declared Empress of India
Socialist march clashed with police and soldiers in Trafalgar Square

1877

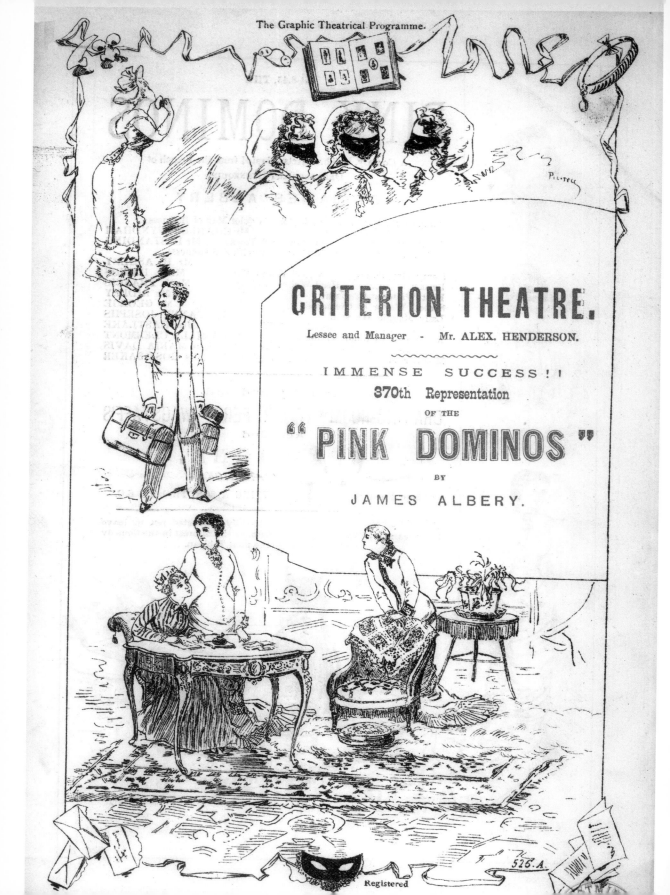

CRITERION THEATRE.

Lessee and Manager - Mr. ALEX. HENDERSON.

IMMENSE SUCCESS !!

370th Representation

OF THE

"PINK DOMINOS"

BY

JAMES ALBERY.

Registered

526.A.

1878

JANUARY 12. William Kendal and Madge Kendal in **Diplomacy**, Bolton Rowe and Saville Rowe's adaptation of Victorien Sardou's *Dora*, at Prince of Wales's Theatre. Squire Bancroft as Count Orloff, and Mrs Bancroft as Countess Zicka. A husband learns on his wedding day that his wife is a spy. It's not true; the real traitress is a Russian countess taking her revenge on the husband who had scorned her. Bancroft visited the British embassy in Paris to get the décor and furniture absolutely right. Such was the play's success that Sir Francis Burnand wrote a burlesque, *Diplunancy*, which was also a great success, the two plays running parallel. Some people, unable to get seats for *Diplomacy*, saw *Diplunacy* instead.

> His playing of the part [Count Orloff] throughout gives fresh proof of Mr Bancroft's fine power of impersonation – a thing somewhat different from acting in the loose sense which is too commonly attached to the word. The character demands an unusual capacity, for indicating rather than expressing s a passionate emotion, and in Mr Bancroft's rendering of it we can find no fault. *Saturday Review*

JANUARY 26. Ellen Terry and Henry Irving in **Olivia**, William Gorman Wills' adaptation of Oliver Goldsmith's *The Vicar of Wakefield*, at Covent Garden Theatre. William Terriss played Squire Thornhill. Scenery and costumes were designed by Marcus Stone, RA. Terry's performance moved audiences to tears.

'Those who are fortunate enough to have seen this actress's performance,' said *The Daily News*, 'cannot have forgotten the terrific power of her expression of hatred and aversion of the man who has so basely betrayed a trusting nature. Henry James, however, writing in *The Nation*,

didn't think 'a pretty collection of eighteenth-century chairs, and buffet, and pottery' were 'a substitute for dramatic composition and acting.' The final act, according to Terry, never worked. 138 performances.

FEBRUARY 11. A. Cook as Falstaff in Otto Nicolai's **The Merry Wives of Windsor** at Adelphi. Opera. Julia Gaylord as Mistress Ford. Josephine Yorke as Mistress Page. 'There is,' said *The Athenaeum*, 'no occasion to make Falstaff such a size as to qualify him to be exhibited as prize fat man in a show carnival.'

MARCH 1. Samuel Phelps as Cardinal Wolsey in Shakespeare's **Henry VIII** at Aquarium Theatre. Phelps collapsed on stage during the 'Farewell, a long farewell to all my greatness' speech. It was his last stage appearance. He died six months later.

RIGHT

Samuel Phelps, leading Shakespearian actor, as Wolsey in Shakespeare's Henry VIII at Aquarium Theatre in 1878. Wolsey was his last role before his death.

253

The audience at Lyceum Theatre in 1878. Prime Minister Benjamin Disraeli can be seen in one of the boxes: he is the gentleman with the curl in the second box from the left on the upper tier.

Henry Irving and Ellen Terry acted together for the first time in Shakespeare's Hamlet at Lyceum Theatre in 1878.

MARCH 9. Henry Irving in Dion Boucicault's very free adaptation of Casmir Delavigne's **Louis XI** at Lyceum Theatre. A second-class play was given a first-class performance. The high spot was Louis' death scene in Act V.

In this elaborate, picturesque representation of a grotesque old tyrant, at once passionate and cunning, familiar and ferocious, he has the good fortune that some of his defects positively come to his assistance … in the actual state of the English stage, there is no actor capable of doing the thing so cleverly and picturesquely as Mr Irving.   HENRY JAMES, *Nation*

Mr Irving never allowed the audience to forget that Louis, with all his squalid crouching over

the fire, his grim, toothless chuckling over mean triumphs, his malign ill-will, his saturnine humour, his senile incipient decay of body and mind, his doting superstition, his hobbling giant and fantastic mopping and mowing, is still a man, is still a king.
ARTHUR GODDARD, *Players of the Period*

MAY 25. George Grossmith as Sir Joseph Porter, Rutland Barrington as Captain Corcoran, Harriet Everard as Little Buttercup and George Power as Ralph Rackstraw in Gilbert and Sullivan's **HMS Pinafore or The Lass That Loved a Sailor** at Opera Comique. A gentle debunking of the Queen's Navee, the British class system and patriotism. Sir Joseph Porter was based on W. H. Smith, the First Lord of the Admiralty, who had never been to sea.

Mr Irving exerts himself to the utmost; his performance is remarkable for its picturesque intensity, its power of self-control, and passionate oratory; the part, however, is not in truth, worthy of so fine an actor.
DUTTON COOK, *World*

So wordy and yet so barren a piece has never before, we should suppose, been ushered on to the stage with such a flourish of trumpets.
The Times

They are so obviously aware of the fact that they are not as other folk are, they are so bent upon making the tragic point out of commonplace conversation and are so vehemently supernatural in their bearing, that they run a very narrow risk of becoming ridiculous.   *Observer*

'A masterpiece of dramatic caricature,' said Arthur Goddard. 'Irresistibly comical,' said *The Illustrated Sporting and Dramatic News*. 'We feel confident,' said *Era*, 'that an entertainment so bright, witty and amusing will attract audiences for a long time to come.' But not everybody agreed. 'Not much humour to balance its studied absurdity,' said one critic. 'Frothy production destined soon to subside into nothingness,' said another. 571 performances.

We cannot suppress a word of regret that the composer on whom before all others the chance of a national school of music depends should confine himself, or be confined by circumstances, to a class of production, which, though attractive, is hardly worthy of the efforts of an accomplished and serious artist.   *The Times*

JUNE 8. Henry Irving and Isabel Bateman in W. G. Wills and Percy Fitzgerald's *Vanderdecken* at Lyceum Theatre. This version of *The Flying Dutchman* was not as good as Edward Fitzball's version and grossly inferior to Wagner's opera. Tedious and over-long, it was not one of Irving's successes.

JUNE 22. London premiere of Bizet's **Carmen** at Her Majesty's Theatre. Minnie Hank as Carmen. Signor Campanini as Jose. Signor Del Puente as the Torreador. Alwina Valliera as Michaela. 'It seems likely,' said *The Times*, 'that Carmen will prove a decided and permanent success.'

JULY 9. Cyril Searle as Bill Sikes and Miss Etynge as Nancy in Cyril Searle's **Nancy Sikes** at Olympic Theatre. A succession of tableaux based on the characters in Charles Dickens' *Oliver Twist*. The critics thought the murder of Nancy was so degradingly brutal that the play should have been banned. 'To disgust and horrify is not the mission of the stage,' said *The Times*. 'The whole exhibition is about as healthy and as much entertainment as the sight of a public execution,' said *The Athenaeum*.

SEPTEMBER 30. *Uncle Tom's Cabin* at Strand Theatre. Adaptation from the French version by Leonard Rae: a jumble of scenes, not a play. The high spots were the plantation songs and hymns sung by a specially selected set of black supernumeraries.

Births

Isadora Duncan, American dancer and choreographer

Georg Kaiser, German dramatist

Deaths

Charles Fechter, French actor (b. 1824)

George Henry Lewes, British critic (b. 1817)

Charles Matthews, British actor (b. 1803)

Samuel Phelps, British actor-manager (b. 1804)

Literature

Thomas Hardy's *The Return of the Native*

Notes

Imperial Theatre opens

Henry Irving assumes management of Lyceum Theatre

Wilton's New Palace of Varieties is opened

Gilbert and Sullivan's *HMS Pinafore* is premiered at opera Comique, Strand (571 performances)

History

Queen Victoria is shown the telephone by Alexander Graham Bell

Congress of Berlin attempts to bring stability to the Balkans

Second Anglo-Afghan war begins

'Cleopatra's Needle' is erected on The Embankment

Freighter *Bywell Castle* collides with pleasure steamer SS *Princess Alice* on the Thames; 640 perish

DECEMBER 30. Henry Irving as Hamlet and Ellen Terry as Ophelia in Shakespeare's **Hamlet** at Lyceum Theatre. Ellen Terry believed that Ophelia suffered from incipient madness from the very start of the play. She had wanted to wear black in her mad scene, not appreciating that the only person who wore black in *Hamlet* was Hamlet. *Punch*, writing of her performance, declared that, 'If anything more intellectually conceived or more exquisitely wrought out has been seen on the English stage in this generation it has not been within Punch's memory.' 108 performances.

The best the stage during the last quarter of a century has seen and it is the best also that is likely, under existing conditions to be seen for some time to come.

JOSEPH KNIGHT, *Theatrical Notes*

1879

FEBRUARY 3. W. H. Vernon and Lotte Vene in Sydney Grundy's **The Snowball** at Strand Theatre.

The Snowball is in danger of melting before its time. Mr Grundy's dialogue is smart and telling, and he has the advantage of great assistance from the hands of Mr W. H. Vernon, who plays the part of the puzzled and worried hero with an admirable simulation of genuine distress. The part of the maidservant who struggles between her greed for bribes and her curiosity is acted by Miss L. Venne with delightful humour. *Theatre*

FEBRUARY 5. Carl Rosa Company. Selina Dolaro in Georges Bizet's **Carmen** at Her Majesty's Theatre. Adapted into English by Henry Hersee.

Her [Dolaro] acting was piquant without vulgarity and graceful without affectation. The offensive tints of the character were subdued. *Observer*

FEBRUARY 13. Caroline Hill in Paul Merritt's **The New Babylon** at Duke's Theatre. This melodrama, which featured Goodwood race course, was one of the most successful plays of the season. Hill played two women who looked exactly alike: the pure-minded heroine and a vicious courtesan.

MARCH 24. Marion Terry in W. S. Gilbert's *Gretchen* at Olympic Theatre. Mr Conway as Faust. Mr Archer as Mephistopholes.

JUNE 2. Charles Warner in **Drink**, Charles Read's adaptation of Emil Zola's *L'Asommoir*, at Princess's Theatre. Coquelin, the great French actor, raved: 'One of the finest dramatic efforts ever seen on stage.' The French critic Francisque Sarcey thought Warner was superior to Gill-Naza who had created the role in Paris but added: 'Those furious outburst, those rollings of haggard eyes, that contorted mouth, those lips wet with unwholesome saliva, may belong to nature, but they have no affinity with art.'

There is a lack of dignity in the whole subject; and a craving after morbid realism which should but rarely be gratified. But granting the task has to be undertaken Mr Warner must be pronounced to have accomplished it almost faultlessly. *Theatre*

He dies on the stage, the audience being spared no detail of delirium tremens. Whether this is legitimate art or desirable effect is a matter for individual opinion. But there can be no question of the power and intensity with which Mr Warner represents the most terrible scene ever presented on the English stage. *Daily News*

JUNE 4. Comédie Française in a season of plays by Molière, Beaumarchais, Racine and Victor Hugo at Gaiety Theatre. High spots included Delaunay in **Le Misanthrope**, Coquelin and Jordelet in **Les Precieuses Ridicules**, Got in **L'Avare**, Coquelin in **Le Marriage de Figaro**, and Bernhardt in **Phèdre** and **Herman**. Such was Bernhardt's nerves on the first night that she pitched her voice too high. Coming off stage, she fainted. She was, nevertheless, a huge success. 'Acting like this has the impress of absolute genius,' said one critic.

Phèdre was the most splendid creation I ever witnessed. The scene lasted only ten minutes yet she worked the audience to a strained pitch of excitement such as I never saw. OSCAR WILDE

JULY 25. Henry Irving as Jeremy Diddler, the ultimate confidence trickster, in James Kenny's **Raising the Wind** at Lyceum Theatre. The farce was a regular stand-by for Irving to alternate with *The Bells*.

AUGUST 9. Frank Mayo in Frank Murdoch's **Davy Crockett** at Olympic Theatre. American drama: idyll of the backwoods in Kentucky. Crockett saves the life of the heroine by thrusting his arm in the staples of a door, from which the bar has been removed, and so keeping out a pack of wolves.

SEPTEMBER 22. Mary Litton as Mrs Sullen, William Farren as Archer and John Ryder as Sullen

1870

World premieres
Henrik Ibsen's *A Doll's House* in Christiania (Oslo)
Pyotr Tchaikovsky's *Eugene Onegin* in Moscow

Births
Jacques Copeau, French manager, director
Albert Einstein, German-born theoretical physicist
Mattheson Lang, British actor-manager

Deaths
John Baldwin Buckstone, British actor, dramatist, theatre manager (b. 1802)
Charles Fechter, French actor (b. 1824)

Literature
Georg Buchner's *Woyzeck* (published for the first time)
Henry James's *Daisy Miller*
George Meredith's *The Egoist*
Robert Louis Stevenson's *Travels with a Donkey*

Notes
First Stratford-upon-Avon festival opens with Barry Sullivan and Helen Faucit in Shakespeare's *Much Ado About Nothing*
John Baldwin Buckstone's ghost is said to haunt the Haymarket Theatre
Augustus Harris, 'father of modern pantomime', becomes manager of Drury Lane Theatre

RIGHT

Ellen Terry as Portia in Shakespeare's The Merchant of Venice at Lyceum in 1879.

in rare revival of George Farquhar's **The Beaux' Stratagem** at Imperial Theatre. Much of the wit was cut due to Victorian prudery.

SEPTEMBER 27. William Arthur Conway, Marion Terry and Mrs Vezin in James Albery's **Duty** at Prince of Wales's Theatre. Son saves his mother's distress by assuming the responsibility of a liaison of his father and, as a result of his act of filial piety, he wrecks his own happiness.

SEPTEMBER 30. Henry Irving as Edward Mortimer in George Colman the Younger's **The Iron Chest** at Lyceum Theatre.

As a picture of despair and desolation, sombre and funereal, illumined by bursts of passion which rend and convulse the frame, and are as yet as evanescent as they are powerful, the performance is marvellous. The grimmer aspects of Mr Irving's powers have never been seen to equal advantage ... Is this thing worth doing at all? *Iron Chest* is one of the worst plays of the worst epoch in our dramatic annals.
JOSEPH KNIGHT, *Theatrical Notes*

NOVEMBER 1. Henry Irving as Shylock and Ellen Terry in Shakespeare's **The Merchant of Venice** at Lyceum Theatre. Radiantly beautiful in her

'*There was no question then of a good Shylock or a bad Shylock: he was simply not Shylock at all; and when his own creation came into conflict with Shakespear's [sic], as it did quite openly in the Trial scene, he simply played in flat contradiction of the lines, and positively acted Shakespear [sic] off the stage.*'

GEORGE BERNARD SHAW

'*The actor struck us as rigid and frigid, and above all as painfully behind the stroke of the clock … Mr Irving's Shylock is neither excited nor exciting, and many of the admirable speeches, on his lips, lack much of their incision: notably the outbreak of passion and prospective revenge after he finds that Antonio has become forfeit, and that his daughter has fled from him, carrying off her dowry.*'

HENRY JAMES, *Scribner's Monthly*

rich costume, Terry looked as if she had stepped out of a painting by Veronese or Giorgione. The production was famous for an interpolation of a scene with Shylock coming home, knocking on the door, and on the third knock, realising that the house was empty and his daughter gone. 250 performances.

Shylock is a bloody-minded monster – but you mustn't play him so, if you wish to succeed; you must get some sympathy for him.
HENRY IRVING

Never before has there been a Shylock for whom it was so easy to feel respect and sympathy.
ARTHUR GODDARD, *Players of the Period*

For absolute pathos, achieved by absolute simplicity of means, I never saw anything in the theatre to compare with his [Shylock's] return

home over the bridge to his deserted house after Jessica's flight.
ELLEN TERRY, *The Story of My Life*

DECEMBER 16. The Children's **HMS Pinafore** at Opera Comique. Master Harry Eversfield as Ralph Rackstraw. Gilbert and Sullivan's opera was acted entirely by children for one matinée performance.

One passage in it was to me sad beyond words. It occurs when the captain utters an oath 'Damn me!' and forthwith a bevy of sweet-innocent looking little girls sing, with bright happy looks, the chorus, 'He said Damn me! He said Damn me!' I cannot fail to convey to the readers the pain I felt in seeing these dear children taught to utter such words to amuse ears grown callous to their ghastly meaning … How Mr Gilbert could have stooped to write, or Sir Arthur Sullivan could have prostituted his noble art to set to music, such vile trash, it passed my skill to understand. LEWIS CARROLL, *Theatre*

DECEMBER 18. William Kendal and Madge Kendal in Alfred Lord Tennyson's **The Falcon** at St James's Theatre. The falcon is killed and cooked by a poet. The play was for the library rather than the theatre. The actors recited rather than acted.

It was unfortunate, too, that neither Mr nor Mrs Kendal could impart to it a reality which might have supplied the place of present interest and action. Both looked extremely well in their handsome clothes and acted in the technical sense of the word, with great propriety, carefulness and effect. But they are both essentially modern actors. *The Times*

THE PIRATES OF PENZANCE

The 1880s

1880

JANUARY 31. Squire Bancroft and Mrs Bancroft opened the refurbished Haymarket Theatre with a revival of Edward Bulwer-Lytton's **Money**. The audience, finding the theatre no longer had a pit, delayed the start of the play by half an hour with their loud complaints.

Lady Franklin, who has marital designs on the gloomy, widowed Mr Graves, reminds him of the French song and the Scottish reel his wife used to sing and dance. Arthur Cecil and Mrs Bancroft in Edward Bulwer-Lytton's Money at Haymarket Theatre in 1880.

APRIL 3. W. S. Gilbert and Arthur Sullivan's **The Pirates of Penzance** at Opera Comique. The opera burlesques tender-hearted pirates, timid policemen, silly romantic girls, orphans, the peerage, the army, Victorian values (especially Victorian duty), opera (especially coloratura), Gothic melodrama, patriotism and Queen Victoria. (The queen was not amused, and Gilbert didn't get his knighthood until after she was dead.) 'It abounds throughout in genial comic humour, untinged by either coarseness and undue flippancy,' said *The Daily News*. When Sullivan was choirmaster at St Michael's Church in Chester Square, Belgravia, in 1861, he drew on the local constabulary for his tenors and basses. He always said that he had had his policemen in mind when he was composing *The Pirates of Penzance*.

MAY 1. Helen Modjeska made her London debut as Camille in James Mortimer's **Heartease** at Court Theatre. An English version of Alexandre Dumas' *La Dame aux Camélias*. In order to get the play past the censor Dumas' name was not mentioned, and it was presented as the work of an English playwright. The management also thought it necessary to change Camille's profession.

The audacity of it all was quite amazing. My success surpassed all my expectations. There was a great deal of weeping during the last act. My eyes were moist, but I kept full control of my voice. HELEN MODJESKA, *Autobiography*

My wife and I were amongst the greatest admirers of Modjeska. When she spoke certain words, her lips, as they passed, seemed to give

A scene from Dion Boucicault The O'Dowd at Adelphi Theatre in 1880.

1880

Births

Grock, Swiss clown
Sean O'Casey, Irish dramatist

Deaths

George Eliot, British novelist (b. 1819)
Gustave Flaubert, French writer (b. 1821)
Jacques Offenbach, French composer (b. 1819)
Adelaide Neilson British actress (b. 1848)

J. R. Planché, English dramatist (b. 1795)
Tom Taylor, British dramatist (b. 1817)

Notes

Duke's Theatre is destroyed by fire
Haymarket Theatre (with remodelled interior) reopens

History

First Boer War
First telephone directory published
Emma Cons, social reformer, re-opens the Royal Victoria Coffee House and Music hall as a 'cheap and decent place of amusement on strict temperance lines'.
Andrew Carnegie donates funds for first 'Carnegie' library, in Dunfermline

---

them a sort of tremulous caress. She was in a version of *La Dame aux Camélias* the supreme type of a Magdalen; you almost had your doubts if she could have sinned, but none as to her salvation. THE BANCROFTS, *Recollection of Sixty Years*

MAY 20. Henry Irving and Ellen Terry in W. G. Wills' *Iolanthe* at Lyceum Theatre. Idyll in one act: an adaptation of Henrik Herz's poem, *King Rene's Daughter*.

No performance in our time possesses in anything like the same degree the power of casting off the special accent of modern life and of passing without effort into the region of ideal fancy. J. COMYNS CARR, *Theatre*

An insubstantial and whimsical affair in which the character assigned to Mr Irving was singularly unsuited to him, that assumed by Miss Terry allowed too much scope for certain fantastic qualities which have rarely, save in its purest form, been absent from her acting, and which should by all means be checked rather than encouraged. *The Times*

JUNE 26. Edwin Booth and Bella Pateman in Bulwer-Lytton's *Richelieu* at Adelphi Theatre.

Richelieu's great speeches are delivered with extraordinary vigour and virulence, the

oratorical frenzy of the actor's manner exercising an electrical effect upon the audience, greatly exciting them and urging them to most enthusiastic applause. DUTTON COOK, *World*

OCTOBER 21. Dion Boucicault's *The O'Dowd* at Adelphi Theatre. The discussion of Irish Reform caused offence. There were many people who did not think the theatre was the place for politics.

NOVEMBER 6. Edwin Booth in Shakespeare's *Hamlet* at Princess's Theatre. 'A very great actor has come among us,' said J. Palgrave Simpson. 'Artificial and uninspired,' said *The Observer*. 'Laboured and tricky,' said *The Times*. 'The days of the old classical school are dead and buried,' said *The Daily Telegraph*.

I hardly think the critics have shown me a kindly spirit. A poor stranger is cold-shouldered as a trespasser. EDWIN BOOTH

DECEMBER 15. W. H. Vernon as Consul Bernick in *Quicksands* at Gaiety Theatre. William Archer's translation of Henrik Ibsen's *The Pillars of Society*. One matinée: the first time Ibsen was performed in England. A Danish critic wryly reported that when the audience called for the author, Archer, without any trace of embarrassment, took the curtain call. Archer later apologised to Ibsen for having produced the play without his permission.

264

*Richard Temple, Frank Thornton and
Durward Lely in Gilbert and Sullivan's
Patience at Opera Comique in 1881.*

*Audience seen leaving Lyceum Theatre in
1881. The Lyceum's fame began with Henry
Irving in Leopold Lewis's The Bells.*

1881

JANUARY 3. William Terriss, Henry Irving and Ellen Terry in Alfred Lord Tennyson's **The Cup** at Lyceum Theatre. Pagan spectacle: a libertine is in love with a priestess. 'I doubt,' said William Archer, 'if a more elaborate and perfect stage picture of its kind has ever been seen, and if so certainly not in England.'

> The play proved to be crude, uninteresting and ineffective ... A play to him is little more than a collection of choice speeches ... possibly the poet is too literate and fastidious for the theatre. DUTTON COOK, *World*

JANUARY 17. Edwin Booth in Shakespeare's **Othello** at Princess's Theatre. Mr Booth, said Dutton Cook in *World*, 'is apt to interpret overmuch: desirous that no word should lose its value, he seems to surcharge the text with meaning, to oppress it with superfluous comment or emphasis.'

FEBRUARY 14. Edwin Booth in Shakespeare's **King Lear** at Princess's Theatre. 'Nothing finer of the kind has been known upon the English stage,' said *Era*. The production was a critical, but not a box office, success.

> They tell me my success is great!!! and all that. But the Press damn me with faint praise – the audiences are cold and dead, truly British. EDWIN BOOTH

MARCH 26. Johnston Forbes-Robertson and Helen Modjeska in Shakespeare's **Romeo and Juliet** at Court Theatre.

> In the whole poetic repertory, she could scarcely have lighted upon a character less suited to her physique, temperament and histrionic method ... In fine Madame Modjeska's Juliet lacks youth and truth, nature, freshness, passion and poetry ... reducing passages of the finest poetry in the language to the rudest prose, to a mere pulp, so to speak, of wrong emphasis, false accent, and mispronunciation. At times, indeed, it seemed questionably whether Madame Modjeska herself understood the speeches she failed so completely to render comprehensible to her audience. DUTTON COOK, *World*

> There seems to me there are only two schools of acting, the one of good acting, the other of bad acting. HELEN MODJESKA

APRIL 16. William Poel directed Shakespeare's **Hamlet** at St George's Hall. It was Poel's first attempt to stage a play by Shakespeare as it would have been staged in Shakespeare's day.

World premieres
Jacques Offenbach's *Les Contes d'Hoffmann* in Paris

Births
Stanley Houghton, British dramatist
Frederick Lonsdale, British dramatist
Pablo Picasso, Spanish artist
P. G. Wodehouse, British novelist, dramatist, lyricist

Deaths
Benjamin Disraeli, British Prime Minister, novelist (b. 1804)
Fyodor Dostoevsky, Russian writer (b. 1821)
E. A. Sothern, American actor (b. 1826)

Literature
Henry James's *Portrait of a Lady*

Notes
Savoy Theatre opens, the first to be illuminated by electricity
Comedy Theatre opens

History
First edition of London's *The Evening News*
New Natural History Museum building on Exhibition Road opens

1881

APRIL 23. George Grossmith as Bunthorne in W. S. Gilbert and Arthur Sullivan's **Patience or Bunthorne's Bride** at Opera Comique. A satire on the affectation and snobbery of the aesthetic movement and a gibe in particular at Swinburne, Rossetti and Whistler. Gilbert perpetuated the popular Philistine idea that the pursuit of the Arts, Music and especially Poetry was a painfully effeminate activity between consenting adults in public. Devotees of the opera have always identified Bunthorne with Wilde. However, in the production Grossmith made up to look like Whistler and he also adopted Whistler's vocal mannerism.

MAY 2 AND MAY 9. Edwin Booth and Henry Irving alternated Othello and Iago in Shakespeare's **Othello** at Lyceum Theatre. Both actors were better as Iago. Ellen Terry was Desdemona. William Terriss was Cassio. William Arthur Wing Pinero was Roderigo.

As far as I know there is no warrant discoverable for attiring Iago as something between a Spanish bull-fighter, and an Italian bandit. These objections admitted, Mr Irving is to be heartily congratulated: his Iago is one of his happiest impersonations: vigorous, subtle, ingenious, individual, an altogether impressive histrionic achievement. DUTTON COOK *World*

Mr Irving is despotic on the stage. At rehearsal his will is absolute law … from first to last he rules the stage with a will of iron, but also with a patience which is marvellous … His patience holds out against any test. Over and over again the line is recited or a bit of action done, until it is perfect. At the Lyceum one sees the perfection of stage discipline, and in Mr Irving the perfection of stage patience. EDWIN BOOTH

Henry Irving's Othello was condemned almost universally as his Iago was praised. For once I found myself with the majority. He screamed and ranted and raved – lost his voice, was slow where he should have been strong. I could not bear to see him in the part. It was painful to me. Yet night after night he achieved in the speech to the Senate one of the most superb and beautiful bits of acting of his life. It was wonderful.
ELLEN TERRY, *The Story of My Life*

MAY 8. The Meiningen Court Company in Shakespeare's **Julius Caesar** and **Twelfth Night** at Drury Lane Theatre. Acted in German. The productions by Georg II, Duke of Saxe-Meiningen, were notable for the fine ensemble work, the high artistic standards, and the historical accuracy of the scenery and the costumes. There was no star system and leading actors were cast in minor roles. The staging and the individuality of the mob in the Roman forum were particularly impressive. The supernumeraries were recruited from German expatriates living in London.

JUNE 11. Sarah Bernhardt in Alexandre Dumas' **La Dame aux Camélias** at Gaiety Theatre. Camille died standing up, a novelty, which did not appeal to London audiences.

AUGUST 6. Henry Merritt and Augustus Harris' **Youth** at Drury Lane Theatre. Military spectacle set in the Khyber Pass. The actors were given real Gatling guns and real rifles. The noise of the blank cartridges and the fumes were overwhelming.

SEPTEMBER 10. Wilson Barrett as hero and W. S. Willard as villain in George A Sims' **The Light o' London** at Princess's Theatre. Scapegrace son, basically a good chap, is rejected by his father. The production was notable for its realistic handling of the crowd scenes and the street-fighting.

If anything it is also too real, too painful, too smeared with the dirt and degradation of London life, when drunkenness, debauchery and depravity are shown in all their hideousness. CLEMENT SCOTT, *Daily Telegraph*

Like a true artist Mr Willard accepted the hisses of the honest critics in the pit and gallery as what they were – the sincerest tribute which they could pay to the excellent art with which he played the villain.
ARTHUR GODDARD, *Players of the Period*

OCTOBER 10. Savoy Theatre opened with Gilbert and Sullivan's **Patience**. 578 performances. The Savoy was the first theatre in London to have electricity.

DECEMBER 29. William Kendal, Madge Kendal and Kate Verity in Arthur Wing Pinero's **The Squire** at St James's Theatre. The similarities to Thomas Hardy's *Far From the Madding Crowd* was much commented on in the Press, and led to a very public dispute, which embarrassed Pinero enormously and which Hardy found demeaning and didn't wish to pursue.

1882

JANUARY 24. Sarah Bernhardt in Octave Feuillet's **Le Sphinx** at Gaiety Theatre. Bernhardt revelled in the melodramatic violence and remained standing after she had taken the poison until her spectacular death-fall backwards. Death scenes were her forte.

MARCH 8. Henry Irving and Ellen Terry in Shakespeare's **Romeo and Juliet** at Lyceum Theatre. William Terriss as Mercutio. Fanny Stirling came out of retirement to play the Nurse. Irving, 44 years old, was somewhat lacking in boyish exuberance. Mrs Irving thought the production was a jolly failure, and that her husband was awfully funny. 161 performances.

> Miss Terry is very charming, but she is not Juliet, and when real tragic passion is wanted, it is not forthcoming.   *The Saturday Review*

> Perhaps I was neither young enough nor old enough to play Juliet. I read everything that had ever been written about her before I had myself decided what she was. It was a dreadful mistake. That was the first thing wrong with my Juliet – lack of original impulse.
> ELLEN TERRY, *The Story of My Life*

MAY 5 TO MAY 9. London premiere of Richard Wagner's **The Ring Cycle** at Her Majesty's Theatre. The first complete cycle. Emil Scaria as Wotan. Otto Schelper as Albrich. Albert Niemann as Sigmund. Therese Vogl as Brunnhilde. 'The listener becomes fatigued by a tedious succession of lengthy speeches,' said *The Observer*.

MAY 30. London premiere of Richard Wagner's **The Meistersingers** at Drury Lane Theatre.

JUNE 20. Hermann Winkelmann and Rosa Sucher in the London premiere of Richard Wagner's **Tristan and Isolde** at Drury Lane Theatre. Conductor: Hans Richter.

> There is no music in existence which makes heavier demands on the executants than that of *Tristan and Isolde*; when, therefore, we say that the performance on Tuesday was all but perfect we are giving no slight praise to all concerned.   *Athenæum*

RIGHT
The playbill for Charles Reade's Drink at Adelphi Theatre in 1882. Charles Warner had a huge success as the drunkard in this adaptation of Emile Zola's L'Assommoir, which was published in 1877.

ADELPHI THEATRE.

DRINK

BY CHARLES READE ESQ

FORMAN & SONS ENGS Leeds.   ENT. STA. HALL.

The only Authorised Version of the French Play "L'Assmoir."

ENTRANCE

STAIRCASE

FOYER

VESTIBULE

TOOLE'S THEATRE.

JULY 3. Mme Chaumont and M. Dubray in Victorien Sardou and Emil de Najac's ***Divorçons*** at Gaiety Theatre. Written at the height of the controversial Divorce Bill of the 1880s, here is the familiar *ménage à trios*, but with the basic difference that the roles of husband and lover are reversed. It is the husband who is sexually attractive, and the lover who is the bore. The critics found it charmingly naughty, but somewhat too risqué for young girls and play-goers of stern and unbending morality.

SEPTEMBER 23. Lillie Langtry as Rosalind in Shakespeare's ***As You Like It*** at Imperial Theatre. The production was badly cast, and Langtry, though popular with the audience, was not admired by the majority of critics, who thought she would be well advised to leave Shakespeare alone and dismissed her Rosalind as 'a species of soubrette … utterly devoid of sentiment … mere recitation of a certain number of lines of verse delivered by a pretty woman.'

JULY 14. Adelaide Ristori in Paolo Giacometti's ***Elizabeth, Queen of England*** at Drury Lane Theatre.

> Madame Ristori is the greatest of European artists in the grandest style of histrionic art, the breadth and force of which none can realize as well as she. It is the opposite of the drawing room style to which we have been so much and so long accustomed on the English boards and we hope may counteract the tendency which that possesses to degrade the drama, substituting the familiar for the ideal.
> *Illustrated London News*

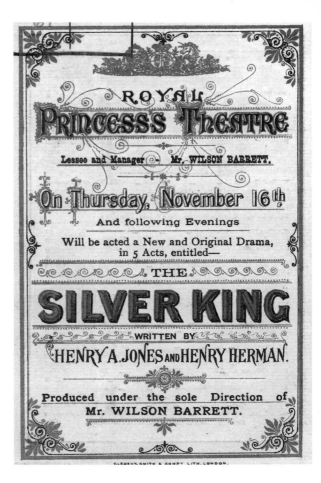

OCTOBER 11. Henry Irving as Benedict and Ellen Terry as Beatrice in Shakespeare's ***Much Ado About Nothing*** at Lyceum Theatre. Irving was 'a soldier first, a lover next, and always a gentleman'. For many theatre-goers Ellen Terry was the incarnation of Shakespeare's merry lady.

> He [Irving] gave me little help. Beatrice must be swift, swift, swift! Owing to Henry's rather finicking, deliberate method as Benedict, I could never put the right pace into my part.
> ELLEN TERRY, *The Story of My Life*

NOVEMBER 16. Wilson Barrett as Wilfred Denver in Henry Arthur Jones and Henry Harman's ***The Silver King*** at Princess's Theatre. A huge hit, which established Jones' reputation. In a combination of spectacle and intimate scenes he told a popular sentimental story of crime, suffering, repentance,

'There was a star danced and under that was I born.' Ellen Terry as Beatrice in Shakespeare's *Much Ado about Nothing* at Lyceum Theatre in 1882.

and made a fortune in the silver mines of Nevada. He returns home five years later to be reunited with his family and clear his name.

> Mr Barrett's pathos is of just the right tone – never whining or lachrymose, but as manly as it is true.
> ARTHUR GODDARD, *Players of the Period*

> The critics are right in thinking that in this work they have something new and highly praiseworthy … the diction and sentiments are natural, they have sobriety and propriety, they are literature. MATTHEW ARNOLD

pardon and redemption, constantly underlining a Christian message. The hero ('three parts drunk and the rest mad') had gambled away all his money. Wrongfully accused of murder and believed to have died in a train crash, he had emigrated to America

NOVEMBER 25. Jessie Bond as Iolanthe and George Grossmith as the Lord Chancellor in Gilbert and Sullivan's **Iolanthe or The Peer and the Peri** at Savoy Theatre. A satire on British party politics, the House of Lords (and its reform), fairies and Arcadian lovers. 'Same set of puppets that

1882

World premieres
Henri Becque's *Les corbeaux* in Paris
Nikolai Rimsky-Korsakov's *The Snow Maiden* in St Petersburg
Victorien Sardou's *Fédora* in Paris
Richard Wagner's *Parsifal* in Bayreuth

Births
John Barrymore, American actor
Harold Brighouse, British dramatist
John Drinkwater, British dramatist
Jean Giraudoux, French dramatist

James Joyce, Irish novelist
Theodore Komisarjevsky, Russian director
A. A. Milne, British novelist
Sybil Thorndike, British actress
Virginia Woolf, British novelist

Deaths
Madame Celeste, French dancer (b. 1810)
Charles Darwin, British naturalist (b. 1809)
Benjamin Webster, British actor, manager (b. 1798)

Notes
Royal Avenue Theatre opens (later renamed The Playhouse)

History
Insane Scot Roderick McLean shoots a pistol at Queen Victoria at Windsor railway station, the final of eight attempts on the queen's life over the previous 40 years
Second Married Woman's Property Act
Militant Irish republicans murder two British officials in a Dublin park
Royal Courts of Justice open
Egypt becomes a British protectorate after unrest

Mr Gilbert has dressed over and over again,' said *Echo*. There were two unexpected sensations: the entrance of the peers accompanied by the band of the Grenadier Guards and the electrically illuminated fairies. The Queen of the Fairies (six foot tall Jessie Bond and looking like Brunnhilde) sang her aria, 'Oh, Captain Shaw', directly at Captain Shaw, the Chief of the Metropolitan Police, who was among the first night audience. Gilbert, as usual, did not attend; he paced up and down the Thames Embankment, arriving at the theatre in time for the curtain call. 398 performances.

House crammed. Awfully nervous; more so than usual on going into orchestra. First Act went splendidly. The second dragged and I was afraid it must be compressed. However it finished well, and Gilbert and myself were called and heartily cheered. Very low afterwards. Came home. ARTHUR SULLIVAN, *Diary*

DECEMBER 9. William Kendal and Madge Kendal in **Impulse** at St James's Theatre. B. C. Stephens' adaptation of Xavier De Montepin and Kervani's *La maison de Mari*. A newly married woman's ex-lover threatens to shoot her husband unless she introduces him into the household. 'British audiences,' said *Theatre*, 'ignorantly imagine that a French play must necessarily be immoral, and they cast stones at it accordingly.'

DECEMBER 26. **Sinbad the Sailor** at Drury Lane. A cast of 650. The high spot was a procession of 36 kings and queens. Their costumes had been copied from books and drawings in the British Museum.

Mary Anderson (1859–1940), the American actress in the 1880s, was the first actress to double Hermione and Perdita in Shakespeare's The Winter's Tale.

1883

MARCH 14. Robert Buchanan's **Storm-Beater** at Adelphi Theatre. Two men, who hate each other, become friends when they are adrift on an iceberg. Based on Buchanan's novel, *God and Man*.

MARCH 24. John Clayton, Marion Terry and Mr Mackintosh in Arthur Wing Pinero's **The Rector** at Court Theatre. Rector believes the lies of a mad tramp.

> Theatres are dear and practical folk like their money's worth. If seats were cheaper there would be more audiences for plays like *The Rector.*   *Theatre*

APRIL 9. E. Rose and C. H. Hawtrey in E Rose's adaptation of F. Anstey's **Vice Versa, A Lesson to Fathers** at Gaiety Theatre. A schoolboy and his father swap identities.

' *Make 'em laugh, make 'em cry, make 'em wait.* '
WILKIE COLLINS

APRIL 11. Ada Cavendish and Mr Bucklaw in Robert Buchanan's **Lady Clare** at Globe Theatre. A loveless marriage between a high-born lady and a wealthy manufacturer. Based on Georges Ohnet's novel, *Le Maitre de Forges*.

APRIL 23. Miss Santley in George R. Sims and Frederick Clay's **The Merry Duchess** at Royalty Theatre. Comic opera. Satire on horse-racing and the idolisation of jockeys.

MAY 5. Mrs Bernard-Beere in Herman Merivale's translation of Victorien Sardou's **Fédora** at Haymarket Theatre. To satisfy English Puritan susceptibilities Fedora was married. The role had been specifically written for Sarah Bernhardt. Mrs Bernard-Beere went to Paris to see the play, and her performance was almost an exact copy of Bernhardt's. 'No interpretation, however, faultless,' said *Theatre*, 'no reception however magnificent – no criticism however brilliant, will ever make *Fédora* a good play.'

MAY 17. Philip Day and Kate Bishop in Joseph Derrick's **Confusion** at Vaudeville Theatre. The confusion was between a baby and a pug-dog.

JUNE 9. Wilkie Collins' **Rank and Riches** at Adelphi Theatre. One of Collins' stage failures: the audience laughed in all the wrong places.

1883

World premieres	Deaths	Notes
Henrik Ibsen's *An Enemy of the People* in Christiania (Oslo)	Junius Brutus Booth Jr, Anglo-American actor (b. 1821)	Royalty Theatre opens
Henrik Ibsen's *Ghosts* in Helsinborg	Richard Wagner, German composer, conductor, poet, author (b. 1813)	Royal College of Music is founded

Births
St John Ervine, Anglo-Irish dramatist
Benito Mussolini, founder of Fascism and leader of Italy

Literature
Robert Louis Stevenson's *Treasure Island* (in book form)

History
Andrew Mearns' tract *The Bitter Cry of Outcast London* exposes conditions in Southwark rookeries
First run of Orient Express, from Paris to Vienna

JULY 4. A banquet at St James's Hall is attended by 500 guests to honour Henry Irving before his departure for America.

AUGUST 29. Arthur Darce in James Willing and Frank Stamforth's **Glad Tidings** at Standard Theatre. *Glad Tidings* was the name of a steamer, and the sensational scene was the steamer on fire. The play was inspired by the recent *Princess Alice* boating disaster. The staging of the identifying of the dead bodies was not only thought to be far too gruesome but also in very bad taste.

SEPTEMBER 1. James Willing's **Daybreak** at Standard Theatre. The Derby was recreated on stage.

SEPTEMBER 8. J. L. Shine and Lottie Venne in Sydney Grundy's **The Glass of Fashion** at Globe Theatre. Satire on society journalism.

> Three long hours of satire and moral teaching would, perhaps, under any circumstances, be hard to endure; but when the scene is the ill-ventilated Globe Theatre and Mr Grundy is the lecturer and operator and the satire and moral teaching take the form of a tedious form in four acts, the result is assuredly depressing … His characters are most unsympathetic creatures, crudely conceived, insincere, unnatural. DUTTON COOK, *World*

OCTOBER 15. Mr Harris and Sophie Eyre in Robert Buchanan and Augustus Harris' **A Sailor and His Lass** at Drury Lane Theatre. The production recreated a Newgate execution which many critics found deeply offensive and quite indefensible.

DECEMBER 1. J. H. Barnes and Mary Anderson in W. S. Gilbert's **Pygmalion and Galatea** at Lyceum Theatre. Anderson was a beautiful statue.

> Mary Anderson has achieved popularity rather by dint of personal charms of a high order than by any exceptional display of talent. *The Times*

> What I have said of Galatea behind your back, I have said to your face. I have too profound a

Henry Arthur Jones (1851–1929, dramatist, was the author of The Silver King (1882), The Case of Rebellious Susan (1894), The Liars (1897) and Mrs Dane's Defense (1900).

respect for you and your art to butter you up with empty compliments.
W. S. GILBERT in a letter to Mary Anderson

DECEMBER 6. Wilson Barrett and Miss Eastlake in W. G. Wills and Henry Herman's **Claudian** at Princess's Theatre. Semi-classical play in verse. In AD 362 Claudian murders a holy hermit and is sentenced to perpetual youth, while all those he loves are condemned to die. The high spot was the destruction of his palace by an earthquake.

> But poetic dialogue and beautiful scenery do not, even with the addition of an earthquake, constitute an interesting play, and diverted of what might be called its accessories – since in drama action is everything – Claudian, must, we fear, be pronounced a rather dull affair. *Observer*

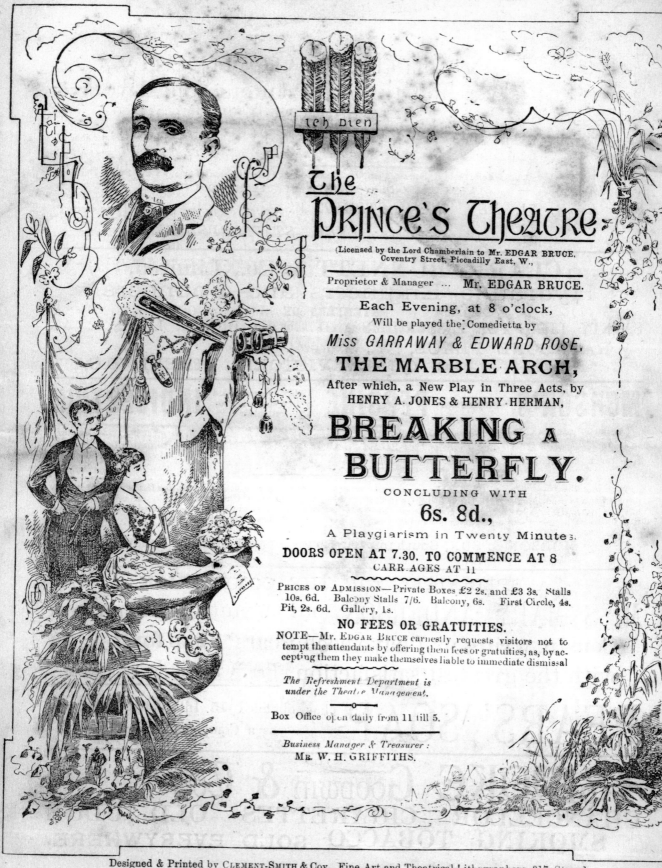

The Prince's Theatre

(Licensed by the Lord Chamberlain to Mr. EDGAR BRUCE,
Coventry Street, Piccadilly East, W.,

Proprietor & Manager ... **Mr. EDGAR BRUCE.**

Each Evening, at 8 o'clock,

Will be played the Comedietta by

Miss GARRAWAY & EDWARD ROSE,

THE MARBLE ARCH,

After which, a New Play in Three Acts, by
HENRY A. JONES & HENRY HERMAN,

BREAKING A BUTTERFLY.

CONCLUDING WITH

6s. 8d.,

A Playgiarism in Twenty Minutes.

DOORS OPEN AT 7.30. TO COMMENCE AT 8

CARRIAGES AT 11

PRICES OF ADMISSION—Private Boxes £2 2s. and £3 3s. Stalls
10s. 6d. Balcony Stalls 7/6. Balcony, 6s. First Circle, 4s.
Pit, 2s. 6d. Gallery, 1s.

NO FEES OR GRATUITIES.

NOTE—Mr. EDGAR BRUCE earnestly requests visitors not to
tempt the attendants by offering them fees or gratuities, as, by accepting them they make themselves liable to immediate dismissal

*The Refreshment Department is
under the Theatre Management.*

Box Office open daily from 11 till 5.

Business Manager & Treasurer :
MR. W. H. GRIFFITHS.

Designed & Printed by CLEMENT-SMITH & COY., Fine Art and Theatrical Lithographers, 317, Strand,
and 1, 2, & 3, Drury Court, and Star Yard, Chancery Lane, London.

1884

JANUARY 5. Gilbert and Sullivan's **Princess Ida** at Savoy Theatre. Operatic perversion of Alfred Lord Tennyson's *Princess*. 'There were not three and a half jokes worth remembering through three and a half hours misery,' said *The World*. *The Sunday Times*, on the other hand, thought, 'It is the best in every way that Sir Arthur Sullivan has produced, apart from his serious work.'

JANUARY 12. Charles Cartwright, Kitty Compton and R. C. Carton in Arthur Wing Pinero's **Low Water** at Globe Theatre. The play got a very bad press. Pinero complained it had been produced in direct opposition to his wishes.

> The fault, the crying fault, of *Low Water*, was, however, Mr Pinero's original sin of laughing at all sentiment and ridiculing the pathetic situations he had himself invented. He irritated his audience to madness, and he will fail, and go on failing, so long as he neglects to study the principles of dramatic effect. *Theatre*

FEBRUARY 28. Tommaso Salvini in Shakespeare's **Othello** at Covent Garden Theatre. 'There is genius in all Salvini does,' said *Era*. 'The force of the actor is as irresistible, his art as incontestable and his influence as absorbing as they were nine years ago.'

MARCH 1. Tommaso Salvini in Shakespeare's **King Lear** at Covent Garden Theatre. The audience was amazed when Salvini actually took a bow in the middle of a scene to acknowledge the applause.

> King Lear, with its monotony of motive, and its lack of varied human interest, is a play which does not act nearly as well as it reads. *Observer*

MARCH 3. Kyrle-Bellew and Miss Lingard in **Breaking a Butterfly** at Prince's Theatre. Translation of Henrik Ibsen's *A Doll's House* by Henry James and Henry Herman. Ibsen was trivialised: anything satirical or unpleasant was cut, and a happy ending was also provided.

MARCH 8. Tommaso Salvini in Shakespeare's **Macbeth** at Covent Garden Theatre. The massive barbaric costumes were designed by Gustave Doré.

> It has become clear that he is not an actor of wide range or that his intellectual insight into the subtleties of dramatic creation is by no means remarkable. *Observer*

MARCH 29. Herbert Beerbohm Tree as Rev. Robert Spalding in C. H. Hawtrey's adaptation of Von Moser's **The Private Secretary** at Prince's Theatre. The farce was hugely successful.

> The curious compound of clerical complacency and natural imbecility made him quite one of the funniest figures of the modern stage. ARTHUR GODDARD, *Players of the Period*

MAY 4. Johnston Forbes-Robertson as Captain Absolute and Eleanor Calhoun as Lydia Languish in Richard Brinsley Sheridan's **The Rivals** at Haymarket Theatre. Arthur Wing Pinero as Sir Anthony Absolute. Mrs Sterling as Mrs Malaprop. The play was tinkered with to allow for a sumptuous recreation of the eighteenth century, but the production did not repeat the success the Bancrofts had had with Sheridan's *The School for Scandal* ten years earlier.

MAY 22. Wilson Barrett in W. G. Wills and Henry Herman's **Chatterton** at Princess's Theatre. A portrait of the life and death of the poet in a garret. An artistic triumph for Barrett.

LEFT

The programme for Breaking a Butterfly, Henry Arthur Jones and Henry Herman's adaptation of Henrik Ibsen's The Doll's House at Prince's Theatre in 1884.

Sarah Bernhardt in one of her most famous roles: the Queen in Victor Hugo's Ruy Blas at Gaiety Theatre in 1884.

JUNE 29. Sarah Bernhardt in a season of plays at Gaiety Theatre: Victorien Sardou's *Fédora*, Henri Meilhac and Ludovic Halevy's *Frou-Frou*, Eugène Scribe and Ernest Legouve's *Adrienne Lecouvreur* and Victor Hugo's *Ruy Blas*. Bernhardt's performance in *Macbeth* (translated into French prose) was considered to be vulgar melodrama. 'She never for one moment seems to get inside her character,' said *The Observer*; 'she uses it as a mere mechanical vehicle for the display of certain stock resources of the stage.'

JULY 8. Henry Irving as Malvolio and Ellen Terry as Viola in Shakespeare's *Twelfth Night* at Lyceum Theatre. Irving looked like a cross between Don Quixote and Shylock.

' *Twelfth Night is not a good acting play. There is so little that is really dramatic in the situation, so little that enlists the sympathy of the audience in the characters or circumstances of the principal figures, and the humour is of such a decidedly old-fashioned flavour.*'

ARTHUR GODDARD, *Players of the Period*

OCTOBER 16. Wilson Barrett in Shakespeare's *Hamlet* at Princess's Theatre. Miss Eastlake as Ophelia.

Tears come into my eyes unbidden when I am acting my best. With an effort I can repress them, but if I am not sufficiently in my part for them to come uncalled, no power of mine can bury them. WILSON BARRETT

Mrs Stirling as Nurse and Mary Anderson as Juliet in Shakespeare's Romeo and Juliet at Lyceum Theatre in 1884. Anderson (1859–1940) had made her debut as Juliet in New York in 1875, when she was sixteen years old.

World premieres
Jules Massenet's *Manon* in Paris

Births
James Elroy Flecker, British
dramatist, poet
Ruth Draper, American
monologist

Deaths
H. J. Byron, British dramatist
(b. 1834)
Charles Reade, British novelist
(b. 1814)

Literature
Mark Twain's *The Adventures of
Huckleberry Finn*
Work begins on *New (Oxford)
English Dictionary*

Notes
Augustin Daly Company first
appearance in England, at
Toole's Theatre
Empire Theatre of Varieties is
opened
Prince of Wales Theatre opens
as The Prince's Theatre

History
General Gordon is besieged in
Khartoum
Fabian Society is founded
to advance peaceful social
democratic reform
Inner Circle Line of the
London Underground is
completed
Greenwich Meridian chosen
as international reference
meridian (the French
abstain)
NSPCC founded in London

NOVEMBER 1. William Terriss and Mary
Anderson in Shakespeare's **Romeo and Juliet** at
Lyceum Theatre. Mrs Stirling as Nurse. The acting
was subordinate to the scenery.

> She is always Mary Anderson. Never once is she
> any one else. The best of it is, the public does
> not want her to be any one else. They want to
> see Mary Anderson and that is all.   *Theatre*

> It would have been a more perfect piece of art
> had there been a little less Terris and a little
> more Romeo in it. Even in his most passion-
> torn moments the actor rarely quite forgot that
> he was behind the footlights.
> ARTHUR GODDARD, *Players of the Period*

> Miss Anderson's Juliet was only saved from
> mediocrity by the actress's personal grace,
> though some indiscreet and self-sufficient
> admirers have loudly proclaimed her the
> possession of genius, or at least of talent of the
> first order.   *The Times*

NOVEMBER 3. Little Tich's debut at The
Marylebone and Forresters Music Hall. Little
Tich (Henry Relph), comedian, patter singer
and eccentric dancer was 4 feet 6 inches and
famous for his Big Boot Dance, which became his
trademark.

*William Terris in Shakespeare's Romeo
and Juliet at Lyceum Theatre in 1884.*

1885

JANUARY 24. William Kendal and Madge Kendal as Rosalind and Orlando in Shakespeare's *As You Like It* at St James's Theatre. Mr Kendal was forty-two. Mrs Kendal was thirty-seven and her gaiety seemed forced. *The Illustrated London News* said there was 'plenty of scenery but very little Shakespeare'. There was even a babbling brook. The spectacular production was set in medieval times.

> Shakespeare nowadays is the hobby of stage directors. More care is taken with the design of one headdress than in the proper delivery of one speech. *Daily Telegraph*

MARCH 14. Rutland Barrington as Pooh-Bah and George Grossmith as Ko-Ko in Gilbert and Sullivan's ***The Mikado or The Town of Titipu*** at Savoy Theatre. Sullivan's masterpiece. Inspired though it was by the Japanese Village Exhibition in Knightsbridge, there was very little that was Japanese about it, except the settings and fabrics. The Japanese were still offended. Pooh-Bah, who holds all the offices of state at the same time, is one of the great comic roles, a monument to perjury, bribery, lies, and the salary that goes with it. Ko-Ko, the Lord High Executioner, has a list of society's offenders, 'people whose loss will be a distinct gain to society'. (The list was, and still is, regularly updated.) *The Evening News* said the opera 'was not likely to add very much to the reputation of either author'. It ran for 672 performances, a record Gilbert and Sullivan, and never surpassed.

> When Mr Gilbert asks for certain things he sees he gets them; he not only suggests, but he expects implicit obedience; he is not only inventive, but he is a man of authority and insists on his wishes being carried out. Perhaps it is to this uncompromising disposition that such good results can be attributed. *Entr'acte*

Madge and William Kendal as Rosalind and Orlando in Shakespeare's As You Like It at St James's Theatre in 1885. The Kendals were a famous husband and wife team, and their stage partnership lasted until his death in 1917.

Some of the lower actors included in the present Savoy Company are denied the vocal gifts essential to satisfactory vocalization, and for them the composer has to write melodies expressly contrived to meet deficiencies which obviously impose fetters on his genius. We have never concealed our opinion that in accepting such a position Sir Arthur Sullivan stoops to a lower rank in art than that for which at one time he seemed destined and has disappointed the hopes of sincere admirers and friends who looked upon him as the possible creator of a revival of English operatic art.
Illustrated Sporting and Dramatic News

W. S. Gilbert and Arthur Sullivan have done more good work for the drama than is generally recognized. They have to a great extent abolished the meretricious opera-bouffe and the flimsy, vulgar burlesque, and have given us in place of these noxious productions a style of entertainment which pleases the imagination and is absolutely free from that touch of coarseness which so often degrades the modern school of comic opera. *Stage*

MARCH 21. Arthur Cecil as Mr Posket and Mr H. Eversfield as Cis in W. Arthur Wing Pinero's ***The Magistrate*** at Court Theatre. Posket, Magistrate of Mulberry Street Police Court, a model of Victorian propriety and decorum, is led astray one night by his stepson. They end up in a hotel of disrepute and have to flee for their lives during a police raid. *The Magistrate* was Pinero's first major success. It had

George Grossmith as Ko-Ko in Gilbert and Sullivan's The Mikado at Savoy Theatre in 1885.

Sybil Grey, Leonora Braham and Jessie Bond as Three Little Maids in The Mikado at Savoy Theatre in 1885.

World premieres

Henri Becque's *La Parisienne*
  in Paris
Henrik Ibsen's *The Wild Duck*
  in Copenhagen
Henrik Ibsen's *Brand* in
  Stockholm

Births

Sacha Guitry, French
  dramatist, actor
Jerome Kern, American
  composer
Jules Romains, French
  novelist, dramatist

D. H. Lawrence. British
  novelist, dramatist

Deaths

Victor Hugo, French poet,
  dramatist, novelist (b. 1802)

Literature

Emile Zola's *Germinal*
Rider Haggard's *King Solomon's
  Mines*
Guy de Maupassant's *Bel Ami*
Sir Richard Burton's *Arabian
  Nights*

Notes

The Bancrofts retires from
  management of Haymarket
  Theatre

London Pavilion opens as a
  music hall
Oxford University Dramatic
  Society is founded

History

First cremations in Britain
Irish terrorists damage
  Westminster Hall and the
  Tower of London

---

always been his ambition 'to raise farce a little from the low pantomime level.' 363 performances.

Farce should have as substantial and reasonable a backbone as a serious play.
ARTHUR WING PINERO

One of the most amusing productions that the English stage has seen for some time. Mr Arthur Cecil was the very perfect of the character. His description of the night's horrors when being chased by the police was inimitable in its more tragic description. Mrs John Wood played the deceiving and indignant wife in her usual laughter-provoking manner, and fairly convulsed the house. *Theatre*

APRIL 4. Charles Warner, James Fernandez, Louise Moodie and Mary Rorke in George R. Sims' **The Last Chance** at Adelphi Theatre. The hero is married to the daughter of the man who is responsible for his family's ruin.

If I were asked – could Mr Sims write a really high-class melodrama for the Adelphi, supposing he were to try, I should say no – because the Adelphi does not want a really high class melodrama and Mr Sims is mentally incapable of producing what is not wanted … Mr Sims writes not for posterity, but for his contemporaries – not for tomorrow, but for

today – not for the critics, but for himself and his managers. SYDNEY GRUNDY, *Theatre*

MAY 18. Marie Roze in Jules Massenet's **Manon** at Drury Lane Theatre. Joseph Maas as Des Grieux.

The music suited her perfectly. She not only sang charmingly she invested her impersonation with so much refinement and grace that the odious qualities of the character were temporarily forgotten. *Illustrated Sporting and Dramatic News.*

MAY 27. Ellen Terry as Olivia and Henry Irving as Dr Primrose in **Olivia**, W. G. Wills' adaptation of Oliver Goldsmith's *The Vicar of Wakefield*, at Lyceum Theatre. William Terriss as Squire Thornhill.

He [Dr Primrose] is altogether a more distinguished personality than Goldsmith imagined, but that is a fault one can easily forgive, since it does not make him less simple or less lovable. The performance is full of masterly touches, but the end of the second act stands out from the rest as one of the finest pieces of pathos Mr Irving has ever compassed.
WILIAM ARCHER, *World*

The scene between father and daughter, and the return of the wanderers was never surpassed in

> ' It is a curious paradox in theatre that the play for
> which every one has a good word is often the play
> which no one is going to see, while the play which is
> apparently disliked and run down is crowded every
> night. '
>
> ELLEN TERRY, *The Story of My Life*

pathos; there was not a dry eye in the house:
even the hardened critics blew their noses and
furtively wiped their cheeks.

H. BARTON BARKER, *History of the London Stage*

JUNE. Marie Lloyd made her debut at Eagle Tavern
or it may have been the Grecian Theatre. She was
15 years old. Her songs, often risqué, included 'The
Boy I Love Lives Up in the Gallery', 'A Little of
What You Fancy Does You Good' and 'She Never
Had Her Ticket Punched Before'. Lloyd was at
the height of her popularity in the music halls in
the 1880s.

JULY 20. Last night of the Bancroft's management
of the Haymarket Theatre. The programme
included the first act of Bulwer-Lytton's **Money**
and Dion Boucicault's **London Assurance** and the
second and third acts of Charles Reade and Tom
Taylor's **Masks and Faces**. All roles in *London
Assurance* were acted by past members of the
Bancrofts' company.

> It is my opinion that the present advanced
> condition of the English stage and throwing as
> it does, a clear natural light upon the manners
> and the life of the people, where a few years
> ago there was nothing but mouthing and tinsel
> – is due to the crusade begun by Mr and
> Mrs Bancroft in the little Prince of Wales's
> Theatre. When the history of the stage and its
> progress is adequately and faithfully written,
> their names must be recorded with honour and
> gratitude. ARTHUR WING PINERO

OCTOBER 31. William Kendal, Madge Kendal,
John Hare and Charles Cartwright in Arthur Wing

Pinero's **Mayfair** at St James's Theatre. Adaptation
of Victorien Sardou's *Maison neuve*. An unprin-
cipled Baron passes out in a lady's boudoir. Her
husband wants to know what he was doing there
in the first place. 'It is curious,' observed *Theatre*,
'that every lady in an adaptation of a French farce,
however compromising the situation she is found
in, is always as pure as the unsunned snow.'

DECEMBER 19. Henry Irving as Mephistopheles,
Ellen Terry as Marguerite and John Conway as
Faust in Goethe's **Faust** at Lyceum Theatre. Adapted
by W. G. Wills. Diabolical and gruesome comedy:
one of the chief attractions was the witches' revelry
in thunder and lightning. 'The first duty of any one
who mounts a piece is to produce a beautiful and
pleasing effect,' said Irving. 'Archaeology must give
way to beauty.' The critics thought the production
was a distorted caricature of Goethe and dismissed
it as claptrap and pantomime. It proved to be
one of Irving's greatest financial successes. 388
performances.

> Mr Wills's creation is unfortunately not Goethe's,
> lacking the trenchant wit of the original, and
> becoming at times unduly declamatory. Within
> the limits set by the belittling of the character
> Mr Irving was all that could be desired: keen,
> hard, cold, cruel, sardonic, cynical, and above all
> picturesque. *Observer*

> The actor [Henry Irving], of course, at moments
> presents to the eye a remarkably sinister figure.
> He strikes us, however, as superficial – a terrible
> fault for an archfiend – and his grotesqueness
> strikes us as cheap. HENRY JAMES, *Century*

DECEMBER 23. William Terris, Mary Rorke,
Jessie Millward and Mrs D. Beveridge in George
R. Sims and Henry Pettitt's **The Harbour Lights** at
Adelphi Theatre. The hero is accused of a dreadful
crime and sets out to prove his innocence.

> Freshness, kindliness, geniality and sympathy
> with all that is brave in man and pure in
> woman are the distinguishing features of The
> *Harbour Lights*. Its comedy and tragedy are nicely
> balanced. *Illustrated London News*

1886

MARCH 26. Arthur Dacre and Lady Monckton in Sir Charles L. Young's *Jim the Penman* at Haymarket Theatre. Mr Brookfield as Detective. Mother and son are totally unaware that dad is a forger.

MARCH 27. Mrs John Wood, Arthur Cecil, John Clayton and Edward Kerr in Arthur Wing Pinero's *The Schoolmistress* at Court. The respectable schoolmistress takes to singing in comic opera in order that she can supplement her income to pay her wastrel husband's debts. 'Wild nonsense,' said *The Referee*.

> A comedy with a hero and heroine so perverse and contemptible that they exhaust the patience, while they never for a moment secure the sympathies of the audience. *Graphic*

> [Pinero] leaves his audience so exhausted with laughter that the critical faculty is entirely suspended in anxiety for the condition of their zygomatic muscles.
> H. SAVILE CLARKE, *Theatre*

MAY 1. Wilson Barrett and Mary Eastlake in Sydney Grundy and Wilson Barrett's *Clito* at Princess's Theatre. Blank verse drama. Clito is a young Athenian sculptor infatuated with a siren. They are both murdered by a mob. E. S. Willard played the Emperor Glaucius. *Theatre* wondered what was 'gained by this sorry spectacle of how low poor humanity may fall?'

MAY 6. Premiere of Percy Bysshe Shelley's *Cenci* at Grand Theatre, Islington. Written in 1818 but not staged until this private performance under the auspices of The Shelley Society. *Theatre* was unimpressed: 'This was the first and possibly the last of the most repulsive plays that have been produced this century.'

MAY 25. Madge Kendal in Sydney Grundy and Sunderland Edwards' *The Wife's Sacrifice* at St James's Theatre. Morbid sentimentality.

> Martyrdom and self-sacrifice in woman is always a very safe card for a dramatist to play … All her [Kendal] tricks and exaggerated facial contortions, that once threatened to become chronic, have disappeared and she holds her own as the first pathetic actress of the English – or for the matter of that, of any other – stage. *Illustrated London News*

Charles Coborn sang The Man who Broke the Bank at Monte Carlo in the 1880s.

Dan Leno in *The Babes in the Wood* at Surrey Theatre in 1886. Leno was the greatest music hall artist of his day.

AUGUST 28. Harry Nicholls, Alma Murray and E. W. Gardiner in Henry Pettitt and Agustus Harris's *A Run of Luck* at Drury Lane Theatre. The first of a long line of sporting dramas. The ladies were handsomely dressed by Worth of Paris.

OCTOBER 18. George Conquest and R. H. Eaton in Mark Melford's *Secrets of the Police or Waifs and Strays* at Surrey Theatre. Melodrama.

OCTOBER 23. John Hare and Madge Kendal in Arthur Wing Pinero's *The Hobby Horse* at St James's Theatre. Kendal was miscast as the philanthropic lady who looks after waifs and strays in the East End. The mixture of sentimental comedy and emotional drama wasn't popular; audiences wanted one or the other, not both in the same play.

OCTOBER 23. Gertrude Hawthorne in *The Governess*, an adaptation of the second part of Mrs Henry Wood's *East Lynne* at Olympic Theatre. Hawthorne, an American actress, had played the role 500 times in the United States.

> Art, much more finished and emotional force far more impressive than hers [Gertrude Hawthorne], might well fail to arouse much pity for the heroine whose hysterical grief leads so monotonously to her melancholy end. *Observer*

OCTOBER 28. John Douglass and James Willing's *A Dark Secret* at Standard Theatre. A Tale of the

---

1886

World premieres
Georges Courteline's *Les Gaities de l'escadron* in Paris

Births
Ronald Firbank, British author
Ben Travers, British dramatist

Deaths
Franz Liszt, Hungarian composer, pianist, conductor (b. 1811)

Literature
Francis Burnett's *Little Lord Fauntleroy*
Rider Haggard's *King Solomon's Mines*
Thomas Hardy's *The Mayor of Casterbridge*
Robert Louis Stevenson's *The Strange Case of Dr Jekyll and Mr Hyde*
Robert Louis Stevenson's *Kidnapped*
Henry James' *The Bostonians*

Notes
In his London debut Charles Coburn sings 'The Man Who Broke the Bank at Monte Carlo' and 'Two Lovely Black Eyes' at Paragon Music Hall.

History
First Home Rule Bill defeated
Tilbury Docks open as new deep-water facility for the port of London
First petrol car patented by Karl Benz

Thames Valley based on an incident in J. S. H. Fanu's novel, *Uncle Silas*. Domestic and sensational drama was notable for the re-creation of the Henley Regatta with real water (213 tons), real boats, a real swan and a real steam launch. The production transferred to Olympic Theatre in 1887.

NOVEMBER 13. Charles Wyndham, Mary Moore and David James in T. W. Robertson's ***David Garrick*** at Criterion Theatre. Wyndham's 'impersonation,' said *The Observer*, 'made up in spirit what it lacks in weight and distinction.'

DECEMBER 26. Harry Nicholls in E. L. Blanchard's ***Ali Baba and the Forty Thieves*** at Drury Lane. A procession of 500 thieves lasted 15 minutes. *The Daily Telegraph* said the production was admired 'by those who consider mere costliness is the essential aim of effect in dramatic art'.

DECEMBER 26. Dan Leno's London debut as Dame Durden in ***Jack and the Beanstalk*** at Surrey Theatre.

> He had, in a higher degree than any other actor I have ever seen, the indefinable quality of being sympathetic. I defy any one not to have loved Dan Leno at first sight. The moment he capered on, with that air of wild determination, squirming in every limb with some deep grievance, that must be outpoured, all hearts were his. MAX BEERBOHM

1887

JANUARY 22. George Grossmith, Durwood Lely, Rutland Barrington and Leonora Braham in Gilbert and Sullivan's ***Ruddygore or The Witches Curse*** at Savoy Theatre. Supernatural comic opera. Ruddygore was changed to Ruddigore. Gilbert had wanted to change it to Kensington Gore.

> Whilst Wagner, Berlioz, Brahms, Saint Saens, and other modern composers of indisputable genius have strenuously endeavoured to prove that ugliness is artistic, our leading musician has stuck to beauty and has been amply rewarded for his unswerving constancy. Unless I am much mistaken, Ruddygore will rank among his chef d'oeuvre. *Theatre*

JANUARY 27. John Clayton as the Dean in Arthur Wing Pinero's ***Dandy Dick*** at Court Theatre. Dandy Dick is a horse. The Dean is tempted by the quick rewards of the Turf, and is arrested while

John Clayton in Arthur Wing Pinero's Dandy Dick at Court Theatre in 1887.

*Arthur Wing Pinero (1885–1934) was the author of
The Magistrate (1885), The Schoolmistress (1886),
Dandy Dick (1887), Sweet Lavender (1888), The
Profligate (1889), The Second Mrs Tanqueray (1893)
and the Notorious Mrs Ebbsmith (1895).*

*John Hare, actor-manager (1844–
1921) spoke for many when he said,
'The more I look around the more
I deplore the lack of State and
municipal aid for theatre.'*

drugging a horse by the name of Dandy Dick. Some people found a clergyman on stage in a farce offensive. Clayton wasn't at his best on the first night, and Mrs John Wood stole the notices as the horsey Georgina Tidmus. 171 performances.

It is certain as anything can be that your *Magistrates* and *Schoolmistresses* and *Hobby-Horses* and *Dandy Dicks* will never be heard of again when their popularity is exhausted. They are for the moment and the moment only.
CLEMENT SCOTT, *Illustrated London News*

APRIL 25. ***Buffalo Bill, Red Shirt and their Wild West Tribe*** in all their paint and panoply of war at Toole's Theatre.

MAY 9. Bill Cody, Annie Oakley and Buck Taylor in ***The American Exhibition or Buffalo Bill's Wild West Show*** at Earls Court. Indians attack an immigrant train and a stagecoach. A buffalo hunt with real buffalo. Three performances: 11 a.m., 3 p.m. and 8 p.m.

MAY 28. Lionel Ellis and Kate Neville in Colonel Stanley and Charles Hermann's ***Buffalo Bill or Life in the Wild West*** at Sanger's Amphitheatre.

MAY 30. George Roberts's ***Buffalo Bill*** at Elephant and Castle Theatre.

JUNE 1. Henry Irving, Ellen Terry and George Alexander in Lord Byron's ***Werner*** at Lyceum

World premieres

Victorien Sardou's *Tosca* in
 Paris
August Strindberg's *The Father*
 in Copenhagen
Giuseppe Verdi's *Otello* in
 Milan

Births

Sigmund Romberg,
 Hungarian-American
 composer
Edith Sitwell, British poet
Arthur Rubinstein, Polish-born
 pianist and conductor
Violet MacMillan, American
 Broadway actress

Deaths

Jenny Lind, Swedish soprano
 (b. 1820)
Alexander Borodin, Russian
 composer (b. 1833)

Literature

Thomas Hardy's *The
 Woodlanders*
Rider Haggard's *She*
Arthur Conan Doyle's *A Study
 in Scarlet*
Thomas Hardy's *The
 Woodlanders*
Rider Haggard's *Allan
 Quatermain*

Notes

Strand Theatre is renamed
 Prince of Wales's Theatre
Herbert Beerbohm Tree
 assumes management of
 Haymarket Theatre

History

Queen Victoria's Golden
 Jubilee celebrations
'Bloody Sunday': many
 injured and 2 dead in
 demonstrations in support of
 radicalism and Irish freedom
Statue of Liberty erected
Hammersmith Bridge opens

Theatre. Sombre drama. 'It is difficult to exaggerate the picturesqueness and uniform consistency of Mr Irving's Werner,' said Clement Scott in *The Daily Telegraph*. 'He has given us few more beautiful or thoughtful pictures.'

JULY 18. Sarah Bernhardt in Victorien Sardou's **Théodora** at Lyceum Theatre. A poor example of Sardou's skill as a dramatist. It owed its success entirely to Bernhardt.

JULY 28. William Terriss and Jessie Milward in Sydney Grundy and Henry Pettitt's **The Bells of Haslemere** at Adelphi Theatre. Melodrama: forgery and blackmail plus picturesque scenes of plantation life in America.

SEPTEMBER 10. Johnston Forbes-Robertson as Leontes in Shakespeare's **The Winter's Tale** at Lyceum Theatre. Mary Anderson played both Hermione and Perdita. 'From her delivery of the text it was not easy to detect if Miss Anderson had studied either woman very much save in externals,' said *The Daily Telegraph*.

DECEMBER 26. Charles Lauri Jr in **Puss in Boots** at Drury Lane Theatre. This was the pantomime that Mrs Kendal took Joseph Merrick (the 'Elephant Man') to see. He sat in a box seat, hidden from the audience's view.

'*Once the curtain is raised, the actor ceases to belong to himself. He belongs to his character, to his author, to his public. He must do the impossible to identify himself with the first, not to betray the second, and not to disappoint the third.*'

SARAH BERNHARDT

1888

MARCH 21. Edward Terry, Brandon Thomas and Maude Millet in Arthur Wing Pinero's **Sweet Lavender** at Terry's Theatre. Wholesome domestic comedy. Sweet Lavender is the pet name for a maid-of-all work. A young man reading for the bar falls in love with her, much to the distress of his father. 684 performances.

MAY 16. Lewis Waller and Julia Neilson in W. S. Gilbert's **Pygmalion and Galatea** at Savoy Theatre. Neilson was beautiful. Waller was scholarly and not very sympathetic.

MAY 29. John Drew and Ada Rehan in Shakespeare's **The Taming of the Shrew** at Gaiety Theatre. This was the play Shakespeare wrote and not the David Garrick version.

> She [Rehan] was irresistible in her forwardness and exquisite in her submission speaking the verse throughout with an intelligence and charm rare among this generation of actors. The same praise is due to Mr John Drew.   *Observer*

JULY 9. Sarah Bernhardt in Victorien Sardou's **Tosca** at Lyceum Theatre. Pierre Berton as Scarpia. Dumeny as Cavaradossi. The play was an even greater success in London than it had been in Paris.

> Were it not for the genius of Mme Bernhardt Sardou's latest production would be looked upon as a very commonplace play and would attract but little … Of the play itself I will only add that it is offensive in its morals, corrupt in its teaching and revolting in its brutality, and yet every one who admires acting is bound to see it. *Theatre*

Sarah Bernhardt in one of her greatest roles: Victorien Sardou's Tosca at Lyceum Theatre in 1888. Today the play survives only as Puccini's opera.

The programme for Gilbert and Sullivan's H.M.S. Pinafore at Savoy Theatre in 1888.

AUGUST 4. Richard Mansfield in R. R. Sullivan's adaptation of Robert Louis Stevenson's **Dr Jekyll and Mr Hyde** at Lyceum Theatre. A tour de force. 'Jekyll is,' said *The Daily Telegraph*, 'a morbid, unsatisfactorily gruesome, uncanny chapter of useless psychological analysis.'

> As a lover he certainly did not shine, but once the transformation took place he fairly appalled his audience as the horrible creature … so utterly vampire-like in its appearance – the tones of voice were those of no human being – the ferocity and bloodlust were those of a beast of prey; and the effect was all the greater that it was so sudden and compassed by no mechanical means or leaving the stage. *Theatre*

SEPTEMBER 7. Sophie Eyre in Edward Rose's adaptation of Rider Haggard's **She** at Haymarket Theatre. The audience was bored rigid. Haggard, speaking from a private box at the curtain call, said that with a little trimming his novel would make a fine play. His observation was greeted with ironical cheers and applause.

SEPTEMBER 22. Leonard Boyne and Winifred Emery in Henry Hamilton and Augustus Harris' **The Armada: A Romance of 1588** at Drury Lane Theatre. Ava Neilson as Queen Elizabeth I. The hero saves the heroine from the stake at the very last minute. Spectacular tercentenary commemoration of the destruction of the Spanish fleet. There was an exact reproduction of Seymour Lucas' painting, *The Game of Bowls on Plymouth Hoe*.

SEPTEMBER 28. Miss Lingard in Alexandre Dumas' **La dame aux camélias** at Prince's Theatre. Lingard had appeared as Camille more than 500 times. The critics wondered if the play was worthy of her talent.

OCTOBER 3. George Grossmith as Jack Point in Gilbert and Sullivan's **The Yeoman of the Guard** at Savoy Theatre. Jack Point, a strolling player, loses the girl he loves to a soldier. It is not clear whether he dies of grief in the final scene. Gilbert said it was up to the audience to decide. The opera, set in the Tower of London during the Tudor era, was their only work to end unhappily. Sullivan told *Strand*

World premieres

Anton Chekhov's *The Bear* in Moscow

August Strindberg's *Creditors* in Copenhagen

Births

Irving Berlin, American composer

James Bridie, Scottish dramatist

T. S. Eliot, English dramatist and poet

Edith Evans, British actress

Eugene O'Neill, American dramatist

Deaths

Eugène Labiche, French dramatist (b. 1815)

Edward Lear, British artist, writer (b. 1812)

Matthew Arnold, English poet and critic (b. 1822)

Literature

Henry James's *The Aspern Papers*

Rudyard Kipling's *Plain Tales from the Hills*

Oscar Wilde's *The Happy Prince*

Notes

Shaftesbury Theatre opens

Madge Kendal takes up the case of Joseph (John) Merrick, the Elephant Man

Court Theatre opens

History

'Jack the Ripper' murders in Whitechapel

English Football League is formed

Match-girls go on strike at Bryant & May's factory in Bow for better terms and less dangerous conditions

---

Musical Magazine it was his favourite opera. Gilbert also thought it was the best thing they had ever done. Many critics commented on the similarity of the plot to Wallace's opera, *Maritana*.

> It remains to be seen whether the former admirers of Gilbert and Sullivan's 'topsy turvy' operas will accept with the same enthusiasm the new departure they have made, exchanging the grotesque fancies and wild extravagancies of the past. *Era*

DECEMBER 27. Henry Irving and Ellen Terry in Shakespeare's **Macbeth** at Lyceum Theatre. 151 performances. The play was adapted to suit the actors' personalities. Lady Macbeth was a far more sympathetic character than the audience was used to. The costume that Alice Comyns Carr designed for her can be seen in John Singer Sargent's painting of Terry in the role. 151 performances.

> The great fact about Miss Terry's Lady Macbeth is its sex. It is redolent, pungent with the *odeur de femme*. Look how she rushes into her husband's arms, clinging, kissing, coaxing, flattering, and even her taunts, when his resolution begins to wane, are sugared with a loving smile. *Star*

It is a most tremendous success, and the last three days' advance booking has been greater than ever was known, even at the Lyceum. Yes, it is a success and I am a success, which amazes me, for never did I think I should be let down so easily. Some people hate me in it; some, Henry, among them, think it my best part and the critics differ, and discuss it hotly, which in itself is my best success of all! Those who don't like me in it are those who don't want and don't like to read it fresh from Shakespeare and who hold by the 'fiend' reading of the character. ELLEN TERRY, *Diary*

> '*Judging from the banquet, Lady Macbeth seems an economical housekeeper and evidently patronises local industries for her husband's clothes and the servants' liveries, but she takes care to do all her own shopping at Byzantium.*'
>
> OSCAR WILDE, quoted by Graham Robertson

1889

MARCH 21. Johnston Forbes-Robertson, Kate Rorke, John Hare and Mrs Gaston Murray in Arthur Wing Pinero's **The Profligate** at Terry's Theatre. The profligate seduces and abandons a farmer's daughter. *The Pall Mall Gazette* in its headline hailed 'a real play at last', but it proved too serious for those who had hoped for another of Pinero's farces.

> If *The Profligate* succeeds – really and solidly succeeds – we shall know there is in England a public of men and women ready and even eager to accept the serious treatment of serious themes. WILLIAM ARCHER, *Theatre*

> ' *It is hardly to be expected that [Ibsen's] plays will appeal to the British public.* '
>
> Queen

JUNE 7. Janet Achurch as Nora and Herbert Waring as Torvald Helmer in Henrik Ibsen's **A Doll's House** at Novelty Theatre. Translation by William Archer. Nora famously walked out on husband and children, slamming the door behind her, an action which was said to have reverberated throughout Europe. Genevieve Ward, the actress, told Achurch that she thought the play was 'a piece of moral vivisection' and 'fit only for an audience of doctors and prostitutes'.

> In spite of Ibsen or any other theorist, it may be confidently asserted that no woman who ever breathed would do any such thing. *Daily News*

> Seldom, outside a doctor's consulting room, have such candid and plain-spoken revelations been heard … strong meat and not fit for babes. *Licensed Victuallers' Mirror*

> It has taken a great deal out of me, and if it had gone on much longer I should have broken down. It is the hardest part I have ever played. Nora is never off the stage for a single moment during the whole of the first and second acts, and in the third she is only absent for five minutes. The part is heavier than that of Hamlet and to go through it eight times a week is too great a strain.
> JANET ACHURCH, *Pall Mall Gazette*

Kate Rorke (1866–1945), actress, would create Bernard Shaw's Candida in 1904.

JULY 5. Francesco Tamagno in London premiere of Verdi's **Otello** at Lyceum Theatre. M. Maurel as Iago.

JULY 9. Sarah Bernhardt in Pierre Berton and Madame de Velde's **Lena** at Lyceum Theatre. Trashy grand guignol. High spots included Lena pleading with the man she has deceived, and dying of cholera. Death scenes were always Bernhardt's forte.

> Is it necessary at this time of day to point out that *Fédora*, *Théodora* and *La Tosca* (leaving rubbish like *Lena* entirely out of the account) are not works of art, but pieces of mechanism … They are vehicles for one and the same personality, mere strings of situations conditioned by that personality; not real plays.
> A. B. WALKLEY, *Playhouse Impressions*

JULY 17. W. H. Vernon and Genevieve Ward in Henrik Ibsen's **The Pillars of Society** at Opera Comique. Translation by William Archer. 'Though Ibsen in the study might be exceedingly interesting,' said *Referee*, 'Ibsen on the stage is an abominable bore.'

> In distant Scandinavia and long-winded Germany they may love this interminable talk. CLEMENT SCOTT, *Daily Telegraph*

It has a powerfully dramatic story, magnificent snatches of dialogue, brilliant sketches of character – but the preacher will preach, and preach inopportunely. *Daily News*

The Pillars of Society introduces us to a stretch of things which could hardly be said to have any existence in a capital like London, but which may still be found in some English provincial towns, and is very common in many foreign ones. *Theatre*

AUGUST 27. E. S. Willard in Henry Arthur Jones's **The Middleman** at Shaftesbury Theatre. A potter is cheated by an unscrupulous businessman, and a father will not allow his son to marry the woman he has seduced.

' *The stage is not real life. Those people who want real life can go into the streets and get it.* '
HENRY ARTHUR JONES
speaking to loud applause to the
National Sunday League Society

September 28. Henry Irving as Landry and Squire Bancroft as Abbé Latour in Watts Philips' **The Dead Heart** at Lyceum Theatre. Melodrama set during the French Revolution and staged to celebrate the centenary of the capture of the Bastille. Landry and Abbé Latour fight a convincing duel to the death with sabres. The duel was even more dangerous than it looked, since both actors were short-sighted. 183 performances.

It may be true that the actors and actresses of 1859 played to the gallery and pit. Why should not the artists of 1889 be allowed to play to the intelligence of the people all over the house? Pantomime and action are all very well but dialogue is still an important factor in an historical play. *Illustrated London News*

What a big name you might have made for yourself had you never come across those Robertson plays – what a pity – for your sake – for no actor can be remembered who does not appear in classical drama.
HENRY IRVING to SQUIRE BANCROFT

December 7. Gilbert and Sullivan's **The Gondoliers** at Savoy Theatre. 'It is not opera or play; it is simply an entertainment,' said *Echo*, 'the most exquisite, the daintiest entertainment we have ever seen.'

The piece is ridiculous rubbish and is, accordingly, hailed as a masterpiece. If it had deserved one half of the encomiums passed upon it, it would have been howled off the stage. W. S. GILBERT to Alfred Austin

I should prefer to please serious musicians in such matters, but one must consider the general public. ARTHUR SULLIVAN

World premieres
Anton Chekhov's *The Proposal* in Moscow
Anton Chekhov's *The Wood Demon*, private performance in Moscow
Henrik Ibsen's *The Lady from the Sea* in Oslo
August Strindberg's *Miss Julie*, banned, privately performed in Copenhagen

Births
Charles Chaplin, British comedian, actor, film writer, director, producer
Jean Cocteau, French dramatist, poet, novelist, film director, designer
George S. Kaufman, American dramatist

Deaths
Robert Browning, British poet, dramatist (b. 1812)

Literature
Jerome K. Jerome's *Three Men in a Boat*
Robert Louis Stevenson's *Master of Ballantrae*
Leo Tolstoy's *Kreutzer Sonata*
Mark Twain's *A Connecticut Yankee in King Arthur's Court*

Notes
Garrick Theatre opens
Albert Chevalier, The Coster Laureate and The Kipling of the Halls, sings 'Funny without Being Vulgar' for the first time, at Avenue Theatre.

History
London County Council is formed
The Eiffel Tower is erected for the Paris Exhibition
Cleveland Street scandal as police raid a gay male brothel; several aristocrats are incriminated or embarrassed
London Dock Strike exposes poor wages and harsh working conditions, arouses middle-class sympathy; strike is an historic success
Savoy Hotel, built by Richard D'Oyly Carte, opens
Jim Connell writes the socialist battle song, *The Red Flag*

1889

The
1890s

1890

JANUARY 4. J. L. Toole in John Poole's **Paul Pry** at Toole's Theatre. Pry, the interfering busybody, was created by John Liston in 1825.

> In low comedy and broad farce it would be difficult to find an actor of equal merit. As Paul Pry he [Toole] keeps his audience in an uproar whenever he is on stage.
> FREDERICK WADDY, *Cartoon Portraits.*

JANUARY 23. Mr and Mrs F. R. Benson in Shakespeare's **The Taming of the Shrew** at Globe Theatre.

> [Benson] clowned to such an extent as to produce the effect of a pantomime rally. Shakespeare intended him to be a gentleman. The lady should be womanly not the coarse-grained vixen that Mrs Benson made of her.
> *Theatre*

FEBRUARY 5. Herbert Beerbohm Tree as Falstaff in Shakespeare's **The Merry Wives of Windsor** at Haymarket Theatre. Bernard Shaw said that Tree 'only wants one thing to make an excellent Falstaff and that is to be born again as unlike himself as possible.'

FEBRUARY 22. John Hare as Benjamin Goldfinch in Sydney Grundy's **A Pair of Spectacles** at Garrick Theatre. Based on Eugene Labiche and Alfred Charlemagne Delacour's *Les Petites Osieaux.* The adaptation was more wholesome than the original. Hare's Dickensian performance was hugely popular. 'His acting is beyond praise,' said *Theatre;* 'indeed it is not acting, it is nature itself, so cheery and happy in its belief, so miserable when struggling against its new formed suspicions.'

APRIL 18. F. R. Benson in Shakespeare's **Hamlet** at Globe Theatre. Mrs Benson as Ophelia.

> Will anyone tell me why Mr Benson has revived Hamlet? ... It would be so easy one would have thought, not to revive Hamlet. A. B. WALKLEY, *Playhouse Impressions*

APRIL 23. Allan Aynesworth in Arthur Wing Pinero's **The Cabinet Minister** at Royal Court Theatre. The audience was confused as to how they were meant to take it. The underlying seriousness seemed at odds with a play that was billed as a farce. The minister's wife has run up so many debts that she has to borrow from a moneylender. In order

to get out of his blackmailing clutches she acts on secret government information in her husband's private papers and buys shares in the Suez Canal. She makes a fortune solely as a result of insider trading, and this is seen, without any cynicism, as a happy outcome. Five years later Oscar Wilde would tell a similar story in *An Ideal Husband*, more dramatically and with greater wit.

MAY 21. E. S. Willard and Olga Bradon in Henry Arthur Jones's **Judah** at Shaftesbury Theatre. A religious imposter fools a Welsh Presbyterian preacher.

JUNE–JULY. Sarah Bernhardt at Her Majesty's Theatre in a season of plays which included Jules Barbier's **Joan of Arc**, Eugène Scribe's **Adrienne Lecouvreur**, Alexandre Dumas' **La dame aux camélias** and Victorien Sardou's **Tosca**. *Joan of Arc* was a succession of melodramatic tableaux. Bernhardt, observed one critic, 'acted with all the earnestness, fire and genius which ever marked her work. She is exquisite as Jeanne, though it is not a part which furnishes her with so many oppor-tunities as some of her other roles.' *The Illustrated London News* said, 'The only serious fault that can be found with the play is that it is no play at all.'

JULY 8. Ada Rehan as Kate and John Drew as Petruchio in Shakespeare's **The Taming of the Shrew** directed by Augustin Daly at Lyceum Theatre.

> The representation of the play itself is an extremely vigorous, feeble; easy, laborious; finished, crude; eye-opening, soporific; magnificent and petty (here supply pairs of contradictory epithets ad lib) performance. The first epithet of each pair is to be applied, if you please, to Miss Ada Rehan and Mr John Drew, the second to the rest of the cast. A. B. WALKLEY, *Playhouse Impressions*

JULY 15. Ada Rehan as Rosalind in Shakespeare's **As You Like It**, directed by Augustin Daly at Lyceum Theatre. Disguised in male attire, Rehan never for one moment let the audience forget that she was a woman and sexy. 'Occasionally a strong American accent startled the ear,' said *The Daily Telegraph*, 'but on our stage it is rare to hear Shakespeare's lines spoken with such dignity, distinctness and musical force.' Ellen Terry thought Rehan was adorable on stage and off, too.

SEPTEMBER 20. Henry Irving and Ellen Terry in Herman Merivale's **Ravenswood** at Lyceum Theatre.

1890

World premieres
Anton Chekhov's *The Wedding* in St Petersburg
Marius Petipa's ballet *The Sleeping Beauty*, to music by Tchaikovsky, in St Petersburg
Victorien Sardou's *Cléopâtre* in Paris
August Strindberg's *The Stronger* in Copenhagen

Births
Karel Capek, Czech dramatist

Deaths
Dion Boucicault, Irish dramatist, actor, theatre manager (b. 1820)

Literature
Sir James George Fraser's *The Golden Bough* (first volume)
H. M. Stanley's *In Darkest Africa*
Oscar Wilde's *The Picture of Dorian Gray*, in US magazine

Notes
Grand Guignol flourishes in Montmartre
Lyric Theatre, Hammersmith, opens
Bransby Williams, monologist and character actor, plays Dickens' Sydney Carton in *The Noble Deed* for the first time. Williams goes on to be the 'Hamlet of the Halls'.

History
First moving picture show in New York
Forth Bridge, first major steel structure, is opened
Vincent van Gogh shoots himself in the stomach and dies two days later
First edition of the illustrated paper *Daily Graphic*
The future king Edward VII is embroiled in the Royal Baccarat Gambling Scandal and is called as a witness
World's first deep-level underground railway, the City & South London Railway, opens from the City to Stockwell

Poetic romance in blank verse: an adaptation of Sir Walter Scott's *The Bride of Lammermoor*. Ravenswood was a compound of Hamlet (a sense of impotence at having to avenge the death of his father) and Romeo (in love with a woman whose family is in deadly feud with his own.)

NOVEMBER 11. George Alexander and Marion Terry in R. C. Carton's **Sunlight and Shadow** at Avenue Theatre. A woman is loved by two men: one is a deformed musician; the other is old enough to be her father. 'Mr Alexander's performance was a surprise even to his admirers,' said *The Observer*. 'It was delicate and refined, revealing unsuspected depths of emotion in the actor's talent.'

NOVEMBER 19. Charles Coghlan and Lillie Langtry in Shakespeare's **Antony and Cleopatra** at Princess's Theatre. Military pageantry plus two ballets, which included a fight between Day and Night.

> Mrs Langtry's Cleopatra is not to be described as a disappointment, for the judicious can have found nothing in the lady's previous career to warrant the expectation that she could play the part. A. B. WALKLEY in *Playhouse Impressions*

Madge Kendal (1848–1935) actress, remembered today chiefly for taking up the case of John Merrick (The Elephant Man).

1891

JANUARY 5. Henry Irving as Benedict and Ellen Terry as Beatrice in Shakespeare's **Much Ado about Nothing** at Lyceum Theatre.

> I must make Beatrice more *flashing* at first, and *softer* afterwards. This will be an improvement upon my old reading of the part. She must always be merry and by turns scornful, tormenting, vexed, self-communing, absent, melting, teasing, brilliant, *sad-merry*, thoughtful, withering, gently, humorous, and gay, Gay, Gay! Protecting (to Hero), motherly, very intellectual – a gallant creature and complete in mind and feature. ELLEN TERRY, *The Story of My Life*

JANUARY 15. Julia Neilson and Herbert Beerbohm Tree in Henry Arthur Jones's **The Dancing Girl** at Haymarket Theatre. Sub-titled a play of modern English life. A dissolute Duke, infatuated with a Quaker girl, who has turned dancer, very nearly kills himself, but is saved just in time when the girl, he has always loved (a nice girl played by Rose Norreys), snatches the phial of poison from his hand.

> *The Dancing Girl* has more affinity with the traditions of the stage than with the manners and customs of the fashionable society it professes to depict. *The Times*

*The 1891 programme cover for London
Pavilion, home of musicals and revue.*

Julia Neilson's powers are tragic, and when
developed will prove of high service to the
stage; but in comedy she is not at home. The
high spirits of the heroine was ineffective, and
she lacked effervescence. *Athenæum*

JANUARY 17. Emma Chambers in *Joan of Arc* at
Opera Comique. Burlesque by John L. Shine and
Adrian Ross. Music by F. Osmond Carr. Joan is led
to the stake, but nobody is willing to burn her.

JANUARY 31. Ben Davies as Ivanhoe and Norman
Salmond as Richard Coeur de Lion in Arthur
Sullivan's *Ivanhoe* at Royal English Opera House.
Adaptation of Sir Walter Scott's novel. Libretto by
Julian Sturgis. A critical and a financial failure:
'The grand finale,' said J. B. Carrlile, 'is very tame
and disappointing and the composer no doubt

wrote it under the depressing conviction that all
the people who could not get out quietly were
looking at their watches.'

FEBRUARY 23. F. R. Benson as Rosmer and
Florence Farr as Rebecca West in Henrik Ibsen's
Rosmersholm at Vaudeville Theatre.

Here and there at intervals a laugh or two broke
the gravity with which the audience received the
strangest play that has ever been seen upon the
London stage. *Black and White*

These Ibsen creatures are neither men nor
women, they are ghouls, vile, unlovable,
unnatural, morbid monsters and it were well
indeed for society if all such went and drowned
themselves at once. MOMUS, *Gentlewoman*

MARCH 7. Kate Rorke, Johnston Forbes-Robertson and John Hare in Arthur Wing Pinero's *Lady Bountiful* at Garrick Theatre. Hare played a man who is totally unaware of how selfish he is. Pinero acknowledged his debt to Charles Dickens' Skimpole in *Bleak House*. 'Clever, brilliant, unconvincing,' said *The Athenæum*. 'The sense of the comic deadens his perception of the true.'

MARCH 13. J. T. Grien founded The Independent Theatre Society and staged Henrik Ibsen's *Ghosts* at Royalty Theatre. Mrs T. Wright as Mrs Alving. Frank Lindo as Oswald. Leonard Outram as Pastor Manders. Sydney Howard as Jacob Engstrand. Edith Kenward as Regina. Written in 1881, the play defended free love, suggested incest was quite normal and acceptable in Norway, and dared to mention such unmentionables as brothels and syphilis. Ibsen was fully aware that his play would cause offence. 'If it didn't,' he said, 'there would have been no necessity for me to write it.' However, the hostility was far greater than even he had envisaged. Bookshops sent the book back to the publisher in their hundreds, and the play was refused performance in Norway, Sweden and Denmark. The London critics had a field day.

The most loathsome play ever to be put on the stage ... an open drain; a loathsome sore unbandaged ... a dirty act done publicly; a lazar house with all its doors and windows open ... unutterably offensive ... revoltingly suggestive and blasphemous ... morbid, unhealthy, unwholesome and disgusting ... a repulsive and degrading work ... garbage and offal ... as foul and filthy a concoction as has ever been allowed to disgrace the boards of the English theatre ... an insult to the common-sense of all playgoer ... a piece to bring the stage into disrepute and dishonour every right-thinking man and woman
CRITICS on Ibsen's *Ghosts*

APRIL 20. Elizabeth Robbins as Hedda in Henrik Ibsen's *Hedda Gabler* at Vaudeville Theatre. Scott Buist as Tesman. Charles Sugden as Judge Brack. Arthur Elwood as Løvborg. Marion Lea as Mrs Elvsted. Translation by Edmund Gosse. One matinée.

Miss Elizabeth Robins has managed to endow the callous selfishness and morbid malignity of the heroine with just enough womanly grace and inconsistent charm to make her bearable for three acts. *Observer*

World premieres
Henrik Ibsen's *Hedda Gabler* in Munich
Leo Tolstoy's *The Fruits of Enlightenment* in Moscow

Births
Arthur Bliss, British composer
Ivor Brown, British critic
Agatha Christie, British crime novelist, dramatist

Deaths
Phineas T. Barnum, American circus showman (b. 1810)

Literature
Thomas Hardy's *Tess of the D'Urbervilles*
George Gissing's *New Grub Street*

Notes
Royal English Opera House opens
Pavilion Theatre opened
New Olympic Theatre opens
George Alexander's becomes manager of St James's
First meeting of the Actors' Association held at Lyceum
Marie Lloyd sings 'Oh, Jeremiah, Don't you Go to Sea' in her London debut
Lottie Collins sings 'Ta-ra-ra-Boom-de-ay' for the first time at Tivoli Music Hall
Eugene Sandow is billed as 'The Strongest Man' in the World at Tivoli Theatre; Sandow was able to lift, with one hand, a live cart horse weighing 600 lbs

George Robey makes his debut at Oxford Music Hall.
Ada Reeve songs include 'What Do I Care?', 'The Little Puritan', and 'I Am a Little Too Tiny to Know You Know'.

History
Charles Parnell, cited in divorce case, refuses to resign and marries Kitty O'Shea
Naval exhibition on Thames attracts 2.5 million visitors
Education Act removes fees for all elementary education
Carnegie Hall opens in New York; Tchaikovsky is guest conductor

1891

Might be interesting to an audience of mad doctors ... To conceive of the Ibsen drama gaining an extensive or permanent foothold on the stage is hardly possible. Playgoing would cease to be an amusement and become a penance. *The Times*

If I were asked if it is a well-made play, a play for the people, a wholesome play, an instructive play, a play that amuses, or elevates, or assists the imagination or fancy, or fairly contrasts the good with the bad, the evil in life with the good, I should answer 'No.'
CLEMENT SCOTT, *Illustrated London News*

MAY 11. Rose Meller as Ellida Wangel and Oscar Adye as Dr Wangel in Henrik Ibsen's **The Lady from the Sea** at Terry's Theatre. Translation by Eleanor Marx. Charles Dalton as the Stranger. 'Five acts of unmitigated rubbish,' said *The Standard*.

If the piece had been presented under any name but Ibsen's, I verily believe it would have been hissed off the stage long before the end of it. *Referee*

Clearly Ibsen's best chance of being accepted as a dramatist rather than a pathological lecturer, is that he should be administered to the public

in small doses and at long intervals. Studies in morbid heredity are very well in scientific treatise. On the stage, put forward as a public entertainment, they tend to perplex, irritate, and repel, besides being useless for practical purpose. *The Times*

MAY 12. Ellen Terry and Gordon Craig in Charles Reade and Tom Taylor's **Nance Oldfield** at Lyceum Theatre. Craig, who was Terry's son, said his mother 'played but one part – herself, and when not herself she couldn't play it'.

JUNE 3. Sidney Herbert Basing and C. Lambourne in W. S. Gilbert's **Rosencrantz and Guildenstern** at Vaudeville Theatre.

If you promise me faithfully not to mention to a single person – not even your dearest friend, I don't think Shakespeare rollicking. W. S. GILBERT

AUGUST 1. Leonard Boyne, Elizabeth Robins and Mrs Patrick Campbell in George R. Sims and Robert Buchanan's **The Trumpet Call** at Adelphi Theatre. Military melodrama. 'Actresses are made, not born,' reported *The Daily Telegraph*, 'and this performance shows that in Mrs Campbell we have the makings of a valuable melodramatic actress.'

OCTOBER 24. Edward Terry, Fanny Brough and E. V. Esmond in Arthur Wing Pinero's **The Times** at Terry's Theatre. A satire on vanity: a parvenu wants to be recognised by society, but is thwarted by the behaviour of his good-for-nothing son who marries the daughter of an Irish landlady. Pinero's 'satire does not titillate,' said *The Times*; 'it sears and destroys. The cup he gives us to drink is a sparkling one, but it has bitter dregs.'

LEFT

Henry Irving, J. L. Toole, and Squire Bancroft in 1891. From a drawing in colour by Phil May.

RIGHT

Edward Terry and Fanny Brough in Arthur Wing Pinero's The Times at Terry's Theatre in 1891.

November 7. George Alexander in Mark Hinton and Henry Hamilton's **Lord Anerley** at St James's Theatre. French melodrama. Gaucho tries to palm himself off as the heir to an earldom. Unbeknown to him, he actually is the earl's first-born son.

The stage has its ardent reformers who clamour for what they are pleased to call truth … Is truth the real aim of theatrical entertainment? Is the stage anything more than a contrivance for exhibiting to an unthinking crowd a more or less pleasing simulacrum of life? *The Times*

December 26. Marie Lloyd, Dan Leno and Little Tich in **Humpty Dumpty or The Yellow Dwarf and the Fair One with the Golden Locks** at Drury Lane Theatre. 'If the loftiness of this lady's salary,' commented one critic, 'is measured according to the height she kicks she is an expensive luxury.' *The Saturday Review* described Tich as 'a veritable imp, with the wizened ace of a fiendish old man and the body of a boy.'

1892

January 5. Henry Irving as Cardinal Wolsey, Ellen Terry as Queen Katharine, William Terriss as King Henry, Johnston Forbes-Robertson as Buckingham and Gordon Craig as Cromwell in Shakespeare's **Henry VIII** at Lyceum Theatre. 'Mr Irving,' said *The Saturday Review*, 'rises to the highest expression of histrionic art.' He looked superb, the very incarnation of evil. The silk for Wolsey's flame-coloured robes had been dyed by the dyers to the Cardinal's College in Rome. The recreation of Tudor London, supervised by Alma Tadema, was so lavish and spectacular that, though the production ran for 40 performances, it still lost money.

The plain truth is that for a good number of average modern Britons this is about the noblest kind of artistic pleasure that they are capable of appreciating … We practise an aestheticism on the cheap. *St James's Gazette*

Henry Irving as Wolsey in Shakespeare's Henry VIII at Lyceum Theatre in 1891.

'Speak, sir! Why is my wife's fan here? Answer me! By God! I'll search your rooms, and if my wife's here, I'll –' H. H. Vincent, Mr Vane-Tempest, Ben Webster, George Alexander and Nutcombe Gold Oscar Wilde's Lady Windermere's Fan at St James's Theatre in 1892.

FEBRUARY 20. George Alexander, Marion Terry, Lily Hanbury and Nutcombe Gold in Oscar Wilde's **Lady Windermere's Fan** at St James's Theatre. The play was originally called *The Good Woman*. Wilde changed the title when his mother said it was mawkish and that nobody would want to go to the theatre and see a good woman.

Mr Wilde has the gift of writing witty and memorable dialogue, full of paradoxical surprises, and pregnant with the wisdom of the boudoir and the cynicism of the club smoking room, while under all this there frequently lurk deeper truths of a wider range. *Sunday Times*

The play is a bad one but it will succeed. No faults of construction, no failure of interest, no feebleness in character drawing, no staleness in motive, will weigh in the scale against the insolence of its caricature. Society loves best those who chaff it most, and society will rush to see Lady Windermere, and will be tickled by her fan. *Daily Telegraph*

One longs for a refreshing breath of sincerity on this barren and dreary waste of epigram. *The Times*

' *Ladies and Gentlemen: I have enjoyed this evening immensely. The actors have given us a charming rendering of a delightful play, and your appreciation has been most intelligent. I congratulate you on the great success of your performance, which persuades me that you think almost as highly of the play as I do myself.* **'**

OSCAR WILDE in his curtain call speech

MAY–JULY. Sarah Bernhardt at English Opera House. Her roles included Cleopatra, Leah, Tosca, Marguerite Gautier, Fédora, Frou-Frou and Phèdre. *The Athenæum*, reviewing *Frou Frou*, said, 'The voice had lost its golden ring, and the performance was inadequate.'

1892. Sarah Bernhardt was in the middle of rehearsing Oscar Wilde's **Salome** when the Lord Chamberlain, Edward F. Smyth Pigott, refused the play a licence on the grounds that biblical characters were not allowed on the English stage.

Wilde said that he would renounce his citizenship and become a Frenchman. The play, written in French and published in Paris, was premiered in Paris with Lina Munte as Salome and Aurelien Lugne-Poe as Herod. The English translation by Lord Alfred Douglas was published in 1894, but London did not see it produced until 1905 and then only for two private performances.

MAY 30. Katharina Klafsky as Brunnhilde, Max Alvary as Siegfried and Henirich Wiegand as Hagan in Richard Wagner's **Ring Cycle** at Her Majesty's Theatre. Conductor: Gustav Mahler.

Among the lesser advantages which she [Klafsky] enjoys may be mentioned the circumstance that she has not the exceedingly massive proportions which Londoners have learnt to regard as inseparable from the finest German singing.   *The Times*

SEPTEMBER 24. Lucille Hall in Arthur Sullivan and Sydney Grundy's **Haddon Hall** at Savoy Theatre. Religious satire.

Each hearer will no doubt have his own opinion as to the propriety of joking with subjects more or less intimately connected with religion, but some of the Puritan speeches and songs sail a good deal nearer the wind than anything that has been seen before at the Savoy Theatre. *The Times*

Marion Terry, actress sister to Marion, Florence and Fred: a theatrical dynasty that would later include John Gielgud.

World premieres

Ruggero Leoncavallo's *Pagliacci* in Milan

Marius Petipa's ballet *The Nutcracker* to music by Pytor Tchaikovsky at St Petersburg

August Strindberg's *Playing with Fire* in Copenhagen

Births

Ugo Betti, Italian dramatist

André Obey, French dramatist

Elmer Rice, American dramatist

Deaths

Alfred Lord Tennyson, British poet (b. 1809)

Literature

Arthur Conan Doyle's *The Adventures of Sherlock Holmes*

Rudyard Kipling's *Barrack Room Ballads*

George and Weedon Grossmith's *The Diary of a Nobody*

Rudyard Kipling's *Barrack-Room Ballads*

Notes

Henry Irving is created Honorary Doctor of Letters, University of Dublin

Duke of York's Theatre opens

Trafalgar Square Theatre opens

School of Dramatic Art opens

History

Shaftesbury Memorial in Piccadilly Circus unveiled

Plessy *v.* Ferguson upholds racial segregation in US

OCTOBER 17. London premiere of Pyotr Tchaikovsky's **Eugene Onegin**, conducted by Henry Wood at Olympic Theatre. Sung in English. Eugene Ondon as Eugene. Fanny Moody as Titiana. Ivor McKay as Lensky. Charles Manners as Prince Gremin.

We cannot accept Tchaikovsky as an operatic composer of the first rank. His dance music is characteristic piquant and excellently orchestrated; but his vocal compositions are, for the most part, of second-rate, not to say inferior, quality. They seldom show originality in their melodies. *Observer*

NOVEMBER 10. Henry Irving in Shakespeare's **King Lear** at Lyceum Theatre. Ellen Terry as Cordelia. William Terriss as Edgar. Frank Cooper as Edmund. Gordon Craig as Oswald. Designer Ford Maddox Brown.

Henry Irving – not to speak it profanely, but in all reverence – in his character of Lear, might have stood for Moses on Mount Sinai, or Noah at the hour of the flood. His appearance is patriarchal, not theatrical. The stage vanishes, and we seem to be in the presence of the sublimest instances of hoary senility.
CLEMENT SCOTT, *Daily Telegraph*

The grand *mise en scene* and Ellen Terry's Cordelia – and never had Shakespeare's heroine a more exquisite interpretation – were the only redeeming feature of a very inadequate production.
H. BARTON BAKER, *History of the London Stage*

DECEMBER 3. George Alexander and Marion Terry in R. C. Carton's **Liberty Hall** at St James's Theatre. A young squire disguises himself as a commercial traveller in order to court his haughty cousin, who is always quick to take offence when none is meant.

After the cynicism and artificiality of *Lady Windermere's Fan*, the simple, direct, homely sentiment of *Liberty Hall* goes to the heart of the public with a force which is not to be gainsaid. *The Times*

DECEMBER 21. W. S. Penley as Lord Fancourt Babberley in Brandon Thomas's **Charley's Aunt** at Royalty Theatre. Two Oxford undergraduates persuade their best friend, Babberley, to dress up and pretend to be a rich aunt and then to act as chaperone to their girl friends. Thomas insisted that the role had nothing whatsoever to do with female impersonation, and that there should not be any suggestion of effeminacy in the acting. 'The man,' he said, 'must walk, talk and move like a man.' Dressed in black satin, white lace fichu, bonnet and wig, Penley looked like a chimpanzee pretending to be Queen Victoria. The future Edward VII, a regular theatre-goer, was not amused. 'I am Charley's aunt from Brazil where the nuts come from,' became a popular catchphrase. The production transferred to Globe Theatre and set a box office record, running for four years.

DECEMBER 26. Marie Loftus, Marie Lloyd and Little Tich in ***Little Bo-Peep, Little Red Riding Hood and Hop O' My Thumb*** at Drury Lane Theatre. The pantomime included a grand procession of the best known nursery rhymes and fairy tales. Book by Augustus Harris and J. Wilton Jones. Music by John Crook. Dan Leno played Daddy Thumb.

W. S. Penley as Lord Fancourt Babberley in Thomas Brandon's Charley's Aunt at Royalty Theatre in 1892. 'I'm Charley's Aunt from Brazil where the nuts come from,' became a much-quoted line in the theatrical profession.

1893

JANUARY 26. Charles Wyndham and Mary Moore in Henry Arthur Jones's **The Bauble Shop** at Criterion Theatre. Romantic drama and politics. 'There is only one word,' said William Archer in *Theatrical World*, 'and that, unfortunately, a French one – to describe the whole conception and execution of the play; it is incurably *naïf*.'

FEBRUARY 6. Henry Irving as Thomas Becket, Ellen Terry as Rosamund de Clifford, William Terriss as Henry II and Genevieve Ward as Eleanor of Aquitaine in Alfred Lord Tennyson's **Becket** at Lyceum Theatre. Tennyson did not live to see the production. On his death-bed he had said, 'I can trust Irving: he will do me justice.'

Becket is a noble and human part, and I will say I do not see how any one could act it and feel it thoroughly without being a better man for it. HENRY IRVING

Mr Henry Irving has created a play out of an undramatic poem … The actor has done splendid things before now, but we regard his Becket as the crowning point of his artistic career … Mr Henry Irving has never done anything so subtle, so delicate, or so artistically graduated, as his merging of the statesman into a saint … the play should be studied and registered as one of the most perfect artistic productions of our time. CLEMENT SCOTT, *Daily Telegraph*

No acting could save the piece from being what it is – a tragedy, though not in the sense which was intended by the author.

Pall Mall Gazette on Ibsen's *The Master Builder*

Henry Irving in Alfred Lord Tennyson's Becket at Lyceum Theatre in 1893. Tennyson died during the rehearsal period. Irving would go on playing Becket until his death – literally.

FEBRUARY 20. Herbert Waring as Halvard Solness and Elizabeth Robins as Hilda Wangel in Henrik Ibsen's **The Master Builder** at Trafalgar Square Theatre. Translation by Edmund Gosse and William Archer. Louise Moodie as Mrs Solness. 'As regards the acting,' said *The Standard*, 'it is impossible to criticise the incomprehensible.'

Herbert Waring and Elizabeth Robins in the leading parts succeeded in holding a full audience in attentive silence during three acts of the most dreary and purposeless drivel we have ever heard in an English theatre. In his latest play Ibsen has finally demonstrated that he is a great man. No one but a great man could get a clever actor and actress to accept and produce upon the stage such a pointless, incoherent, and absolutely silly piece. *Evening News and Post*

MARCH 7. Weedon Grossmith, Fred Kerr, W. G. Elliot, Lily Hanbury, Pattie Brown and Ellaline Terriss in Arthur Wing Pinero's **The Amazons** at Court Theatre. Three young girls have been brought up as boys by their father. The play – a joke about the New Woman – was romantic comedy rather than satire, and Pinero rang some obvious jokes on the contrast between manly girls and effeminate boys. 114 performances.

A whimsicality, a little unpretentious effort, a sort of digestive after dinner. In it I have attempted to find the poetry of farce.
ARTHUR WING PINERO in interview by *Sketch*

APRIL 19. Herbert Beerbohm Tree and Mrs Bernard-Beere in Oscar Wilde's **A Woman of No Importance** at Haymarket Theatre. There were cries of 'Author! Author!' A large gentleman rose in

People love a wicked aristocrat who seduces a virtuous maid, and they love a virtuous maiden for being seduced by a wicked aristocrat. I have given them what they like so that they may learn to love what I like to give them.

OSCAR WILDE

311

'Stop, Gerald, stop! He is your father!' Julia Neilson, Fred Terry, Mrs Bernard Beere and Beerbohm Tree in the climax to Act III in Oscar Wilde's A Woman of No Importance, at Haymarket Theatre, in 1893.

one of the boxes. 'Ladies and Gentlemen, I regret to inform you that Mr Oscar Wilde is not in the house.' The large gentleman spoke with authority. He was Oscar Wilde.

> In intellectual calibre, artistic competence – ay, and in dramatic instinct to boot – Mr Wilde has no rival among his fellow-workers for the stage. WILLIAM ARCHER, *World*

> Mr Oscar Wilde has diligently collected jokes, done them up so cleverly that some sound almost new, and the result is an amusing chitter-chatter of impossible aristocrats. *Sketch*

MAY 19. Fernando de Lucio as Canio, Mario Ancona as Tonio and Nellie Melba as Nedda in London premiere of Ruggiero Leoncavallo's **I Pagliacci** at Covent Garden Theatre. 'The atmosphere is grim, unwholesome and sordid to the last degree,' said *The Athenæum*, 'but it is intensely and pitilessly human.'

MAY 27. George Alexander and Mrs Patrick Campbell in Arthur Wing Pinero's **The Second Mrs Tanqueray** at St James's Theatre. It was as much a theatrical milestone as *Caste* had been in 1867 and *Look Back in Anger* was to be in 1956. Nevertheless, many people refused to see anything more in it

than an effective commercial piece in the mould of popular late Victorian 'problem play'. Paula Tanqueray is that most familiar of all Victorian stage characters: a woman with a past. The play ends with her suicide. 'Hideous and squalid,' said *The Times*. 'A great play,' said *The Evening Standard*. 'A great actress,' said *Echo*. At one performance Mrs Campbell had a fit of the giggles. At the end of the act Alexander sent his man to present his compliments to her and to ask her not to laugh at him on the stage. The actress sent a message back to the effect that she never laughed at Mr Alexander on the stage and that she always waited until she got home.

> He [Pinero] has written a play which Dumas might sign without a blush … It is not merely the seriousness of the subject that distinguishes the play from its predecessors? It is the astonishing advance in psychological insight and technical skill which places the new play in a new category. Technically, the work is as near as possible perfect. WILLIAM ARCHER, *World*

> Not Sarah Bernhardt herself, mistress of all feminine feline arts, as she is, could play the part better than Mrs Patrick Campbell. It is a wonderful performance. *Punch*

MAY–JUNE. Eleanora Duse season at Lyric Theatre. The plays included Shakespeare's **Antony and Cleopatra**, Alexandre Dumas's **Camille**, Victorien Sardou's **Fédora**, Giovanni Verga's **Cavalleria Rusticana** and Henrik Ibsen's **The Doll's House**. 'Duse,' said William Archer in *World*, 'is without exception the most absorbingly interesting actress I ever saw.' Her Cleopatra, said *The Athenæum*, 'is pretty and poetical, dream-like even, but deficient in voluptuousness and passion.'

> In such parts as Marguerite Gautier where gentleness and tenderness are needed, she [Duse] was found to be no unworthy rival to Mme Sarah Bernhardt, though she failed in the more tempestuous scenes of Fedora in which the French actress excelled. *The Times*

JUNE 14. Hebert Beerbohm Tree as Dr Thomas Stockman in Henrik Ibsen's **An Enemy of the People** at Haymarket Theatre. Translation by William Archer. A small provincial town in Norway learns that its health spa is built on a sewer. Stockman feels that the risk to health is so great that the public must be told instantly of the pollution. The Mayor insists that the findings must remain private since the town's livelihood depends upon visitors to the spa.

JUNE 27. Daly's Theatre opened with Ada Rehan as Katharine and George Clarke as Petruchio in Shakespeare's **The Taming of the Shrew**.

World premieres

Gerhart Hauptman's *The Weavers* in Berlin

Gerhart Hauptmann's *Hannele* in Berlin

Engelbert Humperdinck's *Hansel und Gretel* in Weimar

Henrik Ibsen's *The Master Builder* in Berlin

Maurice Maeterlinck's *Pelleas et Melisande* in Paris

Victorien Sardou's *Madame Sans-Gêne* in Paris

Hermann Sudermann's *Magda*

Giuseppe Verdi's *Falstaff* in Milan

Births

Ivor Novello, British composer, actor

Erwin Piscator, German director

Ernst Toller, German dramatist

Mae West, American actress, dramatist

Deaths

Fanny Kemble, British actress (b. 1809)

Pyotr Tchaikovsky, Russian composer (b. 1840)

Literature

Arthur Conan Doyle's *The Refugees*

Notes

Daly's Theatre opened

Prince of Wales's Theatre opened

Vesta Tilley sings 'After the Ball' for the first time

Marie Lloyd sings 'Oh Mr Porter' for the first time.

History

Lumière brothers invent the cinematograph

Henry Ford builds his first car

Rudolf Diesel receives a patent for his oil-burning engine

Independent Labour Party holds its first meeting

Edvard Munch's 'Scream' is painted

OCTOBER 7. Gilbert and Sullivan's **Utopia (Ltd)** at Savoy Theatre. Bernard Shaw said that he had enjoyed it more than any previous Savoy Opera. Most critics, however, dismissed it as 'mirthless travesty'.

NOVEMBER 9. William Poel directed Shakespeare's **Measure for Measure** at Royalty Theatre. The unnamed actors, and especially Poel, who was playing Angelo, were not certain of their lines.

DECEMBER 9. T. Wigney Percival as Sartorius, Florence Farr as Blanche, James Welch as Lickcheese and Arthur Whittaker as Cokane in the Independent Theatre Society's production of Bernard Shaw's **Widowers' Houses** at Royalty Theatre. The first act lulled the audience into thinking that they were going to watch a light romantic comedy, but it proved to be but a curtain-raiser to a powerful indictment of the corruption and the hypocrisy of the ruling classes. Sartorious is the worst slum landlord in London.

In *Widowers' Houses* I have shewn middle-class respectability and younger son gentility fattening on the poverty of the slum as flies fatten on filth. This is not a pleasant theme.
BERNARD SHAW, *Preface to Plays Unpleasant*

It is not dramatic. I only see a number of people arguing round a table. Indeed Mr Shaw's people are not dramatic characters at all, they are embodied arguments.
A. B. WALKLEY, *Speaker*

DECEMBER 26. Ada Blanche as Crusoe in Augustus Harris and Harry Nicholls' **Robinson Crusoe** at Drury Lane Theatre. Little Tich as Man Friday. Dan Leno as Mrs Crusoe. Marie Lloyd as Polly Perkins. High spots: a shipwreck, a submarine ballet, and a grand procession of the kings and queens of England from King William I to Queen Victoria.

DECEMBER 26. Ellaline Terriss in Horace Lennard's **Cinderella** at Lyceum Theatre. Victor Stevens and Emery as the Wicked Sisters.

RIGHT

The programme cover for A Gaiety Girl at Prince of Wales Theatre in 1894.

A GAIETY GIRL
MR GEORGE EDWARDES' COMPANY.
SOUVENIR
PRINCE OF WALES' THEATRE 1894

1894

APRIL 21. Yorke Stephens as Captain Bluntschli, Bernard Gould as Major Saranoff and Alma Murray as Raina in George Bernard Shaw's **Arms and the Man** at Avenue Theatre. Anti-romantic comedy is set during the Serbo-Bulgarian war of 1885–86. Raina is deeply shocked when she learns that a fleeing Swiss mercenary (who invades her bedroom in the best romantic comedy manner) carries chocolates rather than bullets in his pouches. She nicknames him her 'chocolate soldier', an epithet, to be used later in a musical adaptation, that would keep *Arms and the Man* off the stage for years. The comedy was not popular with militarists, who thought Shaw was sneering at military courage. It was equally unpopular with Bulgarians, who were outraged to find themselves portrayed as unwashed, ignorant cowards. At the premiere there was one lone booer. 'My dear fellow,' said Shaw, taking his curtain call, 'I quite agree with you, but who are we two against so many?'

> When I used to read the play before it was produced, people used not to laugh at it as they laughed in the theatre. On my honour it was a serious play – a play to cry over if you could only have helped laughing.
> BERNARD SHAW in a letter to Ellen Terry

> I begin positively to believe that he may one day write a serious and even an artistic play, if only he will repress his irrelevant whimsicality, try to clothe his character-conceptions in flesh and blood, and realize the difference between knowingness and knowledge.
> WILLIAM ARCHER, *World*

> I admit I don't understand everything in *Arms and the Man*. But everything in it – even the things I didn't understand – exhilarated and delighted me beyond measure. My sides are still aching with laughter … the play kept the house in a perpetual roar of laughter. *Star*

One member of the audience booed as the author, George Bernard Shaw, took his bow. Shaw retorted to the man:

'*My dear fellow, I quite agree with you, but who are we two against so many?*'

APRIL 28. George Alexander and Herbert Waring and Mrs Patrick Campbell in Henry Arthur Jones's **The Masqueraders** at St James's Theatre. A satire on vulgar society. A nice girl marries a dissipated gambler. *The Times* said it was 'the freshest, most vigorous, the most splendidly audacious play' that Jones had yet written.

APRIL 30. Ada Rehan as Rosalind in Shakespeare's **As You Like It** at Daly's Theatre. John Craig as Orlando. James Lewis as Touchstone. George Clarke as Jaques.

> No Rosalind known to the present generation of playgoers has equalled or even come within easy distance of Miss Rehan's, which imparts to the most delightful of pastoral plays an incomparable freshness and beauty. *The Times*

MAY 5. W. L. Abingdon as Hjalmar, Charles Fulton as Gregers Werle and Winifred Fraser as Hedvig in Henrik Ibsen's **The Wild Duck** at Royalty Theatre. Mrs Herbert Waring as Gina. Lawrence Irving as Dr Relling. Hjalmar has delusions that he is an inventor manqué. Gregers Werle, his best friend, is a warped idealist, who sees his mission in life is to destroy illusions, and tells Hjalmar that he is not the father of his daughter. Critics and public were confused and didn't know what to make of the symbolism of the lame duck in the attic. Was the play a comi-tragedy or a tragi-comedy? Bernard Shaw admitted to watching it in horror and pity while roaring with laughter.

The Wild Duck is an atrociously true and cruel satire, pitiless and pessimistic.   *Era*

MAY. Eleanora Duse's season at Daly's Theatre included Alexandre Dumas's **La Dame aux camélias**, Victorien Sardou's **Divorçons**, Carlo Goldini's **La locandiera** and Giovanni Verga's **Cavalleria Rusticana**. 'The mixture of intellectual admiration and emotional sympathy, which she excites in her great scenes,' said William Archer in *World*, 'is, in my experience, unique.'

MAY 14. Olga Olgina and Beduschi in London premiere of Giacomo Puccini's **Manon Lescaut** at Covent Garden Theatre. 'If I cannot pretend Puccini is great,' said *The Sketch*, 'I must say he is very clever.'

MAY 19. Arturo Pessina in the London premiere of Giuseppe Verdi's **Falstaff** at Covent Garden. Unanimous praise from critics and public, and instantly recognised as a masterpiece.

JUNE 23. Réjane in Victorien Sardou's **Madame Sans-Gêne** at Gaiety Theatre. Her over-acting delighted the audience.

JUNE 25.   E. S. Willard and Bessie Hatton in J. M. Barrie's **The Professor's Love Story** at Comedy Theatre. The professor does not realise that he loves his secretary. William Archer in

The World dismissed the play as 'a patchwork of extravagant farce, mawkish sentiment and irrelevant anecdote.'

SEPTEMBER 1. Cyril Maude and Winifred Emery in Sydney Grundy's **The New Woman** at Comedy Theatre.

His plays, in short, amuse and delight but they fail to convince. Mr Grundy is in fact, since the truth must be told, a brilliant writer and a poor dramatist. Give him the skeleton of a plot and he will give you a play. He lacks, however, invention.   *Athenæum*

OCTOBER 3. Charles Wyndham and Mary Moore in Henry Arthur Jones's **The Case of Rebellious Susan** at Criterion Theatre. 'My comedy isn't a comedy,' said Jones. 'It's a tragedy dressed up as a comedy.' The subject is marriage and the code of behaviour expected of men and women. Susan has found out that her husband is having an affair. Everybody advises her not to make a fuss, to forgive and forget; however, she decides to pay him back in coin. The question is whether she did or did not take her revenge with a young man in Cairo. (The actors had tampered with the text, so that it remained ambiguous because in real life Wyndham was having an affair with Moore.)

He [Henry Arthur Jones] often writes heavy and flaccid sentences which tax the elocution of the actor and the attention of the audience; and when an opportunity offers for some discreet little verbal felicity, he does not always take it.
WILLIAM ARCHER, *World*

1894

LEFT

The programme for The Shop Girl at Gaiety Theatre.

'*The first rule of playwriting is not to write like Henry Arthur Jones. The other rules are the same.*'

OSCAR WILDE

DECEMBER 7. Henry Irving as Corporal Gregory Brewster in A Conan Doyle's *A Story of Waterloo* at Garrick Theatre. A sentimental one-act play based on Doyle's short story, *The Straggler of Waterloo*, which described the last day of the only surviving soldier who had fought in the battle in 1815. One of Irving's biggest successes. Bernard Shaw was not impressed: 'A little cheap and simple mimicry which Mr Irving does indifferently. The whole performance does not involve one gesture, one line, one thought, outside the commonest routine of automatic stage illusion.'

DECEMBER 26. Ada Blanche as Dick and Dan Leno as Idle Jack in **Dick Whittington** at Drury Lane Theatre. Book by Augustus Harris, Cecil Raleigh and Henry Hamilton.

NOVEMBER 24. Ada Reeve, George Grossmith, Edmund Payne and Seymour Hicks in **The Shop Girl** at Gaiety Theatre. Book by J. W. Dam. Lyrics by H. W. Dam and Adrian Ross. Music by Ivan Caryll. Additional numbers by Lionel Monckton and Adrian Ross. The beginning of a new era for musical comedy. 56 performances. Hit songs included: 'Her Golden Hair Was Hanging Down Her Back' and 'Over the Hills'.

Miss Ada Reeve endows her with all the impudent fascination characteristic of music hall art ... Mr Payne's pantomime business is very droll in a sledge hammer way and it contrasts very well with the more refined animation of Mr Seymour Hicks. *Observer*

Dan Leno, one of the great comedians of the music hall stage, was thought by many to be the funniest man on earth.

1895

1895. Elizabethan Stage Society is founded by William Poel. The Society performed in various halls from 1895 to 1905. The productions were notable for their austerity. Poel's aim was to get rid of the Victorian spectacle, and to produce Shakespeare as he had been in his own time: minimal scenery, platform stage, quick scene changes and an emphasis on the text. His pioneering work had a major influence on the way Shakespeare would be performed in the twentieth century.

'There is nothing which gives Mr Wilde the right to class himself as a playwright either of promise or experience.'

Morning Advertiser

JANUARY 3. Lewis Waller as Sir Robert Chiltern, Charles H. Hawtrey as Lord Goring and Florence West as Mrs Cheveley in Oscar Wilde's **An Ideal Husband** at Haymarket Theatre. Chiltern's fortune is founded on selling a cabinet secret. A scarlet woman, who has got his incriminating letters, threatens to expose him. Chiltern's reaction to scandal and blackmail anticipates Wilde's own fall: 'And now what is there before me, but public disgrace, ruin, terrible shame, the mockery of the world, a lonely dishonoured death?'

The fact remains that Mr Wilde's work is not only poor and sterile, but essentially vulgar.
A. B. WALKLEY, *Speaker*

There is hardly a character in the piece in whom one detects any signs of life. MONOCLE, *Sketch*

Florence West as Mrs Cheveley in Oscar Wilde's An Ideal Husband at Haymarket Theatre in 1895. 'Morality,' says the blackmailing Mrs Cheveley, 'is simply the attitude we adopt towards people whom we personally dislike.'

In a certain sense Mr Wilde seems to me our only thorough playwright. He plays with everything: with wit, with philosophy, with drama, with actors and audience, with the whole theatre. Such a feast scandalizes the Englishman, who can no more play with wit and philosophy than he can with a football or a cricket bat.
GEORGE BERNARD SHAW, *Saturday Review*

JANUARY 12. Henry Irving as King Arthur, Ellen Terry as Guinevere and Johnston Forbes-Robertson as Lancelot in J. Comyns Carr's **King Arthur** at Lyceum Theatre. Genevieve Ward as Morgan Le Fay. Lena Ashwell as Elaine. Overture by Arthur Sullivan. Costumes and armor by Edward Burne-Jones. *The Illustrated London News* said that Terry looked as if she had stepped out of a church window into modern life.

FEBRUARY 14. George Alexander as John Worthing, Allan Aynesworth as Algernon Moncrieff and Rose Leclercq as Lady Bracknell in Oscar Wilde's **The Importance of Being Earnest** at St James's Theatre. Irene Vanbrugh as Gwendolen Fairfax. Evelyn Millard as Cecil Cardew. As Wilde knew, 'In matters of grave importance, style not sincerity is the vital thing.' John and Algernon fall in love with two young women who have a fixation about being married to a man called Ernest.

On 5 April Wilde was arrested on a charge of gross indecency. On 6 April his name was removed from the programme and all advertising. The box office takings collapsed immediately. The play closed on 8 May, having run only 83 performances, and it would not be seen again in London until 1901, and then still without the name of Wilde on the playbills or programme.

It is exquisitely trivial, a delicate bubble of fancy and it has a philosophy that we should treat all the trivial things of life very seriously, and all the serious things of life with sincere and studied triviality. OSCAR WILDE

The Importance of Being Earnest was never for a moment in doubt. To use a current vulgarism, the piece 'caught on' immediately. *Morning Post*

It is easy to find fault with Wilde's latest piece. It is, indeed, difficult to do anything else. *Athenæum*

On the whole I decline to accept *The Importance of Being Earnest* as a day less than ten years old; and I am altogether unable to perceive any uncommon excellence in its presentation.
GEORGE BERNARD SHAW, *Saturday Review*

'Uncle Jack, if you don't shake hands with Ernest, I will never forgive you.' Allan Aynesworth, Evelyn Millard and George Alexander and Evelyn Millard in Oscar Wilde's The Importance of Being Earnest at St James's Theatre in 1895.

MARCH 13. Mrs Patrick Campbell and Johnston Forbes-Robertson in Arthur Wing Pinero's **The Notorious Mrs Ebbsmith** at Garrick Theatre. Mrs Ebbsmith notoriously throws her Bible into the stove and then with a wild scream pulls it out of the fire. 'The last act broke my heart,' said Mrs Campbell. 'The first three filled me with ecstasy.'

Unquestionably the masterpiece, as yet, of Arthur Wing Pinero ... head and shoulders above Mrs Tanqueray in analysis, in excellence of dialogue, in profundity of thought.
CLEMENT SCOTT, *Daily Telegraph*

Amply justifies the verdict that Mr Pinero comes near to being, and yet beyond all question is *not*, a writer of great plays. *Pall Mall Gazette*

A piece of claptrap so gross it absolves me from all obligation to treat Mr Pinero's art as anything higher than the barest art of theatrical sensation ... Mrs Patrick Campbell, in fact, pulls her author through by playing him clean off the stage ... I disliked the play so much that nothing would induce me to say anything good of it.
BERNARD SHAW, *Saturday Review*

Mrs Patrick Campbell in Arthur Wing Pinero's The Notorious Mrs Ebbsmith at Garrick Theatre in 1895. Mrs Ebbsmith was notorious for throwing a Bible in the fire.

World premieres
Henrik Ibsen's *Little Eyolf* in Berlin
Henrik Ibsen's *Emperor and Galilean* in Leipzig
Marius Petipa's ballet *Swan Lake* (full ballet) to music by Pyotr Tchaikovsky at St Petersburg
Arthur Schnitzler's *Liebelei* in Vienna

Births
Lorenz Hart, American composer
J. B. Priestley, British dramatist

Deaths
Alexander Dumas, fils, French dramatist (b. 1824)

Literature
Stephen Crane's *The Red Badge of Courage*
H. G. Wells' *The Time Machine*
Thomas Hardy's *Jude the Obscure*
Arthur Morrison's *A Child of the Jago*, set in the slums of the East End of London and portraying life and violence in the Old Nichol Street Rookery

Notes
Oscar Wilde is sentenced to two years' hard labour
Aubrey Beardsley becomes art editor of *The Yellow Book*
Henry Irving knighted (first actor to be so) at Windsor
Promenade Concerts founded by Sir Henry Wood

History
Guglielmo Marconi invents wireless telegraphy
First ever commercial movie performance, in New York
Jameson Raid fails, but sets scene for Second Boer War

1895

Johnston Forbes-Robertson in one of his best roles: Shakespeare's Romeo and Juliet at Lyceum Theatre in 1895. His Juliet was Mrs Patrick Campbell.

MAY 25. Herbert Beerbohm Tree and Mrs Patrick Campbell in Harman Merivale's adaptation of Victorien Sardou's *Fédora* at Haymarket Theatre. Fedora was 'a part to tear a cat in,' according to Tree. 'It is greatly to Mrs Patrick Campbell's credit,' said Bernard Shaw in *Saturday Review*, 'that, bad as the play is, the acting was worse.'

JUNE 10. Sarah Bernhardt in Hermann Sudermann's *Magda* at Daly's Theatre. In French.

> The childishly egotistical character of her acting which is not the art of making you think more highly, or feel more deeply, but the art of making you admire her, champion her, weep with her, laugh at her jokes, follow her fortunes breathlessly, and applaud her wildly when the curtain falls.
>
> GEORGE BERNARD SHAW, *Saturday Review*

JUNE 12. Eleanora Duse in Hermann Sudermann's *Magda* at Drury Lane Theatre. Acted in Italian. Clement Scott preferred Bernhardt in the role. Bernard Shaw preferred Duse.

SEPTEMBER 21. Johnston Forbes-Robertson and Mrs Patrick Campbell in Shakespeare's *Romeo and Juliet* at Lyceum Theatre. Charles Coghlan as Mercutio. Robertson thought his own performance 'tame, lacking in fire and the buoyancy of youth'.

> Mrs Patrick Campbell gives us – as no other actress to my knowledge has given us – the child in Juliet. A more delicious embodiment of Juliet I do not hope to see. A. B. WALKLEY, *Speaker*

OCTOBER 16. Winifred Emery in Arthur Wing Pinero's *The Benefit of the Doubt* at Comedy Theatre. When a faithful wife finds out that her husband actually believes she has been unfaithful, she does the sensible thing: she leaves the house and goes to the home of her supposed lover.

MARCH. Theatre de L'Oeuvre at Opera Comique in a season of plays: Henrik Ibsen's *Rosmersholm* and two plays by Maurice Materlinck: *Péléas et Mélisande* and *L'Intruse*.

> For the bulk of the company it is impossible to say anything whatever. They stand nervously and ashamedly on stage, are badly made up, unable to walk, and know not what to do with their hands. *Athenæum*

Herbert Beerbohm Tree as Svengali and Hilda Baird as Trilby in Paul M. Potter's Trilby at Haymarket Theatre in 1895. Tree scored a big success, but he knew the play was hogwash.

OCTOBER 30. Herbert Beerbohm Tree as Svengali and Dorothea Baird as Trilby in Paul M. Potter's **Trilby** at Haymarket Theatre. Based on George du Maurier's novel. Baird looked as if she had stepped out of one of du Maurier's drawings. The production was the biggest financial success of Tree's career. He loved playing Svengali; but he had no illusions about the play, which he always dismissed as 'hogwash'.

Never before, we will venture to say, has the actor's genius for make-up been exercised with such remarkable effect. The stage Svengali, with his long, matted black hair and beard, his hooked nose, his unwholesome, sallow face, his piercing eye, and his lazy, octopus-like limbs is positively demoniac. *The Times*

Mr Tree is simply doing what comes easiest to him, luxuriating in obvious and violent gestures and grimaces, expending no more thought on the matter than is involved in the adroit use of personal advantages and the mechanical resources of stage effect. WILLIAM ARCHER, *World*

Tree's flair for make-up was truly remarkable, far exceeding that of any other actor; he could alter the shape of his head as easily as he could rearrange his features, but unfortunately he could not remodel his hands, which were the weak part of his physique. Although the cares of production might cause him to be a little vague about his words on a first night, it was always evident that, word-perfect or not, he not only looked but really felt the character he was assuming.

SIR GEORGE ARTHUR, *From Phelps to Gielgud*

❛ *It is nearly impossible for a woman to remain pure who adopts the stage as a profession.* ❜

CLEMENT SCOTT

1896

JANUARY 4. Maud Jeffries and Wilson Barrett in Wilson Barrett's *The Sign of the Cross* at Lyric Theatre. Franklyn McLey as Nero. Persecution of the early Christians. The critics thought the play in dubious taste and also expressed their concerns about hearing Holy Writ on the stage. 700 performances

JANUARY 7. George Alexander, Evelyn Millard and Lily Hanbury in Edward Rose's adaptation of Anthony Hope's novel, *The Prisoner of Zenda*, at St James's Theatre. 'One great advantage of this class of play,' said William Archer in *World*, 'is that it does not tax the talents of the actors.'

JANUARY 15. Johnston Forbes-Robertson and Marion Terry in Henry Arthur Jones's *Michael and His Lost Angel* at Lyceum Theatre. A man has to choose between his religion and a woman. Mrs Patrick Campbell was originally cast as the woman, but resigned during rehearsals. 'There was something about the play I could not stomach,' she said.

MARCH 7. Walter Passmore in Gilbert and Sullivan's *The Grand Duke or The Statutory Duel* at Savoy Theatre. 'Mr Gilbert has stood still, but Mr Sullivan has advanced,' said *Man of the World*. 'Mr Gilbert has lost all his gaiety and nearly all his old brilliance,' said *City*.

LEFT

Lena Ashwell (1872–1957) actress and theatre manager. She appeared in J. Comyns Carr's King Arthur at Lyceum Theatre in 1895.

ABOVE

Wilson Barrett in Wilson Barrett's The Sign of the Cross at Lyric Theatre in 1896.

325

George Alexander in Anthon Hope's The Prisoner of Zenda at St James's Theatre in 1896.

Evelyn Millard in The Prisoner of Zenda at St James's Theatre in 1896.

Why reproach me? I didn't write the book!! … another week's rehearsal with WSG and I should have gone raving mad.

ARTHUR SULLIVAN, to Frank Burnand

APRIL 25. Marie Tempest, Hayden Coffin, Letty Lind and Molly Seamore in **The Geisha, A Story of a Teahouse**, at Daly's Theatre. Book by Owen Hall. Lyrics by Harry Greenbank. Music by Sidney Jones. 760 performances.

APRIL 29. George Giddens in Georges Feydeau and Maurice Desvallière's **A Night Out** at Vaudeville. English version of *L'hotel du Libre Echange*. 'Its

vulgarity,' said one critic, 'is redeemed by its jovial and irresistible gaiety.'

JULY 2. William Poel directed Christopher Marlowe's **Dr Faustus** for the Elizabethan Stage Society at St George's Hall. A great number of the roles were played by women.

AUGUST 26. William Terriss, W. L. Abingdon and Evelyn Millward in Haddon Chambers and Comyns Carr's **Boys Together** at Adelphi Theatre. The boys, mortal enemies since their schooldays, end up fighting over an abyss. The hero tries to save the villain from falling, but he fails.

> ‘ *Mr Irving does not merely cut plays; he disembowels them.* ’
> GEORGE BERNARD SHAW

SEPTEMBER 22. Ellen Terry as Imogen and Henry Irving as Iachimo in Shakespeare's **Cymbeline** at Lyceum Theatre. Designer: Lawrence Alma-Tadema. Bernard Shaw dismissed the play as stagey trash of the lowest melodramatic order, abominably written, intellectually vulgar, foolish, offensive, indecent and exasperating.

NOVEMBER 23. Courtenay Thorpe as Alfred Almers and Janet Achurch as Rita Almers, in Henrik Ibsen's **Little Eyolf** at Avenue Theatre. Elizabeth Robbins as Asta Almers. Mrs Patrick Campbell as The Rat-Wife. Stewart Dawson as Eyolf. The sexual innuendo shocked audiences.

Gloom, depression, and a sense of the remoteness of the action from all living human interests overcome the spectator, whose abiding impression of the play is that of having seen in a dream the patients of a madhouse exercising in their yard. *The Times*

Mrs Campbell was admirable – a *tour de force* of weirdness and intensity … Mr Courtenay Thorpe was not even a brilliant failure; he simply failed. *Pall Mall Gazette*

It was not Mrs Patrick Campbell's fault that the part suggested the old doubled-up witch in the pantomime and we expected every instant that her rags would be whisked to the floor and she would stand before us as a Fairy Queen or another Paula Tanqueray, radiant in jewels and sheeny satin. *Daily Telegraph*

NOVEMBER 28. William Poel directed Shakespeare's **The Two Gentlemen of Verona** for the Elizabethan Stage Society at Merchant Taylor's Hall. Monotonous and inaudible.

DECEMBER 2. Julia Neilson as Rosalind and George Alexander as Orlando in Shakespeare's **As You Like It** at St James's Theatre. H. W. Vernon as Jaques. Henry Irving played Oliver as if Oliver were Iago. H. V. Esmond played Touchstone as a pantomime demon.

DECEMBER 19. Henry Irving in Shakespeare's **Richard III** at Lyceum Theatre. Genevieve Ward as Margaret. Maud Milton as Elizabeth. One of the most electrifying moments was when Irving, in the tones of Richard, told Miss Milton, in blank verse, to get further up the stage.

World premieres
Anton Chekhov's *The Seagull* in Moscow
Alfred de Musset's *Lorenzaccio* (condensed) in Paris
Alfred Jarry's *Ubu Roi* in Paris
Puccini's *La Bohème* at Turin
Oscar Wilde's *Salome* in Paris

Births
Antonin Artaud, French director, dramatist, theorist
Ira Gershwin, American lyricist
William Arnold Ridley, English playwright and actor
A. J. Cronin, Scottish novelist

Deaths
William Morris, artist, writer and socialist (b. 1834)
Edmonde de Concourt, French writer (b. 1822)
Harriet Beecher Stowe, American writer (b. 1811)
John Everett Millais, British painter (b. 1829)
George du Maurier, French born British cartoonist (b. 1834)

Literature
A. E. Housman's *A Shropshire Lad*
H. G. Wells' *The Time Machine*

History
Anti-German demonstrations in Britain
Daily Mail is founded
Yorkshire score a record county innings of 887 runs
Tsar Nicholas II visits Queen Victoria at Balmoral
First modern Olympics held in Athens: Britain win seven medals in total
Klondike Gold Rush; since the first discovery of gold in the Yukon, nearly 400 tons have been extracted
Glasgow Underground (second in Britain) begins operations

1896

1897

APRIL 10. Ellen Terry in J W Comyns Carr's adaptation of Victorien Sardou and Emile Moreau's ***Madame Sans-Gêne*** at Lyceum Theatre. Henry Irving played Napoleon. 'It seems to me,' wrote Terry in her diary, 'on some nights as if I were watching Napoleon trying to imitate H.I.' Bernard Shaw dismissed Napoleon as 'nothing but the jealous husband of a thousand fashionable dramas, talking Buonapartiana.'

MAY 24. Louis Calvert and Janet Achurch in Shakespeare's ***Antony and Cleopatra*** at Olympic Theatre. Bernard Shaw said that Achurch 'suddenly drops from an Egyptian warrior queen into a naughty English petite bourgeoise'.

JUNE 12. Hebert Beerbohm Tree in Shakespeare's ***Hamlet*** at Her Majesty's Theatre. 'My dear fellow,' said W. S. Gilbert to Tree, 'I never saw anything so funny in my life and yet it was not in the least vulgar.'

> Sir Herbert Tree's Hamlet was magnificent in theory. When he discussed it with me I sat enthralled at the imagination which he brought to bear … yet when he acted it, something went out of the performance and away went the imaginative quality which had so enthralled me.
> MADGE KENDAL

> ❛ *With the single exception of Homer, there is no eminent writer, not even Sir Walter Scott, whom I can despise so entirely as I despise Shakespear [sic] when I measure my mind against his.* ❜
> BERNARD SHAW, *Saturday Review*

JUNE 16. Sarah Bernhardt in Alfred de Musset's ***Lorenzaccio*** at Adelphi Theatre.

> It is never for a moment Lorenzaccio. She [Bernhardt] is a dignified, languid, eminently respectable personage, as diverse as possible from the vicious stripling De Musset has drawn for us, hollow-eyed and hectic with debauchery. WILLIAM ARCHER, *World*

JULY 1. Murray Carson as Napoleon and Florence West as the Strange Lady in George Bernard Shaw's ***The Man of Destiny*** at Grand Theatre, Croydon. A battle of wits over some French letters in which the young Napoleon is out-manoeuvered. Shaw was the first to admit it was hardly more than a bravura piece to display the virtuosity of the two principal performers and he had intended it for Ellen Terry and Henry Irving; but they never acted it. After reading the play, Terry sent Shaw a telegram. 'Delicious,' she said. Shaw was not so enthusiastic. 'This is not one of my great plays,' he wrote. 'It is only a display of my knowledge of stage tricks.'

JULY 23. Charles Wyndham, Mary Moore, T. B. Thalberg, Henry Bishop, Vane Tempest, Irene Vanbrugh, Sarah Brooke and Janette Steer in Henry Arthur Jones's ***The Liars*** at Criterion Theatre. One of the most successful comedies of the 1890s. It belongs to an era when men who behaved badly were expected to go off to the furthest flung post of the Empire and atone, preferably in Darkest Africa, a place of 'heat, hunger and disease'. The condescension towards women is all the more outrageous for being off-hand: 'The curious thing is that ever since the days of the Garden of Eden, women have had a knack of impaling us honourable men on dilemmas of this kind, where the only alternative is to be false to the truth or false to them … My dear fellow, she's only a woman. What are they? A kind of children, you know. Humour them, play with them, buy them the toys they cry for, but don't get angry with them. They're not worth it.' 328 performances.

Henry Arthur Jones is an Englishman and has a style of his own. He thinks for himself and hits out very often straight from the shoulder. But he writes admirably, and in *The Liars*, has given us a comedy that will live. *Daily Telegraph*

AUGUST 2. Florrie Forde, Australian music hall singer, made her first appearance in England at the London Pavilion. Forde, buxom in feathers, sequins and tights, was famous for such songs as 'Oh, Oh Antonio', 'Hold Out Your Hand You Naughty Boy', 'Down at the Bull and Bush', and 'Good Bye'ee'.

SEPTEMBER 11. 47-year-old Johnston Forbes-Robertson in Shakespeare's **Hamlet** at Lyceum Theatre. Mrs Patrick Campbell played Ophelia quite mad. *The Times* found her sweet and winning. *The Pall Mall Gazette* thought she was uninspired and ordinary. *The Observer* thought her casting was an obvious mistake. William Archer thought nobody, except Forbes-Robertson, rose above mediocrity, but regretted that he under-played the madness. 'Artistic self-restraint is a very good thing, but in this case it verges on timidity.' For many, however, he was the finest Hamlet of his generation. The performances inspired Shaw to write *Caesar and Cleopatra* for him and Mrs Campbell. Forbes-Robertson did play Caesar in 1907. Mrs Campbell never played Cleopatra.

OCTOBER 2. London premiere of Giacomo Puccini's **La Bohème** at Covent Garden Theatre. Umberto Salvi as Rudolph. Alice Esty as Mimi.

The plot is morbid and unpleasant; the music is extremely effective and, in a measure, inspired. It is difficult to understand why the operatic composer of the present day shows such a predilection for unwholesome subjects. *Athenæum*

NOVEMBER 6. Cyril Maude and Winifred Emery in James Barrie's adaptation of his novel, **The Little Minister**, at Haymarket Theatre. Set in the early part of the century in Scotland, an earl's daughter (masquerading as a gypsy) sets her sights on a shy, young minister. *The Observer* thought the play 'pretty but just a trifle childish in its unsophisticated dramatic methods'.

DECEMBER 16. As he was about to enter the Adelphi Theatre stage door to perform in Haddon Chambers and Comyns Carr's play on Wellington, **In the Days of the Duke**, William Terriss was stabbed to death by Richard Arthur Price, a deranged actor.

World premieres
Henrik Ibsen's *John Gabriel Borkman* in Helsinki
Ruggero Leoncavallo's *La Bohème* in Venice

Births
Michel Saint-Denis, French director
Thornton Wilder, American dramatist

Deaths
Johannes Brahms, German composer, pianist (b. 1833)
William Terriss, British actor murdered (b. 1847)

Literature
Henry James's *The Spoils of Poynton*
Bram Stoker's *Dracula*
H. G. Wells' *The Invisible Man*

Notes
Tate Gallery opens in London
Squire Bancroft is knighted
Henry Irving recites selections of Alfred Lord Tennyson's *Becket* in Canterbury Cathedral
A statue to Sarah Siddons is unveiled by Henry Irving in Paddington Green

History
Oscar Wilde is released from prison; he spends his last three years of life in penniless exile in Europe
Queen Victoria's Diamond Jubilee
National Gallery of British Art is founded; later renamed as the Tate Gallery
British troops besieged and then relieved at Malakand in North West Frontier
Ferdinand Graf von Zeppelin began construction of his first airship
Blackwall (road) tunnel opens

1897

1898

JANUARY 20. Dion Boucicault as William Glover, James Erskine as Arthur Glover and Irene Vanbrugh as Rose in Arthur Wing Pinero's ***Trelawny of the Wells*** at Court Theatre. Pinero remembered a major turning point in British theatre in the 1860s when what might be described as the 'Vincent Crummles School of Acting' was about to be swept away by the new realism. Tom Wrench, the unrecognised playwright, is a portrait of the young playwright Tom Robertson, who wanted doors to have real handles and real locks, and his stage characters to talk and behave like live people. William Archer said it was 'one of the most delightful works of a great and original humorist'. Bernard Shaw confessed, 'The whole play has touched me more than anything else he has ever written.'

JANUARY 22. Herbert Beerbohm Tree as Mark Antony, Lewis Waller as Brutus and Franklin McLeay as Cassius in Shakespeare's ***Julius Caesar*** at Her Majesty's Theatre. Charles Fulton as Caesar. Lily Hanbury as Portia. Evelyn Millard as Culpurnia. Lawrence Alma-Tadema's lavish and costly sets and costumes got the most praise.

APRIL 12. Edna May and Dan Dally in ***The Belle of New York*** at Shaftesbury Theatre. Book by Hugh Morton. Music by Gustave Kerker. A Salvation Army lass becomes the heiress to a fortune. The musical fared better in London than it had done in New York, and its success was due in no small measure to the loveliness of the English chorus girls. 693 performances.

BELOW

Irene Vanbrugh and Dion Boucicault in Arthur Wing Pinero's Trelawany of the Wells *at Court Theatre in 1898.*

RIGHT

Coquelin, the popular French actor, in his most famous role: Cyrano in Edmond Rostand's Cyrano de Bergerac *at Lyceum Theatre in 1898. Coquelin played the role 400 times*

1898

World premieres

Gustav Kerker, Charles McLellan and Hugh Morton's *The Belle of New York* in New York

Nikolai Rimsky-Korsakov's *Sadko* in Moscow

Edmond Rostand's *Cyrano de Bergerac* in Paris

Births

Bertolt Brecht, German dramatist, poet, director, theorist

George Gershwin, American composer

Michel de Ghelderode, Belgian producer

Gertrude Lawrence, British actress

Lotte Lenya, Austrian born actress and singer

Frederico Garcia Lorca, Spanish dramatist, poet

Henry Moore, British sculptor

Paul Robeson, African-American actor

Deaths

Helen Faucit, British actress (b. 1817)

Literature

Henry James' *The Turn of the Screw*

H. G. Wells' *The War of the Worlds*

Oscar Wilde's *The Ballad of Reading Gaol*

Notes

23-year-old Lilian Baylis, Emma Cons' niece, is appointed acting manager of the Old Vic Theatre

George Robey makes his debut in the music halls in the role of a tramp.

History

Kitchener victorious at Battle of Omdurman and enters Khartoum

Statue of Boudicca unveiled on Embankment

Kowloon and New Territories added to Hong Kong as part of new 99-year lease to UK

Emile Zola publishes *J'Accuse* letter in support of Dreyfus

JUNE 21. Martin Harvey and Mrs Patrick Campbell in Maurice Maeterlinck's **Péllèas et Mélisande** at Prince of Wales's Theatre. Johnston Forbes-Robertson as Goluad. Music by Gabriel Fauré. *The Athenæum* said the play was an intellectual delight. *The Times* said that Harvey looked as if he had walked out of a painting by Perugino. In 1904 Campbell would act Mélisande, in French, opposite Sarah Bernhardt.

> Mr Martin Harvey's melancholy face, his curious timbre of voice, his scholarly delight in cadence helped him to invest the part of Péllèas with an unearthly glamour, and Mr Robertson's classical profile, manly voice and general distinction were invaluable.
> MRS PATRICK CAMPBELL, *My Life and Some Letters*

JULY 9. Coquelin in Edmond Rostand's **Cyrano de Bergerac** at Lyceum Theatre. Maria Legault as Roxane. Coquelin's vivid performance was highly praised. 'The actor's large and expressive gestures are superb; his swagger sublime,' said *The Referee*.

OCTOBER 17. Johnston Forbes-Robertson and Mrs Patrick Campbell in Shakespeare's **Macbeth** at Lyceum Theatre. The actors were mis-cast and there was no spontaneity.

> He becomes loutish where he should be stalwart and massive, and almost cowardly in manner where he should be perplexed and overawed. The part, in short, does not fit in with Mr Robertson's special gifts of intellectual refinement and subtlety. *The Times*

> One of the most hopelessly uninspiring Lady Macbeths that I remember to have seen. Her murderous counsels are delivered without conviction, while her remorse is without a shred of plausibility or pathos. Nothing in her rendering of the part conveys the smallest thrill or shudder to the house. *Academy*

NOVEMBER 1. Herbert Beerbohm Tree as D'Artagnan in **Three Musketeers** at Her Majesty's Theatre. Sydney Grundy's adaptation of Alexandre Dumas' novel. Franklyn McLeay as Richelieu.

Herbert Ross as Louis XIII. Mrs Brown Potter as Milady. Frank Mills as Athos. Louis Calvert as Porthos. Gerald du Maurier as Aramis. 'All is sacrificed to spectacle,' said *The Illustrated London News*. 'Mr Tree has little to do but posture, fight and look distinguished.'

NOVEMBER 29. William Poel as Shylock and Eleanor Calhoun as Portia in Shakespeare's ***The Merchant of Venice***, directed by William Poel for the Elizabethan Stage Society at St George's Hall. Poel wore the once traditional red wig and his interpretation was harsh, without pathos and without dignity.

1899

FEBRUARY 16. John Martin Harvey as Sydney Carton in Freeman Wills's ***The Only Way*** at Lyceum Theatre. Adaptation of Charles Dickens' *A Tale of Two Cities*. N de Silva as Mimi. Herbert Sleath as Darnay. 'Success, absolute and indisputable,' said *The Daily Telegraph*. Harvey made the role his own and secured his position as a leading actor-manager. The exquisite pathos of the farewell ('It is a far, far better thing that I do …') would become indelibly engraved on the collective memory of theatre-goers. His performance was so popular that he would still be playing Carton in 1939, when he was 67.

MARCH 20. Lillah McCarthy as Gwendolen in Algernon Charles Swinburne's ***Locrine*** directed by William Poel for the Elizabethan Stage Society at St George's Hall. Locrine was the son of Brutus, the first King of England. Gwendolen was his mother and she incited her son to take up arms against his father.

> He [Swinburne] read with a voice like a choric chant. The voice sounded strange and wonderful … I chanted as he had done … Imagine my delight when I heard Swinburne exclaim: That is right, you have a fine vibrating voice; appealing in its heroic quality.
> LILLAH MCCARTHY

APRIL 8. John Hare and Irene Vanbrugh in Arthur Wing Pinero's ***The Gay Lord Quex*** at Globe Theatre. A scheming manicurist's efforts to entrap Quex constantly come unstuck. It acted like a play by Oscar Wilde, but without Wilde's redeeming wit.

> The long run of Lord Quex is a sign that the public grows less and less particular as to the aim of the playwright so long as he provides something spicy to whet their jaded palates. In spite of its great success and the excellent acting of Mr Hare and Miss Irene Vanbrugh one cannot but regret that a dramatist of Mr Pinero's gifts should be content merely to sketch a number of disagreeable characters concerned in a discreditable intrigue. *The Times*

APRIL 15. Henry Irving and Ellen Terry in Victorien Sardou's ***Robespierre*** at Lyceum Theatre. One of the high spots was the scene when Robespierre is haunted by the ghosts of the guillotined Marie Antoinette, Georges Danton and Camille Desmoullins. A spectacular production, with 355 actors and musicians.

> Perhaps it was inevitable that Sir Henry Irving should adapt the temperament of Robespierre to suit his own individuality and lend the cold-blooded intellectual a dignity, a fervour and an occasional touch of remorse alien to the character. *Illustrated London News*

JUNE 12. Sarah Bernhardt is Shakespeare's ***Hamlet*** at Adelphi Theatre. *Punch* said the only thing needed to make it perfect was for Henry Irving to play Ophelia.

Martin Harvey as Sydney Carton, in Freeman Wills' The Only Way, an adaptation of Charles Dickens' A Tale of Two Cities, at Lyceum Theatre in 1899. Harvey was the definitive Sydney Carton, and would go on playing the role for the rest of his life.

Herbert Beerbohm Tree as D'Artagnan in The Three Musketeers at Her Majesty's Theatre in 1899.

I cannot even imagine any one of more than a hollow pretence at taking it seriously … Alas! She betrayed nothing but herself, and revealed nothing but the unreasoning vanity which had impelled her to so preposterous an undertaking. For once, even her voice was not beautiful. MAX BEERBOHM, *Saturday Review*

JULY 31. Lilly Langtry in Sydney Grundy's **The Degenerates** at Haymarket Theatre. *Succès de scandale.* 'Nothing better pleases most audiences,' said *The Times*, 'than to be told that society is altogether rotten.'

SEPTEMBER 20. Herbert Beerbohm Tree in Shakespeare's **King John** at Her Majesty's Theatre. J. Fisher White as Faulconbridge. Julia Neilson as Constance. The five acts were reduced to three, and Shakespeare's omission of the signing of Magna Carta was rectified. The production was hugely successful. The *Illustrated London News* described Tree as 'subtle and impressive, though a little over-emphatic in detail and at one point needlessly hysterical'.

SEPTEMBER 26. Murray Carson as Dick Dudgeon, F. H. Macklin as Pastor Anderson and Grace Warner as Mrs Anderson in George Bernard Shaw's **The Devil's Disciple** at Prince of Wales's Theatre. Set during the American Revolution of the 1770s. Shaw said his 'shameless pot-boiler' did not contain one single passably novel incident. It had all the ingredients of popular nineteenth-century melodrama: will-reading, abused orphans, a mother's curse, mistaken identity, arrest, heroic self-sacrifice, court martial and last-minute reprieve at the gallows. The play works at two levels: as a popular melodrama in its own right, and as a satire on a popular melodrama.

If Mr Shaw would give his mind to writing farces, he would achieve a success which his more serious plays have hitherto failed to attain. *The Times*

OCTOBER 16. Evelyn Millard and Herbert Waring in Hall Caine's **The Christian** at Duke of York's Theatre. Melodrama. A priest makes it his life's work to rescue prostitutes. The critics loathed Caine's adaptation of his novel. The public loved it.

RIGHT

Lillie Langtry (1853–1929), mistress to King Edward VII. Lillie was a great beauty, but never a great actress. She made her London stage debut as Kate Hardcastle in Oliver Goldsmith's She Stoops to Conquer at Haymarket Theatre in 1881.

1899

World premieres
Anton Chekhov's *Uncle Vanya* in Moscow
Edward Elgar's *Enigma Variations* in London
Giacomo Puccini's *Tosca* in Rome

Births
Noel Coward, British dramatist, actor, composer, lyricist
Alfred Hitchcock, British film director
Charles Laughton, British born actor
Armand Salacrou, French dramatist

Deaths
Lewis Carroll, British author, mathematician, logician, deacon, photographer (b. 1832)
Maria Ann Keeley, British actress (b. 1806)

Notes
Irish Literary Theatre, Dublin, is founded by W. B. Yeats and Lady Gregory
Wyndham's Theatre opens
Stage Society is founded to produce plays of artistic merit but unlikely to be performed in commercial theatre

Literature
Serialisation of Joseph Conrad's *Heart of Darkness*
Henry James' *The Awkward Age*
Stephane Mallarme's *Poems* (published posthumously)
Leo Tolstoy's *Resurrection*

History
Second Anglo-Boer War begins
German chemist Felix Hoffmann patents aspirin
Queen Victoria lays the foundation stone of the V&A in South Kensington

NOVEMBER 11. Evie Green, Willie Edoiun, Florence St John and Nina Severing in *Florodora* at Lyric Theatre. Book by Owen Hall. Lyrics by Ernest Boyd-Jones and Paul Rubens. Music by Leslie Stuart. Florodora is a perfume, and the recipe is stolen. Hit number: 'Tell me pretty maiden are there any more like you?' The beautiful chorus girls were very much part of its success. 455 performances.

> One has been more or less amused, it is true, by a three-hour representation of what one already knows from *The Family Herald* and the comic papers; but one has not encountered a single surprise of wit and humour, or picked up an idea of life which, for any novelty of its own, is worth taking to mind again.
> *Illustrated Sporting and Dramatic News*

Programme cover for Shakespeare's King John at Her Majesty's Theatre

NOVEMBER 26. Yorke Stephens as Valentine and Mabel Terry-Lewis as Gloria in George Bernard Shaw's *You Never Can Tell* produced by the Stage Society at Royal Theatre. Shaw set out to write a commercial play that would appeal to theatre managers and their audiences. A mother, an advocate of Women's Rights, is unexpectedly reunited with her estranged husband, who used to beat her. Her eldest daughter falls in love with an impoverished dentist, who is a compulsive flirt and fortune-hunter. James Welch as the old and wise waiter, deferential, yet never servile, stole the notices with immense tact and affability.

DECEMBER 26. Dan Leno as Dame Trott in *Jack and the Beanstalk* at Drury Lane Theatre. The giant's name was changed from Blunderbore to Blunderboer. When the giant was dead, children, dressed in full army uniform, marched out of his pocket, a direct retort to the Boer's leader's boast that he could 'put the British army in his pocket'.

The audience cheered.

Index of performances

Illustrations

The illustrations in this book are drawn from the collections of Westminster City Archives, and are reproduced with their permission. The images may be consulted at WCA and the list below gives the archive reference number of each image

Venice), ref. A09A3779; page 177 (Great American Circus), ref. A09A3780; page 178 (Royal Italian Opera House), ref. A09A3724; page 179 (Ira Aldridge in *Othello*), ref. A09A3782; page 180 (*Henry V*), ref. A09A3785; page 182 (interior of New Adelphi Theatre), ref. A09A3966; page 183 (*Asmodeus or The Devil of Two Sticks*), ref. A10A4252; page 184 (poster for Strand Theatre), ref. A10A4253.

THE 1860s Page 185 (Charles Mathews, John L. Toole and Samuel Phelps), ref. A09A3903; page 186 (*The Colleen Bawn*), ref. A09A3964; page 187 (Charles Fechter), ref. A09A3881; page 188 (John Baldwin Buckstone), ref. A09A3955; page 192 (Edward Askew Sothern), ref. A09A3869; *The Octoroon*, ref. A09A3968; pages 194–5 (Strand Music Hall), exterior ref. A09A3713, interior ref. A09A3712; page 196 (Marie Wilton), ref. A09A3916; page 198 (Tom Taylor), ref. A09A3840; page 192 (*The Ticket-of-Leave-Man*), ref. A09A3790; page 199 (crowds at Adelphi Theatre), ref. A09A3962; page 200 (Kate Bateman in *Leah*), ref. A09A3950; page 202 (Edward Askew Sothern), ref. A09A3764; page 203 (scene from *Streets of London*), ref. A09A3842; page 205 (Joseph Jefferson), ref. A09A3891; page 207 (scene from *Ours*), ref. A09A3843; page 207 (Thomas William Robertson), ref. A09A3860; page 209 (The New Amphitheatre, Holborn), ref. A09A3796; page 210 (Marie Wilton and John Hare in *Caste*), ref. A09A3766; page 211 (Sir Arthur Sullivan), ref. A09A3910; page 212 (scene from *Antony and Cleopatra*), ref. A09A4065; page 214 (plays at Drury Lane and Holborn theatres), ref. A09A3795; page 215 (plays at Covent Garden and Lyceum theatres), ref. A09A3793; page 217 (scene from *The King of Scots*), ref. A09A3799; page 218 (Charles Dickens), ref. A09A3876; page 220 (scene from *Black and White*), ref. A09A3939; page 221 (scene from *Lost at Sea*), ref. A09A3951.

THE 1870s Page 223 (Henry Irving and Isabel Bateman *Richelieu*), ref. A09A3932; page 224 (Henry Irving), ref. A09A3888; page 225 (scene from *The Vicar of Wakefield*), ref. A09A3800; page 227 (scene from *The Woman in White*), ref. A09A3801; page 229 (Henry Irving in *The Bells*), ref. A09A3819; page 230 (Dion Boucicault), ref. A09A3940; page 231 (scene from *The Last Days of Pompeii*), ref. A09A3802; page 232 (Isabel Bateman), ref. A09A3803; page 233 (scene from *False Shame*), ref. A09A3805; page 234 (Henry Irving in *Charles I*), ref. A09A3814; page 235 (scene from *The Lady of the Lake*), ref. A09A3807; page 236 (scene from *The Wandering Jew*), ref. A09A3969; page 238 (Henry Irving in *The Fate of Eugene Aram*), ref. A09A3925; page 240 (Henry Irving in *Hamlet*), ref. A09A3926; page 241 (scene from *Clancarty*), ref. A09A3924; page 243 (H. J. Byron), ref. A09A3904; page 245 (programme for *The Shaughraun*), ref. A09A4029; page 247 (Jennie Lee in *Bleak House*), ref. A09A3849; page 250 (Arthur Cecil and Mrs Bancroft in *The Vicarage*), ref. A09A3768; page 251 (programme for *Pink Dominos*), ref. A09A4028; page 253 (Samuel Phelps), ref. A09A3919; page 254 (the audience at Lyceum Theatre), ref. A09A3717; page 255 (Henry Irving and Ellen Terry in *Hamlet*), ref. A09A3818); page 256 (Henry Irving in *The Flying Dutchman*), ref. A09A3820; page 259 (Henry Irving in *The

Merchant of Venice*), ref. A09A3887; page 259 (Ellen Terry in *The Merchant of Venice*), ref. A04A1715.

THE 1880s Page 261 (*The Pirates of Penzance*), ref. A09A3872; page 262 (Arthur Cecil and Mrs Bancroft in *Money*), ref. A09A3767; page 263 (scene from *The O'Dowd*), ref. A09A3959; page 265 (*Patience*), ref. A09A3930; pages 266–7 (audience leaving Lyceum Theatre), ref. A09A3718; page 271 (playbill for *Drink*), ref. A09A3945; page 272 (Toole's Theatre), ref. A09A3719; page 273 (programme for *The Silver King*), ref. A09A4057; page 274 (Ellen Terry in *Much Ado about Nothing*), ref. A09A3979; page 275 (Mary Anderson), ref. A09A3906; page 277 (Henry Arthur Jones), ref. A09A3990; page 278 (programme for *Breaking a Butterfly*), ref. A09A3711; page 280 (Sarah Bernhardt in *Ruy Blas*), ref. A09A3898; page 281 (Mrs Stirling and Mary Anderson in *Romeo and Juliet*), ref. A09A3933; page 282 (William Terris), ref. A09A3864; page 283 (Madge and William Kendal in *As You Like It*), ref. A09A3823; page 284 (George Grossmith), ref. A09A3883; page 284 (*The Mikado*), 3927; page 287 (Charles Coborn), ref. A09A3836; page 288 (Dan Leno in *The Babes in the Wood*), ref. A09A3981; page 289 (John Clayton in *Dandy Dick*), ref. A09A3846; page 290 (Arthur Wing Pinero), ref. A09A3845; page 290 (John Hare), ref. A09A3884; page 292 (Sarah Bernhardt in *Tosca*), ref. A09A3978; page 293 (programme for *H.M.S. Pinafore*), ref. A09A4052; page 295 (Kate Rorke), ref. A09A3909; page 296 (*Dead Heart*), ref. A09A4040.

THE 1890s Page 298 (J. L. Toole), ref. A09A3866; page 299 (John Hare in *A Pair of Spectacles*), ref. A09A3975; page 301 (Madge Kendal), ref. A09A4027; page 302 (programme for London Pavilion), ref. A09A4038; page 304 (Henry Irving, J. L. Toole, and Squire Bancroft), ref. A09A3769; page 305 (Edward Terry and Fanny Brough in *The Times*), ref. A09A3935; page 306 (Henry Irving in *Henry VIII*), ref. A09A3886; page 307 (*Lady Windermere's Fan*), ref. A09A3859; page 308 (Marion Terry), ref. A09A3972; page 310 (W. S. Penley), ref. A09A3874; page 311 (Henry Irving in *Becket*), ref. A09A3813; page 312 (*A Woman of No Importance*), ref. A09A3863; page 313 (George Alexander and Mrs Patrick Campbell in *The Second Mrs Tanqueray*), ref. A09A3844; page 315 (programme for *A Gaiety Girl*), ref. A09A4049; page 318 (programme for *The Shop Girl*), ref. A09A4031; page 318 (Dan Leno), ref. A09A3982; page 319 (Florence West in *An Ideal Husband*), ref. A09A3997; page 320 (*The Importance of Being Earnest*), ref. A09A3987; page 321 (Mrs Patrick Campbell in *The Notorious Mrs Ebbsmith*), ref. A09A3991; page 322 (Johnston Forbes-Robertson), ref. A09A3994; page 323 (scenes from *Trilby*), ref. A09A3936; page 324 (Lena Ashwell), ref. A09A3878; page 325 (Wilson Barrett), ref. A09A3988; page 326 (Evelyn Millard), ref. A09A3983; page 326 (George Alexander), ref. A09A3984; page 330 (Irene Vanbrugh and Dion Boucicault in *Trelawny of the Wells*), ref. A09A4050; page 331 (Coquelin), ref. A09A3867; page 334 (Martin Harvey), ref. A09A4045; page 335 (Herbert Beerbohm Tree), ref. A09A4035; page 337 (Lillie Langtry), ref. A09A3740; page 338 (programme for King John), ref. A10A4250.